Saint John

Saint John

THE MAKING OF
A COLONIAL URBAN
COMMUNITY

T.W. ACHESON

UNIVERSITY OF TORONTO PRESS

Toronto Buffalo London

© University of Toronto Press 1985
Toronto Buffalo London
Printed in Canada

ISBN 0-8020-2586-2

Canadian Cataloguing in Publication Data

Acheson, Thomas William, 1936–
Saint John: the making of a colonial urban
community
Includes bibliographical references and index.
ISBN 0-8020-2586-2
1. Saint John (N.B.) – History. I. Title.
FC2497.4.A24 1985   971.5'32   C85-099412-8
F1044.5.S14A24 1985

This book has been published with the help of a grant from the Social Science
Federation of Canada, using funds provided by the Social Sciences and
Humanities Research Council of Canada, and from the Publications Fund of the
University of Toronto Press.

To the memory of

Sarah Ada (Pomeroy) Christie

and

George William Christie

The Saint John Bicentennial Inc. was created by the City of Saint John to suitably commemorate three years of bicentennials: in 1983, the landing of the Loyalists; in 1984, the founding of the Province of New Brunswick; in 1985, the incorporation of Saint John as a city, Canada's first.

Over the three-year period, the Bicentennial has produced, managed, and funded many varied projects. As part of its historical publication series, The Saint John Bicentennial Inc. is proud to sponsor this publication.

Contents

Acknowledgments

A number of people and institutions have rendered valuable assistance in the preparation of this work. I wish to express my gratitude to the Social Sciences and Humanities Research Council of Canada for support given this project through the leave fellowship program. Additional support for research and typing expenses was provided by the School of Graduate Studies and Research and the Dean of Arts at the University of New Brunswick. The staffs of the Provincial Archives of New Brunswick, the New Brunswick Museum, the Archives of the University of New Brunswick, and the Saint John Public Library were always willing to assist in the research endeavour and to share their extensive knowledge of the collections. Among the many individuals who have helped I would single out Richard Ramsay, Monica Robertson, Gary Hughes, and my colleagues at UNB, especially Ernie Forbes, Steve Turner, Elizabeth McGahan, Murray Young, Gail Campbell, and Stephen Patterson. Phyllis Miller and Becky Daniels typed full drafts of the manuscript and Susan typed the first impossible draft. Finally, Marge has lived with this project as long as I have.

T.W. Acheson

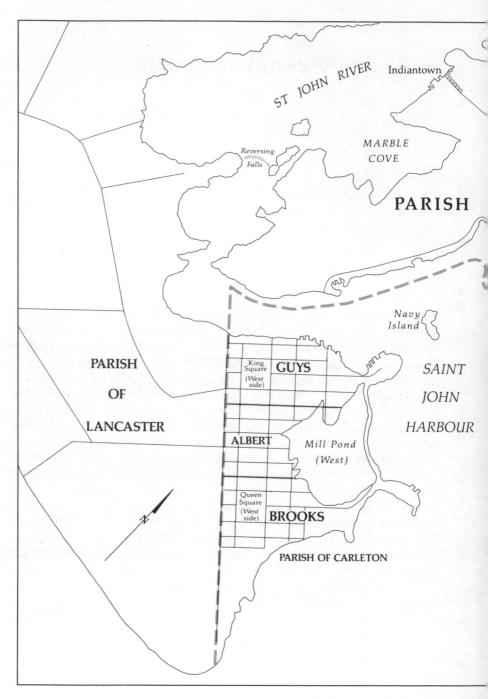

ST JOHN RIVER   Indiantown

MARBLE
COVE

Reversing
Falls

PARISH

PARISH

OF

LANCASTER

King
Square
(West
side)

GUYS

ALBERT

Queen
Square
(West
side)

BROOKS

Mill Pond
(West)

Navy
Island

SAINT

JOHN

HARBOUR

N

PARISH OF CARLETON

Plan of the city and harbour of Saint John, using as a base map the surve

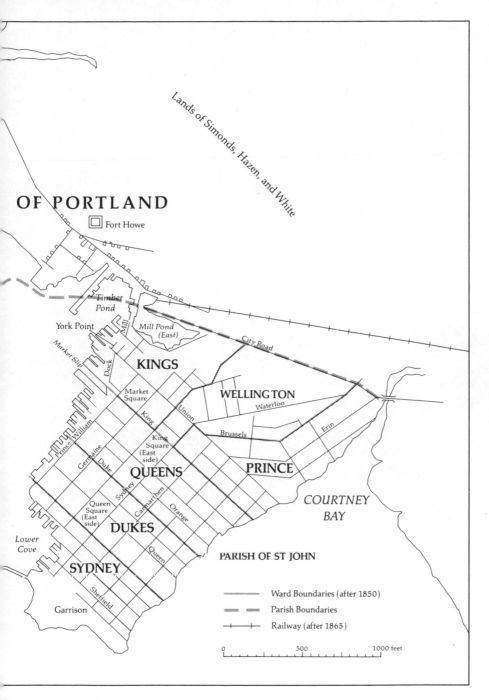

OF PORTLAND

Fort Howe

Lands of Simonds, Hazen, and White

Timber Pond

York Point

Mill Pond (East)

City Road

Market Slip

Dock

Mill

KINGS

Market Square

King

Union

WELLINGTON

Waterloo

Prince William

Germaine

Duke

King Square (East side)

QUEENS

Brussels

Erin

PRINCE

Sydney

Carmarthen

Orange

COURTNEY BAY

Queen Square (East side)

DUKES

Queen

Lower Cove

SYDNEY

PARISH OF ST JOHN

Sheffield

Garrison

——————— Ward Boundaries (after 1850)
– – – – – Parish Boundaries
+—+—+—+ Railway (after 1865)

0   500   1000 feet

y John Cunningham and published for Isaac Gage (New Brunswick 1835)

Saint John

Introduction

In the half-century following Waterloo a significant anglophone society emerged in British North America. The small scattered remnants of the Second British Empire, anchored around the strongholds of Quebec City and Halifax, rapidly evolved from frontier fragility into complex colonial societies. A population of perhaps half a million in 1815 grew to nearly three-and-a-quarter million by 1860, a growth rate far exceeding that in any other comparable period of Canadian history since 1700; in Upper Canada and the Maritimes population rose by 750 per cent.[1]

Land settlement and trade values experienced even more striking rates of growth.[2] The engine that initially powered this development was the decision of the British government to provide the colonies with a virtual monopoly of the British market for timber and timber products. This reassertion of mercantilism came in the wake of the Napoleonic threat to Britain's vital Baltic supplies. It remained in place until 1842 and produced a scramble to erect the infrastructure and organization needed to conduct this largest enterprise in the North Atlantic commerce.[3] Accompanying the timber trade was the mass migration of British peoples to British North America. The movement was provoked by the pull factors of cheap public land, jobs, and commercial opportunity, and by the push factors of famine, destitution, and a feeling on the part of many that the age of the artisan and the small tenant farmer was passing in the face of agricultural and industrial reorganization.[4] Whatever the reasons, perhaps 1,200,000 people from the three kingdoms entered British North America between 1815 and 1860, and a large proportion of these became permanent settlers.[5] The extension of European settlement and European values into the North American wilderness has been a common theme in Canadian and American historical writing.[6] Also important were the twin problems of the structural impact of the staples trades and the accompanying commercial system upon the colonial societies, and the integration of the army of strangers that continued year by year to flood through the ports of British North America. The growing complexity of the colonial social order was reflected in the variety of political, religious, and ethnic institutions that emerged in the period, in the array of voluntary organizations, in the temperance and reform movements, in the growing numbers of wage-earners, and in the extremes of wealth and poverty that came increasingly to characterize the society.[7]

Although most British North Americans lived in rural settings, the conduit through which the Old World reached and organized the New was a handful of commercial and administrative centres found at strategic locations on the colonial coasts and waterways. In 1815, apart from Montreal, these were mainly towns created in the imperial interest that also served as distribution centres, an urban form Gilbert Stelter describes as mercantile.[8] The next generation witnessed the dramatic growth of these centres – literally a transition from town into city in most cases – and the development of networks of subsidiary towns and villages that emerged in the rapidly expanding rural hinterland.[9] The economic functions of the cities became more diffuse and significant: local production of goods and services and the significance of the colonial markets themselves, for example, became important concerns.[10] The urban population grew much more rapidly than did that of the colonies as a whole. The cities and larger towns became complex social laboratories in which the often conflicting demands and needs of a variety of interest groups were worked out. Here was seen the exercise of power, the influence of culture and class in social relationships, the place of status and wealth in determining position, the integration of newcomers and new ideas, the creation of voluntary institutions, the struggle for control of public institutions and for the material and policy benefits that control conferred. In all this activity, the community of the small mercantile towns was remade in various forms reflecting the combination of circumstances present in each.[11]

The Atlantic seaboard colonies shared the general pattern of British American development in the early nineteenth century. Indeed, these trends were accentuated in New Brunswick where the river system permitted early exploitation of an extensive timber stand, encouraged the development of a major shipbuilding industry, offered extensive opportunities for British, American, and local capitalists, and provided a vast area of crown land available for settlement.[12] The population of the colony rose from perhaps 50,000 to more than 250,000 during the period. A similar pattern of growth was experienced in the neighbouring state of Maine where the forest-based economy permitted the growth of a population that by 1860 reached three-quarters that of Massachusetts.

As the principal urban centre of New Brunswick, Saint John became a microcosm of the economic and demographic changes that were altering the social fabric of the province. The population of the town grew from perhaps 5000 in 1815 to 20,000 in 1840 to 38,000 in 1861. By American standards it was a modest city – about the same size as Richmond, the 25th ranked city in the United States at the outbreak of the Civil War – but throughout most of the period it was the third-largest urban centre in British North America and the largest on its Atlantic seaboard.[13] Located on a fine harbour at the mouth of the St John River and near the mouth of the Bay of Fundy, the town was admirably suited as a centre for the prosecution of the timber trade that developed in response to the new mercantilism. The large shipbuilding industry, the cheap transatlantic fares offered by its returning timber ships, and an extensive hinterland permitted the port to establish a metropolitan influence over the Bay of Fundy watershed.

The demands of the expanding economy and the needs of those who came or remained in response to those demands produced profound changes in the city itself.[14] The most obvious of these was the spread of the material city. From a collection of small market villages huddled around the harbour, the city expanded to fill the available lands on the east-side peninsula by mid-century and then pushed into neighbouring Portland. This was accompanied by the expansion of harbour facilities and by a dramatic rise in the population density of the harbour-front area as dock workers moved into tenements near their place of work. Congestion created a city of strangers in which the older devices of accommodation and social control worked less well. It also produced problems that were distinctly urban: livestock could no longer be easily kept in the city; water supplies and waste disposal became increasingly difficult to obtain; even the organizing of an adequate food supply required considerable supervision; and struggles erupted among the military, the civic corporation, and business interests in the competition for limited space and resources. Growth and high-density population were accompanied by economic diversification as immigrants drawn by the growing local markets began producing a variety of commodities formerly imported. This in turn produced a marked diversification of occupations. The timber trade remained important, but it was increasingly challenged by shipbuilding, construction, sawmilling, and a variety of small crafts and trades.

Saint John was thirty years old in 1815. Newcomers and new ideas faced an established order on their arrival. Like its principal rival, Halifax, Saint

View of Saint John, 1814
by J.B. Comino
(courtesy, New Brunswick Museum [NBM])

John had been created in the imperial interest. A garrison town and an imperial trading centre, its society was highly stratified. Deference and loyalty were the cardinal virtues. Status in the early mercantile city had been largely based on presumed service to the crown. As the transition to a commercial city began, entrepreneurial success increasingly joined the older virtues as a mark of high status. The crown remained a powerful influence in the public life of the city. The appointments of public officials and the actions of municipal agencies were carefully monitored at each step of the constitutional hierarchy. As in most North American towns, this produced a powerful social élite of public officials and great merchants that played a dominant leadership role in the life of the community.[15] This élite contained many of the elements of a genuine class, particularly in its ownership of property. In the early nineteenth century, its leadership was usually assumed and rarely challenged within the city.[16]

When challenges did emerge, they came from a growing producers' interest, which became more prominent as the transition from mercantile to commercial town accelerated. The groups contained within this interest covered the spectrum from manufacturers through large and small masters and shopkeepers to most artisans and tradesmen. As such, the interest contained elements of both the business and working classes described by Michael Katz,[17] including the petite bourgeoisie, the artistocracy of labour (artisans), and a large and highly unstable group of working masters.[18] The influence of this interest was considerable in a number of voluntary and public institutions after 1830, and its members from time to time displayed many of the characteristics of a class.

Important though it was, the producers' interest was only one of several often interrelated factors that contributed to community formation in Saint John between 1815 and 1860. The most significant of the others were cultural, particularly those centred on religious or ethno-religious traditions. The broad Erastian Protestant orthodoxy that formed the Church of England establishment within the Loyalist order represented one ideal around which the community could, and in some measure did, organize in the early nineteenth century. The immigrant influx from both the United Kingdom and the Maritime hinterland created large constituencies not easily integrated into the existing order. And the pressure of different people was supplemented by that of different ideas as the great popular movements emanating from New England and Old England were integrated into the community of the port. Irish Catholicism is the obvious example of an ethno-religious transfer that occurred in every major port on the Atlantic coast of North America in the mid-nineteenth century.[19] After 1820 there was a broadly based and growing evangelical culture determined to reverse the secular trends of the nineteenth century. While the evangelical influence was found across the spectrum of civic society, it was particularly powerful among the artisan and small-business interest. Catholic culture attempted to create voluntary social institutions that paralleled those found in the city, while evangelicals attempted to capture and remake the existing community. Churches were important not only for their ideological framework but also because, like the family, they were institutions of primary identity gathering people from all conditions and from most social origins. Each church provided an experience of community – for many people the only one in which they participated. And together with lodges and fraternal organizations, they offered a status – a stability and respectability – to their followers. In Saint John, religion in the mid-nineteenth century 'continued to bear most of the institutional responsibility for community values.'

Community found its most obvious public expression in the city's political and administrative institutions. In 1815 Saint John was a series of ward-villages huddled around the harbour, each governed by its alderman-magistrate. On the first Tuesday of every April, the electors of each ward assembled in one place to elect their governors. The members of this political community were generally known and often linked by ties of blood and marriage to each other. Other necessary civic services were performed by volunteers from among the electors. The neighbourhood civic community of Saint John gradually diminished over the next generation and was replaced by the civic bureaucracy and by an image of the city rather than the neighbourhood.[20] In the process, politics increasingly became a means of managing conflict rather than establishing and enacting the community consensus. The division between public and private functions, almost indistinguishable in the early century, had become pronounced by 1860. So, too, was the tendency to restrict the public community to the native population. At times the pressures created by the urbanizing process, and the tensions among the principal social groups within the city, strained the community to its breaking point. The 1840s saw much of the fabric of the older community destroyed and replaced by new instruments of accommodation and control. Ultimately, as in all commercial cities, the most important decisions affecting the economic well-being of the community were made outside by external agents.[21] Tariffs, navigation acts, market access, and even railways were matters decided by imperial or provincial governments often in consultation with private consortia operating outside the city. The city and its leading business interests could react to these decisions and could build the infrastructure necessary to take advantage of them. They could do little else.

This study is an attempt to explore the changing nature of community in Saint John from the beginning of the transition from town to city in the early nineteenth century to the entry into the 'golden age' of the 1850s. The first two chapters explore the political and economic institutions around which the material and administrative life of the city was organized. Chapters 3 and 4 examine two influential social groups – the great merchants and the artisans – illustrative of the social structure of the city and of the relationship between that structure and the uses of power. Chapters 5 and 6 focus on religion and ethnicity, the most powerful cultural influences in the city. The remainder of the work consists of a series of case studies that explore the implications of culture, social structure, and urbanization for the community of Saint John, particularly in the period after 1840. Temperance, the instruction of the young, charter reform, harbour and utilities development, and protection of persons and property each reflected the changing nature of community in the city. Finally, in chapter 12, the family and occupational structure of the formed city at mid-century is examined. Tables in the appendix provide details.

~1~

The Urban Economy

The American Revolution and the St John River were the cardinal facts that led to the creation of the port of Saint John. The city was built on the estuary of a major river system and was created as the outpost and regional centre for a defeated imperial power. Like most early Canadian towns, Saint John was a planted community designed to encourage a more general settlement in the area, and its initial form bore the marks of the familiar grid pattern preferred by the engineers of the British army.[1] The early economy was dominated by the imperial fact. The British garrison played an important role as dispenser of treasury notes. Even more significant was the commercial activity of the harbour that was directly linked to policy decisions made in London. After the initial Loyalist settlement in 1783 and a few years of modest prosperity, the port entered a period of lethargy when the British government admitted the Americans to the West Indies carrying trade in 1791. The permanent population, which numbered about 3500 in 1785, probably totalled no more than 4500 in 1810.[2]

It was the Napoleonic blockade that revived British interest in the resource potential of the North American colonies. The threat the blockade posed to the essential Scandanavian timber supplies rekindled the old British debate over the question of cheapness versus national security, a debate in which the interests of national security prevailed. There was no doubt that the most secure supply of timber could be obtained from the North American colonies. The capital costs of developing the skills and facilities needed to produce these supplies, however, would be enormous and the freight costs were considerably higher than those from Scandanavian ports. The Liverpool merchants who dominated the British timber trade were unwilling to enter the new arrangement unless they were given assurances that protection for the trade would be guaranteed beyond the immediate crisis.

The new regulations came into effect in 1809. They initially provided an advantage of about 45s. per load – a measure weighing a little less than a ton – to colonial timber shipped in British vessels. When the higher freight costs were included, colonial producers were left with an effective protection of about 30s., providing a tariff of over 100 per cent. The regulations underwent a variety of modifications in the years following the Napoleonic wars, but until 1840 the effective protection of the preference never fell to less than 50 per cent of the value of the timber shipped. By 1821, colonial timber held 75 per cent of the British market, and the appetite of the rapidly growing British economy for even this high-priced colonial produce increased timber imports from 200,000 loads in 1800 to 1,318,000 in 1844.[3]

The result of such a policy was predictable. The exploitation of the timber resources of British North America proceeded apace. New Brunswick produced about one-third of the colonial output of this period.[4] The size of the harvest varied dramatically from year to year, reflecting market conditions in England, but in the best years more than 300,000 tons of timber with a local value of £1 sterling a ton was exported from the province. Added to this was a smaller quantity of timber processed into long planks called deals and other wood products. The labour and enterprise involved in this undertaking was so extensive that Arthur Lower has described the province as one great lumber yard with virtually every activity in society subordinated to this undertaking.[5]

Throughout this period the St John River watershed accounted for from half to two-thirds of all wood products exported from the province. The process through which the harvest was accomplished was complex. Sometimes the exporters of timber to the British or West Indies markets sent crews into crown land and on to their own holdings to make timber. The more common practice was for local business men or farmers in a hundred villages throughout the watershed to procure the timber and sell it either to their Saint John suppliers or to an intermediary who finally sold it to a supplier.[6] Whatever the process, the annual harvest made its way by water to the city, where it was either shipped as squared timber or processed into building materials before export.

The arrival of the timber in the city was only one step in the process leading to its final marketing in Great Britain. The movement of timber down the river was a comparatively simple and efficient matter. Its transport after its arrival required the seasonal services of a small army of cartmen, draymen, and ship labourers. Cartmen and draymen were

Vessels loading in Saint John Harbour, c. 1870 (NBM)

The West Head Steam sawmill, c. 1870 (NBM)

usually small business men who owned their own horses and wagons. Depending on the season, they could command a respectable living by hauling materials through the city streets. Ship labourers were wage labourers whose function was to load and unload many of the 1500 to 2000 vessels that entered the port of Saint John each year. The work was heavy, slow, and arduous, requiring large numbers of poorly paid labourers. A labour force of perhaps 500 was required to load and unload vessels in a typical year.[7] The work of this labour force was seasonal and the wages low. The continued influx of impoverished Irish immigrants played an important role in keeping these wages down and, as the preferential tariff on colonial timber declined after 1845, in keeping New Brunswick timber competitive with Scandanavian timber on the British market. This labour force worked either directly for the merchant responsible for the ship being unloaded or for stevedores who acted as contractors and hired their own labourers.[8]

The sawing of timber for local and West Indies markets had been common from the 1760s and early merchant settlers had vied for the best water-power sites on the province's streams. The rise of the British market with its demand for ton timber eclipsed the early sawmill activity: as late as 1826 the province exported 279,000 tons of timber and only 10.7 million feet of deals. The difference between the export of processed and unprocessed wood was important to the producer and to the provincial economy. A ton of timber in 1826 brought, on average, just under £1 at Saint John; a thousand feet of deals, roughly the same quantity of timber when the 20–30 per cent wastage from sawdust produced by the broad saws is taken into consideration, was worth 100 per cent more.[9] The various processed materials could often be made from smaller pieces of timber, a particularly important consideration as the great waterside timber stands disappeared. The transition from ton timber to lumber was dramatically illustrated in the decade of the 1830s: timber exports grew very slowly through the decade (from about 200,000 to 250,000 tons), but the quantity of deals nearly tripled, from 30 to 80 million feet. By 1847 deals exceeded ton timber in value and by 1852 in weight. In 1860 the province exported 275 million feet of deals with a total value of £540,000.[10]

This shift had particular implications for the economy of Saint John. The city had been the port of shipment for most colonial ton timber before 1830 and while it briefly lost this position to the north shore in the next decade, it reasserted it in the 1840s. From the beginning, however, most processed timber was exported from Saint John. Moreover, most of the processing of that timber took place in and around the city. The editor of *The New Brunswick Courier* spoke with obvious relish in 1838 on the expansion of the sawmilling industry that had occurred in the previous few years.[11]

The tidal mills at Carleton had always been an important facility but now large mill complexes – sometimes employing as many as seven saw gates and using water-power generated from burning sawdust and other by-products – peppered Saint John, Carleton, Portland, Lancaster, and Indiantown.[12]

The years 1835 to 1841 witnessed both a substantial expansion of the city's industrial capacity and a considerable integration of the manufacturing and commercial functions of the port. Most early sawmill operators had not been merchants but the newer, larger, capital-intensive mills in the city area were largely constructed at merchant initiative. The census of 1851 revealed 26 sawmills in Saint John, Lancaster, and Portland, each employing an average of 28 men, while the other 538 mills in the province averaged only 6.[13] The expanded milling operations introduced still another seasonal labour force to the city. While the mill operators drew from the same pool as the stevedores for much of their labour, the art of the sawyer was an exacting skill and it is unlikely that any ship labourer unaccustomed to working with wood could have made the transition. Depending on the market, as many as 700 men found seasonal employment in the sawmills in and around the city at mid-century, about half of them in Portland. The rapid expansion of the period provided an additional advantage to the technology of the industry. Almost all new mills were outfitted with gang saws, rather than the sash saws that dominated the sawmill industry of Maine and New York in the period. This technological advance must have given the Saint John industry an advantage in competition with foreign lumber in the next decade.

The timber trade produced the shipbuilding industry. No issue in Maritime history has been the subject of greater debate in the past decade than the question of the nature of the shipbuilding industry and the impact it had upon the growth of the regional economy. Peter McClelland has argued that the industry at its height accounted for less than 3 per cent of the gross value of goods produced in the province, employed little more than 2 per cent of the labour force, and stimulated few significant backward or forward linkages in the local economy.[14] By contrast, shipbuilding may well have accounted for 20 per cent of the value of goods produced in Saint John and Portland and employed 10–15 per cent of the male work-force at mid-century. The happy confluence of endless cargo, cheap and plentiful building material, and a labour force with considerable experience in woodworking inevitably led to the development by 1820 of a small but thriving shipbuilding industry producing for local merchants and steadily adding to the Saint John fleet. Even at this early period, the Saint John vessels were sharply distinguished from those of other Maritime ports by their large size.[15] As the volume of the timber trade expanded between 1820 and 1840, so too did the size of new Saint John vessels, which increased from 241 tons on average in 1824–26 to 322 in 1839–41 to 569 in 1855–57.[16]

Despite its growth and importance, the shipbuilding industry saw few structural changes in the colonial period. It began as a small craft-oriented enterprise. Most early shipyards were expanded artisans' workshops employing members of several trades, and that model underwent little change throughout the nineteenth century. The master shipbuilders were originally men of limited resources who frequently acted as contractors to merchants wishing to have vessels built. The merchant provided the materials and capital advances while the builder provided the workers, equipment, yard, and supervisory skills. Although some of the leading builders began to use their vessels in trade on their own account by mid-century, they rarely did so in the earlier period; and despite the important contribution they made to the economy of the port, it is doubtful if any of the shipbuilders of the port would have been among its wealthier or more prominent citizens in 1850.[17]

Although the structure of the industry changed little throughout the period, its significance did. Many early vessels had been of questionable quality but experience resulted in a better commodity and this, coupled with a rising British demand for shipping, led to a growing market for Saint John ships outside the region. Saint John merchants had frequently sold their vessels in the United Kingdom, but after 1830 there was a growing demand for new New Brunswick vessels from British merchants. The numbers of vessels sent from New Brunswick under governor's pass rose from 2200 tons in 1838 to 5400 tons in 1849 to 10,500 tons in 1854.[18] In a single year, 1854, a total of 10,578 tons of new shipping was built for English customers and another 2154 tons for foreign clients. In all 27,258 tons of new shipping was transferred to other ports in that year, much of it the result of sales of vessels by their first owners. At a value of £7 to £8 a ton this represented at least £90,000 in clear sales, £140,000 if it is assumed that half the transfers were also sales, and £200,000 if all the transfers were sales. As early as 1840, trade in ships had come to play a vital role in the commerce of the port and the province. Throughout the colonial period, the New Brunswick economy operated in a perpetual imbalance in terms of its commodity trade, one that sometimes exceeded £500,000 a year on a £2,000,000 trade. The deficit ordinarily ran at more than £300,000. Against commodity exports of £639,000 in 1842, the Saint John Chamber of Commerce estimated that the value of New Brunswick vessels sold in the United Kingdom amounted to £181,000.[19] The chamber was doubtless exaggerating to make the point, but there can be little doubt that sale of shipping and of shipping services played a vital role in enabling city merchants to balance their London and Liverpool accounts. After 1840 the annual export of vessels from the province ordinarily exceeded £100,000. Even more important and more difficult to calculate was the value of the carrying trade, which the Chamber of Commerce estimated at £335,000 in 1843.

Whatever the merits of McClelland's views on the significance of the shipbuilding industry to New Brunswick, there can be no doubt of its role in the urban economy of Saint John. Just as the processed-timber trade was more concentrated in the city than was ton timber, so too was shipbuilding even more an urban function than was the making of lumber.[20]

The importance of shipbuilding to the economy of the city is inestimable. The marine craftsmen constituted one of the most highly paid group of artisans in the city. Like ship labourers, sawyers, and construction tradesmen, most marine craftsmen were subject to a seasonal work year and to the vagaries of the British market for timber and ships. An 11,000-ton year, like 1841, could be followed by one of fewer than 6000 tons. But except for such extremes, the seasonal work year was part of a broader culture in which artisan families normally expected to spread nine months' wages over twelve months or to engage in some less lucrative activity in the interval. Ship carpenters and their ilk were a numerous and well-paid tribe by mid-century standards. In 1854 Moses Perley estimated half the cost of every ship was paid to labour and that, on average, ten-days' labour was expected on the building of every ton of shipping.[21] This scale would yield wages of £4 a ton or 8s. a man per day. The year 1854 was unusually prosperous and many of the tradesmen employed would probably be transient, but the average annual production of the port suggests the presence of perhaps a thousand tradesmen in the Saint John labour market who would normally make a substantial part of their living from the construction of vessels – a number exceeding the size of the ship labourers work-force – an estimate confirmed by the freemens' rolls and the 1851 Census of the east side of the harbour.[22] After 1833, ship artisans made up a steadily growing proportion of the labour force, and played an important role in the urban growth of the 1830s and the 1850s.

New Brunswick shipbuilders produced vessels to a value of about £650,000 in 1854, a figure comparable to the value of all timber and deals exported from the province in that year.[23] Moreover, the timber product consumed by the shipbuilding industry across New Brunswick probably accounted for 15–20 per cent of the timber produced in the province. This was by far the most valuable timber produced in the province. If a ton of wood brought £1 when sold as square timber and £2 as deals, its manufacture into ships yielded more than £6 in 1854.[24] Shipbuilding

The Alexander Yeats, a full-rigged ship
under construction near Long Wharf, 1876 (NBM)

The Bank of New Brunswick (erected c. 1826)
and Prince William Street (NBM)

certainly created unprecedented local demand for lumber, deals, and masts. The extent of the demand is difficult to assess because no figures were ever kept on total timber output. But the construction of 30,000 tons of wooden shipping in 1838 amounted to about 12 per cent of the province's ton timber exports; by 1854 the 81,000 tons amounted to more than 23 per cent of the total weight of the ton timber and deal exports. In the face of only very gradual growth in the timber-export trade of the 1850s and 1860s (McClelland estimates the growth at 1 per cent a year), shipbuilding undoubtedly played an important role in fostering local demand for the timber staple.

At the same time, there is little evidence to support the view that shipbuilding stimulated the development of other more sophisticated ancillary industries. Local foundries undoubtedly supplied part of the iron needs of the industry, but primary iron, along with chain and anchor, sailcloth, steam engines, and other ships commodities, was mainly imported for the use of the shipbuilders. In the long run, the weakness of the industry was structural. The 1870 industry functioned much as that of 1820 while the changing needs of the industry required a more complex corporate structure, a substantial capital outlay, and a much higher degree of integration of the building firm with its supplier.[25]

The Saint John fleet was much the largest possessed by any port in British North America in the nineteenth century and, reflecting the dependence of the city's commerce on the British timber trade, its vessels were significantly larger than those of other Maritime ports. Virtually the entire fleet was built at Saint John and its outports, or on the Fundy shore of Nova Scotia. Ownership of the fleet was spread over hundreds of Saint John inhabitants, although most of the larger timber ships were owned solely or by some combination of a dozen prominent Saint John merchant firms and shipbuilding families.[26] The number of vessels constructed fluctuated in response to the demands of the timber trade and what British merchants perceived as the prospects for the trade. The general movement was not just to larger vessels but also to more of them. Tonnage peaks in each decade rose sharply. The peaks in 1826, 1840, and 1853 for example, saw the additions of 24,000 tons, 43,000 tons, and nearly 71,000 tons.[27] The city fleet had long represented a wide variety of vessels built to serve a number of purposes – wood boats, small vessels designed for the coasting trade, barques for the West Indies trade, and the inevitable timber ships – but as the fleet improved in quality and efficiency toward the mid-century, it was more and more concerned with the carrying trade, quite independent of the transport of staples from the Fundy littoral.[28]

The economy of Saint John rested on more than its production and shipping functions. What distinguished the city from the other urban centres of the province and provided the basis of its dominance of provincial commerce was the presence of financial institutions. Much the most significant of these were the banks. The development of the early Saint John banking closely paralleled that of Nova Scotia and Upper and Lower Canada and for many of the same reasons. Before 1820 each shipping merchant was, in effect, a private banker attempting to ship sufficient staples and acceptable notes to his English and Scottish suppliers to keep his account solvent. Within the city virtually every coinage of Europe and the Americas circulated in a legally defined relationship to each other. The arrangement was adequate for neither the private nor the public sectors of the provincial economy. Merchants needed both a more controllable circulating medium and a means through which they could borrow on the security of the notes they received to facilitate both internal and external trade. Government needed an agency that could carry its debt and provide an orderly arrangement for meeting the government's obligations on a day-to-day basis. From the needs of both of these groups emerged the Bank of New Brunswick. Chartered in 1820 with a capital of £50,000, its directorate reflected the locus of political and commercial influence at that time. Its thirteen provisional directors included members of both the political and commercial élites of the city.[29]

The expanding commerce of the late 1820s led to a demand for a second bank that would provide both more extensive capital and an alternative to the monopoly of the official institution. The demand provoked a long bitter struggle within the city's business community. The Commercial Bank was finally incorporated in the autumn of 1834 only when the lieutenant-governor procured a royal charter over the veto of the Legislative Council.[30]

The new institution quickly became the major element in financing the commercial expansion of the late 1830s, easily surpassing its older rival in notes discounted and in notes in circulation. Both institutions grew rapidly and by 1837–38 their discounts and those of the smaller City Bank may have totalled £2,300,000.[31] Saint John bank loans in that year may have been equal to the entire trade of the province. The banking capital of the city at the time amounted to £250,000.[32]

The expanded accommodation made possible the dramatic expansion – some critics claimed the over-extension – of trade in the decade before 1842. If the experience of the Bank of New Brunswick was also characteristic of the Commercial Bank – and observers of the late 1830s argued that it was – the banks of the city provided very large accommodations for a small number of leading merchants. In 1837–38, apart from government borrowings and the discounts of other financial institutions, nearly 85 per cent of the Bank of New Brunswick's discounts were made to just eighteen merchants.[33] The only substantial non-mercantile account was that of the foundry firm of Barlow and Ketchum, which was the fifth largest account with the bank. Significantly few, if any, small merchants with purely local interests were found among the bank's customers. Significantly, too, not a single shipbuilder was involved in the use of the bank's resources. Accommodation at the Bank of New Brunswick was confined to the great general merchants who controlled their own firms and participated in the wholesale trade on a large scale on their own account, and in either the British timber trade or the West Indies fish trade.

The needs of the same group of men gave rise in the 1820s to the demand for ship insurance companies. In so hazardous an undertaking as shipping, only the most desperate owner would trust his unprotected investment to the mercies of the North Atlantic. Traditionally, Saint John vessels had been insured with Lloyds and other British consortia, an often costly arrangement since the low ratings Lloyds accorded most colonial shipping resulted in high premiums and the complaint that much of the benefit of the carrying trade was diverted into the hands of English financiers. In 1831, at the behest of thirty-seven merchants, the legislature created the New Brunswick Marine Insurance Company with a capital of £50,000.[34] The company was an instant success. Operating with a paid-up capital of £10,000, the underwriters insured risks of more than £500,000 a year throughout the late 1830s and early 1840s. The business was severely cut in the crises of the 1840s, but by 1845 it was joined in the market by a second Saint John insurance company,[35] the Globe, and by 1851 the two firms were underwriting more than £600,000 of marine risks.[36] The insurance firms carried only a fraction of the total risks incurred by Saint John shipping but they were a source of considerable profit to the shareholders, whose annual dividends ranged from 10 to 40 per cent.[37]

Finance, the carrying trade, shipbuilding, sawmills, and timber were all part of a seamless web structured around the British market. At its heart was the imperial promise of preference and protection for its own. Even when this promise was kept, the rapidly shifting needs of the metropolitan market resulted in a very unstable economy creating a boom-and-bust psychology in the colonial business community. This instability was compounded by the continued efforts of British free traders to destroy the Old Colonial System in the interests of British consumers. The nightmare that the free traders might actually succeed in their purpose, following the election of Sir Robert Peel in 1842, in part precipitated a crisis of public confidence in the timber and colonial shipping industries. That crisis was followed by the gradual reduction of the colonial preference that left colonial timber on an equal footing with Scandinavian timber by 1846.

Three years later, the Navigation Acts were repealed and colonial shipping left to compete directly with American shipping for the commerce of the empire.

The colonial economy survived those blows surprisingly well. Despite the premonitions and prophecies of collapse, none of the commercial difficulties of the middle and late 1840s approached that of 1841–43. In fact, New Brunswick deals competed successfully on the British market and expanded rapidly during the 1840s, while Saint John shipping competed successfully with American in the North Atlantic trade. Only the squared-timber trade suffered serious consequences from the removal of the imperial preference.

None the less, the failure of the imperial promise engendered a major back-to-the-land movement and created a crisis of confidence in the traditional staples system. Abrogation of the colonial system had implications for all elements of the economy. The most immediate was that traditional imperial barriers to free trade with the United States were removed and thousands of small colonial artisans and farmers producing for the domestic market felt their livelihood threatened. The demand for protection against American and British produce became an important theme in the public debate over the economy that developed as the imperial policy of protection faded. As the population of Saint John and its hinterland expanded, these producers came increasingly to see their welfare in terms of a more restricted but controlled market.

Between 1824 and 1861 the population of New Brunswick increased more than two-and-one-half times, from 74,000 to 250,000; that of urban Saint John nearly quadrupled. By the later date, Saint John was home to 15 per cent of the people of the province. The settlements of the region existed in varying degrees of dependence upon the city. Saint John merchants possessed a monopoly of the commerce of the St John River valley and its tributaries, the centre and focus of the province in the nineteenth century, either as purchasers, forwarders, or agents for that commerce. The city dominated the commercial life of the Bay of Fundy counties of New Brunswick and Nova Scotia. In 1824 the population of the St John valley totalled 40,000. By 1840 it reached 88,000 and in 1861 nearly 140,000. The Fundy counties – exclusive of Saint John – developed in the same period from 65,000 to 101,000 to more than 165,000 inhabitants divided between New Brunswick and Nova Scotia on a 4:6 ratio in 1861. This hinterland growth from 104,000 to 310,000 between 1824 and 1860 created a market that became increasingly influential in its own right and offered an alternative to the staple-export emphasis that had marked the economy. The most obvious immediate effect of the growing migrant population was the rapid growth of the import trade.

The narrowly based New Brunswick economy described by Arthur Lower, with a thinly spread population dedicated to the gathering of a few commodities destined for the export market, reached its peak between 1809 and the mid-1820s. Wood gathering was the primary occupation of 85 per cent of the male population in the early nineteenth century, but the timber exports of the province reached their largest amounts between 1824 and 1826 at a time when the total population was only about 70,000. After 1826, the form of the wood exports changed, as did its value but the total volume never exceeded that of 1825.[38]

The fragmentary data on colonial trade available for the early 1820s indicate that most consumer goods, including food, and virtually all producer goods were imported into the province mainly from Great Britain. As a result of the influx of immigrants, colonial imports expanded much more rapidly than the exports, but it seems likely that before 1820 a reasonable trade balance between the staples output of timber, ships, and fish and the material needs of a population of perhaps 50,000 people was maintained. As the population rapidly expanded beyond this figure, alternative economic activity had to be developed to consume the surplus labour available in the economy. Some was used in the processing of the timber staple: sawmills and shipyards employed more and better-paid labour than did the ton-timber industries. But sawmill workers and ship artisans would account for only a small part of the labour pool created between 1820 and 1860. Ultimately, most migrants and Loyalists' children made the greater part of their livings from agriculture and the production of consumers and producers goods for the regional market.[39]

The growth of population in a comparatively undeveloped economy like that of New Brunswick resulted in larger and larger trade imbalances throughout the 1830s. Between 1825 and 1839, the value of imports rose from £694,000 to £1,433,000, while exports grew from £501,000 to only £701,000. Much of the £700,000 shortfall on the colony's 1839 current account was made up by the sale of New Brunswick vessels on the British market and the military expenditures of the British government in the province, but most of it had to be in the form of sterling and immigrants' notes payable in the United Kingdom.[40] For the merchants and other business men within the colony, the wholesale import trade was significantly more important than the traditional staples trade in 1839.

Paralleling the growth of the import trade was the emergence of an internal producers' economy in the province. The construction industry played an important role, particularly in Saint John. Across the province, however, the increase of improved land from 435,000 acres in 1840 to 885,000 in 1861 is indicative of the increasingly important role agriculture had come to play.[41]

A similar development occurred in the manufacturing and construction sectors. Only the most general estimates can be made of the construction industry of the period, but the censuses clearly indicate that between 1824 and 1861 the number of houses in the colony more than quadrupled, quite apart from any public buildings or the ravages of fire or the extensive infrastructure of roads, bridges, dams, and wharves. A variety of manufacturing activities producing both consumer and producer goods emerged in a hundred towns and villages after 1820. The cordwainer and tailor had long practised their crafts, but with the expanding local market they extended their operations and were joined in the 1820s and 1830s by a number of technical trades, notably the iron, brass, and later the copper founders. By 1861, colonial artisans produced virtually all the soap and candles, iron castings, furniture, and more than 75 per cent of the leather, footware, saddlery, machinery, nails, and spikes consumed in the province. Even clothing, long the most significant import and the basic staple import from the United Kingdom, was becoming a New Brunswick product. Nearly 40 per cent of the cloth and clothing used in the province was produced there, while between 1840 and 1861 the value of British cloth declined from perhaps 90 per cent to little more than 60 per cent of the cloth consumed in the New Brunswick market.

The major themes and tensions recurrent in colonial society at large were intensified in the city of Saint John because the city was the stage upon which the leadership of the old and the new economies played. The city was port of shipment for close to half the colony's exports between 1820 and 1860. Even more important was its role as wholesale distribution centre for New Brunswick and the Fundy coast of Nova Scotia. In most years, fully 80 per cent of all goods legally imported into the province passed over the wharves of Saint John, either for use in the city area or for reshipment into the hinterland. In 1851, the city contained well over half the merchants and other business elements in the province.[42]

At the same time Saint John was the centre of the province's artisan-oriented manufacturing industry. The city and Portland produced nearly half, by value, of the province's manufactured output and contained over half the artisans of the province.[43] By mid-century, for an increasing number of people, the city was becoming less a hinterland extension of Liverpool and more the centre of its own metropolitan system. Basic to such a system was the place of the city as a market for the surrounding hinterland. The role of the hinterland as food shed and wood shed for the city was a prominent theme in the early nineteenth-century community. The growth of Saint John to one of the largest urban centres in British North America by mid-century greatly expanded that market. The city was the primary meat and dairy market for most of the farms of the lower

St John valley and the Bay of Fundy settlements, as well as for the fishermen of the harbour and the bay, where a small fleet of wood boats moved from the private woodlots of the food shed to the market wharf of the city. This internal system was maintained by its own body of secondary business interests within the city, including grocers, butchers, and traders. The same market provided the stimulus for numerous small trades like leather, footwear, saddlery, blacksmithing, flour making, bakery products, candle and soap making, clothing, and the dozen trades and needs of the construction industry.

The significance of the producers' groups in the mid-century city is perhaps best illustrated in the 1861 Census. This document demonstrates that, despite the presence of ship labourers and mariners and millmen, Saint John was essentially a city of artisans. In the city alone, artisans outnumbered labourers 2600 to 1600 and with Portland added by 4000 to 2700.[44] When the thousand artisans associated with the shipbuilding trades are removed from the latter figure, the remainder reveals something of the size and significance of this powerful interest of domestic producers.

The development of a more broadly based provincial economy continued unabated in the 1860s. Gordon Bertram has demonstrated that the 1871 per capita output of New Brunswick manufacturing industries rivalled that of Ontario and Quebec and was nearly twice that of Nova Scotia.[45] At that time nearly half the industrial output of New Brunswick – more than $8.3 million (Canadian) in value – was produced in and around the city of Saint John. Not surprisingly the largest components of the city's industrial output were sawmill products and wooden ships. Apart from these staple manufactures, virtually every industry that had received even a modest degree of protection in the previous generation flourished. The manufacture of foundry products, footwear, and clothing all exceeded shipbuilding in value, while furniture and carriage making, boiler making, saw and file manufacturing, tin and sheet-iron output, and leather making all played significant roles in the local economy. Shipbuilding produced vessels to the value of $538,000 (£135,000) and employed 647 men, while foundry output exceeded $786,000 (£195,000) and employed 407, and 565 boot- and shoe-makers produced $539,000 worth of footwear. In terms of employment, all these activities were dwarfed by the clothing trades, which employed 1033 people, 828 of them women, and produced more than $826,000 (£206,000) worth of clothing.[46] The provincial demand for cloth and bar iron was being met in large part by the output of the Parks Cotton Mills and the Coldstream Rolling Mills at Saint John. The city's woollen and cotton mills may have provided as much as half the cloth consumed in the clothing trades.[47]

The North and South Market wharves
and Market Slip, c. 1870 (NBM)

Market Square, Saint John, c. 1870 (NBM)

By the end of the colonial period, two economic systems – each possessing its own institutions and work-force – had emerged in Saint John. The older system, structured on the great timber staple, had been in relative decline after 1825. Increasingly, its needs were challenged by a newer, more dynamic system centred on the production of goods for the domestic market, the supporters of which argued for the development of a stable internally integrated economy. A city that had only made the transition from mercantile dependency to artisans' shops in the early century was by 1860 home to interests that seemed capable of transforming the city into an industrial centre.

~2~

The Common Council

Like the early economy, the political institutions of Saint John were formed in response to imperial needs and reflected the structure of their English counterparts. Saint John became an instant centre of population in 1783 with the arrival of some thousands of refugee Loyalists from New York. That fact alone would not have ensured the creation of urban political institutions: communities the size of Montreal, Quebec, Halifax, and later Toronto were governed as rural parishes well into the nineteenth century. Saint John received the institutional form of a city in 1785 when Thomas Carleton, the new governor of New Brunswick, conferred the status by royal charter.[1] This special dignity provided a focus for the community and sharply distinguished the city parishes from the unorganized villages and towns surrounding it. The new city was only a part of the Loyalist settlement at the mouth of the St John River; the mainland of St John County and even the northern shore of the harbour remained outside and cut the city into two unlinked pieces. From 1785 onward, it is possible to speak of Saint John 'within-the-walls' and of the suburbs without. The southern portion of Portland parish, lying along the city 'walls,' had been granted to three pre-Loyalist families; even though it developed into a significant urban area, it remained without municipal form.

The city itself was an English creation and its models were entirely British. While the charter permitted considerable participation on the part of citizens in the public life of the community, it was designed to maintain a deferential society and restrict democratic excess. The royal charter created a public corporation under the style of the mayor, aldermen, and commonalty of the city of Saint John.[2] The corporate powers were exercised by a Common Council composed of a mayor, six aldermen, and six assistant aldermen. Members of the Common Council played legislative, executive, and judicial roles. Sitting as a Common Council, they had authority to promulgate laws and policies for the better governing of the city. As individuals or as members of council committees, they personally undertook to administer many of the policies they had made corporately. Finally, the mayor and aldermen always held commissions as justices of the peace, of the quorum, and of the common pleas. As such they were magistrates of the county court of quarter sessions, sat on a rotating basis as police magistrates, and any one member, together with the common clerk, constituted the city court of common pleas empowered to hear all civil cases up to £5.

The charter powers granted the corporation were extensive and could not be altered by the province without the consent of Common Council. The geographic area of the city, including its harbour, was an area of special jurisdiction within which the Common Council possessed authority to maintain public order; to regulate commerce and the trades; to conserve and control the river, bay, harbours, piers, wharves, and streets; to lay out and maintain all streets, highways, and bridges throughout the county and city of Saint John; to appoint and supervise all parish officers; and to create freemen who alone possessed the franchise and the right to carry on any craft, business, or profession within the city.

In common with the other counties of New Brunswick, local government in St John County was administered by an appointed magistracy of prominent freeholders known as the sessions. For county purposes the city constituted two parishes: St John on the east side of the harbour and Carleton on the west. The authority of the St John sessions was curtailed by the presence of the city and its Common Council. While the sessions performed most of its traditional duties in the rural parishes, its function in the city was primarily custodial. Through the overseers of the poor, the magistrates administered the provincial poor laws. They also took primary responsibility for the construction and maintenance of those institutions concerned with the care of the poor and the deviant – notably the poor house, court house, gaol, almshouse, house of correction, house of refuge, immigrants and seamen's hospitals, penitentiary, and asylum. Yet even in these areas the Common Council members played an important role. The mayor and aldermen were always the active magistrates in the county and their opinions weighed heavily in matters related to concerns of the city.

In creating the first (and for nearly half a century the only) Common Council in British North America, Governor Carleton and his aides attempted to incorporate the tripartite principles of monarchy, aristocracy,

View of the City of Saint John from the upper east side, 1827 (NBM)

The Hon. John Robinson, mayor, province treasurer, merchant.
Son of Col. Beverley Robinson and uncle of Sir John Beverley Robinson,
chief justice of Upper Canada, c. 1825
(courtesy, Provincial Archives of New Brunswick [PANB])

and democracy that were so fashionable at the time. In imitation of the English municipal charters, the political constituency of Saint John was defined as its freemen and freeholders.[3] But that group, 'the commonalty,' no longer played a direct role in the administration of the city, instead deferring to the aldermen and assistant aldermen whom they annually elected to undertake the corporation's business. Within this structure, it was assumed that the aldermen would be representative of the respectable freeholders of the city while their assistants would be drawn from the respectable tradesmen. The point at which Governor Carleton's charter diverged most sharply from that of English practice was in the appointment of the mayor and the legal officers of the corporation. English common councils normally elected their own mayors from among the prominent aldermen and appointed their own servants; Carleton incorporated the mayoralty as one of the great offices of the crown in New Brunswick. Perhaps he feared the thrust of a rude democracy even among the Loyalist freemen in the frontier environment and perceived this office as a means of retaining control of the municipal executive authority. Whatever his reasons, this crucial condition in the charter remained inviolate until 1851. The mayor was a personal appointee of the governor. He chaired the Common Council and the county sessions and was chief magistrate and chief executive of the county and the city. He alone could use the city seal, grant licences, and issue freedoms.

More important than any political power or economic benefit was the social status accorded the holder of the office. The mayor was agent to the lieutenant-governor. The stature of the office was further enhanced by the personal stature of its holder. The first four incumbents, who held the mayoralty for a total of forty-eight years, were all members of the city's great patrician and merchant families and came to the office while holding the dignity of member of His Majesty's Council for New Brunswick.[4] Colonel Gabriel Ludlow was a brother of the first provincial chief justice, William Campbell was a prominent merchant, John Robinson was the son of New Brunswick's premier Loyalist, Colonel Beverley Robinson, and William Black had been a leading Scottish timber merchant.

In addition to the mayoralty, the lieutenant-governor appointed the corporation's law officers. The recorder was usually an ambitious young attorney from good family for whom civic office was the first step in a career progression that led from recorder to solicitor general, attorney general, and supreme court judge. The common clerkship, since it entailed four offices (common clerk, clerk of sessions, clerk of common pleas, and county clerk) and was a full-time position, always went to a less-distinguished family than did the part-time recordership. None the less, able incumbents in both offices who possessed views acceptable to the lieutenant-governor could make very successful careers within the provincial service. Both the older and younger Ward Chipman served as recorders of the city, the former finishing his career as administrator of the province, the latter as chief justice; and so did Robert Parker, who ended as chief justice of New Brunswick, and Edward Jarvis, who became chief justice of Prince Edward Island.[5] Charles and James Peters, uncle and nephew, held the lucrative office of common clerk from 1799 until 1847.

The citizens of this little commonwealth were its freemen and free-holders. Freeholders were simply real-estate owners who automatically possessed the political privileges of freemen because they were perceived as having a stake in the community. The concept of freemen was rather more complex. It went far beyond ownership of property. The freedom was a way of protecting the political and economic interests that citizens possessed by virtue of their family's long tenure in the community.

The original Loyalist arrivals had been offered their freedom on payment of fees of office: about 500 of 1100 males between 16 and 60 took advantage of that offer.[6] After 1785, the freedom was restricted to those sons and unmarried daughters of freemen who had served an apprentice-ship with the master or merchant in the city. Clearly the charter's intention, as the city's recorder, Robert Parker, noted in 1829, had been to restrict the freedom of the city to the original freemen and their offspring forever.[7] The charter did however allow the mayor to admit others to the freedom through purchase. Throughout the colonial period the Common Council maintained a schedule of fees for this purpose. By payment of a sum ranging from £5 to £1.10.0, strangers were permitted to obtain citizenship. Fees were arranged by occupation in a way that reflected the social rankings within the city. Gentlemen and merchants paid the full £5, followed in second rank by masters, ship captains, grocers, and tavern-keepers, in third by journeymen and captains of small vessels, and so on down to labourers and school masters at the bottom. All those who had served an apprenticeship in the city paid £1.[8]

Possession of the freedom also provided an important economic benefit. The city protected the occupations of its freemen by denying employment to non-freemen. Theoretically this prohibition would have excluded even common labourers and servants from the urban labour force. In reality it was only enforced against the higher- and middle-status occupations. Most menial workers never obtained the freedom and were permitted to spend their entire working life in the city. At the same time, the prohibition did provide some protection to artisans, tradesmen, grocers, manufacturers, merchants, and professionals. Its enforcement had partic-ular implications for Americans. Since only British subjects could become freemen, Americans could legally work as servants, or live outside the city, or pay an annual £25 fee to secure a licence permitting them to work in the city.

Between 1785 and 1840, about 3000 people – almost all of them male – were admitted to the freedom of Saint John. In the next twenty years they were joined by another 4000. While it is impossible to determine the number of freemen living in the city at any given moment, analysis of the 1851 census reveals that about one in five males twenty-one years and over and one in four male heads of households were freemen. When freeholders who were not freemen are added to this figure, it is probable that about one-quarter of all adult males and one-third of all male household heads were citizens of the city.[9] The proportion of freemen in the population at mid-century compared favourably to that found in English cities such as Birmingham and Ipswich and even Leeds; it was considerably smaller than that found in American cities like Boston and New York.[10]

There were in Saint John by 1815 six legal divisions into which all men and single working women were gathered: freeholders, freemen, non-freemen British subjects, aliens, blacks, and business women. Only the first two categories possessed the franchise. The third was able to acquire it through purchase, and the fourth through naturalization and purchase although the former process would take at least five years. Blacks could not become freemen under the charter. Unmarried working women were required to purchase their freedom but were permitted no electoral rights.

Given the comparatively small number of freemen, it is tempting to assume that they composed something of a closed élite drawn from high-status occupations. An examination of freemen's rolls does not confirm this premise. While the proportion of merchants and professionals who were freemen was obviously higher than that of people in the lowest ranks of society, it is significant that the freemen labourers made up by far the largest occupational group admitted to the freedom. Indeed, before 1850 there were nearly as many labourers admitted to the freedom as all persons from high-status and white-collar occupations combined. In the decade 1808–19, labourers constituted nearly one-third of all admissions, a proportion that rose to more than two out of five in the 1820s. Artisans and tradesmen were even more numerous than labourers among the civic electors. Composing nearly two-fifths of all freemen admissions in the colonial period, they often possessed property within the city and qualified as freeholders as well.

None of this is to suggest that labourers would elect other labourers to Common Council or that they possessed the influence over public policy that their numbers would indicate. Even in New England and New York communities, where the franchise was more broadly based than in Saint John, poor taxpayers consistently elected well-to-do citizens as their representatives.[11] A sense of deference and the pressures that could be brought to bear in an election held as a public forum diminished the influence of lower-status electors. Ultimately, power within civic institutions was exercised by the elected aldermen and assistants.

The relative strength of freemen to freeholders is difficult to establish since the only complete surviving record of freeholders is that for 1856. At that time there were about 1000 male and 37 female freeholders, many of whom were non-resident or deceased. Comparison of the 1851 Census sample with the freeholders' and freemen's rolls indicates that about 40 per cent of the electorate on the populous east side of the harbour were freeholders and freemen. Propertyless freemen made up a clear majority of the electors. That conclusion is confirmed by the poll books of the 1848 civic election in Kings and Queens wards where those owning property in 1854 accounted for only one-quarter of the total votes cast.[12] Freeholders could also purchase their freedom and about 60 per cent of those in the 1851 Census sample did so.[13]

The most important political benefit conferred by the franchise was the right to vote in the annual civic elections where freemen and freeholders met as equals to elect the Common Council of the city. The charter of 1785 brought together two peninsulas and the harbour between them to form the city. The east-side peninsula, Parrtown, which contained the overwhelming mass of the population, was divided into four wards; the west-side peninsula, Carleton, became two. For electoral purposes, each ward was a constituency returning an alderman and an assistant to the council. Usually each aldermanic candidate headed a ticket consisting of himself and of candidates for the offices of assistant alderman and constable.

The two senior offices were inextricably linked, yet were fundamentally different in status. The alderman was a gentleman permitted by custom to attach the coveted 'Esquire' to his name. This status was confirmed by the king's commission he held as justice of the common pleas. Although aldermen and assistant aldermen sat together at the council board and had an equal vote in council decisions, the chairmanship of important council committees and recommendations on matters concerning the ward almost never fell to the assistant aldermen.

Between 1815 and 1860, only a handful of great merchants, few professionals, and virtually no great functionaries sat on Common Council and those who did remained for only one or two years.[14] Several minor merchants also belonged to the council but, particularly before 1840, the aldermanic office was dominated by a petite bourgeoisie of masters, fishermen, grocers, captains of small coasting vessels, and artisans. The social distinction between aldermanic and assistant aldermanic offices was reflected in the middling status occupations of the occupants of the latter. Before 1840, almost two-thirds of the assistants were carpenters, tanners, coopers, printers, bakers, and assorted other artisans. In contrast to the experience of most small English cities where large proprietors controlled the councils, the Saint John council was dominated by its small proprietors.[15]

As a group, the aldermen and their assistants represented longevity and varying degrees of material success in the Saint John community. Their dominant social characteristics were upward mobility, the ownership of real property, longevity of city residence, and preference for religious dissent. The surprising thing about them was the number who began their careers as labourers and ended them as business men and city aldermen. The impression of upward mobility is reinforced by the numbers of young men of modest social origins who began their political careers as assistant aldermen and eventually became aldermen, a process characteristic of about one-third of the aldermanic incumbents of the period.[16] Moreover, since those who began their careers at lower stations in life tended to remain on the Common Council for longer periods than did those from better families, well over half the aldermanic terms between 1815 and 1840 were served by men who had experience as assistant aldermen.

The great majority of aldermen and assistant aldermen were freeholders. While it is difficult to ascertain the information for the early period, examination of common councillors from 1845 to 1860 suggests that at least two-thirds of the aldermen and two-fifths of the assistants were freeholders. The latter figure is interesting because the group was concentrated in the artisan occupations. While several merchant councillors of the period were not freeholders, all of those of the humbler origins were. Although many Irish and English immigrants were found among their numbers, a majority were drawn from the sons and grandsons of Loyalists, both from the city's original grantees and from rural migrants. Finally, like the common councils of most early nineteenth-century English cities, the Saint John council was marked by the high proportion of Protestant (non-Anglican) dissenters found among its members. This fact is especially significant in view of the small proportion of dissenters among the members of the provincial legislature and in the ranks of the appointed magistracy. Most striking was the strong Baptist presence among the aldermen in the period before 1830. Although there were no more than a few hundred adult male Baptists in the city, Calvinist Baptists rivalled the much more numerous Methodists on the council. Part of the explanation for this early Baptist activity may have to do with the pietism of the Methodists, but it also reflects the fact that a number of early nineteenth-century Baptists had achieved considerable economic success in this rapidly expanding timber colony. At the other extreme, Irish Catholics and Scots Presbyterians were largely absent from the council board before 1860.[17]

This, then, was the composite Common Council that directed the development of the city of Saint John in the early- and mid-nineteenth century. The council drew largely from the ranks of the Saint John 'commonalty' of the late eighteenth century. These were men who, like their fathers, began work as labourers, mariners, tanners, shipwrights, fishermen, bakers, coopers, printers, tailors, grocers, clerks, or tavern keepers. What they generally had in common was a traditional residency in the city and an extensive kinship network. Their life experience suggests a pattern of slow but careful accumulation of capital resources, usually the result of a combination of moderate risk-taking ventures, simultaneous involvement in several undertakings not directly concerned with their trade or business, and ownership of real property in or near the city. Typically, they had inherited some part of a small estate from their fathers, perhaps title to a single city lot, and then over a lifetime added to this modest beginning. Their attitude toward private property in general and to land in particular was obsessive: it was viewed as the final act of security never to be alienated. They were united in their frugality, industry, acquisitiveness, their sense of community and family, their ideology and progress and social mobility, their belief in the rewards of virtuous living, and, in most cases, their acceptance of the Loyalist tradition and of their place within the world-view on which it was predicated. In short, regardless of the extent or nature of their resources, they were the petite bourgeoisie of Saint John – a conservative, often inward-looking middle class, similar in outlook to their English counterparts.[18] Through their kinship and friendship network and their ability to develop a wide-ranging system of patron/client relationships by effective use of the extensive patronage in the gift of the councillors, they both reflected the views and origins of their constituency and remained in control of the Common Council throughout the colonial era.[19]

Control of the Common Council did not necessarily mean domination of the public life of the city. Great merchants and patricians had access to a variety of mechanisms through which they could exercise power. Yet, as John Garrard has demonstrated for mid-nineteenth-century English cities, influence within council was not so much a result of wealth as of a willingness to work at the often onerous tasks of civic administration.[20] The Saint John councillors who survived more than a few terms were those who worked unceasingly at the complex tasks that, in the pre-1840 city, played an important role in the formation of community. Their responsibilities embraced every aspect of public life in the nineteenth-century city. In an age of limited provincial and imperial responsibilities – limited in part because of the inconsequential civil service and lack of technology to more closely bind the domain – the municipal government became for its citizenry the provider of most vital services, ranging from basic transportation facilities, through public safety, welfare, water-supplies, and regulation of food supplies. Some of these functions were the responsibility of the sessions, but by the 1820s the Saint John experience paralleled that of the English boroughs where, because they were active, the elected borough magistrates became the dominant influence in the administration of the county.[21]

Unfortunately, while the charter provided ample scope for public intervention by the Common Council, this potential was severely limited by the taxing powers granted in the charter. These restricted council revenues to licence fees and rents from the city's common and corporation lands.

Given these limitations to its taxing authority and the extensive responsibilities required to maintain an increasingly complex urban society, council was able to function only through the extensive voluntary efforts of its citizens. The large corporate endeavours needed to maintain a night watch and a fire department required the enlistment of all adult males, particularly freemen and freeholders. Firemen were regarded as so essential in this wooden city that they were in time relieved of militia and jury service, as well as of poor taxes and statute labour. And since the firemen were drawn largely from the ranks of the artisan-freeholders, this class was almost entirely exempted from the payment of any direct taxes or services.[22]

The public service of the city before 1840 functioned through the use of private enterprise to accomplish public ends, part-time user-pay civil service, and voluntary leadership of the harbour and harbour facilities. The second feature of the system was the use of a part-time civil service. Some of these officers, like the mayor, held charter offices and were rewarded for their work through fees of office on a user-pay basis. A much larger second group of professional and supervisory officials, including the assessors and collectors of taxes, the supervisors and surveyors of roads, the harbour master, and inspectors of wheat, bread, meat, fish, firewood, and coals, were paid either a periodic per diem wage or a percentage of the revenues they collected. Still a third group, the city labourers, might end up on the payroll either as hourly employees or, in the case of street lighters, as contract labour paid on a monthly basis for a particular piece of work. In all, in any given year in the 1820s, perhaps as many as 500 of the city's 2000 adult males might participate in the functions of civil government, most as labourers, cartmen, or firemen, but

Sydney Ward, end of Prince William Street, c. 1870 (NBM)

Duke Street facing the harbour, c. 1870 (NBM)

Queen Square, c. 1870 (NBM)

Saint John from Fort Howe
showing part of York Point in the foreground, 1864 (NBM)

King Street facing King Square, c. 1870.
The tower containing the work bell is in the centre (NBM)

Queens Ward housing (possibly Carmarthen Street), c. 1870 (NBM)

a significant number as officers of the city, posts usually held by men of some stature and status in the community.

At the centre of this system, enabling and manipulating the whole, were the principal voluntaryists, the members of the Common Council. Their role was that of an unpaid administrator overseeing the whole range of civic activities. The system certainly encouraged patronage and, over time, the client/patron relationship that characterized so much of pre-industrial social relationships in England. But it was, in the main, efficient and workable in the relatively small homogeneous community that was Saint John before 1820.

The alderman and his assistant operated at the level of the ward, the city, and the province. The most time-consuming and socially significant of these activities were those involving the ward. In many ways, the city's six wards were villages of extended neighbourhoods each possessing most of the basic material accoutrements of an urban society – streets, markets, squares, public wells – and an often unique combination of social characteristics. The typical ward was about 150 acres in size, an area that as late as 1830 included a number of open meadows and pastures. The east-side wards cut across the peninsula dividing it latitudinally into four segments, each of equal length. The business district of the city faced the harbour and since all four parishes shared the harbour, each contained a portion of this central district.

But there the similarity ended. Sydney, the smallest ward in both size and population, shared the southern tip of the peninsula with the British garrison. Here were found a disproportionate share of the professions that fattened on meeting the needs of a peacetime garrison: tavern keepers, prostitutes, and crimps. Here, too, were many of the sailors' boarding houses. Freemen were present as well – although they were a smaller proportion of the population than in any other ward in the city – but they also reflected the general population of the ward. Generally, they were poorer freemen, an image that the presence of a half-dozen merchants did little to modify.

Next to Sydney was Dukes Ward, an intermediate zone containing a number of minor merchants and small business men, but dominated by its artisans and mechanics. Like neighbouring Queens, which it most resembled socially, Dukes was a centre of the native population of Loyalist origins. Queens Ward, the very heart of the city, contained in its population the largest proportion of business men of any ward. Queens, Guys – directly across the harbour – and the eastern end of Kings Ward constituted the centre of the city's tradocracy. Queens was characterized by its Protestant dissenters and by a later reputation as the centre of the famous prohibitionist 'Smashers' tradition. At the head of the peninsula was Kings, the largest, most densely populated, and most polyglot ward. Its east side was dominated by a population of largely Protestant artisans and shopkeepers, while its harbour shore, the centre of the city's business life, housed both great merchants and the poorest of Irish-Catholic dockworkers. Between 1850 and 1860, Kings was divided and Wellington and Prince wards were created out of its east side.

The aldermen's function was to represent the ward in the Common Council and to implement the decisions of that council within the ward. The most useful aldermen became the paterfamilias of their constituencies – known, respected, and easily accessible. Accessibility, in fact, was the most important characteristic that aldermen and assistants possessed. More than any other public figures, councillors were subject to the will (some would have said to the whims) of their electorate. On this account alone, there was no more arduous public position in the province. The relationship was an intensely personal one. Councillors were subject to the arrival of constituents at their door in connection with any number of immediate and often controversial matters. The annual election could be a fearsome adventure, sometimes fraught with violence and threats of violence. In 1842, Alderman Henry Porter of Kings actually withdrew from the fray after a mob of his constituents tore down the platform on which he was speaking and drove him from the streets. Many of these partisans were doubtless freemen; many others were not.

The most effective and enduring aldermen were those who carefully cultivated the interests of their ward and used the authority of their office to develop an intricate network of relationships with their freemen through blood, service, and patronage. The aldermen controlled the patronage for road work financed by those who commuted their statute labour for money. This involved nearly 4000 man-days of employment as early as 1828 and by 1842 exceeded 10,000.[23] Aldermen in Kings and Queens wards each had in excess of 2000 man-days by the later date and could offer 3s. a day to their workers.[24] As well, the aldermen could usually name the cartmen at a wage of 10s.

Nor were the aldermen's gifts limited to those of low status and limited means. The letting of contracts for public works done within a particular ward was frequently delegated to the alderman and assistant from that ward and they would normally constitute the supervisory committee to oversee not only contract projects but also the faithful performance of all public functions within the ward.

An even more important source of patronage was the influence wielded by the aldermen in the matter of appointments to the hundreds of part-time municipal offices. These included the annual rentals of all corporation revenues, leases on the several municipal wharves, weighage, and anchorage, as well as appointments of more than a hundred part-time public officials.[25]

Finally, through their control of the harbour and the corporation lands, the councillors possessed the richest natural resources in the province, including not only the harbour, its wharves, water lots, tidal power, flats, and water front, but also the most valuable salmon fishery on the Atlantic coast. Ultimately even the greatest city merchant had to make his peace with council in order to acquire long-term leases to the land and harbour resources he needed to exploit.

In addition to this extensive system of patronage, the aldermen wielded considerable influence among their constituents through their roles as magistrates. The magistracy conferred upon aldermen an authority that was to be found nowhere else in the political system. Each alderman served as police magistrate. The most important court in the city was the fortnightly common pleas, in which an alderman sat as chief justice. It is difficult to overestimate the value and significance of this court. It was the first trial court and the only one in which swift and relatively cheap justice could be obtained. Its significance is revealed in the only surviving colonial record, a summary of hearings at six sittings between September and December 1843. In that period, the court issued 1641 summons and attachments, 243 executions, and committed 39 people to gaol for debt. This was the court in which debts were collected and sailors sued their captains for wages.[26]

Equally important in the public mind was the alderman's role as guardian of the peace and public morals. In minor criminal matters, the alderman could dispatch the constables to arrest an individual, have the culprit hauled before him, and send him or her to the House of Correction or the penitentiary for up to sixty days.[27] An alderman's presence at a public function made even the boldest think twice before indulging in a show of spirits. The extent of this judicial influence depended very much on the willingness of the aldermen to play such roles. Because the exercise involved judgment, the most popular aldermen involved themselves as little as possible. However, some took this role very seriously. Alderman Peters, for example, would walk through the Irish ghetto at York Point on a Sunday afternoon calling on the proprietors of each open shop and tavern and threatening them with fines if the violation of the sabbath were repeated.[28]

Through the devices of personal association, service, and patronage, some aldermen became the expression of their constituencies, played influential roles in the formulation of public policy, and survived the annual elections to achieve long public careers. Most notable among these were Thomas Harding, George Bond, and Gregory Van Horne who served, respectively, 29, 23, and 25 years in the office for Dukes, Brooks, and Sydney wards. Other important figures included Henry Porter (Kings, 12 years), John M. Wilmot (Kings, 10 years), and David Ansley (Queens, 8 years). With the exception of George Bond, all were native New Brunswickers and long-time residents of their ward. All were business men or master artisans: Wilmot and Porter were merchants, Harding and Ansley were tanners, and Bond was a sawmill operator. The group had strong evangelical roots: Harding, Bond, and Wilmot were leading Calvinist Baptists and Ansley was a Methodist.

Secure in their wards, the aldermen and their assistants met as a Common Council to administer the city. Central to this meeting was the question of whether they met as a city council or as representatives of six separate entities confederated for certain common purposes. That question was never fully settled before 1840. The Common Council was the place where the broad public interest was defined, where regulation of goods, social relationships, and fees for the protection of society were prepared, and where the distribution of patronage, office, and contracts occurred.

Until the late 1830s, the Common Council worked through a system of committee of the whole. Specific tasks of the council were assigned to individuals or to ad hoc committees, but all matters had to be considered by a full council before decision was taken. The mounting pressure of business was modified in 1839 by the creation of four standing committees – finance, land, protection, maintenance – that would deal with their respective problems in separate meetings and bring forward final resolutions for the consent of council.[29] The new structure enjoyed considerable success and in 1841 the system was expanded to thirteen committees, each having administrative responsibility for one or two municipal functions. These three- to five-man committees prepared policy proposals for council and superintended the activities of employees and contractors concerned with the activity.

If the aldermen and assistants were creatures of their ward and their freemen, the mayor, presumably, was the symbol of the city's unity. Holding office at royal pleasure, a strong patrician mayor was frequently able to moderate the sometimes bitter animosities that disturbed the council board. As chairman of the meeting, he was able to decide its agenda and establish its rules of order. But apart from his personal and procedural authority, the mayor possessed certain charter rights that gave him a veto over certain kinds of council decisions. Most of these related to the issue of licences and the use of the city seal. The council could set a scale of fees for the admission of freemen, but the mayor could refuse to issue the licence to any individual for reasons of his own. Similarly, tavern and retail licences and the licences required by surveyors of lumber, fish, and other commodities were all issued under the mayor's authority. As the city's chief executive officer, the mayor was responsible for the peace, order, and good government of the city on a day-to-day basis. His most important role was that of intermediary between the city on the one hand and the provincial and imperial governments on the other. The mayor made frequent reports to the lieutenant-governor on the state of the city, and the latter replied with a spate of advice ranging from a demand that animals be removed from the streets, to offers of assistance following major fires, to requests for specific public improvements, to advice on how to deal with Irish immigrants.[30] The influence the governor possessed in the Common Council stemmed not so much from his vice-regal position – although that certainly got him a hearing – as from the provincial funds he was able to make available to projects meeting his approval.

New sources of revenue was something the council desperately needed in the 1820s and 1830s. The charter revenues – drawn largely from rentals and fees – rose slowly between 1820 and 1840, but did not nearly meet the capital requirements of a rapidly growing city. Even with the use of volunteer and fee-receiving functionaries, the basic costs of administering the city far exceeded the revenues by 1830. The result was a series of begging appeals from the Common Council and the sessions requesting assistance in erecting a penitentiary, a house of correction, a house of refuge, to provide aid to distressed immigrants, funds to cut down and open new city streets, grants to build landing places for the new steam ferry and for ocean-going steamships.[31] In addition to the possibility of obtaining grants through an order in council, there was the hope that the governor would intercede with the assembly on issues of particular interest to the city.

Even more important, the city attempted, whenever possible, to use the lieutenant-governor as an ally in its frequent wars with its enemies to the south and the north. To the south was the imperial garrison, the commanders of which were locked in almost incessant struggle with the Common Council over the disposition of strategic lands within the city and the regulation of taverns and bawdy houses in the Sydney Ward area.[32] To the north were the estates of the great proprietorial families, notably the Simonds, Hazens, and Whites, who owned most of the land surrounding the city, including part of the upper harbour and the lower reaches of the St John River where the owners and their lessees operated sawmills. The council endeavoured to prevent these local magnates from putting sawdust into the river and from claiming any property rights below the low-water mark in the north end of the harbour.[33]

Quite apart from its relationship with the provincial executive, the Common Council maintained a close relationship with the House of Assembly. The charter of the city created a corporation with power to govern a seventeenth-century market town. Any kind of modernization required special legislation conferring the necessary authority on the Common Council and providing it with provincial grants.[34]

Under normal circumstances the point of contact between the corporation and the assembly was the mayor and the assembly members for the city. During Robert F. Hazen's tenure in the mayoralty, the senior Saint John assemblyman, John R. Partelow, favoured the mayor with a running commentary on the progress of the city's requests and of the strategies he developed in order to achieve them. At the 1839 sitting he reported each of his prizes to the mayor – on 2 February 'Got £500 for Madras School'; on 25 February 'got £1250 for the Corporation wharves and £500 for the Mill Bridge widening in the Committees. Have yet to look at Saint John and Portland Poor, Breakwater, and Russell Street. Claims for emigrants ... referred to select Committee'; on 5 March 'Wharves and Bridge grants through Legislature, Breakwater got £500, Board of Health for medical doctors £327'; on 10 March 'House of Correction £500 – got it through by offering to take convicts from all over the province. £800 for Saint John poor and £1000 for the asylum.'[35] It was reasonably good hunting that year, but then Partelow was one of the most astute politicians in the province.

There was a second, purely negative reason for the great interest the council took in the proceedings of the legislature. Like its English counterparts, the corporation of Saint John was particularly conscious of its charter rights and jealously guarded those prerogatives. Like their English counterparts, the civic law officers carefully scrutinized each proposal before the assembly to determine its implications for the city. Intrusions on the charter rights could occur through general laws applied to the whole province, and through bills aimed specifically at a certain problem within the city. In such cases the Common Council prepared counter-petitions opposing the proposals and then usually sent delegations of councillors or civic functionaries to lobby against the bill on the grounds that it contained matters that were not within the authority of the provincial legislature.[36]

The issue of the inviolability of the royal charter lay at the heart of each of these confrontations. The Common Council never retreated from the position that its prerogative was derived directly from the throne and could not be modified, saving with its consent, by any provincial authority. It was a view generally respected by the legislature. In the few cases where the issue was tried, the city always won. In 1807, for example,

the colonial secretary disallowed a provincial statute extending ownership of land along the river front to the low-water mark on the grounds
that it infringed the city's charter rights.

The most famous test case occurred following the disastrous fire of 1839.
That fire, the second major conflagration in the city in less than three
years, was made possible by the tightly packed three-storey wooden
buildings and the narrow streets into which they were jammed. At a
special sitting of the legislature called to deal with the emergency, Sir John
Harvey – that most conciliatory of all New Brunswick governors –
introduced legislation to widen certain streets in the burned district and
to establish regulations designed to prevent further destruction from fire.
A majority of the Common Council opposed the governor's unilateral
action.[37] In the animated and frequently bitter debate following, the
venerable and highly respected Thomas Harding, in the true Independent tradition, placed his arm on the council table and declared that he
would sooner sever it than surrender one iota of the rights guaranteed in
the charter.

The council protested the proposals and when this did not deter the
governor, several members determined to carry a petition to the foot of the
throne asking for redress of their grievance. That proposal, with its clear
challenge to the governor's authority, split the council itself. On a 7 to 5
vote, the majority determined to prepare the petition arguing that the
province had no right to intervene. The recorder prepared a paper
defending the legislature's right to override the charter and advised the
mayor to neither sign the petition nor forward it to London.[38] The grateful
mayor eagerly complied with this advice. Undaunted, the dissidents took
control of the council and by resolution had the common clerk engross the
petition. The Saint John delegation was received by an irate Harvey,
who, after scolding the recalcitrant burghers, forwarded the petition
to London, together with his letter of disapproval and the recorder's
opinion on the subject.[39]

The Common Council won its war. The Colonial Office suspended the
offending legislation, vindicated the dissidents, and sustained the
principle of the inviolability of the city charter. Unfortunately the
interests of local democracy and community welfare sometimes did not
coincide. The principle may have been important but the issue was a poor
one. Having proved their point, the council moved a resolution of thanks
to the Queen, as defender of the rights of her subjects, and then agreed to
allow the legislation to go into effect.[40]

The 1841 triumph marked the high point of the corporation's influence.
Designed to serve a seventeenth-century market town, it had demonstrated a considerable resiliency and adaptability to the needs of the

urban community. Its great strength lay in its capacity to permit a close personal relationship between the governors and the governed and to extend informal control through the involvement of large numbers of men in the common good. And while the Common Council had many of the weaknesses of its English counterparts – particularly the lack of authority to tax and innovate – it was always a more popularly based body than almost any English corporation. Finally, the council membership reflected its position in the political hierarchy of the province: the great merchants and functionaries dominated the provincial legislature, while leaders of the artisans' interest were increasingly found in the Common Council seats.

~3~

The Merchant and the
Social Order

At the centre of the mercantile economy of early nineteenth-century Saint John was a merchant élite that played a central role in determining the economic priorities of the city. The Saint John experience paralleled that of most eighteenth- and nineteenth-century English and North American ports. Indeed, the most powerful statement in mid-twentieth-century Canadian historiography is Donald Creighton's depiction of the Montreal merchant élite as the primary nation builders of the first half of the nineteenth century.[1] While Creighton's view of the motives of this élite has recently been challenged by Gerald Tulchinsky, perceptions of their influence and social position remain undiminished.[2] Similar views of the Halifax merchants have been advanced by David Sutherland.[3] And while Gunther Frank would argue that these were colonizing élites fulfilling the aims of their metropolitan masters,[4] no one would challenge the view that such élites were able to set the local agenda and create the ideological framework within which discussion and major decisions were taken.

The Saint John merchant directed the wholesale import trade of the province, controlled the export of staples, bought and sold through his agents on the British, American, and West Indian markets, owned most of the fleet upon which the prosperity of the city so much depended, employed the ship labourers and cartmen, built and maintained the wharves around which the port centred, and organized and directed the banks and other financial institutions (and through them the monetary policy of the colony). Indeed, his influence has been perceived by some scholars as so extensive that much of the accepted analysis of colonial society has been seen in terms of a contest for power between the Saint John commercial interests and the official bureaucracy centred in Fredericton. Stewart MacNutt's view of the crown-lands crisis of the 1830s is predicated on the assumption that an organized and self-conscious provincial merchant community moved to destroy a competing élite of functionaries that attempted to sustain a program inimical to merchant interests. Saint John merchants, like those of Montreal and Halifax, have been perceived as leaders of a dominant provincial élite. More important, they have been seen as a social type with peculiar and commonly held values and characteristics. If any clearly identifiable class or community of interest existed in colonial Saint John, it was surely to be found in this influential group of great proprietors.

In many ways, the merchants are the most easily defined social group in the city. They were numerous, prominent, and often played public roles. The merchant was a legally defined status in colonial Saint John. The esteem in which merchants were held is reflected in the £5 fee required of those British subjects seeking admission as freemen merchants. Between 1785 and 1860, a total of 702 men were admitted to this status, although the numbers varied sharply from decade to decade throughout the period.[5] In addition, a number of men who began their careers in another occupation became merchants. The links between mariners and merchants and clerks and merchants were particularly close, and while most clerks did not achieve the status of capitalist, a number did so.[6]

In all, perhaps as many as 1000 men performed the function of merchant in colonial Saint John, a figure that is somewhat misleading because it includes a large number of transients and provides little sense of the size of the merchant group at any given moment. A clearer picture is provided by the 1851 Census in which 159 individuals identified themselves as merchants on the east side of the harbour.[7] Adding those to be found in Carleton and those mariners who also functioned as merchants, it is probable that the number of practising merchants in the city was about 200 at that time. A 20 per cent sample of the households from 1851 Census data reveals 38 merchants living in the 587 households found in the sample. In addition, two others, identified as a mariner and an insurance agent, were recognized as merchants. This would seem to indicate that about 7 per cent of Saint John households contained merchants and that about 7 per cent of employed males in the city were engaged in this function.

The composition of the sample group provides a useful insight into the social characteristics of the Saint John merchant at mid-century. Just over half – 21 of 40 – were native New Brunswickers, roughly twice the proportion of natives among the city's household heads. The remainder were Scots, Irish, and English in that order. In terms of the population of the city, the Irish were greatly under-represented, the Scots over-represented. Thirty-seven of the 40 headed their own families, while 2 of the 3 bachelors were lodgers. The 40 represented a high degree of social mobility, reflecting the social effects of the economic expansion between 1820 and 1850. The social origins of 30 of the 40 can be identified. Of these, only 16 began their careers as merchants. The others included 3 mariners, 2 traders, 2 tailors, 2 labourers, a lawyer, a grocer, a clerk, and a commercial agent.

This sense of disparateness continued in the size and scope of merchant commercial activities. These ranged from the limited retail-grocer activities of William Durry, a 51-year-old Irish migrant, and the merchant tailor, William Robertson, to the great shipowners and importers like Stephen Wiggins and John Wishart. Between these extremes were an assortment of insurance agents, commission merchants, and general wholesalers. Like nineteenth-century merchants everywhere, those of Saint John engaged in a number of commercial functions. All participated as entrepreneurs in the movement of goods through the port. Wholesaling activities were the most common function but these were almost always done in conjunction with other commercial activities. The most important were import and export. But even in these cases, some firms shipped goods in their own vessels while some bought space in the vessels of others. It is possible, then, to speak of at least two distinct statuses – great and minor – when discussing colonial merchants.

Even when only the great merchants are considered, the striking fact is their social diversity. A list of forty merchants who dominated the commercial life of the city between 1820 and 1850 reflects the same social characteristics of the 1851 sample group.[8] A bare majority were of Loyalist origin; most of the remainder were Scots. The rest consisted of a few Irish Protestants and an Englishman. Even this list reflects evidence of social mobility, although less than for the broader merchant group in the 1851 Census.

Regardless of the economic interests that merchants shared, occupational status was only one of several factors determining their social standing in colonial society. The leaders of Saint John society were a group of patricians composed largely of high-status Loyalist families, the 'Loyalist elite.'[9] Members of these families monopolized the principal offices of the crown. There is little evidence, however, that they had the traditional distain of trade characteristic of the English aristocracy. Several leading Loyalist families such as the Jarvises, the Wards, and the Wigginses engaged in trade from the first settlement. Others, like the Millidges and the Robinsons, were active merchants in the early nineteenth century. Even John Robinson, son of the great Virginia landowner, Colonel Beverley Robinson, engaged in trade as did his son, George Duncan. Robinson's case is also significant because of his marriage to the daughter of another leading member of the élite, Chief Justice George Ludlow. Robinson went on to hold the offices of province treasurer and mayor of Saint John. Three of his sons married daughters of the Millidge family.

Other early Loyalist merchants, such as the Jarvises, were readily accepted as part of the patrician élite. Munson Jarvis's older children married into the Leonard and Hazen families and his youngest son was appointed to the Supreme Court. The Jarvises provided leadership in the principal élite activities, such as the subscription assemblies, associated with the Loyalist patricians and the officers of the British regiments in garrison. As Mary Jarvis pointed out in 1825, 'as we are acquainted with all the people in N-S- and N-B-, if not personally, by name, of course we take an interest in what concerns them.'[10] The experience of the Jarvis family was repeated for the Millidges, the Simonds, the Gilberts, and the Wigginses. All of these clans had the virtue of accepting religious conformity. But even a prominent Loyalist family that embraced dissent, like the Wilmots, had little difficulty finding acceptable wives among the élite. John M. Wilmot married into the Wiggins family and his brother married the daughter of the Honourable Daniel Bliss.

Scottish merchants of long standing, like Hugh Johnston, were acceptable to the Loyalist élite. They intermarried with each other and with officers of the garrison. They served as officers of militia and participated in the city's élite social functions. They attended the subscription assemblies, danced at the ball given by Captain the Honourable John Robertson of the 1st Battalion in honour of the birth of the Princess Royal,[11] at the militia officers' grand balls to celebrate the British victories in India and China,[12] and at the great Masonic ball, 'the ball of the season ... composed of the elite of our city,' where the 300 guests danced until 4:00 am on Thursday morning.[13] At the other extreme, a merchant like the Irish Protestant William Parks seems to have played little role in the broader life of the community, but like his Catholic counterparts served as ethnic leader of the substantial Irish-Presbyterian group in the city.

The status of those whose good fortune had permitted them to rise from the ranks was even more problematic. For example, Nehemiah Merritt's father had been a fisherman, an activity in which he had been joined by his son in the 1790s. Possessing considerable initiative and a keen eye for business, young Merritt gradually acquired the trappings of a merchant and by 1840 was one of the principal shipowners and wholesalers in the colony.[14] In addition, he was a major property holder in the city and possessed a large inventory of real estate scattered through Upper Canada, New York City, Nova Scotia, and the interior of New Brunswick.

In 1832 his daughter attracted the attention of William Wright, the son of the collector of customs for Saint John, a sinecure exceeded in financial benefit only by the lieutenant-governorship of the province. The Wrights had married well. Their daughter was the wife of Mr Justice Ward Chipman, who in turn was a son of a chief justice and the grandson of the Honourable William Hazen. The marriage of young Wright to a Merritt created a family scandal, the newlyweds moved into one of Merritt's numerous city properties, and Mrs Chipman publicly expressed her disgust that her brother would marry the daughter of an 'old Fisherman.'[15] In 1832 wealth alone could not achieve acceptability in Saint John society.

Other honours came more easily. Loved or not, the great merchant was also a major property holder and on the recommendations of the mayor (almost always a substantial business man himself), commissions were freely granted to merchants who supported either the English or the Scottish established churches. Hugh Johnston Sr, John Ward, and Ralph Jarvis became magistrates and members of the general sessions in 1818 and were joined the following year by Lewis Bliss and in 1821 by Charles Simonds and Lauchlan Donaldson.[16] The 1830s saw the height of merchant influence in the general sessions. In 1832 the lieutenant-governor appointed five great merchants to the court and the following year they were joined by another seven. By 1833, nine of the thirteen appointed magistrates from the city were great merchants and two others were involved in business, a lead they continued to hold for the rest of the decade. The first challenge to the control of the great merchants came during the financial collapse of 1841–42 when the magistracy became much more socially diverse and contained newspapermen, small merchants, brewers, and shipbuilders, in addition to the great merchants and a few lawyers. But in all, thirty-four of the forty designated great merchants served on the general sessions for some period of time in the first half of the nineteenth century. By mid-century the position was one of honour rather than responsibility. The clerk reported in 1849 that eleven of the city's magistrates, including most of the great merchants, never attended general sessions. Yet the commission itself was a symbol of gentility conferring on its holder the status of gentleman and permitting him to style himself as esquire. The title of squire was coveted by most successful colonials and the office was handed down from father to son among the most prominent merchant families.[17] It was fought for by those who perceived their exclusion as part of a declining status.[18]

The pattern of appointments to the county militia was similar, although here the officer corps was restricted even more to the traditional Loyalist merchant class and the Scottish migrants. Conspicuous by their absence from both the appointed magistracy and the militia were the small merchants, those of Irish origins, Protestant dissenters from the Church of England, and total-abstinence and prohibition leaders.

All the great merchants were men of property. In a special sense they were proprietors of the city. A case in point concerns Hugh Johnston Jr, son of the premier Scottish merchant of Saint John. In 1826 the firm of Crookshank and Walker possessed assets of over £50,000, including ownership of four vessels, two stores on the Market Wharf, a house and property at York Point, and two houses in Portland. In addition, on his own account, Johnston owned the Marsh Farm in Portland and a number of city lots in Prince William Street, Queen Street, and Queen Square in the very business centre of the city.[19] Similar tales are legion. John Robertson was assessed city taxes on real and personal estate valued at £40,000 in 1849, and this included neither the large Carleton sawmill he constructed a few years later nor more than 100 city lots he had acquired on long-term lease through his brother.[20] At his death in 1843, the 'old Fisherman' (Merritt) left a personal estate, exclusive of ships and business stock, of over £40,000.[21] The most successful of the bluenose merchants, Stephen Wiggins, left $704,000 (£175,000) to his heirs in 1863. This included an investment in ships, wharves, stores, and material of just under £100,000, investments in local banks, gas stock, water debentures, and city bonds totalling £43,000, and a further £20,000 in American bank and railway stocks.[22]

Even the more modest fortunes were invested in the city. Noah Disbrow owned twelve city lots and five houses in addition to his business premises in 1850.[23] Given the pressure on limited land resources between 1820 and 1840, the investments certainly paid handsome capital gains to their owners. Some indication of the value of these undertakings is to be found in the Johnston accounts. Johnston acquired five Queen Square lots in 1818 for £265, collected rent on them for twenty-one years, and sold them in 1839 for £630. A house and lot on King Street bought for £375 in 1839 was sold for £1000 a decade later.[24] Some merchants bought up substantial tracts of suburban land after 1815, apparently in anticipation of the development of the 1820s. The Marsh Road area north and west of the city was part of the Hazen estate. Beginning in 1819, most of that land was purchased by several merchants as building lots and farms.[25]

The most important role the Saint John merchant played in the city was that of organizer and director of the principal means of production. Ownership of vessels, wharves, stores, and banks meant effective control of the urban economy before 1830. There were few competitors. Most small business men were dependent upon the great merchant for financial accommodation and, in an age of small shop producers, the only other significant capitalists were the shipbuilders who were essentially clients of the merchant. Even in the decade of the 1830s, when the major expansion of the domestic producer's economy began, the only substantial enterprises were those of the iron founders and even these probably represented a total capital investment of no more than £30,000 in 1841. By contrast, the port of Saint John had nearly 90,000 tons of shipping on its registry in 1840.[26] While ownership in terms of vessels was widely held, about half the tonnage of the port, comprising almost all of its larger vessels, was held by the great merchants. Assuming an average price of £5 a ton, the shipping of Saint John represented a capital investment of £450,000 in 1841, and the fleets of individual shipowners like James Kirk and Stephen Wiggins would have been worth £30,000 to £40,000. A similar investment was found in the harbour. In 1842, a total of twenty-eight merchants held perpetual leases on the east-side water lots that permitted them to build and maintain the wharves of the port and to collect users fees from shipowners.[27] Finally, in the late 1830s, as the square-timber trade gradually gave way to the trade in deals, several great merchants invested in the construction of large sawmills. John Robertson was the leader in this movement but significant operations were conducted in Carleton by Stephen Wiggins, R.D. Wilmot, the Barlows, Nehemiah Merritt, and Robert Rankine & Co. (the Saint John branch of Gilmour and Rankine).

The question of ownership, however, extended to much more than control of real estate and the principal means of production. By 1842 the municipal-funded debt totalled £112,000 of which 40 per cent was held directly by merchants and their families and another 20 per cent by local financial institutions, including the city banks, the Fire Insurance Company, and the New Brunswick Marine Insurance Company.[28] The directorates of all three banks were consistently dominated by the city's leading merchants and there is evidence to suggest that in the late 1820s a majority of the shares of the Bank of New Brunswick were held by seven or eight great merchants and office holders.[29] More than 80 per cent of the Marine Insurance Company stock was held by city merchants in 1841.[30]

In addition to the proprietorial nature of their relationship to the city, the merchants played an important role in its political life. Because of their numbers, the leisure that their resources permitted, and the esteem in which their abilities were often held by the freeholders of the county and city and the freemen of the city, merchants were consistently found among the six assemblymen sent to Fredericton. Two or three merchants were always found there and during periods of internal crisis their numbers swelled as economic issues united the freemen and freeholders behind a mercantile leadership. During the bank and crown lands crises of the 1830s, merchant representation rose to four of six members in the election of 1830 and six of six in 1834 at the height of the crown lands issue, a development that supports Edward Pessen's contention that the very wealthy participated in the political process only when an issue critical to their interests was at stake.[31] Even more important than their numbers was the quality of leadership the merchants provided in Fredericton. During their long assembly tenure before 1820, the Scottish merchants Hugh Johnston and William Pagan were among the most powerful figures in the lower house. They were replaced in 1822 by Charles Simonds, who led the battle for the crown lands, served for many years as Speaker of the House, and in 1837, along with his merchant-nephew, Hugh Johnston Jr, became the first assemblyman admitted to the executive council of New Brunswick.[32] Other Saint John merchants, such as Isaac Woodward and John Ward, were among the assembly leaders in the 1830s.

Merchants played a less important role in the Common Council. While the largest single occupational group among the aldermen from 1820 to 1860 consisted of merchants, most of these were drawn from the lesser ranks. The great merchant was certainly seen by the articulate public as the basis and source of the prosperity of the community. This perception was extremely important to the moral authority merchants were able to wield. The great public meetings called by the high sheriff to deal with crises of common concern were inevitably dominated by the lawyers and the merchants, but it was the great merchants whose opinions were listened to with the greatest respect. Given their control of the economy, their access to political power, and their standing in the community, it seems reasonable to assume that the leading merchants of the city could impose their values upon the city and create a climate of public opinion that identified their interests with the welfare of the society at large. Apart from the existence of other influential social groups, the major impediment to merchant domination was their inability to act as a class on many issues, an experience similar to that noted in English industrial towns of the period.[33]

The social complexity of even the leading merchant group has already been discussed. Even more complicated was the colonial business system itself. If business men included all of those who did not work for wages or salary and who made their livelihood from the purchase of goods and the sale of goods and services, then they composed a substantial part of the gainfully employed population of Saint John. In addition to the leading merchants, there was a large number of minor merchants of limited means and status. Then there were the traders and grocers and retailers, the professional bankers and agents, the tavern owners, the sawmill owners and shipbuilders, the masters from a variety of trades, such as the

Lawrences in cabinet making and the Tilleys and Smiths in pharmaceuti-
cals. They composed the business interest and any program had to be
acceptable to most of these groups. At the nub of the problem was the
inability of even the leading merchants to agree among themselves on a
number of priorities. Auction licences granted a few merchants the
privilege of importing foreign goods at 2.5 per cent duty to the detriment
of other shippers.[34] Grain bounties and wheat, flour and bread duties,
designated to promote provincial agriculture, created a milling industry in
Saint John and a flour interest among merchants who proposed to import
British wheat for milling.[35] This provoked bitter resentment among
shipowners for whom cheap bread was an article of faith.

The campaign to break the banking monopoly of the official party began
Auctions and wheat bounties were minor issues by comparison with
the banking crisis that began in the mid-1820s and remained the city's
major commercial question throughout the early 1830s. The issue was
particularly bitter because it combined a genuine grievance with self-
interest. Because of the potential for abuses, the question of colonial
banking was taken very seriously by His Majesty's Council for New
Brunswick. The Bank of New Brunswick had been created in 1820 and
given effective control of the province's financial system. Small regional
banks were permitted in other colonial centres but the Bank of New
Brunswick, by virtue of its size, the government accounts it handled, and
the government debt it financed, could effectively control the monetary
policy of the colony. Its directors, composed of merchants and functionaries of the highest reputations, were expected to maintain a responsible
institution in keeping with its vital function. In return, the bank was given
considerable autonomy and the small group of merchants and functionaries had effective ownership of the institution. In 1834, the directors of
the bank held 42 per cent of its stock.[36]

The campaign to break the banking monopoly of the official party began
in earnest in 1832 when a bill to create the Commercial Bank with a capital
of £60,000 was passed by the assembly and rejected by the Legislative
Council.[37] Realizing the impossibility of breaking the council's position,
the new bank promoters petitioned the king for a royal charter to no
avail.[38] In the end, the Commercial Bank proponents won by winning the
endorsement of the New Brunswick business community at large. The
1834 petitions favouring the Bank of New Brunswick were signed by only
73 business men. The Commercial Bank, by contrast, received 400
signatories in Saint John and the support of leading business interests in
Westmorland, York, Sunbury, and Carleton counties.[39] Over the veto of
the Legislative Council the new bank advocates appealed to the colonial
secretary, who authorized the creation of the Commercial Bank by royal
charter.[40]

Despite conflicts of interest and the intrusion of cultural issues into the business system, there is little doubt that on most important economic issues before 1840 virtually all merchants were in agreement. When they closed ranks they were able to override any opposition within the city. The only serious obstacle to that influence was the government élite working in connection with the lieutenant-governor. The official voice of the merchants was the Saint John Chamber of Commerce, the closest thing to a genuine class organization in the first half of the nineteenth century. Despite its championing of the timber trade, the chamber seems to have reflected reasonably faithfully the desires and needs of Saint John merchants – at least until the collapse of the mercantilist system.

The world the Saint John merchant sought to create and maintain is clearly visible through the chamber's petitions to the municipal, provincial, and imperial governments. It was a world shared by Montreal and Halifax counterparts, a not surprising development since the merchants' organizations generally co-operated on economic matters concerning their common economic welfare within the imperial system.[41] The central feature of this world was the maintenance of the mercantilist policies of colonial preference and navigation acts. The British Empire was a large commercial free-trade area, the internal commerce of which was to be carried in vessels of British registry. Within the security of this imperial economic framework, the merchant in each colonial commercial centre proceeded to build the commercial and financial infrastructure necessary to maintain the system. Ultimately, since it was the carrying trade rather than any particular commodity that was of greatest importance, the merchant's final objective was to create an entrepôt into which a dozen different forms of commerce would flow. Because of its strategic location at the entrance to Upper Canada and to the Ottawa valley, Montreal merchants were most successful in the creation of a major entrepôt, but merchants in all other major ports made the attempt with varying degrees of success.

Economic interest joined the political interest of the élite and combined with the sentiment of American refugee and British migrant to create the tie of loyalty to things British that marked community in Saint John. The great merchant was as much a symbol of that economic connection as the lieutenant-governor was of the political. That point was made repeatedly in every part of the public press: the timber trade was the great engine of progress, and the merchant was the risk taker upon whose efforts the economic progress of the community depended.[42] The evidence of this proposition was to be seen everywhere. The great ton-timber moving down the river, the sawmills, the shipyards, the scores of vessels crowding the summer ports, the high wages of artisans, the profits of all business men and masters, the large-scale employment provided labourers were all visible signs of this economic grace. Economic life outside British mercantilism was unthinkable. Clearly any policy that worked to the commercial benefit of the great merchant was of benefit to the community. It was the general acceptance of this moral economy by society at large that provided the real basis of the merchants' authority.

The square-timber staple was the great engine of growth between 1808 and 1830 and merchant attention shifted more and more to the problems of maintaining this trade. Here the struggle was twofold. Constant vigilance was required to ensure that British politicians did not tinker with the mercantilist policies so as to diminish the preference enjoyed by colonial timber products on the British market. In this struggle, the Saint John Chamber of Commerce spoke for virtually the entire province and worked with other colonial chambers of commerce and the powerful British timber interest of Liverpool and London, as well as with sympathetic colonial officials such as Sir Howard Douglas, the lieutenant-governor of New Brunswick from 1824 to 1831.[43] Such debates were always treated as major crises in Saint John. Inevitably they were the subject of a public town meeting convened by the mayor where the usual sentiments were expressed and the strongest resolutions favouring the imperial system were passed. This great ritual had the further advantage of casting the merchants as the forceful defenders of the interests of the larger society. The defeat of such efforts by the arch-villain free traders was always greeted by great public demonstrations of loyalty and rejoicing.[44]

A second struggle for the timber trade was fought within the province. Timber merchants demanded that the interests of the trade be protected against the needs of any other element of provincial society, including those of the government itself. Fundamental to the trade was the timber supply itself. The greatest prize of all was the crown land and it was the competing claims of government and merchant that precipitated the provincial crown-land crisis. The merchants' hands were strengthened by the clash of personalities within the political oligarchy and by the fears generated throughout the province by the arbitrary actions of the surveyor general. Throughout the debate, the merchants demanded the right to exploit the resources of the province for a minimal fee. The assurance of a protected supply of cheap wood was a sine qua non to further development of the system; it was a proposition that was bound to win the support of the army of wood producers in the villages and rural areas of the province.[45] The 1830s debate split the patrician community and saw the merchant president of the Bank of New Brunswick providing leadership for the popular cause in the issue.

The timber trade required protection of a highly mobile property and the capacity to collect debts and enforce debtors laws in a remote part of empire and even in areas remote from Saint John. Severe penalties were demanded (and usually granted) for those stealing timber, or supplying lumber, timber, fish, and flour of inferior quality. When public discussions of the morality of imprisoning men for debt occurred, the system was defended by merchant spokesmen on the ground that the threat of prison must be maintained to assure British creditors of the colony's stability and its willingness to protect the interest of investors.[46]

Equally as important as the supply and protection of the staple system was the protection of the colonial market. From the merchant perspective this involved a reciprocity of colonial staples for British produce. While there is little evidence that merchants ever actively attempted to prevent the development of locally produced consumer goods, it is abundantly clear that they were not prepared to tolerate any intervention that would interfere with the free movement of British Empire produce through the city and the province. Mercantilism presumed such a system and certainly prevented the natural competition that Boston merchants might have provided. At the same time, the provincial government depended for revenue on import and export duties and could impose duty on British imports. The provincial duty in the early nineteenth century was a 2.5 per cent ad valorum and every effort to raise that general impost encountered fierce resistance from the merchants. The legislature raised the general duty to 5 per cent in 1834. After a general appeal for disallowance had failed,[47] the principal officer of the Chamber of Commerce, Isaac Woodward, successfully contested the 1834 general election in the merchant interest on the grounds that, as a *Courier* commentator noted, 'the mercantile community is now sensible of the need to have themselves represented by intelligent and experienced fellow merchants. Witness the odious and most unjust tax recently laid upon the import of British goods.'[48] For Saint John merchants the concept of the port as a great entrepôt remained paramount. The home market for the entrepôt was, however, a divided political jurisdiction. Commercial control of the St John River basin was assured but the Fundy shore of Nova Scotia was an important market that required that New Brunswick duties never exceed those of Nova Scotia. And constant vigilance was required to ensure that duties in food imports were kept to a minimum.[49]

The other major concern of the commercial interest was the matter of judicial cases, particularly those involving seamen's wages. Repeatedly merchants attempted to get the cost of justice reduced by increasing the amount of debt that could be dealt with by the inferior courts and by transferring cases involving seamen's wages from the court of vice-admiralty to the common pleas.[50] With few exceptions these merchant requests were accepted.

Within the hinterland they controlled, leading merchants were prepared to encourage a wide range of development related to resource
processing and to expanding the carrying trade of the port. The
commercial boom of 1824–25 produced the Marine Insurance Company,
the St John Water Company, the Labrador Fishing Association, and the
expanded Bank of New Brunswick with a total capital of £60,000.[51] The
expansion of the early 1830s produced the Commercial Bank (with an
initial capital of £150,000), the New Brunswick Fire Insurance Company
and the Merchant Exchange,[52] the St John Bridge Company, the new
water company, and the New Brunswick East India Company (each with
an initial capital of £20,000), and the City Bank.[53] Even more significant
in terms of the development of the province was the rush for energy
resources to meet the demands of the milling industry. In 1831, a number
of merchants led by T.L. Nicholson attempted to form a joint stock
company to explore the coal resources in Grand Lake, some fifty miles
from the city. They invested about £10,000 in the project between 1831 and
1835.[54] The most ambitious undertaking by the merchants was the attempt
to cut a canal parallel to Reversing Falls. The new water-power would
drive the extensive mill operations expected from the growing demand for
deals and lumber.[55] Incorporated as the St John Mill and Canal Company,
the merchants succeeded in these efforts. By 1839 they had cut a canal,
erected dams and mills at Reversing Falls, and employed the provincial
dredging machine to remove shoals near the works.[56] Meanwhile, the
leading city merchants combined forces to form the Sheffield Mills and
Land Company.[57]

The most ambitious development proposals involved transportation.
Like leaders in every major Atlantic port, the merchants of Saint John were
anxious to structure an internal commercial network around their city.
Saint John lacked any direct commercial access to the north shore of the
province. Moreover, although the St John River basin remained the great
captive hinterland of the city, the river was only easily navigable to
Fredericton and access to the upper river was a costly and time-consuming
effort. In 1835, a number of leading merchants formed the Saint John
Steamboat and Railway Company with a capital of £20,000. They
proposed to run a line of steamships from Saint John to the bend of the
Petitcodiac River. There a railway would be laid across the fourteen level
miles between the bend and the village of Shediac on the Northumberland
Strait. The village would become the connecting point of a steamship line
that would service the north shore of New Brunswick and have its other
terminal in Quebec.[58] Although this scheme was not completed it became
the basis of the European and North American Railway. The following
year, Launchlan Donaldson and twenty-two other merchants proposed

R.D. Wilmot,
merchant, mayor, and protectionist,
c. 1860 (NBM)

William Parks,
Irish merchant and cotton-mill owner,
c. 1860 (NBM)

Lucretia Gilbert, c. 1870 (NBM)

to improve the navigation of Grand Lake at Jemseg, sixty miles from the city. The move would permit both the exploitation of the Grand Lake coal reserves and the navigation of the lake and the Salmon River flowing east into Kent County almost to the Northumberland Strait.[59]

The rapid change and threat of change in the early 1840s produced a crisis of confidence in the mercantilist assumptions that had dominated the province since Loyalist times.[60] The proposed elimination of imperial protection in 1843 threatened further disaster to an already badly demoralized community. Coupled with the earlier set-backs, it produced an acrimonious debate between those prepared to follow the mother country into free trade and those who argued that the productive classes of the colony were being destroyed by such policies and the wealth of the colony dissipated in the interest of shippers. These protectionist views were strengthened by the emergence of a significant mechanics' revolt against what was perceived as the tyranny of the merchant and of a system that had failed. Out of the thriving mechanics constituency that had developed in the 1820s was founded the Provincial Association, which brought together the producers of the province in a union against the imperial system.

The merchants were ill prepared to meet this assault. Many had been severely mauled in the collapse of 1841–42, and the survivors perceived the British free traders as the major threat to their security. As a group, the timber merchants had little choice but to defend the system on which their own prosperity depended. A producers' association that threatened that system by raising protective walls against even British produce was intolerable. The Chamber of Commerce had always been the preserve of the great shipowner. Its initial reaction to the association and proposals to divert provincial resources from the timber trade into manufacturing and agriculture was negative. In strongly worded petitions to the provincial and imperial authorities, it reiterated its support for the traditional mercantilist policies in the timber trade, and a maximum 5 per cent duty on provincial imports, and reiterated its traditional opposition to any duty at all on flour.[61]

Yet there was increasing evidence that the merchants themselves were divided on the issue of protection. A significant number came out in support of the Provincial Association and its policies of economic diversification and protective tariffs.[62] Among the heretics were R.D. Wilmot, William Parts, the Jarvises, Henry Gilbert, John Walker, Noah Disbrow, Charles Ward, and Walter Tisdale. Indeed, when the Provincial Association entered the political arena with its platform of the 'new New Brunswick,' Wilmot was returned to the House of Assembly where he replaced his cousin, L.A. Wilmot, as the province's leading protectionist.

Of the thirty-seven great merchants still living in the city after 1842, sixteen lent their support to at least some significant part of the protectionist program and twelve of these consistently supported its general objective.[63]

Not surprisingly, the merchants split on the issue of protection in terms of the emphasis their business activities gave to the timber trade. Those with the most significant trading concerns – like John Ward, John Wishart, John Robertson, and Stephen Wiggins – remained largely divorced from the concerns of other elements within the broader community. These were also the major shipowners and their focus remained on the transatlantic community. They did not, necessarily, oppose the protective element per se, but they did fear its emphasis on economic self-sufficiency, its inefficiencies, and particularly the stated goal of transferring resources out of the timber industry and into manufacturing, agriculture, and fishing.[64] Other leading merchants, including a few with shipping interests, were prepared, with a few reservations, to support the new order proposed by the protectionists. Although it is difficult to generalize about these men, they tended to be those with more local interests. While they were men of substance, none could match the personal fortunes amassed by the more substantial timber merchants, particularly those with heavy investments in ships. At his death in 1853, Noah Disbrow left over $80,000 (£20,800) to be divided among his six daughters and two sons; three years later, William Jarvis, a prominent dockside merchant, left $50,000.[65] The next year William Parks placed a value of £17,484 (about $70,000) on the assets of his firm.[66] All three men supported the Provincial Association. By comparison, Stephen Wiggins's share of the firm of Stephen Wiggins and Son was valued at $389,000 (£97,000) in 1863, most of which would have been in shipping.[67]

Those who identified most closely with the city were generally most willing to commit capital to its internal development; those with strong British ties and alternatives were usually much less willing to make this commitment. Thus, a relatively high proportion of merchants of Loyalist origins supported the Provincial Association and its objectives. These were men who viewed Saint John as the central element in a limited regional economy, in preference to its position in the larger metropolitan economy. It was the merchants who had developed these more limited horizons and who saw their future in terms of local enterprise who came to the support of the manufacturers and artisans of the city. Many of them became involved in the secondary industry of the city. William Henry Scovil had established his cut-nail factory in the early 1840s; wholesale grocer William Parks ended his career as the proprietor of one of the first cotton mills in British North America; and the Jarvises established a rope factory in the city in the 1850s.[68]

The division among the merchants seriously threatened their hegemony within the city. Throughout 1843 and 1844, the timber-trade merchants were unable to control the situation. The loss of control was reflected in the legislature where the protectionists succeeded in increasing provincial duties on a number of consumer products in the 1844 session.[69] The Chamber of Commerce itself was publicly castigated as an oligarchy of five or six prominent merchants in no way representative of the commercial interests of the city.[70] Shaken by the disintegration of their order, the leading merchants attempted to adjust to the new political reality. In an effort to restore a semblance of unity among the divided merchants, the Chamber of Commerce was reorganized in the spring of 1845 and the membership of its new directorate more faithfully reflected the range of merchant opinion.[71] Wilmot, Scovil, Parks, and Robert Jardine for the protectionists joined Robertson, Woodward, and Wishart at the chamber board.

These efforts muted but could not entirely conceal the tensions between the free traders and protectionists. Despite the return of prosperity in 1845 and 1846, the producers' movement did not die away. The timber merchant moved to meet the timetable for economic decolonization set by the British government. Leading surviving timber merchants like John Robertson rapidly moved to the construction of new and larger sawmills in the Saint John area to meet the demands of the British market. For other producers, however, the prospects of free trade were daunting.

It was in an effort to pacify these anxieties and to set the political community on a new course that the New Brunswick Colonial Association was formed in Saint John in 1849. The Chamber of Commerce played an important role in the new organization, which brought together the city's most distinguished citizens in an effort to define the province's role in the new economic order.[72] Charles Simonds presided over this mid-century effort to re-create a consensus around which a community could be structured after the economic and ideological devastation of the 1840s. The new economic order had to reconcile the interests of both commercialists and producers, something that could be done only by emphasizing the possibility of developing a reasonably self-sufficient provincial economy. The association and its nine-point program of political reform and economic development rapidly became a province-wide movement. While its initial idealism was modified in the face of the realities of the provincial political process, its program provided the intellectual underpinnings for the reformist coalition that gradually supplanted the old political order after 1854.

The uneasy compromise achieved by the organization was seen in the association's 1849 program, which urged the encouragement of home industry, and the 1850 proposals, which offered reciprocity with the United States as the sole panacea for the province's economic ills.[73] The nature of the compromise was most clearly seen in the province's fiscal policy. The artisan and manufacturer were granted a moderate tariff on material not required in the prosecution of the wood trades, while virtually everything necessary to the lumber industry, the timber trade, the building of wooden ships, and the victualling of crews was admitted free to the New Brunswick market. This included anchors, chains, canvas, cordage, tackle, felt, sails, spikes, cotton ways, and iron bolts, bars, plates and sheeting, as well as rigging, tin and copper plate, sheathing paper, grain, flour, meal bread, meats, fruit, and vegetables.[74] All other produce made or grown in the province was offered tariff protection up to 15 per cent. All remaining goods were admitted at the traditional 5 per cent tariff. The most important victory of the protectionists was the imposition, after 1849, of both general and protective tariffs on British goods. By surrendering at least part of their import function, the timber merchants managed to preserve the important elements in the timber trade and to retain control of those functions essential to the carrying trade.

The still-important role played by the merchant in the city was undertaken by those merchants of limited means and essentially local interests. The new men were enamoured by the use of the new railway technology to speed commerce and open new areas of the province to settlement and exploitation. They were supported by the urban working class who saw the opportunity for both work and local investment in this new endeavour. John Robertson participated in the planning of the first railway system, but its leaders were minor merchants, grocers, and druggists rather than the traditional merchant leadership of the province.[75] Despite this withdrawal from public life, the timber merchants retained a formidable influence. The trade in lumber products remained the most important element in the commerce of the port and the making of ships remained its most important manufacturing activity. The merchants continued to direct much of this activity and to control the banks, the wharves, and the fleet of the urban economy. The carrying trade reasserted itself, particularly with the opening of the American market following the 1854 reciprocity agreement, but this was a much more complex arrangement as shipbuilders themselves increasingly entered the trade and built fleets for their own purposes.

Meanwhile the divisions among the merchants and between the traditional merchant leaders and the powerful new influences which were remaking the Saint John community continued to widen. The temperance movement was a case in point. Most of the leading merchants had at least given lip service to the early temperance movement when it emerged in the 1830s. Several followed it into total abstinence. Only a few became prohibitionists. Instead, a number of leading merchants actively opposed the activities of the prohibitionists and a large number were among those who petitioned in 1853 for a postponement of the prohibitory act.[76] Prohibition also revealed the internal divisions among the merchants. A substantial number of minor merchants with local interests supported the movement and as a group played leadership roles in it quite disproportionate to their numbers.

In the final analysis, it is possible to speak of several merchant statuses in colonial Saint John that often functioned as a class. The whole merchant interest could generally be summoned to the defence of basic economic concerns, such as private property, low levels of taxation, control of the crown lands, and, while hope remained, the mercantilist system. At the height of the protected timber trade, leading merchants were able to determine what were the desirable material goals of the city and the strategies necessary to achieve them. This perception of merchants as creators of property added to the esteem in which they were held. The great merchants shared with the lieutenant-governor himself the distinction of being one of the great links that bound the city and the community to its British metropolis. So long as the ideal of a unitary society informed by the values of a single dominant culture prevailed, and a British government willing to maintain the tory ideal remained, the system was effective. After 1840, divisions over economic policy tended to divide the merchant interest. The great merchant increasingly withdrew from direct intervention in public affairs, and proved less able to set the agenda of questions that would or would not be the focus of public discussion and decision.

Merchants proved to have a cultural dimension beyond their common economic concerns and could frequently be counted upon to act upon these other imperatives. They sometimes became leading representatives of cultures that challenged the place of the dominant culture. The most obvious case was that of Irish merchants who consistently took the position of their compatriots even when the dictates of order and social control suggested that this was not the wisest course. But the prohibition and protection debates often produced similar behaviour on the part of other segments of the merchant interest. This fragmentation accelerated after 1840, as most prominent public roles in the community were played by younger minor merchants and other lesser business men.

~4~

Bone and Sinew:
The Artisans and the
Social Order

If merchants and merchant leaders were able to dominate the community agenda, particularly before 1840, the opposition to this domination came not from the manual labourers dependent on their system but from the producers' interest. That interest bound together a number of status groups, ranging from apprentice artisans to shopkeepers to established small manufacturers, led by a petite bourgeoisie of small masters. It is an interest that Michael Katz described as a class in his early work on mid-nineteenth-century Hamilton; in his later study of Hamilton and Buffalo he argued that the journeymen and masters were members of competing classes.[1] Other historians have been more tentative in judgment. All agree that an artisanal interest existed in the eighteenth century and that it was gradually eroded in the face of nineteenth-century industrialism. In her study of nineteenth-century Newark, Susan Hirsch argues that artisan deference to the merchant élite had waned by the time of the American Revolution and that a significant artisanal system in which most journeymen were able to become masters by the time they were forty flourished until at least 1830. A similar community of interest among Kingston artisans is described by Bryan Palmer.[2] British studies suggest that even in the late nineteenth century the aristocracy of labour and a petite bourgeoisie of small proprietors remained closely linked.[3] The experience of the artisan group in Saint John demonstrates that it was not just an economic interest but a politically self-conscious social group.

Tentative and episodic evidence abounds for class perceptions on the part of those occupying the lower and middling social strata within Saint John society. The late eighteenth-century debate between residents of the Upper and Lower Coves in the city, which erupted into near violence in the 1785 elections, had as its basis an intense antagonism between an élite of prominent Loyalists who had received many favours and offices of high status and who had asked for considerably more, and a large number of Loyalist commoners who resented the pretensions of their social betters.[4] Echoes of the 1785 contest could be heard periodically in the nineteenth-century debates of the Common Council. Similarly, much of the denominational antagonism of the early nineteenth century contained the seeds of class conflict. The leadership of the early Wesleyan movement was almost entirely drawn from the tradesmen and labourers of the city, in sharp contrast to that of the churches of England and Scotland. Comparison of the social origins of Wesleyan and Church of England clergy reveals the same kind of social gulf that existed between the leading laymen of the two institutions.[5]

Yet to view denominations simply as manifestations of class can be a treacherous undertaking. The characteristic attitude of leading Wesleyans toward their social superiors during the period of lower-status domination was deference. It was precisely at the point that Wesleyans came to occupy and to perceive themselves as entitled to occupy positions of higher status that their antipathy toward the colonial élite burst forth. But if the concept of Wesleyanism as a class movement encounters difficulties, the social groups from which the Wesleyans draw most heavily – the artisans – do provide the most distinctive and persistent example of class behaviour in colonial Saint John.

Artisans composed nearly half the original Loyalist freemen of 1785.[6] Throughout the first half of the nineteenth century they rather consistently composed about a third of freeman admissions, a proportion confirmed by the 1851 Census. Comprising a wide variety of occupations and wide range of incomes, the artisans were always a powerful interest and on a number of important issues they did act as a class. By mid-century they perceived themselves, and were perceived by observers of the scene, as the 'bone and sinew' of the community. In terms of economic function, artisans were distinguished from those of higher and lower status in one important way: other groups were concerned with the provision of services, but craftsmen produced all the goods made in the city apart from the simple mechanical process of sawing deals.

In no way did the early city so faithfully reflect the late medieval origins of its institutions as in the means through which the townspeople organized themselves for the production of goods. Production was equated to craft and each craft was structured around a trade, which in turn was organized on the traditional triad of apprentice/journeyman/master. The importance accorded the trades was reflected in the city's constitution, which attempted to restrict both the franchise and the benefit of the trade to those who had served a satisfactory apprenticeship under a master who was a freeman of the city. The apprenticeship process was central to the trades system.[7] Not only did it provide a critical form of educational and skills development, but it instilled the pride, confidence, and sense of apartness that distinguished the training of professionals. This formation of the artisan usually began in early adolescence when the youth was bound over by his parents to a master craftsman. The standard indenture of apprenticeship was a legal document formally assented to by a magistrate binding the young man to a life of servitude in his master's household for a period of from four to eight years. *The Courier* editor, Henry Chubb, 'voluntarily and of his own free will,' was bound to a master printer for seven years at the age of fifteen. The contract, borrowed from traditional English models, provided that the master should teach the art, trade, and mystery of a printer and provide board, lodging, washing, and a new suit of clothing for his apprentice. In return Chubb was required to serve faithfully, keep his master's secrets and commands, neither to damage nor waste his master's goods. He was further forbidden to commit fornication, contract matrimony, play at cards or dice, buy or sell goods without his master's permission, or frequent taverns or theatres.[8]

The control that masters were given over their charges was an attractive feature to civic authorities since it played an important role in the maintenance of order and good discipline among a large segment of the city's male population during the sometimes difficult passage from adolescence to manhood. The exercise of this authority by the masters was encouraged by Common Council, which placed responsibility for the public misdemeanours of apprentices clearly on the shoulders of the masters.[9] The rigorous control was frequently not appreciated by the prentices, and the search for fugitives became a regular feature of the daily press before 1850. By 1817, Henry Chubb, now Master Chubb, was beset by problems with his own apprentice, 'Peter James Wade, 16, smart but a drunkard,' who had fled his master's service.[10] Chubb offered 5s. for the return of the apprentice and £5 for information leading to the conviction of those harbouring him. The complaint was not uncommon, but as the law made the harbouring of a fugitive apprentice a hazardous undertaking, most fled the city.[11] As late as 1841, Sam Wilson was arrested for absconding from his master, the sailmaker and assistant alderman Robert Ray, and sentenced to two months at hard labour for assaulting the city marshal who made the arrest.[12]

Despite these commotions, and restrictions, the apprentice system had a good deal to offer young men.[13] In the short run, there was promise of a skill and a paid series of night courses. In the long run, there was a respectable status, admission to the freedom of the city, and the possibility of becoming a master with ownership of a shop.[14] Among a number of Loyalist families, the artisan's status became a tradition that engendered a native tradeocracy comprising an intricate pattern of fathers, sons, grandsons, nephews, uncles, and cousins. Many young second-generation natives could combine a respectable trade with their father's freehold and shop, a sure guarantee of becoming both master and burgher. The Bustins, the Hardings, and the Olives provide characteristic examples of the great trades families of the city. Fifteen Bustins, sixteen Hardings, and sixteen Olives were admitted as freemen between 1785 and 1858. The Bustin clan included five carpenters, four butchers, three harness makers, two masons; the Olives, six ship carpenters, three carpenters, two ship wrights, and a joiner; the Hardings, four tanners, two shoe-makers, and a blacksmith.[15]

Only toward mid-century did the ranks of this tradeocracy begin to break as young third-generation members began to move toward commerce and the professions. The Hardings were particularly successful in this: three became medical doctors, two were merchants, and one entered the law. This mid-century shift out of the trades on the part of young natives is confirmed by the 1851 Census. A sample of 732 east-side households reveals 23 apprentices almost equally divided between natives and Irish arrivals in the 1840s. By contrast the ranks of the young merchants' clerks expanded rapidly in the 1840s and by 1851 their members rivalled those of the apprentice artisans. More than two-thirds of the clerks were natives. Confirmation of the trend out of the crafts, particularly on the part of young natives, is found in the late 1850s in the complaints of *The Courier* editor who bewailed the abandonment of the crafts by young men of artisan families and scolded their parents – particularly their mothers – for denying the dignity of manual work and for placing a premium on any occupation that permitted its occupant to wear a white collar.[16] The decline of the crafts among native families was probably a reaction against the admission of Irish tradesmen who depressed the wages and reduced the importance of the status of artisans. The native-Irish tension was reflected in the matching of masters and apprentices. Native masters accepted only native apprentices, a fact which meant that almost all journeymen boat and coach builders would be natives while the shoemaking trade was given over to the Irish.[17] The native preferences doubtless reflected a traditional pattern of fathers apprenticing their sons to friends and acquaintances in the fathers' craft or in other similar crafts.

The purpose of the apprentice system was to train an exclusive body of skilled workers dedicated to the craft and determined to restrict its practice to those of like formation. The journeymen craftsmen constituted a broad and influential cross-section of the city's population. Together with the masters, they comprised about 35 per cent of the freemen and 35 per cent of all employed males in the city.[18] Thus they easily formed the largest electoral group in the city, outnumbering all commercial freemen by a ratio of two to one.

In 1851, more than three of every four artisans were family heads living in tenements or freeholds of their own. A very small number – about one in fourteen – were single men living with their parents and the remainder – about one in six – were lodgers, one-third of whom lived with employers. Although all were legally required to be freemen to practise their trade, only about two out of five of those in the sample did so. Virtually every master was a freeman but journeymen, particularly in the lesser trades, frequently failed to acquire their freedom. The proportion of freemen rose to half among the native tradesmen, fell to two in five among the Irish, and to little more than one in five among the other groups. It was remarkably low among those of English, American, Nova Scotian, and Islander origins – doubtless indicating a view toward a temporary residence in the city on the part of members of these groups.

The most important crafts were those relating to the use of wood. Domestic carpenters – a group embracing carpenters, joiners, and cabinet-makers – accounted for 27 per cent of the east-side artisans in the 1851 Census. When combined with the shipbuilding trades (13 per cent of the census sample) and the furniture and coach-making crafts, the woodworkers composed some 42 per cent of the total artisans found in the 1851 Census. Another 18 per cent were employed in the leather trades, including tanners, cordwainers, and saddlers, and another 14 per cent in the metal trades – blacksmiths, whitesmiths, tinsmiths, machinists, and foundry men. Together these six categories accounted for 70 per cent of the city's artisans, the remainder being scattered through dozens of skills, the largest of which related to the production of clothing and food.

There were significant differences in the wages received for service within the various trades. These ranged from the 45s. a week that a millwright could command in 1841 to the mere 15s. paid to a baker, who received little more than the day labourer. In terms of remuneration there were three general categories of trades. The aristocrats were the wood craftsmen (carpenters, joiners, shipwrights, cabinet-makers), the tailors, and the painters, all of whom could expect 40–45s. a week when work was to be found. A second group were the 'smiths, butchers, masons, and shoe-makers, whose wages ranged between 29s. and 34s. Finally, there were the bakers and wheelwrights. Artisans' wages, of course, like all others, fluctuated in response to the demands of the local market. The year 1846 was a period of recession. Donaldson's figures for 1831, while not easily comparable because of the categories used, would indicate a weekly wage of about 45s. for a good journeyman carpenter or joiner, compared with 43s. eleven years later; a common labourer received 18s. compared with 15s. in 1841.[19] Wages of Saint John carpenters appear to have been comparable to those received by their counterparts in Upper Canada.[20]

Most wages declined after 1841. By 1846 average wages were probably not more than 75 per cent of those in 1831, although, since prices also fell, living standards were probably not notably lower. The differences in wages were important but since the suffering seemed to be general, the wage declines in any one craft were probably not viewed as the results of discriminatory treatment.

More significant than the rise or decline of wages generally was the relative position enjoyed by a particular skill within the economic hierarchy of trades. In good times, journeymen joiners and ship carpenters employed servants and ate salt beef, fresh pork, and bread made from American wheat flour; they enjoyed an income comparable to that of most small business men and non-conformist clergymen of the period. By contrast the shoe-maker kept no servant and mixed a good deal of fish with his meat, while the baker, like the common labourer, fed his family on fish and potatoes.[21] Three pennies would buy the working man two pounds of fish and three pounds of potatoes at most times of the year, as compared with a third of a pound of salt beef, or a quarter-pound of butter, or one pound of oatmeal, or a half-pound of sugar, or three eggs, or one pint of milk. Certainly the evidence suggests that a journeyman carpenter enjoyed an income closer to that of a master carpenter than to that of a journeyman shoe-maker.[22]

Still another dimension to the artisan movement was stratification based on ethnicity. The 1851 Census revealed sharp ethnic patterns among particular trades. The proportion of artisans from each ethnic origin corresponded closely to that which the ethnic group bore among the heads of households as a whole, the sole exception being Irish arrivals after 1840. Native artisans, for example, accounted for 27 per cent of all craftsmen in the city. Their proportions, however, varied sharply from trade to trade. The natives were usually strong in all of the wood trades and among painters. They equalled the Irish in the domestic carpentry trades, outnumbered them almost two to one in the shipbuilding trades, and comprised all the coach and furniture makers in the city. By contrast, the leather trades, particularly shoemaking, were an Irish preserve by 1851, where Irish outnumbered natives almost eight to one. The same Irish predominance characterized the metal, clothing, and food trades, and the workers in stone. Significantly, the trades dominated by natives were also those that provided the largest remuneration, while those providing the poorest remuneration, such as shoemaking, were largely staffed by newer Irish arrivals whose presence made impossible the regulation of the trade by the city masters.[23]

Sharp differences in size and organization existed not only among the trades but also within them. The 1851 Census required master shoemakers to give information on the number of workers employed and on the value of output. While the answers to the latter question doubtless grossly undervalued the product, they do provide a clue to the variations present in this trade. Most shoemaking shops were small, consisting of a master, one or two journeymen, and perhaps an apprentice. Masters admitted to values of from £75 to £1000. The same differences were found through out most other trades. It is impossible to determine with any accuracy either the status or income of a master. Donaldson indicated in 1831 that master carpenters and joiners, who worked for supervisor's wages in the construction industry, received about 20 per cent more than did a first-class journeyman. It is likely that comparable differentials existed between journeymen and the minor master shoe-makers and tailors, but it is clear that the greater masters in some trades were in the process of developing independent means that enabled them to meet smaller merchants on equal terms.

The traditional and emerging trades structures were both plainly visible in 1851. A significant number of master artisans, particularly in the footwear and clothing trades, maintained households that contained both their journeymen and their apprentices. At the other extreme, some individual firms had grown so large that the enterprises might more accurately be described as small factories. Most notable among these were the iron foundaries. The Portland blacksmith James Harris had expanded his operations to include a block of buildings employing more than seventy men and boys. Within the city Thomas Barlow employed another sixty-five, and the city's other founders employed comparable numbers. The wage spread between the blacksmith and the foundry-engineers in the metals trades was no greater than that between the small master cabinet-makers employing a few journeymen in their shops and a leading furniture maker like J.W. Lawrence, who employed sixteen men and boys in making furniture to the value of £2250.[24]

Expanding local markets brought about a rapid change in the structure of the traditional trades. Master tradesmen responded to these opportunities in a variety of ways. Immigration produced large numbers of shoe-makers and tailors. These trades required only limited capital – in some cases artisans even owned their own tools – and the result was a profusion of small shops and small masters.[25] By contrast, those trades permitting the application of steam-generated energy tended to remain concentrated in the hands of relatively few masters who added to their shops and employed an increasingly sophisticated technology.[26] Thus, while the shoemaking shops increased in number, offering numerous opportunities for ambitious young tradesmen to possess their own shops, the tanneries were concentrated in the hands of a few masters who came to employ more men in a more structured fashion and to play increasingly important roles in the life of the city. Daniel Ansley, who entered the trade as freeman tanner in 1809 at the age of eighteen and became a leading master tanner, finally classified himself as a merchant in the 1851 Census. Already possessing substantial shops in the early 1830s, four of the tanners greatly increased their capacity after 1840 by the installation of steam engines.[27] The same development occurred in the flour trade. Grist-mill owners had constructed sixteen plants by 1840, each costing between £3000 and £5000 and each capable of grinding between 7000 and 12,000 barrels annually.[28] The most important elements in the city's industrial activities were the sawmills and iron and brass foundries, which became increasingly capital intensive as steam engines largely replaced water-driven mills.

The principal masters of that trade provide a useful insight into the successful trades leadership of the city. James Harris came from Annapolis as a young man and began to practise his blacksmith's craft. He gradually added machine, pattern, and fitting shops to his blacksmith's enterprise. In 1831 he added a blast furnace. Over the next few years a stove shop, a car shop, and a rolling mill completed the New Brunswick Foundry. His partner was a Scottish machinist, Thomas Allen, who completed his apprenticeship in Glasgow and settled in Saint John in 1825. Allen's son Thomas apprenticed as a machinist in his father's foundry, and a second son, Robert, became a moulder through the same process; a third son, Harris, studied as a brass founder. All three came to be owners of Saint John foundries by the early 1860s.[29] The Saint John Foundry was established in 1825 by Robert Foulis (a Scottish scientist and inventor and graduate in medicine of Aberdeen University) and was later taken over by a Fredericton merchant, T.C. Everitt, and two Saint John men, John Camber, a blacksmith, and James Wood, a machinist. George Fleming established the Phoenix Foundry in 1835. Fleming had served as a machinist's apprentice at the Dumferline Foundry in Scotland and then had worked as a journeyman in Glasgow, Cork, Pictou, Saint John, Boston, and Baltimore. His partners included a local carpenter, Thomas Barlow, an iron moulder, John Stewart, and later a long-time clerk with the firm, Thomas Humbert.[30] The city's ten iron and brass foundries in

Mrs Thomas Nesbit,
née Margaret Graham, c. 1850 (NBM)

J.W. Lawrence,
furniture maker, 1870 (PANB)

The Ossekeag passenger steam engine, 1859 (NBM)

1860 were thus distinguished by their Scottish and native ownership, by their structure as multiple partnerships that enabled them to bring together the necessary capital resources, and by the size of their producing units.

The foundries were the largest producing units in the city by the end of the colonial period. Three hundred journeymen and apprentices worked in them in 1850;[31] by 1873 the New Brunswick Foundry alone possessed a work-force of 300. The foundries were clearly operating on the factory system. In these, as in the bakery, carriage and cabinet making, tanning, and milling trades, the application of steam power and new technology to create a more efficient system of production was well under way by 1840. The founders, of course, were using steam power before 1830. Barzilia Ansley first brought steam power to a tannery in 1838. Thomas Rankine, a product of a Scottish bakers apprenticeship, introduced hand machinery to his business in 1844 and steam power eight years later. G.F. Thompson did the same in the paint trade in 1850. Four years later, Joseph and George Lawrence introduced steam power to the furniture-making firm their father had established in 1817. That same year Jeremiah Harrison applied steam to the carriage-making trade.[32]

The application of newer techniques to the traditional trades and the consequent growth of the firms between 1830 and 1860 certainly led to the growth of a group of prosperous masters having less and less in common with their journeymen and, conversely, limited the opportunities for those journeymen to acquire their own shops.[33] Yet the effect of this should not be overplayed. The growth of larger producing units was a slow process and in most firms involved a master artisan who had been a long-time resident of the city. Most important, apart from the iron foundries and a few sawmills, none of the producing units before 1850 could be described as factories in the sense that they employed more than twenty-five people in a plant powered by steam engines or water paddles. Most Saint John artisans in 1851 worked either in artisans' shops employing no more than five people or in the shipyards.[34] Moreover, the trades represented as much a social as an economic status. James Harris, Daniel Ansley, and the baker Stephen Humbert might become prominent, prosperous burghers, might even hold the Queen's Commission of the Peace with the right to style themselves 'Esquire.' Yet they remained artisans, married the daughters of artisans, and expressed the attitudes and biases of artisans, were perceived as tradesmen by their social superiors, and supported the interests of artisans. Throughout the colonial period – despite the changing structure and work relationships within some trades – that ethos remained a powerful source of identification binding most elements of the trades into a common interest.

This is not to suggest that loyalty to that interest was not sometimes divided or that elements of the interest did not war among themselves. The masters' use of the law to enforce obedience upon the apprentices has already been mentioned. Richard Rice has demonstrated the presence of Friendly Societies of carpenters, joiners, cabinet-makers, and painters as early as 1837, but no evidence that any of them took action against the masters.[35] Confrontations between masters and journeymen, usually over rates of pay or slow payment, occasionally occurred. As early as 1830 the journeymen tailors of the city threatened to withhold their labour until the masters agreed to make payment of wages within three days of the completion of their work and to charge no more than 12s. board each week. No further evidence of confrontation occurred until 1841 when a mechanic wrote to the smiths and moulders of the city in the columns of *The News* calling for a one-hour reduction in the workday.[36] In 1856 journeymen printers at *The Courier* withdrew their services because their employer had taken an extra apprentice into the office.[37] Significantly, although Eugene Forsey has provided evidence of a ship carpenters organization, there is no evidence of any confrontations in the shipyards of Saint John.[38]

But incidents of this nature, although indicating an underlying tension within the interest, were relatively few. More important, they were short-lived and left few permanent scars. For the deeply alienated journeyman, Boston lay near and emigration provided a final solution when insoluble problems arose. By contrast, the activities of masters and journeymen, whether working alone or in concert with other groups within the city, revealed something closely resembling a genuine class consciousness.

In the 1830s the artisan leadership erected and attempted to erect a number of distinctive tradesmen's institutions. Throughout the period 1830–60, this leadership maintained a clear and strongly worded program designed to defend the social and economic interests of the artisan. The enemy was perceived to be the great merchant, and in these artisans' organizations the merchants found the most organized and persistent opposition to their domination of the colonial economy. The leadership of the crafts varied, depending on the point at issue. The most persistent spokesmen for the artisanal interest were the small masters whose families had enjoyed a long residence in the city, such as the Blakslees who for three generations had operated a candle and soap-making shop, and the sail-making Rays and Robertsons, the baking Rankins, and the wood-working Nesbits and Lawrences. Many were families with deep roots in the rocky soil of Saint John whose credentials as founding fathers were as respectable as those of the patricians. Like their followers, they were active supporters of the evangelical and temperance causes in the city. In sharp contrast to their mercantile opponents, they represented a localist emphasis that had the city at the centre of its world-view. They were unfailing in their resolve to employ the authority of the state to protect the economic interests of the 'bone and sinew' of the colony and to provide the kinds of development that would eventually lead to the relative self-sufficiency of the province.

Between 1835 and 1839 serious efforts were made to create three artisan institutions, followed in the late 1840s by a fourth. The reasons for this sudden discovery of occupational community cannot be accurately determined, although it was doubtless associated with the rising fortunes and expectations of most craftsmen in the heady days of the mid-1830s. Certainly the idea of the unity of the crafts and of the necessity to band together to further the interests of artisans closely paralleled the rising tide of religious dissent that culminated in the rejection of all social inequalities in the 1840s. Since the leadership of the two movements involved much the same personnel, they may well have shared similar perceptions and values.

The first of these co-operative efforts was the creation of a joint stock company to undertake the hunting of whales. Exploitation of the great southern whale fishery was just well under way. The combination of imperial and provincial tariffs provided 100 per cent protection on black oil and 30 per cent on sperm oil in the British and colonial markets. Saint John possessed the marine personnel capable of such long and arduous marine undertakings. A petition to establish a joint stock concern to be known as the Mechanics Whale Fishing Company was forwarded to the legislature and enacted into law in 1835. The act provided for the creation of a corporation possessing authority to raise a £50,000 capital through sale of 5000 shares of stock each with a par value of £10.[39]

The firm was an artisanal concern at the beginning. The original petition had been signed by 162 men, 71 of whom can be identified.[40] Two-thirds of these were tradesmen and most of the remainder were shipbuilders, grocers, and merchant mechanics. Among the petitioners was John Grey, first vice-president of the House Carpenters and Joiners Society of Saint John.[41] Its directors included the shipbuilder John Duncan, the hatter C.A. Everitt, the newspaper editor Henry Chubb, and the merchant John Wishart; its long-time president, Thomas Nesbit, was a master cabinet-maker. In 1837 the company was owned by 160 individuals drawn mainly from the trades most concerned with the making and outfitting of vessels and the processing of whales – most, but by no means all, masters. In addition, there was a sprinkling of grocers and other small business men, and a few merchants and professionals.

The enterprise was a financial success. Once the initial voyages were completed, the investment proved both profitable and safe. That very success proved its undoing as an artisan's enterprise. The merchant community began to invest heavily in the stock after 1840 and artisans, particularly in the financial crisis of 1841–42, were often forced to sell their holdings to merchants at prices well below their normal market value.[42] By 1846, only 53 of the 160 stockholders of 1838 remained in the company. They had been joined by a number of great merchants and banking institutions. The tradesmen each generally owned between four and thirty shares of stock, each valued at about £10 in 1847. The stock held by the newcomers was much more substantial. For all practical purposes the company had ceased to be a 'mechanics' enterprise by that time.[43]

The second trades institution developed from the top down. Mechanics institutes had by 1835 become the most fashionable organization among leading British artisans.[44] Dedicated to progress and the enlightenment of the working man, the institution was viewed with some scepticism by the more conservative elements of British society. The movement for the institute actually began as part of a more general interest in the nature and possible applications of new scientific knowledge. In Saint John, as in England, the leadership in promoting this interest in scientific theory was taken by a group of professionals led by several judges, clergymen, and physicians. In June 1836 they formed the New Brunswick Philosophical Society. Five months later they capped their success by enrolling sixteen 'of the most respectable master mechanics [a term used for artisans in the metal crafts] in the city' in the society.[45] From this point onward, there was persistent talk of the educational advantages that a proper mechanics institute, with its lecture series, library, and museum, could provide for the tradesmen of the city. The impetus for the institute certainly came from the society and when the decision was finally made to create an institute late in 1838 the society members, under the leadership of patricians like Chief Justice Chipman, Mr Justice Parker, and Beverley Robinson, decided to continue their guidance of the new organization by merging the society with the institute. It was a curious and unequal marriage. Forty-two members of the Philosophical Society joined 175 tradesmen to create the new organization.[46] A 10s. entrance fee and annual dues of 15s. ensured that the institute would be restricted to the aristocracy of labour. None the less, the institute found strong support among the large numbers of craftsmen in the city. Within fourteen months its membership was approaching 400, and by 1851 it reached 1250.[47]

The institute initially suffered an identity crisis. At heart was the question of whether it was to provide broad scientific instruction for the city at large or a specialized technical instruction for the benefit of the tradesmen. Leadership in the organization was taken at first by former Philosophical Society members who dominated the early executive committees and mounted lecture series on geology, ethics, and astronomy – much to the chagrin of many artisans who demanded instruction in practical mechanical principles.[48] The debate between the social leaders of the city and the practical mechanics continued for the next three years.[49] One *Chronicle* correspondent argued as early as December 1838 that the gentlemen who were running the institute thought the mechanics a mass of semi-barbarians incapable of making any kind of responsible decision. He demanded that all propositions the executive wished to implement be presented in writing to the general membership, discussed, and voted on by secret ballot.[50] The debate continued into the spring of 1839 with demands for executive responsibility to the general membership and threats that artisans would withhold their subscriptions.[51] The bill to incorporate the institute was a particularly controversial issue because it had been prepared by the provisional directors and its contents were not revealed to the membership at large before being sent to Fredericton.[52] Rumbles of discontent were heard as late as 1841, but any hope Chipman had of being able to direct the affairs of the organization were soon dashed.

The institute remained a forum for public discussion and education, but after 1840 its leadership passed more and more to the tradesmen, particularly the master tradesmen, of the city. By 1842 the directorate contained the iron founders T. Barlow, G. Fleming, J. Harris; the cabinet-makers Thomas Nesbit and Alex Lawrence; the shipbuilders John Duncan and J. Lawton; the druggists S.L. Tilley and J. Sharp; the printer and editor Henry Chubb; and the merchant tailor William Robertson; together with a doctor, a lawyer, and two merchants.[53] As the decade progressed, its leaders became more and more involved in the important social and economic issues of the day. The final break with the city's patricians occurred in 1844 when the directors opened their hall for Sunday services by the Scottish cleric and Evangelical Alliance leader W.T. Wishart, against the express wishes of Chipman.[54]

The institute served a number of purposes apart from arranging public lectures series. Day and night schools were offered from the beginning, the latter designed particularly for the benefit of apprentices and masters. By 1845 many institute leaders, imbued with much of the evangelical ideology associated with the temperance movement and the Evangelical Alliance, succeeded in attaching the British school to the institute. In 1855, masters and journeymen combined to form the Mechanics Charitable Association to aid distressed tradesmen and to 'elevate' labour.[55] The strength and unity of the artisans was most impressively displayed in 1840

The Saint John Mechanics Institute, constructed c. 1840 (NBM)

Parade celebrating sod turning of European and
North American Railway, 1853 (NBM)

on the occasions of the opening of the Mechanics Hall and the arrival of
the governor general. On the first of these, about 1200 craftsmen paraded
the streets of the city in military formation, each craft marching en bloc, its
members arrayed in the traditional insignia and symbolism of the trade.
First, in point of honour, came the blacksmiths, followed by the founders,
the hammermen, carpenters, tailors, painters, bakers, and shoe-makers.[56]
Two months later, the arrival of the governor general was heralded by
more than 1500 artisans marching under the banner of the Mechanics
Institute.[57] In addition to the crafts present in May, the procession
included the riggers, coopers, and shipwrights.

It is very doubtful that these parades can be seen as evidence of
trade-union activity. Master and journeymen certainly marched together
under the common banner of their trade and some apprentices may have
done so as well.[58] Led by the city's master artisans, the institute remained
the most obvious symbol of the views and interests of the masters and
most respectable journeymen artisans throughout the remainder of the
colonial era. Its only competition for the artisans' allegiance was the
short-lived Chamber of Trades, which in the early 1840s attempted to play
the same role among craftsmen that the Chamber of Commerce played
among merchants. Again, if the list of 1841 officers is any indication, the
Chamber of Trades was composed of both masters and journeymen.[59]

The remaining two efforts to create distinctive artisanal institutions
were both destroyed by political powers against which the artisans could
not prevail. The creation of a Mechanics Whaling Company and the
Mechanics Institute was followed in 1839 by the demand for a mechanics
bank based on the Scottish banking system. The reasons for the demand
are not hard to find. The inability or unwillingness of the Bank of New
Brunswick directors to make available sufficient accomodation to satisfy
many business men had led to the formation of the City and Commercial
banks in the 1830s. Master tradesmen had played a role in both of these
formations, yet, for a second and third time, they found their expectations
frustrated. All three institutions proved to be unwilling to serve the needs
of the trades. In the financial crisis of 1839, the banks strongly discriminat-
ed in favour of the merchant community, which controlled the bank stock.

In January 1839, a public meeting of mechanics was held at the Albion
House for the purpose of discussing the possibilities of establishing a
bank in which 'the property of the working and middle class of society
[would] be represented.' Arguing that these classes had been disregarded
in the operation of the existing banking establishments and that 'the
greatest portion of the wealth of this Province [is] owned by the
operatives of this country,' many of whom were stockholders in the
existing banks, the meeting proposed to create a Mechanics Property

Bank with a capital of £150,000 to £500,000, to be operated on the Scottish system.[60] The meeting concluded when 199 artisans petitioned the legislature for the creation of a non-mercantile bank with an initial capital of £100,000, which they proposed to raise.[61] Not surprisingly the list of petitioners was dominated by artisans with strong support from the master mariners, the grocers, and the Baptist clergy of the city.

The problems faced by the tradesmen in dealing with the provincial political establishment were reflected in the handling of the petition. It was introduced to the assembly by Isaac Woodward, a Saint John member, merchant, and long-time spokesman for the Chamber of Commerce, who moved that it be referred to the Committee on Colonial Banking. That committee, chaired by Woodward, brought back a negative recommendation arguing that compliance would 'increase the difficulty and embarrassment of monetary affairs' by increasing the number of banks in the province.[62]

The fourth attempt at creating trades institutions occurred in 1848–50 when the city's leading shipbuilders, arguing that Carleton was largely populated by tradesmen, proposed to create a joint stock company to contract the building and sale of sailing vessels. The proposal had important implications for the shipbuilding industry of the province. Its organizers included virtually every leading citizen of Carleton, headed by William Olive and six members of his shipbuilding clan, George Bond, Thomas Coram, John Littlehale, R. Stockhouse, Henry Nice and four members of his family, William and Joseph Beatteay and three members of that family.[63] The Olives were among the earliest shipbuilders in the province and, together with the smaller yards of the other builder clans of Carleton, constituted an important element in the provincial shipbuilding industry. Supported by 258 Carleton artisans, a bill to incorporate the Carleton Mechanics Shipbuilding and Navigation Company passed the Legislative Assembly at its 1849 sitting but was defeated in an 8 to 6 division in the Legislative Council.[64] Undeterred, the petitioners returned in 1850 only to repeat the same process, this time suffering a decisive defeat in the council.[65]

The expressions of occupational community that gave rise to distinctive institutions devoted to the interests of craftsmen in the 1830s were only a forerunner of the demands for protection made by artisans in the 1840s. Only freemen could legally carry on a craft in the city. About two of every five artisans were freemen, including virtually all masters. Although the law was frequently broken or occasionally even misapplied – as when the mayor admitted Americans as freemen in 1810 – that right remained a legal whip that could be (and frequently was) used against Americans and other non-freemen operating within the city.[66]

The extent to which this threat was used depended upon the diligence of the mayor and the willingness of artisans to bring complaints. Robert Hazen, for example, was sympathetic to the interests of artisans in the late 1830s. His city inspector regularly reported the tailors, painters, carpenters, and other non-freemen craftsmen working within the city. Hazen apparently regularly tried and fined the offenders, a practice that had the effect of forcing British immigrants to purchase their freedom and of driving the Americans out or at least into less conspicuous positions.[67]

In times of economic difficulty, the freemen artisans were more likely to act as their own police, reporting offenders and in some cases mounting public protests against aliens. Americans, sometimes operating with the co-operation of the masters, sometimes in competition with them, were the principal culprits. The situation was particularly acute within the building trades. The major problem for local journeymen was the arrival in the city of numerous American craftsmen seeking temporary employment at wages below that normally paid to members of the trades. So many Americans arrived at the height of the building boom following the fire of 1839 that the journeymen gathered in public meeting in the autumn to prepare a petition to Common Council asking that their rights of citizenship be protected.[68] If the prayers of that petition were granted, it was only a temporary respite. The following summer, a 'Carpenter' complained that house carpenters were denied employment and that merchants and other townspeople were giving preference to 'a gang of Yankees who flock to the city in summer and work for less and are free from taxes, road work etc.'[69] As the depression of 1841 began the situation became still more tense. In early April, some 2000 journeymen gathered in Queens Square demanding that all foreign journeymen be prohibited from entering the city.[70] The meeting was held at 4:00 pm on a weekday and the lack of public comment on this act would seem to indicate that it was held with the consent of most masters. Despite public fears raised by the size and nature of the meeting, the journeymen proceeded to the St John Hotel where they organized an executive to accomplish their purpose.[71]

The artisans were not without allies in this crusade. A large proportion of the men concerned were freemen and, despite a determined effort on the part of many within the city's merchant community to remove all restrictions on trade and labour within the city, the protectionists were able to elect a strong contingent of supporters to Common Council and to bring considerable pressure to bear on the mayor. The long-time Sydney Ward alderman Gregory Van Horne and his assistant, John Hagarty, were particular champions of the artisans' position, and the support of George Bond and artisan councillors Robert Ray and Ewan Cameron was usually assured. In the spring of 1840, Hagarty and Van Horne succeeded in carrying a resolution in Common Council to prevent foreigners from taking contracts or from doing work in the city that was in any way injurious to freemen mechanics.[72] After a challenge to their authority to prosecute non-freemen was successfully beaten back in the Supreme Court, the mayors of the city quite regularly prosecuted any offending American artisans in the 1840s. The results of these efforts were reflected in the 1851 Census, which revealed that not many more than 2 per cent of the city's artisans had been born in the United States. None the less, the struggle continued. Liberal reformers like Henry Chubb were scandalized by the economic restrictions imposed on Americans and argued that the capital and skills that American business men and manufacturers had to offer the city would do much to advance its interests. And this contention was strongly supported by a substantial part of the merchant community in a petition to the House of Assembly in 1850, but to no avail.

The efforts toward the maintenance of the traditional economic privileges of freemen paled by comparison with the struggle after 1840 to protect the products of city tradesmen from those of their American counterparts. This question, more than any other, divided the society of Saint John into clearly identifiable classes.[73] Protection of goods was never a simple matter in colonial New Brunswick. The principal competitor of the colonial tradesman was not the American but the British producer, and the mercantilism of the empire admitted no defence against the free importation of British goods. Only the modest transportation costs and a very small revenue tariff served as protection for the colonial tradesmen.

As early as 1827, the 'mechanics of Saint John,' complaining of competition from American manufactured products, petitioned for an increase in the provincial tariff on a broad range of commodities. A similar request was made in 1834.[74] Further demands were made by a number of particular trades: the leather makers in 1835 and the millers and bakers in 1828, 1835, and 1840.[75] Despite these sporadic protests, however, the combination of imperial and provincial duties provided a margin of protection for most commodities sufficient to prevent the American producer from posing a serious threat to his Saint John counterpart.[76]

The situation changed rapidly after 1840. The confluence of the 1841–42 commercial collapse with the decision of the Peel government to abandon the imperial tariff produced the kind of economic chaos and social despair that added greatly to the sense of group consciousness evident among the growing body of artisans in the 1830s. The depression produced a devastating effect on the artisanal community of Saint John. Masters and journeymen alike were involved in the common ruin as local markets largely disappeared. Between 1840 and 1842, the number of tailors in the city decreased from 400 to 60 and shoe-makers from 300 to 60.[77] The decline in membership in the Mechanics Institute was so severe that the institution was threatened with bankruptcy.

Yet, while numbers of artisans joined most of the labouring classes on the dole in the terrible winter of 1841–42, and many others took their skills to the urban centres of New England, craftsmen as a group displayed a high degree of cohesiveness in the face of the general ruin. Lieutenant-Governor Sir William Colebrook was approached by a number of 'respectable mechanics' who offered to mortgage their homes to obtain funds to settle on wilderness land. With Colebrook's encouragement and the assistance of Gesner and Perley, the artisans formed themselves into associations and proceeded to petition for block grants of crown land in the countries surrounding Saint John. The initial association of twenty-three craftsmen under the leadership of Azor Betts, a housejoiner, was settled on the Pollet River in Westmorland County in early September. A second group headed by the saddler David Collins and totalling 108 associates were placed in Kings County.[78] The Mechanics', Teetotal, and Eel River settlements were almost entirely created by Saint John artisans. The settlements so made were not particularly successful.[79] The problem was not too serious, however. The provincial economy revived by 1844 and the city was capable of absorbing a large number of its erstwhile citizens.

The crisis of 1841–42 was compounded in 1842 by the decision of the British government to begin dismantlement of the great instruments of imperial economic policy. For most Saint John artisans, this shift in imperial policy posed a threat and offered a rare opportunity. On the one hand, their local markets lay exposed to American produce, which could, in most cases, enter duty free. On the other hand, by 1846, there was a clear possibility that the provincial legislature would be able to protect colonial craftsmen even from their British competitors.

The tensions between the artisans and the governing élites that had underlain much of the artisans' protests and institutions in the 1830s were heightened by the crises of the 1840s. The first shot in the war for the tariff was fired at the 1843 sitting of the provincial legislature when 299 protectionists petitioned for the imposition of a high provincial tariff aimed at the protection of local goods against 'inferior American manufactures.' The document was important not only for the force of its argument but for the strong united front of artisans that it represented. It was accompanied by an even more radical proposal from the city's iron founders. Arguing that they were capable of supplying all castings for ships, mill machinery, stoves, and ploughs needed in the province, and pointing to the sufferings they and their journeymen had endured the previous few years, they asked the legislature to impose a duty on British manufactured goods.[80]

The 1843 protectionist petition was not a large one, but what it lacked in numbers was compensated for in quality. Its signatories included an impressive contingent of leading masters from virtually every trade in the city. When these efforts failed to produce the desired concessions, the leaders of the movement moved to create a formal organization that could be used as a common front behind which rural and urban producers from across the province could be organized. Using the Mechanics Institute as their base, leading protectionists attempted to weld craftsmen, fishers, and farmers into an alliance against the common enemy.

In January 1844, shipbuilder John Owens and miller and flour dealer J.W. McLeod convened a meeting of 'people friendly to protection of agricultural and domestic manufacturers.' Some 500 supporters attended the meeting. The organizers enunciated an explicit class purpose: 'our interests we have much reason to believe have been neglected in the Halls of Legislation. The time, it is hoped, will come when the industrious classes will be able to send men from among themselves who have a community of feeling with them and an identity of interests.'[81] To fulfil this aim, the meeting formed the Provincial Association, elected an executive committee for the new organization, and passed resolutions denouncing all free-trade proposals. The association authorized its executive committee to petition the legislature for a scale of duties to protect the economic interests of all classes.

The committee lost no time in printing and distributing circulars outlining the association's program. Within a month, branch associations were formed at Kingston and Hampton. Among the first recommendations made by the executive committee were proposals to impose a substantial duty on cordage and canvas, to bonus farmers for growing hemp and flax, to construct model farms, and to organize mechanics' fairs. Members of the association were also encouraged to bind themselves to use, consume, and wear only New Brunswick products. The strength of the new producers' common front was reflected in the mammoth petition presented by the Provincial Association of New Brunswick to the 1844 sitting of the legislature. More than 2500 association supporters in Saint John, Kings, and York counties prayed that the legislature provide protection for the farmers, fishers, and manufacturers of the province.[82] This show of strength accomplished what the smaller group of 1843 petitioners had been unable to do: the legislature agreed to impose tariffs of 10–20 per cent on a number of products, including castings, footwear, cut nails, bricks, furniture, and agricultural implements, and specific duties on cattle , oxen, horses, and apples. Of the major Saint John trades groups, only the tailors and bakers and millers were denied any significant protection.[83] The issue did not lie there. The free traders struck back the following year and managed to restore most of the lower 1843 tariff. It was only after the 1846 general election that the protectionists were able, finally, to secure a policy of moderate protection.

The issue of protection divided the city in the 1840s just as thoroughly as did that of prohibition in the following decade. Indeed, the personnel of both groups frequently coincided. Most of the feeling generated against the mercantile free traders was tinged with a strong sense of group consciousness, a sense on the part of many urban tradesmen that the enemy had in some way abused them for its own ends and that it was an enemy that felt itself to be masters of the society. This hostility broke forth in a seemingly trivial incident in spring 1841 when a prominent patrician and merchant, G.D. Robinson, made the public comment that 'the mechanics of Saint John had more wages than mechanics at other places, and that in consequence their wives were dressed in furs and silks and that they looked more like x x x x than decent women.' The comment became the focus of heated debate in the city, meetings of tradesmen were held, a committee was established to investigate the case, and the News editor, George Fenety, felt constrained to defend the dignity and respectability of the city's mechanics, noting that, like 'mechanics in all places,' those of Saint John carried their heads higher than most men because 'they are the bone and sinew of every land.'[84]

The sense of injustice intensified in 1844 at the height of the public debate over the Provincial Association and its program. Courier editor Henry Chubb plainly sided with the merchants in this debate. One commentary in his paper denounced the association as a group of tradesmen who, instead of attending to their business, proposed a tariff that would enable 'them to live in a style far above their station.' It was commerce that must suffer for this – 'that commerce which pours its wealth into our laps' and 'which cannot be advantageously maintained unless our ship owners be permitted to buy their supplies and materials in the cheapest market and to procure their labour at the lowest possible price.'[85] The attacks on the protectionists by The Courier were mild, however, compared to that mounted by Loyalist editor Thomas Hill. Hill saw in the leaders of the protectionist all the elements of Saint John society he so much despised: prohibitionists, Evangelical Alliance supporters, malcontents who would threaten even the imperial connection in their pursuit of their own material gain. Early in 1845 he wrote a play entitled The Provincial Association, which parodied a number of well-known Saint John mechanics and two of their wives. The play, in the words of The

News, was 'intended to bring contempt not only on the respectability of the gentlemen in question but upon their moral rectitude and the virtue of certain ladies in St. John.' After initial performances in Fredericton, the play was brought to Saint John in April. The first performance occurred without incident, although the satire was so obvious and so telling that *The News* was astonished when the mayor did not close the theatre after the first night. The following evening a large number of tradesmen led by 'persons whose standing in society should have caused them to respect themselves' filled the theatre, while another mob, estimated at 300 strong, gathered outside.[86] In the ensuing riot, the doors of the theatre were torn off and the interior literally torn to pieces, while the mayor and police stood by helplessly. *The Courier* thought the play was all in fun and Mayor Donaldson, long a spokesman for the timber interests, permitted another performance during work hours for the benefit of those citizens who were prepared to pay 5s. and sign a requisition.[87]

Hill's attack was certainly the most provocative made upon the Saint John artisans. As prosperity returned in 1845 and 1846, tensions between craftsmen and merchants lessened. Even so, strong feelings remained that were reinforced in the provincial election of 1846 in which protection and religious equality were the crucial issues. John Owens and J.W. McLeod ran on behalf of both the Provincial Association and the Evangelical Alliance. They were defeated, as was their Free Presbyterian counterpart. Ultimately, among the Saint John protectionists, only R.D. Wilmot secured election and soon became spokesman for the protectionist movement. The movement, though less intense and focused on specific industries rather than on the principle of protection, remained a potent force throughout the remainder of the decade.

The rain of petitions by individual crafts that began in 1843 continued unabated throughout the colonial period. The shoe-makers petitioned in 1844 for reciprocal duties with those in the United States. They repeated the petition in 1846 and the following year returned with the support of a large body of tanners, merchants, and other tradesmen.[88] Their prayers were only occasionally heard. At the 1847 sitting of the assembly, their petition was laughed out of the chamber by a group of anti-protectionist assembly men led by Isaac Woodward, a Saint John member and Chamber of Commerce officer. Woodward replied to the shoe-makers by proposing that the assembly act on a petition from the Chamber of Commerce that would remove the tariff from every commodity with the exception of beans. The treatment meted to the shoe-makers was repeated with the tailors, who also asked for reciprocity of duties with the Americans. Iron and brass foundry owners, the bakers, the leather manufacturers, the carriage makers, and the millers all made similar demands.[89] As a result of these repeated representations, the legislature imposed a modest level of protection on a limited range of consumer products made in the city. Footwear, leather, furniture, machinery, iron castings, agricultural implements, wagons and sleighs, veneers, hats, cigars, and pianos were all subject to a 15 per cent tariff.

The recession of 1849–50, occasioned in part by the final demise of British mercantilism, resulted in the migration of hundreds of artisans and labourers from the city and sparked a revival of the protectionist cause. In February 1850, a series of meetings organized by leaders of the Provincial Association were held in St Stephen's Hall. Advertised as meetings of the Friends of Protection to Home Industry and Domestic Manufacturers, the meeting convened under the chairmanship of Thomas Allen, Esq., and heard J.W. Lawrence urge a partial withdraw from the timber industry and the development of an extensive manufacturing capacity within the province. The petition, demanding 'a higher and more decidedly protective tariff' for manufactured and farm produce, was signed by 1234 men headed by the traditional trades leadership.[90]

When the city mobilized in 1851 to press the provincial government for construction of a railway system for the province, artisans met apart from the commercial groups to present their views. At a meeting in the Mechanics Institute chaired by the mayor, they offered to take stock in the rail line provided they were offered employment on it.[91]

The sharp divisions of opinion between merchant and artisan interests evident in economic issues were manifest in other areas as well.[92] Perhaps the most obvious were the attempts in 1835 and 1843 to restrict admission to the freedom of the city to the prosperous. This issue was somewhat confused because the sons of freemen who served an apprenticeship in the city would still have been admissible on payment of the fees of office. None the less, the response of freemen merchants, artisans, and labourers to the 1843 proposal reflected marked differences of opinion. Eight out of ten merchants supported the restriction while more than two-thirds of the artisans and twenty-one of the twenty-two freemen labourers were opposed. The artisans who opposed the proposal were drawn almost equally from native and Irish backgrounds.

Among other matters on which numbers of freemen artisans expressed an opinion were temperance and protection. However, both of these issues received considerable support from the merchant interest and it is difficult to speak of a clear division based on occupational interest. The concerns that provoked the most reaction among freemen artisans in the colonial period were those related to secret societies and to education. A large number of artisans opposed efforts to prohibit secret societies in 1844 and a decade later supported incorporation of the Orange Order.

Given the length of time between the two petitions and their differing purposes, it is not surprising that few names appeared on both. More striking is the fact that while support for religious but non-sectarian schools in 1858 was as high as for Orange incorporation, only 17 per cent of the petitioners signed both petitions. In contrast, merchants appear to have played a much less significant role in efforts either to prevent the prohibition of secret societies or to ensure passage of the 1858 schools bill. They played virtually no part in the attempts to incorporate the Orange Order. Superficially it would appear that such differences in behaviour and attitude were largely class based. However, since a majority of freemen artisans were Irish-born and the great majority of merchants were not, these differences may well have been the result of ethnic factors.

The evidence of the period suggests that there was an artisans' interest in the city from at least 1820. As it grew in size and influence, it took on many of the manifestations of a class. The strength of the interest lay in the persistence and proprietorial attitudes of its leadership toward the community. They shared with the patricians and leading merchants a place in the Loyalist myth. They played dominant roles within the Irish cultures. Many of their number were small freeholders and many more were freemen. By 1840, much of their leadership could claim both respectability and three generations of residency in the city; a handful of masters even aspired to the magistracy. Although they were found in all cultures, the artisans were concentrated in that tightly knit evangelical tradition in which were found so many of the city's respectable artisans, masters, and small proprietors who played such an important role in shaping the values of the mid-nineteenth-century community. Coupled with this strong cultural base was the considerable political influence that the producers' interest enjoyed. Because of the distribution of constituencies, the interest could often control the Common Council and the election of city assemblymen. Finally, as they demonstrated on a number of occasions in the colonial period, artisans could act in a concerted and self-conscious fashion in defence of their economic interests. Altogether, they alone possessed the influence, the status, and the numbers to challenge patrician and merchant interests for control of the community.

~5~

Irishmen and Bluenoses

In most North American nineteenth-century towns, the strength and impact of interest and class were mediated by the influence of ethnicity and religion. Indeed, while a variety of explanations have been offered, detailed studies of mid-century Philadelphia demonstrate that powerful cultures centred on the traditions of native evangelicalism and Irish Catholicism dominated the public life of that city.[1] Similar though less well-documented conclusions may be drawn for New York, Boston, and Toronto.[2] The general conclusion seems clear: before 1860 the effect of economic concerns was largely confined to the work place; the perceptions of most urban dwellers were generally informed by a culture based on ethnicity and religion rather than economic class. There were exceptions, of course, and in some cases it may be argued that particular ethnic and religious groups were in fact surrogates for class. It also seems that ethnic and religious factors had been less significant at the turn of the century and their growing prominence reflected fundamental changes in the structure and nature of urban society.[3] The central, often interrelated, changes were the arrival of large numbers of immigrants from what were viewed as alien traditions by the native population, and the economic and technological advances of the period, which led to problems of accommodation. Immigrant studies have repeatedly demonstrated that ethnicity remained a primary sense of identity and that most ethnic groups made a serious attempt to modify the host environment through the creation of associations and institutions designed to maintain the integrity of particular values and customs. Many historians would argue that this was done only after it was evident that they would not be accommodated in native institutions.

The largest group of migrants to nineteenth-century Saint John were Irish, and they were to play the principal role in changing the social character of the city. In many respects, the Irish experience in Saint John was similar to that in Philadelphia, Boston, and Liverpool. Their numbers, sense of cultural distinction, and concentrated settlement, together with the discrimination they faced from the native population, created insurmountable obstacles to their social integration. And yet the Saint John experience differed fundamentally from the others. At its height, the Irish immigration overwhelmed the city: by 1851 well over half the heads of households were Irish. A high proportion of the migrants were Protestant. That, and the city's role as outpost of empire, produced a situation more akin to that in the Upper Canadian capital of Toronto than in any other North American port. Irish migration began by 1820. In the expansive years before 1842 the migrants were generally well received in the city. Apart from the psychological impact they created, the famine migrants constituted only a small proportion of the resident Irish population. The communal experience of the Irish between 1820 and 1860 may be perceived in three segments: a period of quiescence between 1818 and 1828 when they were viewed as simply another British group, a time of tension as a self-conscious Irish middle class challenged the native proprietors, and the disintegration of the Saint John Irish nation into Roman Catholic and Protestant communities after 1840.

The development of an Irish community in Saint John was inextricably linked to the migration patterns that emerged in the years following the Napoleonic wars. These, in turn, were inseparable from the province's timber trade. Because of the enormous surplus capacity on the return voyage, Saint John shipowners could offer meagre accommodation at bargain prices: a poor man could transport his family from Cork to Saint John for half the price of regular accommodation to Boston.[4]

Once set in motion, the migration continued without serious interruption until 1850. In any four-year period between 1820 and 1840, the number of British migrants exceeded the population of the city. The urban labour market could not absorb such numbers. Fortunately it was rarely necessary to do so. Many had never intended to remain in the city and moved off for Portland and Boston or to the rural areas of New Brunswick within days or weeks of their arrival.[5] It is difficult to determine the numbers leaving for the States, but the estimates of authoritative contemporary observers seem to indicate that from one-quarter to seven-eighths of migrants left the province each year depending on the opportunities available in Saint John and on the state of the Boston market.[6] Considerable effort was made to persuade the remaining immigrants to occupy the intervale lands of the interior rivers and streams.

Those that remained in the port either possessed special skills that made them particularly valuable additions to the urban economy, or had neither resources nor skills and hence no means of leaving.

The major difficulty was the city's inability to match the labour supply to the needs of the local labour market. Like all timber ports, Saint John was subject to the vagaries of the British market. A downturn in British timber needs was reflected six months later in a severe downturn of the urban economy. This process occurred once or twice every decade between 1820 and 1850. In 1827, the magistrates of the county sessions bitterly denounced the shipowners who took their profit and cast a starving Irish peasantry on the care of the city. They demanded, unsuccessfully, the imposition of 15s. head tax to be paid by each captain before the immigrant landed.[7] At the height of the 1831 recession Saint John merchants distributed handbills through much of Ireland describing the high wages available in New Brunswick.[8] At the same time, the magistrates complained of the dumping of 450 'filthy, poverty ridden' smallpox-infected Irish in the city.[9] At the height of the 1837 recession, 5000 immigrants were dumped in the port in a three-month period. Owing to the commercial collapse in the United States, few pressed on and most went on relief.[10] The story was repeated in the recession of 1839 and in the collapse of 1841–42 when the arrival of thousands of destitute Irish occurred simultaneously with the emigrationof hundreds of native workers fleeing to Boston to escape the general ruin.[11] With large-scale prolonged unemployment came the inevitable problems of crime and disorder and the inevitable complaints of the Common Council that the immigrants were 'the lowest class of idlers and prisoners from Ireland.'[12]

The immediate impact of the immigration was felt in the social costs of short-term and long-term relief. Throughout the 1820s, the poor-house commissioners housed and fed indigent immigrants. The need to protect the resident population from the risk of smallpox contamination brought by the poorer Irish migrants persuaded the magistrates to construct a pest house on Partridge Island where all immigrants would be forced to remain until cleared by medical authorities.[13] By 1833 the city was spending in excess of £600 a year on the Partridge Island establishment, in addition to substantial amounts for hospital and poor-house accommodation and for outdoor relief.[14] Major problems were created by those who became permanent charges on the public purse and in time it was necessary to construct institutional facilities to care for them. The largest of these institutions was the provincial lunatic asylum. More than 80 per cent of the patients accommodated there in the 1840s and 1850s were Irish immigrants.[15]

None of the regulations or institutions that had been put in place in the

St John's Irish Presbyterian Church, c. 1870 (NBM)

Mrs Moses Perley, c. 1870 (PANB)

1830s were able to anticipate or cope with the crisis of the late 1840s. The composition of the immigration began to change in the early 1840s and was characterized by a high proportion of agricultural labourers – a euphemism for those possessing neither urban skills nor knowledge of the more important agricultural technologies. The emigrant agent, Israel Perley, reported that in 1845 some 82 per cent of the immigrant workers entering the province were agricultural.[16] The presence of such a large pool of unskilled labour severely depressed wages in the city throughout the 1840s and early 1850s. James Johnston noted that, as late as 1851, wages for unskilled labour in and around the city were 20 per cent less than those paid anywhere in the interior of the province.[17]

The early famine migrations were only a prelude to the terrible spring, summer, and autumn of 1847 when 15,794 starving, disease-ridden bits of humanity staggered ashore from their floating coffins, a high proportion of them aged and infirmed paupers shovelled out of Ireland by their landlords and parishes.[18] Between 7000 and 8000 immigrants lived for at least part of the summer of 1847 in the hospitals and tents of Partridge Island. Hundreds of well migrants who had been allowed to land in the city later ended up in the migrant and almshouse hospital, the victims of disease that their weakened systems were unable to resist.[19]

The 1847 influx was the last major immigration in the history of New Brunswick. Only 4000 arrived the next year and in the face of the depression in the timber trade, more than 3000 set off for New England. After 1850, immigration declined to a few thousand each year.

Native perceptions of immigrants in general and of Irish immigrants in particular were in large measure shaped by the manner of their arrival. In the initial enthusiasm for development, migrants were welcomed with open arms. By the late 1820s, however, public comment had veered to the judgment of the Irish.[20] The session's resolution of 1827 complained specifically of the 'Irish peasantry' being thrown on the city, and that of 1830 explicitly described the Irish arrivals as 'filthy' and 'poverty ridden.' Like most articulate native British North Americans, the magistrates of Saint John seemed offended by the poverty, 'raucous behaviour,' intemperance, and arrogance of the Irish arrivals.[21] The feeling was reciprocated by migrants who found the best farm lands, the public offices, and the seats of authority monopolized by the native population. Demands that the head tax on immigrants be doubled to meet the costs of providing for indigent arrivals in the early 1830s were met by the argument of the Sons of Erin that the existing head tax should be removed because 'we are British and this is our country purchased by the treasure and blood of our ancestors.'[22]

The early Irish experience in Saint John sharpened their sense of ethnicity. All migrants, as Oscar Handlin has argued for Boston, bring an awareness of group identity to their new environment, but the use they make of that identity depends upon the reception they receive in the host community.[23] The first institutional manifestations of a distinctive Irish ethnicity slowly built in response to native reaction to their growing numbers. Even religious structures, as in London and Toronto, developed only over a long period of time.[24]

Irish migrants were absorbed into the city's existing religious institutions. Even St Malachi's Chapel, constructed in 1815–16, had taken institutional form in 1820 with the arrival of a Canadian priest.[25] Constructed originally by the handful of Irish émigrés in the city to serve the needs of Catholic soldiers from the garrison, St Malachi's remained the centre of Catholic faith in the city and its environs for a generation. Leadership in the infant parish was provided by a number of small business men, most of whom had been involved in the construction of the chapel and continued to be its principal support – playing a dominant role in the life of the parish notwithstanding the growing influx of Irish immigrants in the 1830s.[26] In policy and social outlook, the congregation resembled those of the Protestant churches that surrounded it.

Distinctive Irish Protestant congregations were late in developing. The Church of Ireland, particularly in the south, was the most evangelical section of the Episcopalian (as the Church of England was called) communion.[27] Irish Episcopalians settled into Old Trinity with the Loyalists without much difficulty. As their numbers grew in the 1820s, they seem to have played a more influential role in Trinity than in most other bluenose institutions, reflecting a common evangelicalism that most of them shared with the Loyalist rector, Benjamin Gray, and the lay leadership of the parish. Gray was also careful to ensure that when the new Church of England parishes were erected in the 1840s they were served by suitable Irish rectors.

Just the Irish Episcopalians settled in with the Loyalists; the incoming Presbyterians moved into St Andrew's Church with the Scots. The only distinctive Irish congregation to develop before 1840 was that founded in the 1820s by the Reformed Presbyterian Church of Ireland. And even this group did not complete its meeting house until 1835.[28] The partnership of Irish and Scots in St Andrew's Church was not always a happy one. As the proportion of Irish in the congregation grew in the 1830s, there were demands that a greater role in congregational life be given to the Irish members. Irish Presbyterianism was characterized by a strong strain of evangelical sentiment that probably did not sit well with the broad and rather tolerant latitudinarianism of the Church of Scotland.[39] Matters came to a head in 1842 on the resignation of the minister of St Andrew's.

The Irish trustees of the church, led by William Parks, wrote to the moderator of the Presbyterian Church of Ireland inviting him to nominate an Irish minister to compete with a Scot for the vacant pulpit.[30] The moderator, Dr Cooke, Ireland's leading evangelical, complied. The Scots elders rejected the proposal.

The refusal of the St Andrew's elders to compromise on the issue led to the secession of the greater pat of the Irish membership of St Andrew's and the formation of the Free Presbyterian Church in Saint John.[31] Parks once again entered into negotiations with Dr Cooke and succeeded in securing the Rev. Robert Irvine, who was called for life to the new congregation. Four years later, the congregation was incorporated as St John's Presbyterian Church.[32]

The most important elements in the formation of an Irish groups' identity in the 1830s were the secular organizations that attempted to gather the diffuse Irish groups into a single interest. The earliest of these was the St Patrick's Society. Formed in 1819 for 'gentlemen of Irish descent,' the society was transformed by the migration of the 1820s into a militant champion of Irish rights and a vehicle of Irish consciousness. It brought together Irish officers from the British garrison, a number of great and small business men, the city's two Irish physicians, a priest, and a handful of tradesmen. This was clearly a leadership of the successful and upwardly mobile Irish elements of the mercantile community.[33] Almost all the identifiable members had been raised in Ireland and had come to Saint John between the ages of 18 and 31.[34] Forty per cent of the group were merchants and another 15 per cent were in trade. A large majority were Protestants, but several leading Catholics played prominent roles in the organization. Notably absent from the group were any functionaries or individuals prominent in the public life of the city or province.

Aggressive and self-confident, the society took as its special responsibility the definition and care of the Irish community in the city, the maintenance of Irish rights, and the interpretation of the Irish cause to the larger community. The first of these responsibilities was an enormous undertaking. In the 1820s and early 1830s, the society raised between £40 and £50 a year for the relief of Irish immigrants through quarterly levies on its members. As the immigrant tide rose after 1830, the society petitioned the legislature for assistance and proposed the creation of an immigrant fund through a small levy to be assessed on each vessel bringing immigrants to the city.[35] It maintained a presence as the principal voluntary organization committed to the welfare of Irish immigrants.[36] The society never backed away from its identification with the migrants.[37] Throughout the early 1830s, its leaders engaged in a running debate with natives apprehensive over the society's determination to maintain a strong Irish identity, and with temperance advocates who felt the society should set an example to their compatriots.[38]

The élite concerns of the society were reflected in the claim that the Irish were denied opportunities for participation in the public life and service of the province. Its members championed the cause of the surveyor general, Thomas Baillie, whom they viewed as a symbol of Irish success. Baillie's humiliation and dismissal from office at the hands of prominent bluenoses (native New Brunswickers) was seen as a conspiracy to deprive Irishmen of their only influential leader. His subsequent vindication and restoration to office in 1842 was hailed as a national triumph. At a special meeting, the society expressed its 'joy and satisfaction' with Baillie's restoration to the offices of surveyor general and commissioner of crown lands, and offered him a hearty 'ceadh mille fealtha.' The president, William End, offered the further observation that it was 'as Irishman, not as politician, that the Society have addressed you.' Baillie replied: 'That my case should have called forth the congratulations of Irishmen is one of the many proofs that the national will is not to be impaired by climate, time or distance; but is the same, whether in the forests of New Brunswick, or the green fields of our native land.'[39]

It was the unwillingness of the St Patrick's Society to take any partisan political stand that differentiated it from the much larger though less influential organization known variously as the Friendly Sons of Erin Society and the Friendly Sons of Ireland. Formed around 1830 to further the interests of Ireland, it had a much younger and more numerous membership than did the St Patrick's Society. Its support was drawn primarily from among grocers, traders, and artisans. The most significant characteristic of the organization was the presence of the non-Irish-born within it. Fully 30 per cent of those whose birthplace can be established were born in New Brunswick, England, or Scotland, and another 20 per cent had been brought to New Brunswick as children.[40] It was among the Sons of Erin that the process of cultural transmission of a particular ethnic tradition is most evident.

Meeting monthly at James Nethery's Hibernian Hotel, the Sons dwelt at great length on the subject of Ireland, Irish politics, and Irish grievances. The meetings, usually lasting from seven until midnight, were given over to stirring rhetoric accompanied by the consumption of large quantities of alcoholic beverages, a combination that gave rise to considerable anxiety on the part of many neighbours. The political faith of the organization was drawn from Daniel O'Connell's Repeal Association, which aimed at the dissolution of the 1800 union of Great Britain and Ireland and the restoration of the Irish parliament under the British monarchy.

In some fashion the Saint John Sons managed to comprehend both

Catholic and Protestant traditions within this ideology. While the Catholic presence was much more significant in the Sons than in the St Patrick's Society, a substantial proportion of the membership of the former was composed of Protestants. Higher-status Catholics, such as William Doherty and John Dougherty, were found in both societies. With few exceptions, the Sons' Protestants were from lower-status occupations than their counterparts in the St Patrick's Society. The emphasis in the organization was on an Irish unity. The divisiveness of the Irish religious traditions was deliberately played down. Characteristically, the high altar to Irish nationalism at the 1832 St Patrick's Day celebrations of the Sons featured a central harp surrounded by shamrocks and orange lilies entwined to form the motto United We Stand: Divided We Fall.[41]

In their occasional public pronouncements, the Sons showed themselves to be blunt and pugnacious. Unlike their compatriots in the St Patrick's Society, the Sons flatly rejected the principle of a head tax on British immigrants and demanded their settlement as a matter of right of conquest.[42] Similarly the letter from 'Hibernicus' objecting to the claim of an English candidate in the 1834 election that he represented the 'old countrymen' of the city may have been written by a St Patrick's Society man, but its tone and rhetoric were much more characteristic of the Sons of Erin. The writer described the candidate as a '*refuse* Englishman! ... Does the abominable egotist think we can find no better man than he in the whole community of Irish citizens ... have we not a *Peter McBride* and a Paddy McCann?'[43]

The typical Irish-born members of both of these ethnic organizations in 1835 had left Ireland sometime between 1817 and 1829. Their ethnic views, which emphasized the centrality of an Irish heritage and a mildly secular Irish nationalism, were a typical response to the problems of Ireland in the 1820s. All of this changed over the course of the next fifteen years. A religious revival in Ireland produced a militant evangelicalism within the Church of Ireland and the Presbyterian Synod of Ulster. This was paralleled by a growing militancy within the Roman Catholic Church. By 1840 these issues began to impinge on the Irish nationalist movement, which became increasingly Catholic in orientation. The nationalist leader Daniel O'Connell declared 1843 to be the year of repeal of the union of Great Britain and Ireland, by force if necessary. Faced with this appeal to force, the Roman Catholic hierarchy denounced O'Connell and supported British efforts to control the apprehended insurrection.[44]

The sequence of events had profound impact on the Irish overseas communities. In Boston, Philadelphia, and London, tens of thousands of Catholic Irish swelled the ranks of repeal clubs, and the movement consumed the energies of its participants for nearly a decade.[45] In Saint

John, the emergence of the Ulster Constitutional Association, O'Connell's perception of the Irish state as a Catholic state, and his advocacy of extra-parliamentary means to achieve the goal of repeal produced a tragic effect. The Sons of Erin continued to follow O'Connell in the early 1840s, but many Protestants apparently abandoned the organization.

In January 1841 an advertisement appeared in *The Chronicle* announcing a public meeting at which it was proposed to establish a newspaper devoted to Irish interests.[46] The new paper, *The Mirror*, was nearly eleven months in the making. Its prospectus, issued in November 1841, announced that it would be 'decidedly liberal,' avoid religious issues entirely, and stand with the natives of the country in their efforts to achieve commercial prosperity. Among other things, strong support was offered for education, the mechanics institute, temperance, assistance to immigrants, and constitutional reform.[47] The directors of the journal were six Irish Catholic merchants: Francis Collins, Pat McCullough, Henry McCullough, William Doherty, William Doherty Jr, and Francis McDermott. Whatever the merits of the paper, it destroyed the unity of Ireland in Saint John. The centre of the controversy was the editor's support of repeal of the union of Great Britain and Ireland by violent means. The debate split even the paper's editorial staff. At mid year the editor of *The Mirror*, J.R. Fitzgerald, resigned his post explaining in a letter to *The Courier* that he did so because of the extreme opinions expressed in its editorial columns.[48] None the less, O'Connell's call for 'repeal year' in 1843 was answered in Saint John by the creation of a Repeal Association apparently prepared to decide the issue by force of arms if necessary. The leaders of the association were prominent Catholic laymen who generally opposed clerical control of the church.

The issue of repeal was one of two that divided the Irish of Saint John in the early 1840s. The second was the growth of Catholic ultramontanism in the city and the province. Early Irish Catholicism in New Brunswick had faithfully reflected the state of the Irish church. And if the early nineteenth-century experience in Ireland and London was repeated in New Brunswick, probably not more than one-third of the Catholic arrivals practised their faith.[49] The mission of Catholic leadership, then, was to create a Catholic culture and catholicize an indifferent laity. Under the aegis of the See of Quebec until 1828, always more Irish than Catholic, the small Irish parishes on the New Brunswick sea coast, like those of Upper Canada, had developed a strong tradition of lay participation in the administration of the parishes.[50] The absence of episcopal authority had been further compounded by an undisciplined clergy and by local controversies.[51] The situation improved after 1830 during the clerical incumbency of Dollard and his successor, James Dunphy, but as late as

1843 there prevailed a strong tradition of lay participation in the parish. A strong-willed, hot-tempered Irish prelate of good family and considerable wealth, Dunphy was at once an upholder of clerical supremacy and a source of debate within the parish. his authority and popularity were unquestioned among the great mass of Irish labourers and tradesmen; as their numbers increased in the late 1830s and early 1840s, so too did his influence. His bêtes noires were the influential laymen who had traditionally dominated the parish.

The first major confrontation between Dunphy and these laymen occurred in 1841 when plans were made for the construction of a second church in the city to accommodate the growing Catholic population. The principal contributors, who had already purchased the land for the church, refused Dunphy's demand that title be vested in the bishop. The result was an acrimonious dispute in which Dunphy recommended against construction and publicly condemned his opponents from the pulpit.[52] Dunphy was supported by a majority of the building committee, but the minority, which apparently included the major contributors to the undertaking, outlined their case in a widely distributed pamphlet.[53] The pamphlet was answered by a public letter from fourteen pew holders, applauding Dunphy and condemning the dissidents. The dissidents in this case were led by the 'nine Puritans' – as one of the loyalists described them – men who, like Cromwell, were prepared to hold land from the church. The 'Puritans' represented the most respectable Catholic lay leadership in the city and were leaders of the repeal movement. Most of the Irish Catholic merchants were found in their ranks.[54] Six of the nine were leaders in the Sons of Erin, and five were directors of The Mirror.[55] The controversy over the new church died out in the fall of 1841 and no further action on church expansion in the city was taken.

In the meantime, Dunphy proceeded to create ancillary institutions that would further promote the development of a Catholic culture within the city. In February he organized the Catholic Temperance Association.[56] The society was a closely held instrument of denominational policy and outreach. Dunphy's other outreach instrument was a newspaper, The Liberator, established in 1843 or 1844, through which the bishop and the claims of the church were defended and those who questioned clerical authority sometimes violently assailed.[57] The authority of the church was greatly strengthened in 1842 with the consecration of William Dollard as first bishop of New Brunswick. The first two years of Dollard's episcopacy were largely taken up with the problems emanating from Saint John.[58] Finally, the bishop announced his intention to transfer the seat of his see from Fredericton to Saint John in an effort to bring order and stability to those parishes.[59]

The bishop was greeted on his arrival by a deputation of twenty parishioners, professing to speak for a much larger number, who demanded three conditions 'necessary and requisite to ensure the future welfare and tranquility of the parish.'[60] These included the removal of Dunphy, the election of church wardens by the people, and control of parish finances by the pew holders. The deputation included, once again, the leading dissidents.[61] Dollard's treatment of these requests and his subsequent correspondence suggest that by 1844 his course of action was already planned. Above all else, discipline must be restored, the supremacy of the church assured, and the dissidents – whether opposed to the secular authority of the bishop in principle or to Dunphy personally or prepared to take up arms on behalf of O'Connell's Irish dream – must be made to submit themselves to the higher authority and greater good of the church. The last would be done by persuasion if at all possible, but by legal and ecclesiastical sanctions if necessary.[62]

Fortunately for the bishop's cause, there were close connections between some of the dissidents and the leaders of the movement for repeal of the union of England and Ireland. Reverberations of the 1843–44 crisis in Ireland were being felt in New Brunswick and the lieutenant-governor, Sir Archibald Campbell, more than a little apprehensive of repeal sympathizers in Saint John, was quite willing to accommodate the bishop in his efforts to restore and maintain order among the city's Irish Catholics.[63] The bishop decided to settle once and for all the issue of the church temporalities. A bill to vest in the diocese ownership of all church property was introduced at the 1845 sitting of the New Brunswick legislature under the sponsorship of the lieutenant-governor.[64] The bill passed the Legislative Council only to encounter a Saint John-based opposition resulting in a number of amendments on the floor of the assembly.[65] In the face of opposition from both Protestants and Catholics who opposed the bishop's secular authority, the bill was postponed.

The battle was again joined at the 1846 legislative sitting. On 4 January the bishop announced that a new episcopal corporations bill would be brought to the legislature. Opponents to the bill argued that the meeting called to approve the bill had been advertised as a temperance matter attended only by supporters of the Catholic temperance movement and that 'apart from Michael McGuirk and John McSweeney,' none of the respectable Catholics in the city were temperance men.[66] The wardens of St Peters Church (Portland) and 112 other parishoners in the city, headed by Thomas Watters, prepared a petition opposing the bishop's incorporation bill. The bishop's supporters responded with a petition bearing the names of 1400 people favouring the bill. The seriousness of the struggle was revealed when Dunphy publicly threatened to withhold the sacra-

The Most Rev. William Dollard, c. 1850 (PANB)

Rev. Ezekiel MacLeod, c. 1860 (PANB)

Cathedral of the Immaculate Conception, Saint John, c. 1853 (NBM)

ments from those opposing the bill. After the local furore, the bill passed without amendment. Through the spring of 1846, *The Liberator* was used with great effect to undermine the position of those who had challenged the primacy of the bishop among the city's Irish Catholics.[67]

Repeal and the Catholic revival were critical to the fragmentation of the Irish community in the 1840s. The process was accelerated by the arrival of unusually large numbers of Catholics as a result of the Irish famine. This slowly broke the rather delicate balance that existed between the Irish Catholic and Protestant groups.[68] It produced, as well, an Irish majority within the city. The new migrants arrived among a group that was becoming more conscious of itself as being a Catholic culture within a Protestant community rather than an Irish culture within a bluenose community.

Dollard became the focus for that Catholic culture. He spoke for the Catholic people, his advice was sought by governors and political leaders, and his pronouncements were perceived as the will of the culture. As early as 1846, there was a recognition that Catholic Irish had so little in common with their Protestant counterparts that they must be separately represented within the coalition of interests that were coming to participate in the administration of the province, the county, and the city. In a letter to the bishop that year, Charles Doherty noted there was only one Catholic magistrate in the county and city of Saint John and that 'the Home Government in their late appointments evince a desire to extend justice to all, and thereby begat confidence in the administration of justice by selecting for places of trust members of every Christian denomination.'[69] Recognizing that the lieutenant-governor would insist upon the bishop's imprimatur in appointing any Catholic to public office, Doherty asked Dollard to intercede on behalf of a prominent clerical loyalist, Hugh Sharkey. Mr Sharkey received the Queen's Commission the following year.

Recognition of the Catholic right to participation in the common life of the city finally took public form in 1848, following the seleciton of grand jurors for the summer assizes.[70] Not a Catholic was included in the group. A mass protest meeting of Catholics, chaired by the pastor of St Malachi's, was held at the Temperance Hall. The meeting proposed that every Christian body was entitled to equal rights and privileges under the British Constitution, and that the exclusion of any body was a 'gross insult' to the body and a 'positive violation of the constitutional privileges of the subject.' However imperfect the constitutional understanding of the Saint John Catholic leaders, there was no doubt of the political threat implied in their meeting.[71] In further resolutions, they declared that Catholics had lost all confidence in the executive council of the province and called upon Catholics in each county to assemble and adopt measures for the redress of their grievances. The transition to an Irish Catholic identity was complete. After 1848, the assembly slate from Saint John would always contain a Catholic, just as it would normally have a Protestant dissenter.

The emergence of Catholic Ireland in the city was paralleled by that of Protestant Ireland. Once the lines of development began, the two interacted with each other in a complicated snowballing of cause and effect. The Irish Protestant counterpart to the radical repeal and ribbon organizations found among the Catholics of the early 1840s was the Orange Order. Founded in 1796 in Armagh as a secret quasi-military organization designed to protect the interests of Protestants, the Order in both Ireland and England had become associated with a violence that made it suspect even in the eyes of the British government whose authority it claimed to uphold in the second kingdom.[72]

The presence of a large and aggressive body of Irish Protestants and their distinctive Orange tradition sharply distinguished the communities of anglophone British North America from those of the United States.[73] Houston and Smyth have determined that Irish Protestants outnumbered Irish Catholics in Upper Canada by a ratio of two to one.[74] The ratio was not dissimilar to that which existed in southern and central New Brunswick in 1871.

It was inevitable that Orangemen should be numbered among the Saint John immigrants of the 1820s and 1830s and that their influence should be reinforced by the large numbers of Orangemen found in the British regiments that composed the Saint John garrison. Military lodges may have existed from 1818 and the first civilian lodge in the province was operating in 1831.[75] One of Mayor Robert F. Hazen's correspondents noted in 1837 that there had been a long-standing animosity between several Orangemen and 'others of the Catholic party in the Marsh Road neighbourhood.'[76] In some cases, small groups of Orangemen gathered informally on 12 July at private homes to celebrate the Battle of the Boyne (the Glorious Twelfth).[77]

The first public indication of organized Orange activity occurred in July 1838 when *The Chronicle* carried the information from 'Verex' that a 'select number of the United and Loyal Protestants of St. John' willing to celebrate the Crossing of the Boyne dined at the Hibernian Hotel.[78] In the spring of 1840, a group of Orangemen returning from the funeral of one of their number walked down Church Street wearing their Orange armbands. *The Courier* editor condemned such conduct and called upon the Common Council to prevent such demonstrations.[79] In response, the leader of the group, James Nethery, claimed that he had invited seventy-four Orangemen to a private celebration of the Twelfth at his 'home' and there was not a 'worthy, enlightened or liberal Catholic in the community' who would find difficulty with what had transpired.[80] Nethery's leadership in the Orange organization was significant because he was also an officer of the Sons of Erin. In 1840 the two roles did not seem incompatible.

The earliest associations of the order were with the Church of England. The presence of a strong evangelical tradition in the Loyalist Episcopal churches provided the basis for a happy marriage with the dominant evangelicalism of the Irish Episcopalians. The Irish brought to the union their high views of the nature of the church and the establishment. They provided much of the support for *The Chronicle* and the high tories in the political system who had as their cardinal rule of faith the preservation of the established Church of England. As Orangeism evolved into institutional reality, it worked through the agencies of the Church of England. The Orange journal hailed the rector of Saint John, B.J. Gray, as 'the father of the Protestant Church in New Brunswick.'[81] In March 1842, an organization styled the Protestant Conservative Association – a euphemism for the order – called a meeting at the Madras School and there claimed to have admitted at the Madras School and there claimed to have admitted nearly 600 men to its membership.[82] Within a month, the prospectus for a new newspaper, *The Loyalist*, edited by Thomas Hill, was announced.[83] Orangeism had come of age in Saint John.

Like transplanted cultural movements in every age, Orangeism was forced to adjust to the exigencies of a local situation. In Ireland, the order had been the expression of an English Protestant community; its centre was the Church of Ireland and it was comparatively weak within Irish Presbyterianism.[84]

The situation in New Brunswick was quite dissimilar to that of Ireland. The province contained a substantial Protestant majority that effectively controlled all the avenues to wealth and political influence. Even among the Irish settlers in the province, Protestants outnumbered Catholics.[85] But here again religious geography came to play a critical role in the perceptions of Orange leaders. Irish Protestants composed a large majority of the freehold Irish in the watershed of the St John River; in the city of Saint John – as in Fredericton – Irish Catholics clearly outnumbered Irish Protestants by the mid-1840s. And their numbers were growing.

Since the numbers and influence of the bluenoses were essential for the achievement of their goals, Orange leaders deliberately set about the task of grafting the anti-Catholic loyalism of Irish Episcopalianism onto the more benign tree of mid-nineteenth-century New Brunswick loyalty. The synthesis was cleverly done. The 'Protestant Conservative Association' did not betray an Irish reference that might have repelled the bluenoses. The newspaper, appropriately, was the *The Loyalist* (sometimes with *The Protestant Vindicator* added). The masthead depicted a group of refugees landing in a primitive woods, surrounded by the caption, 'We left our foes our All For a Home in a British Land.' Any Loyalist offspring might be forgiven the assumption that the newspaper was concerned with the plight of American Loyalists. Within two years of its beginning, *The Loyalist* claimed to have the largest circulation of any newspaper in the province, a claim denied by neither *The Courier* nor *The News*.[86]

The Loyalist was a powerful instrument in the formation of a Protestant Irish culture. It shared with the bluenoses the ideology that loyalty to the crown, the British connection, and Protestant civilization were all part of a seamless web. From this proposition flowed all of the other Orange positions. Responsible government and assembly initiative in policy making were evils because they both weakened the British connection and introduced the partisan disputes of venial and mediocre men into the deliberations of high policy. Repealers were anathema. So too was the 'St John Teetotal, the Repeal and Ribbon Association.'[87] But above all, in the face of political and constitutional debate, in the face of local riots and disorders, *The Loyalist* continuously portrayed the Orange Order as the final bastion of the British Constitution and the Protestant faith. It could not 'be charged in this province – as a body – of showing an intolerant spirit or doing anything to wound the feelings of those who are prejudiced against them.'[88] Over and over again this view of a tolerant, generous, good-spirited patriotism was presented as the hallmark of Orangemen who answered their opponents' arguments in the public press, and who were usually the victims of a violent vindictive Catholic enemy, which had respect neither for honest differences of opinion nor for the Queen's peace. The campaign had considerable success. Public events in the early 1840s seemed to confirm *The Loyalist* stereotypes. Throughout 1840, 1841, and 1842, the city experienced a series of riots, assaults, and murders.[89]

Through all of this *The Loyalist* portrayed the Orangemen as victims and claimed, with some justification, that every effort was made to avoid situations that would lead to confrontations with Catholics. The Glorious Twelfth was never celebrated in the city after 1841. Instead, brethren from Saint John to Fredericton usually assembled in the Protestant stronghold of Gagetown, forty miles from the city. The rhetoric and the moderation of the order were all designed to recruit young bluenoses. Their finest prize was William Needham, a Saint John attorney, grandson of Loyalist refugees and leading Baptist layman. Needham moved quickly through the order, reaching the grand master's chair in 1846, from where he could be counted upon to declare that no loyal man could refuse to support the connection between church and state.[90]

The rising tide of violence, the claims of the Orange leaders, and the growing identification of Irish loyalism with that of the Loyalist Refugees produced a rapid growth in the Orange Order in the 1840s. The city contained ten Orange lodges by 1846, and the reaction of many concerned citizens of the period suggests that a growing proportion of the recruits were drawn from among the young grandsons and great grandsons of Loyalists and pre-Loyalists. The growth of the order in the 1840s is reflected in the experience of Wellington Lodge in Portland. Founded in June 1844 with 19 members, the lodge reached 100 active members by January 1847.[91]

Many prominent natives were apprehensive about the intrusion of this tradition into their culture. Liberal Episcopalians such as Henry Chubb were particularly aware of the threat that Orangeism posed to their own tradition. On 17 February 1843, *The Courier* published a lengthy letter from 'Argus' that challenged the claims of Orangeism to the Loyalist tradition. Examining the origins of the order, Argus found in it a 'monster,' which for the sake of the province 'must be smothered at once and so effectively that it shall never resuscitate.' Many young native New Brunswickers had been brought into the order by Irishmen 'who have introduced the demon of discord into the country ... They are the guilty parties who instead of trying to bury the recollection of the crimes of their fathers attempt to perpetuate them.' Argus then proposed to prepare a petition to the legislature calling for the suppression of all secret societies,[92] and such a petition was prepared in early 1844. Its 266 signatories included representatives from all major social interests in the city – the grand jury, prominent merchants, lawyers, doctors, functionaries, Episcopalians, Protestant dissenters, and Catholics, including the editors of the city's three leading non-Orange newspapers.[93]

The petition was answered almost as soon as it began. Hearing of the proposal to suppress the order, a number of supporters prepared a counter-petition. In a single day they secured the support of 1400 adult males to their cause. Headed by the 78-year-old retired rector of Saint John B.G. Gray, the signatories included a number of leading citizens in addition to a large number of the middling orders of Saint John society.[94] Analysis of a 10 per cent sample of the signatories reveals a group that was more than 60 per cent Irish, heavily Episcopalian in background, and drawn from high-status occupations. Nearly three-quarters were found in the upper three occupational categories, about three-fifths of these in the first two. This was no mob of ship labourers. It composed much of the city's articulate, prosperous, and prominent citizenry.

Equally significant were the prominent citizens whose names were found on neither petition. Most notable by their absence were the leading Protestant dissenters and temperance supporters. Not a single active clergyman signed either petition, a fact that reflects the widespread confusion and indecision on the part of most dissenters. Their reaction to the debate was perhaps best reflected in the behaviour of Alderman Thomas Harding, third-generation native and leading Baptist, who initially signed the petition for suppression and a few days later, as a magistrate, signed the counter-petition. The suppressionists returned with an even larger petition, but the signatories there were almost entirely Catholic. In the end the legislature did nothing and the order was left free to expand.

The events of the next few years fully justified the apprehensions of the suppressionists. As the Orangemen grew in strength, they more and more confronted Catholics during the period of the Irish high feasts. Virtually all the fatalities before 1845 had been Protestant; after 1845 they were largely Catholic. There were riots in March 1844 following the shooting of a Catholic man by an Orangeman at York Point.[95] But this was only a preview of the conflagration that developed the following year. Beginning in January, the city was plagued by a series of incidents involving Orangemen and Catholics that quickly developed into riots. On three occasions between January and March, troops from the garrison were called out to aid the civil authorities, the second time on St Patrick's Day when parades of armed Irishmen from both parties were held in the city's streets in defiance of a mayor's proclamation prohibiting all processions and public gatherings on the seventeenth of March.[96] A number of casualties and several deaths resulted directly from the riots. By year's end the York Point area of the city was turned into a no man's land into which no non-Catholic dared to venture at night. Those who did were beaten and abused for their efforts.[97]

The climax to the violence occurred on the anniversary of the Battle of the Boyne in 1849. In many ways the riot was inevitable.[98] Before 1849, Orange leaders had held their often rambunctious troops in line in an effort to avoid direct confrontation with Catholics. Father Dunphy had served as a moderating influence on the Catholic side. The earlier affrays usually involved small groups of Orangemen acting on their own. At some time in 1849, an element within the order determined to confront the Catholics on their home ground. The issue that provoked the 1849 procession was doubtless one of the numerous assassinations that had characterized the conflict in the late 1840s.

It is not at all certain what the 1849 parade organizers hoped to accomplish. It may have been an attempt to demonstrate to the public at large that only the order possessed the strength to maintain control of the city's streets. Or it may have amounted to a simple desire for revenge on an ancient enemy. The comparatively small number of Orangemen who participated in the march seems to confirm the suspicion that the Orange leadership was split on the strategy and that the more respectable moderates had lost control of the organization. The leaders of the march – William Anderson, Squire Manks, and Joseph Coram – seemed to be the sergeants rather than the commanders of the order. The march itself was a desperately dangerous and ill-advised game. The decision to move into the Catholic residential area seemed aimed at precipitating a civil war. Even from the Orange viewpoint, there seemed little to be gained from such a confrontation. Catholic strength in the city would seem to make the outcome extremely dubious. Numerical superiority for the order could only be established by bringing the village Orangemen from the St John River valley.

If this were the expectation, it was not fulfilled. In the early morning of 12 July, the steamship from the middle valley landed about 140 Orangemen at Indiantown. There they were met by about 70 from Portland and 400 from the city – who had already passed through York Point without incident – and proceeded in a body to Portland. At St Luke's Church they were met by a magistrate, Jacob Allen, who delivered a message from the mayor directing the Orangemen to return through the Valley Road and bypass the York Point area. The leaders refused to comply with this order.[99]

About an hour later the Orangemen passed into York Point with flags flying and drums beating. They proceeded up Dock Street until they came to a pine archway that the Catholics had erected over the street. When the marchers attempted to remove it, the entire situation degenerated into a wild mêlée. The Dock Street environs were a warren of narrow winding streets bounded by three- and four-storey tenements occupied by Catholic families. From windows and roof-tops the Catholics threw stones and building materials onto the marchers below, and the brawl quickly degenerated into a battle fought with guns as well as fists. Jacob Allen, who had followed the marchers, estimated that more than 500 shots were exchanged in the narrow alleys before the Orangemen managed to tear down the archway and move out of the district into the centre of the city. There they were met by the mayor who had secured his military support. The mayor twice read the Riot Act and then separated the combatants by marching the military between them.[100] That was about noon. The bloodied but unbowed Orange battalions reassembled in the upper part of the city and with bands playing, prepared to advance into York Point again. They were only finally stopped when the troops counter-marched through them.

The number of casualties resulting from the mêlée is unknown, since both sides jealously guarded their dead and wounded. The grand jury found three official deaths, the lieutenant-governor estimated the number at not fewer than six or eight, while *The Courier* editor placed it closer to a dozen. The number of injured must have been very large on both sides. Nor was this the end of it. The Orangemen claimed victory.[101] They had marched through the geographic heart of Saint John Catholicism, torn down a symbolic arch, and emerged more or less intact. After the mêlée, the Orangemen continued to march unopposed through the remainder of the city for nearly five hours. So ended one of the bloodiest confrontations to occur between Irish Protestants and Irish Catholics in the nineteenth century.

Reaction to the crisis was not long in coming. Official opinion was one of outrage. The lieutienant-governor, Sir Edmund Head, laid most of the blame for the riot at the feet of the Orangemen, noting that 'the provocation given by the Orange Party was most deliberately renewed' and that 'they are generally speaking men in a better station in society and better educated than the mis-guided whom they provoke to break the peace.'[102] Of 14 Orangemen charged with bearing arms, 9 were freemen, including 4 shoe-makers, 2 grocers, and a tin-plate worker, although, significantly, none were freeholders.

The native reaction to the riot reflected a decade's experience of Irish violence. Within that context, approval or disapproval of Orange activities was generally a factor of the political and religious views of the natives. On balance it seems reasonably clear that, by 1850, Orange efforts to capture and integrate the Loyalist ideology had succeeded in some quarters. Conservative Protestants saw the order as a necessary ally, the only disciplined group in the city, apart from the military, that could secure the city from disorder. Indeed, many natives of this ideological bent, including members of such distinguished Episcopalian families as the Crookshanks and the DeVebers, had joined the order.[103] The violence of 1849 does not appear to have deterred support from this quarter. Two years later, when the agitation for incorporation of the Orange Order began in earnest, the movement commanded about 5000 followers in the St John River valley, of whom 900 were in the city and 800 others in Portland and adjacent areas.[104]

Opposition to the order was found among political reformers and radical evangelicals. Among Protestants, the most explicit denunciation came from the Free Will Baptists. Following the 1849 riots, the General Conference of the Church admonished the order in strong language. Relations between the church and the order grew more strained until 1857 when, under the leadership of their Saint John minister, Ezekiel Mac-

Leod, the conference proceeded to excommunicate all church members belonging to the order.[105] The Free Will Baptists are particularly interesting because they represented perhaps the most North American religious tradition in the province. But few notable Protestant dissenters or Sons of Temperance leaders were found among Orangemen supporters. Among those who petitioned for incorporation of the order in 1851 and 1854, more than 70 per cent were Irish born or sons of Irishmen, a substantial increase from the number who signed the earlier petition to preserve secret societies. That petition had been supported by large numbers of high-status Protestants. The 1854 petition, headed by the city's first elected mayor, James Olive, was dominated by artisans, cartmen, and labourers.[106] Again, the Irish Orangemen appeared overwhelmingly to come from Episcopalian origins; fewer than 10 per cent can be identified as Presbyterian.

The attitudes of the natives toward the Irish, however, were shaped by ethnicity as well as religion. And in this respect, native views in the 1850s had not changed much over the previous two decades. Protestant Irish might be more tolerable than Catholics to many natives, but they were all Irish, and as a group they were a stubborn, poor, and often overbearing people. James Johnston commented repeatedly on the Irish 'problem' in his 1849 tour of southern New Brunswick. They were the great obstacles to the development of a proper agriculture because of their indolent nature, their unwillingness to indulge in hard work, and the pretensions they often had.[107] He was particularly apprehensive of their habit of settling in neighbourhoods where they were unmixed with other populations.[108] As a group, he argued, the Irish had to be 'managed.'

That same theme was noted by Lieutenant-Governor Colebrook in his 1842 correspondence with the colonial secretary on the issue of Irish immigration to New Brunswick. 'The party distinctions they have assumed,' he noted, 'have tended to engender amongst the old colonists a mistrust of that class of settlers ... which has tended to discourage an active co-operation in measures of the Government.'[109] The emigrant societies of the province were actually promoting English and Scottish migration in an effort to offset the Irish influence. Five years later, the lieutenant-governor argued that the inhabitants of the province were 'justly apprehensive' of any growth in the Irish numbers; so much humanity had been shown in the reception and care of sick immigrants and in providing comfort and employment and yet nothing seemed to tame their barbarism.[110] The same sentiment was expressed a decade later by the moderate liberal editor of *The Courier* in discussing the problems encountered by Americans in dealing with their immigrants.[111]

The sense of apprehension surrounding so many natives' perceptions of the Irish was perhaps best reflected by David Waterbury, an illiterate old Loyalist, who died in 1837 leaving his small possessions to his wife and three sons, and the sum of £200 to his grandson, Duncan McLeod Waterbury, 'provided he does not marry Miss Nethery to whom he now seems attached.'[112] Waterbury's point was well taken. Intermarriage was the final step of accommodation, the final indication of acceptance.

It was at this level of personal relationship that as late as 1850 native Saint Johners continued to reflect their attitudes toward their Irish guests. The 1851 Census revealed a high degree of discrimination against the Irish on the part of native brides and grooms, a discrimination that did not extend to those of other ethnic origins. Intermarriage of Catholics and Protestants had always been infrequent but was probably becoming rare by mid-century. But there is impressionistic evidence suggesting that as late as 1850 unions of natives and Irish Protestants were not common and that final acceptance of most of these half-way people would require at least a generation's residence in the province.

Despite, or perhaps because of, their separateness the Irish did much to define the nature of community in mid-nineteenth-century Saint John. The central fact in the experience was the emergence of a self-conscious and effective Catholic community firmly placed in a culture that was at once Catholic and Irish. The effect of the church's triumph within the community in the 1840s was to secure the domination of a traditional social value and the exclusion of the liberal philosophy and values inherent in so much of the early Irish nationalist movements. The community that remained was paternalistic, hierarchical, and autonomous.[113] Boston, Philadelphia, and Toronto Irish Catholics had by 1860 erected Catholic societies within and yet apart from the larger societies.[114] Saint John Catholics did likewise. The effect was not so much to create a pluralistic society as one containing two distinct castes, each possessing the institutions necessary to its survival and linked at the leadership level by a series of conventions.

Anglo and Scottish Ireland, with its garrison mentality, tended to reinforce rather than challenge the values and tendencies of the Saint John community. Orange leaders shared with native Catholics and native tories a faith in a structured conservative unitary society. Their strategy was to capture and re-make the community of the natives into their own image. They certainly in part succeeded in this objective and the influence of the tradition and the numbers of its supporters did much to make toryism a viable social philosophy in the mid-century city. Reflecting a long Ulster-based tradition, the Scots Irish demonstrated a greater sympathy for the more liberal values of a pluralistic society with its emphasis on individual merit.

~6~

The Evangelical Movement

The ethno-religious tradition of Irish Roman Catholicism provided a powerful source of primary identification for a significant part of the population of Saint John by the mid-nineteenth century. Another equally powerful tradition was evangelicalism. Saint John evangelicalism was distinguished by its catholicity.[1] It drew from American, English, Scottish, and Irish sources and from every Protestant denomination in the city. Focused on a few well-defined, powerful ideas, it came closest of any philosophy to reflecting the spirit and temper of the age. Evangelicals did not react against the moral decay of the city; rather they saw it as an opportunity they were able to exploit successfully. Their weakness was their division into moderate and radical wings and their inability to deal with the issue of the religious establishment. Their great strength was the ability to persuade large numbers of people of the validity and necessity of the call to seriousness and their ability to involve a substantial part of the laity in leadership roles as class leaders, Sunday-school teachers, and in a dozen voluntary organizations that developed as expressions of the evangelical sensibility.[2]

Evangelicalism was perhaps the most influential movement in the English-speaking world in the first half of the nineteenth century. Born in an eighteenth-century world of doubt and deism, its leaders saw their task as one of conversion of the individual with a final view to christianizing the nominally Christian but effectively pagan population of the United Kingdom and the United States. Although it has been closely identified with the Methodism of the Wesleys, the movement embraced most moderate Calvinists including Congregationalists, Baptists, Presbyterians, and a significant part of the Church of England.[3] Perhaps the distinctive characteristic of evangelicalism was the doctrine of vital religion. Faithfulness could not be fulfilled simply by giving assent to doctrine or even by the good works of worship and celebration: at its heart the Christian faith could only be achieved by a confrontation between the supplicant and his faith out of which the supplicant was changed and became in some respects a new being. Wesley's 'strangely warmed heart' was the classic statement of this change, but it was a process that might occur in many forms, sometimes instantaneously, sometimes through a series of events over a considerable period. After these experiences, the faith of the evangelical required that every act, every motive, and every issue be tested to ensure that what was done, thought, or said tended toward the glory of God and the fulfilment of His Kingdom.[4] The movement re-emphasized the Reformation doctrines of the sole authority of scripture as the rule of life and the priesthood of all believers. A unique feature was its anti-sectarian position. Believing that there was an essential core to the faith, evangelicals were generally prepared to accept the validity of many denominational paths provided that they contained the essentials. In sharp contrast to the high churchmen within their tradition, Church of England evangelicals regarded their communion as simply one of many valid Christian bodies.[5] The evangelical tendencies toward personal conversion and perfection were reflected at a corporate level in efforts to convert and make better the society in which they found themselves.

The implications of this faith led evangelicals to propound and support policies with considerable potential for social change. They were missionary agents of the faith creating a public life that at least tended toward good rather than evil, and that provided opportunities for every person to achieve to the Kingdom. In pursuit of these objectives, they supported private benevolences, fought the slave trade, founded hospitals, and formed missionary societies, religious tract societies, the British and Foreign Bible Society, and the British and Foreign School Society.[6]

By the end of the century, the movement had leaped the Atlantic and taken firm root in New England and New York, where the influences of deism, eighteenth-century rationalism, and the ideas of the political radicals posed a threat to the traditional Calvinist Christianity that had dominated the religious and intellectual life of these colonies. Smarting from the threat of Unitarianism in Boston, the Congregationalists by 1813 were making overtures to a wide range of evangelical opinion – Presbyterian, Episcopalian, Baptist, and Methodist – in an effort to form a common front against the variety of secular and religious heresies threatening the orthodox faith.[7]

Religion played a critical role in shaping the social views and institu-

St Andrew's Church of Scotland,
built c. 1814 (NBM)

Trinity Church, built c. 1789 (NBM)

Germaine Street (Queen Square) Methodist Chapel,
built 1808 (NBM)

tions of nineteenth-century Saint John. The measurement of religious commitment and the impact it had on the lives of any group of people have been at best a hazardous and impressionistic undertaking. What hard data do exist for Saint John seem to confirm the hypothesis of a religious people. Censuses of church attendance taken at irregular intervals between 1827 and 1846 indicate that attendance grew more rapidly in the period than did the population of the city. By the mid-1840s, perhaps two out of every three permanent residents of the city and surrounding suburbs may have attended services on a typical Sunday although, as in England, the proportion of adherents in attendance varied sharply with the tradition.[8] The influence of religion permeated most public issues. As the city developed after 1820 it spawned more than a dozen separate newspapers each of which was distinguished from its fellows by the denominational or theological position it upheld. Until the late 1820s, articulate Saint Johners were more likely to express themselves publicly on religious issues than on any other in the columns of the secular press; religious issues fuelled much of the political debate after 1830.

These commitments and public attitudes were reflected in the religious geography of the city. For the first thirty years following its foundation, the city was a bastion of the established Church of England. Loyalist leaders constructed Trinity Church on the height of the city overlooking the harbour in 1789. The Wesleyans established their circuit three years later. But despite numerous complaints by the rectors of Saint John of the activities of the sectaries in and around the city, these remained the only religious institutions in the city until 1810. Indeed, the notable feature of early Saint John life was the virtual monopoly possessed in the town by the Church of England (the adherents of which were commonly called Churchmen or Episcopalians). That monopoly was social as well as religious. The rector of the city possessed a status only slightly less distinguished than that of the mayor. The pews of Trinity Church were occupied by virtually the whole of the indigenous society of Saint John; the efforts of the rector and the values he represented were ably seconded by the champlains and officer corps of the military garrison of the city. The Saint John tradition was latitudinarian in emphasis. Comprehensiveness rather than doctrine was the test of membership. Scots Presbyterian Loyalist merchants like William Pagan found no difficulty in conforming to the established church. As late as 1804, the Wesleyans had only 80 converted members, indicating no more than 400 hearers in a population of perhaps 4000; nominally at least, the remainder were parishioners of the rector of Saint John.[9]

That hegemony was one of the first victims of urbanization.[10] In a series of revivals beginning in 1805, the Wesleyans gathered a large number of converts from beyond the closed Methodist circle.[11] Working from their Germaine Street and Centenary chapels and using the vigorous Wesleyan circuit organization, they built a strong and flourishing Methodist institution in the city by mid-century, one that Robert Cooney, no easy critic, described as 'more healthy and superior to Methodism in most other places.'[12] The number of hearers of the twenty-one Wesleyan chapels and preaching places almost certainly exceeded those at Church of England services throughout the nineteenth century.[13] Saint John Wesleyans, like their English counterparts, were particularly strong within the respectable working class. Artisans – mechanics, shipwrights, and carpenters – together with a number of labourers, grocers, and a few minor merchants composed the communion.[14]

As the urban expansion began after 1807, the religious differentiation of the city continued with the formation of two Calvinist congregations. Presbyterians represented a genuine institutional transfer from the United Kingdom. In 1814, a number of city Scots proceeded to the formation of a church.[15] The new congregation was marked by the high status of its members and their sense of equality with the Church of England. St Andrew's Church was formed under the authority of the Presbytery of Edinburgh. Its first minister was Dr George Burns, a prominent Midlothian divine, and its genesis was marked by protracted and exceedingly bitter theological and political debates waged in the public press between Church of England and Church of Scotland partisans.[16] Joined later by strong contingents of the Irish Presbyterians, the communion was sundered after 1844 into State Church and Free Church factions.

The Baptists' arrival constituted the advent of the frontier and frontier values in the city. The first Calvinist Baptist church was formed in 1810. While a few native Saint John families were found among the early Baptist members, the leadership of the early church was centred on zealous Baptist converts from the rural areas of Kings and Queens counties.[17] The movement experienced considerable difficulties in its early period. Viewed with suspicion by much of Saint John society, the Baptists were greeted with an open antagonism that stemmed from doubts as to their loyalty, their often successful aggressive proselytizing among the children of the respectable, and their unwillingness to treat any religious establishment with respect.[18] Baptists were the ultimate dissenters. In Saint John, as in Halifax, young Episcopalians of prominent background would sometimes purge their old selves in the Baptist movement, usually to the mortification of their families.[19] A second, more radical Baptist denomination emerged in Saint John in 1842.[20] The most indigenous religious denomination in the province, the Free Will Baptists (sometimes described as immersed Methodists because of their doctrinal similarity to the Wesleyans) had begun a decade before as a small autonomous denomination in the upper St John River valley. By dint of zealous evangelical activity, they became a significant social force in the province by the 1860s. The Baptists shared the social and residential characteristics of the Methodists. Both were concentrated in the city centre on both sides of the harbour. Together with the Free Presbyterians, they turned Queens Ward into an evangelical centre described by T.W. Anglin as the 'Smashers stronghold.'

The last major religious institution to emerge in the city was the Roman Catholic. From a small, largely military community in 1815, the communion grew to challenge and finally, by mid-century, to surpass the Church of England. Leadership initially came from an active group of small merchants, grocers, tradesmen, and contractors. But the largest part of its constituency was drawn from the urban labourers clustered in tenements at either end of the eastern peninsula. Kings Ward, encircling the upper wharf area, became the Catholic centre of the city.

Two behavioural models were evident among the emerging institutions of religious dissent in the 1820s. One of these, represented by the Wesleyans and Catholics, was essentially passive and pietistic, aimed at the withdrawal of the faithful from the world and the creation of the institutional structures that could sustain this separatist existence. The Wesleyans possessed an elaborate system of classes, prayer meetings, love feasts, celebrations, class leaders, exhorters, local preachers, and stewards – all designed to modify the former habits and behaviour of their followers (a process called conversion) and to sustain and encourage the converted in the face of a hostile environment.[21] The Wesleyan organization provided alternatives to virtually all secular leisure activities. So, too, on a more limited scale, did the Catholic Church, which in the late 1820s attempted to create an elemental educational system.

By contrast the Calvinists – both Church of Scotland and Regular Baptist – directly challenged the existing order in an effort to force it to accommodate them. The issue for the Presbyterians was a share in the social and political establishment of the city and province. Under the banner of Scottish nationalism, they claimed an equal place with the Church of England in the imperial order. Their spokesmen were the great merchants of the St Andrew's Society and their articulate Scottish minister, Dr George Burns. From 1817 onward, they engaged in a running debate with Episcopalians over the biblical and historical validity of the episcopacy.[22] From the Baptist viewpoint, the establishment was scripturally and socially irrelevant. It was, however, a political reality and possessed a status and authority that not only allowed its members a virtual monopoly of the functionary class of the province but made Churchmen of all dissenters by forcing them to have their marriages performed within the Church of England.

The decade 1810–20, which witnessed the genesis of Baptist, Presbyterian, and Roman Catholic institutions in the city, was a period of bitter sectarianism as each communion sought its justification. Religious debate was by far the most significant public issue in the community of the period, occupying more newspaper space than all other local news combined.

Denominational antagonism was compounded in 1818 with the establishment of the Madras School. Created by provincial legislation and supported by substantial provincial grants, the school employed the monitorial system in which more advanced students taught their juniors. It was particularly valuable for poor families whose children could be offered free instruction. The enterprise was an immediate success and quickly became the most popular public school in the city. However, since its teachers and directors were all Churchmen, and its core instructional program included the catechism of the Church of England, the school was seen by all dissenters as a means through which the established church could proselytize the children of poor families within other communions. In reaction, other denominations moved to create an extensive Sunday-school system. The Methodists had maintained a denominational school staffed by volunteers since 1807. But within days of the Madras School opening in 1818, the 'Scotch Church' Sunday school was established, and the Baptists organized one shortly thereafter.[23] The Catholic response was somewhat delayed because of the lack of leadership, but finally manifested itself in the middle 1820s through efforts to create a school for poor Catholics.[24]

The very vehemence of these disputes produced a reaction against the parochialism of denominationalism. Throughout 1819 and 1820, there were repeated calls for unity and a return to the common essential elements of the faith. Inevitably such appeals came to turn on matters of authority (that of scripture over catechism or historical tradition), of the demands biblical theology made upon commitment, manners, and morals, and of the practical problems that confronted the faithful in the secular world.[25] Those common elements shared by most Saint John Protestants centred around a reverence for biblical tradition and the evangelical doctrines of salvation by grace through faith and the priesthood of all believers. Ultimately the appeal was made to a common evangelicalism. The earliest organized evangelical tradition in the city was Wesleyan, but this was reinforced by the growing Baptist presence after 1810, and a dimension of respectability was added by the adhesion of a growing number of Churchmen and Presbyterians. By 1819 the strength of the tradition was reflected in *The City Gazette*, published by Alexander McLeod, perhaps the most prominent Methodist layman in the city. In his efforts to effect evangelical unity, McLeod was even willing to repudiate Canadian Methodists who challenged the marriage laws of their colony and, by implication, the Church of England establishment.[26]

McLeod was addressing a growing party within the Church of England. An evangelical tradition had been present among the Loyalist settlers. Dr John Calef, a leading Churchman, was a pronounced evangelical and had served as pall bearer to George Whitefield. While these views were not acceptable to the bishop of Nova Scotia, the tradition flourished in the city and, following the appointment of Benjamin and John Gray to the parish of Saint John in 1825, became dominant. The Grays, father and son, were the most significant Church of England clergymen in nineteenth-century New Brunswick. Between them they filled the office of rector of Saint John from 1825 to 1868. The elder Gray was the last of the practising Loyalist clergy and his views on church polity reflected that experience. Prepared to defend the interests of their parish against the authority of the episcopacy, deeply suspicious of any ascription of supernatural powers to the priesthood, and fired by evangelical activism, the Grays proved to be enormously popular among both the substantial burghers who dominated their parish and the most humble folk who crowded their galleries. The core of their teachings was summarized by the younger Gray in 1864:

Because [God] knows it to be impossible to extend the blessings of friendship to them in their present state ... unless they are changed and brought to a very difficult one, their souls will perish forever ... All other considerations are of little moment in comparison to this.

... *Be sure you do not mistake the nature of true religion.* Remember, it is not forms, or doctrines, or transient feelings, but the holy affection of love to God and the children of God ... having the Divine Spirit for its author, holiness and all good works for its effects, and heaven as the scene for its full and final expansion. Such is true religion ... never imagine that you can be saved without it ... aim at possession of a new heart and a right spirit.[27]

The first attempt at evangelical co-operation among these groups involved the British and Foreign Bible Society. Perhaps the most characteristic institution of British evangelicalism, the Bible Society had been brought to Nova Scotia as early as 1810, where it flourished particularly in the Presbyterian communities in Halifax and Pictou. Its progress through

Rev. J.W.D. Gray, c. 1860 (PANB)

Rev. W.T. Wishart, daguerreotype, c. 1845 (NBM)

British North America was marked by the strong opposition of the Church of England episcopacy and the Society for the Propagation of the Gospel. The latter paid the salaries of most of the Episcopal missionaries in the colonies, and perceived the Bible Society as a competitor to the Society for the Propagation of Christian Knowledge, which produced denominational literature for the Church of England.[28] Leadership in the movement to form a New Brunswick auxiliary of the society was taken by the recently arrived Church of Scotland minister, Dr George Burns. The first officers of the organization reveal the range of denominational support it was able to command. Apart from the clergy, these included four evangelical Churchmen, five Methodists, four Baptists, and three Presbyterians.[29]

The Bible Society quickly emerged and remained as the principal vehicle of ecumenical activity in the community. After the arrival of Dr Gray as rector of Saint John in 1825, Church of England participation in the organization became even more pronounced. Despite a contretemps over the place of the apocrypha – the Saint John members argued that they had no place in the Bible – the auxiliary remained an active part of the English organization.[30] Through the 1830s and 1840s, the annual meetings of the society became virtual conventions, with large crowds gathering for the presentation of reports. The organization enjoyed a public respect given to few institutions in the city.

The debates that had led to the formation of the Bible Society in 1819 had produced a profound suspicion of any organization that might provoke sectarian controversies. Consequently, the Bible Society was not accompanied by a tract society. It was only in 1832, probably as part of his Temperance Society activities, that Dr Gray founded the inter-denominational Religious Tract Society ('to disseminate evangelical religious knowledge'), which was supported by matching grants from England.[31] The society shortly came to enjoy the support of the same constituencies – evangelical Churchmen, Methodists, Presbyterians, and Baptists – that maintained the Bible Society, but never achieved the degree of popular support that characterized the earlier organization.[32] Other signs of inter-denominational co-operation among evangelicals were evident during this period. Special offerings for the aid of the poor, especially at Christmas, had been occasionally practised in some congregations for some time. By 1820, this practice became increasingly institutionalized, with the major Protestant churches and the masonic order contributing to a common fund.[33]

At a more practical level, evangelicals attempted to educate the children of the poor through the use of the Sunday school. In the spring of 1823, a number of leading evangelicals formed the Saint John Union Sunday School Society, which co-ordinated the activities of the parochial Sunday schools. By June, it had five schools and upwards of 400 children – fifty-one of them black – and was preparing to open a sixth among the poor immigrants at York Point.[34] The society schools taught basic reading and writing skills but the core of the curriculum at the Baptist school was the Bible; at St Andrew's Church and the Methodist chapel schools it was the Bible and the denominational catechism.[35] The decision to place a school in the centre of the Roman Catholic neighbourhood at York Point would seem to indicate a mixture of motives embracing both charity and a desire to proselytize: in common with all evangelicals, those in Saint John assumed that exposure to the scriptures would permit the Holy Spirit to speak to the young.

Although the activities of the non-Madras schools were publicly attacked by the rector of Saint John, leading Churchmen continued to play an important role in the activities of the union.[36] After Benjamin Gray's arrival in 1825, relationships between the church Sunday schools and those of the dissenters improved, and, through a procession of common rallies, picnics, teachers meetings, and teas, became an important element in the social life of the city.[37] Sectarian advantage, though sometimes quietly sought, was publicly deemed a narrow and unworthy cause. Important though co-operative endeavours were, it was in the reformation of public morals that the evangelicals found the greatest area of common agreement and the widest scope for action. On the question of sabbath observance, most evangelicals were prepared to act. The issue traditionally had considerable legal sanction behind it and could count on the support of the established church. As early as 1822, *The Gazette* carried letters and editorials decrying the profanation of the sabbath by many immigrants.[38] The magistrates of the city were urged to enforce both provincial and city sabbath ordinances. Despite the difficulties encountered in coping with a rapidly expanding population, the magistrates applied the law with some vigour in the 1820s.

Emboldened by their success and their rapidly growing strength, the evangelicals widened the range of their attack. By the late 1820s, *The Gazette* turned its attention to the flourishing theatre in the city in which so many people were wasting their substance, and to the grog shops that seemed to be the centre for so much social violence and disorder.[39] The theatre issue culminated in 1828 when the acting company parodied the scriptures in its performance. Led by Dr Gray, the evangelicals descended on the mayor and justices and, over the repeated appeals of the owner, secured the withdrawal of the theatre licence on the grounds that it posed a threat to public morals.[40]

The work of this united front continued with the creation of a temperance society later in 1829. The occasion was a visit to the city by the leading Boston evangelical, Dr Justin Edwards, a founder of the American Temperance Society a few years earlier.[41] Following the visit, Dr Gray, Dr Burns, and Alexander McLeod participated in the formation of the new organization. To evangelicals like McLeod, temperance appeared as the golden touchstone that could ameliorate most of the obvious evils with which society was plagued. While temperance could not in itself perfect society, he argued, it could remove a great danger from the weak. Moreover, a strong temperance movement should be followed by a revival in religion.[42] McLeod died the following year but the organization he helped to create became an instant success, joining the Bible Society as one of the great engines of moral reform in the community. Within a year of its formation, all of the clergy and numbers of other leading business and professional men had joined the organization.[43] The climax of these united-front activities occurred in 1834 in the foundation of the Female House of Industry, which supported destitute females and provided training for them and nursery and educational facilities for their children. Managed by a committee of prominent women, the house received its major support from the Church of England, the Church of Scotland, and the Wesleyan and the Baptist congregations.[44]

The founding of the temperance movement and the Female House of Industry marked the last major efforts of a united evangelicalism in Saint John for more than a decade. The reasons for the division were complex. Two broad streams of evangelical thought had always existed in the city. In some ways these corresponded, on the one hand, to the feeling of disadvantage that characterized so much of the thinking of the religious dissenters and, on the other, to the proprietorial attitudes of the Churchmen. At another level the distinction seemed to be one of sensibility. Moderate evangelicals tended to be more comfortable with the world than were their more radical brethern. Both shared a tendency toward the 'Great Mission' and toward reform, but radicals demanded a higher standard of purity in their personal and public lives and drew sharp lines between the 'world' and things of the spirit that bespoke a great alienation from a social environment they could not control. Moderate evangelicals might attend the subscription assemblies or public banquets; radicals would never waste their time or substance in such worldly enterprises.[45]

The division between these two views occurred in the 1830s over the issue of church/state relations. It was a controversy that divided evangelicals and non-evangelicals alike. Evangelicals split largely on the basis of their experience. Native dissenters and Irish Presbyterians generally opposed the religious establishment; Irish Episcopalians strongly supported it. Native Churchmen who were not high tories seemed generally willing to take a conciliatory attitude designed to share the benefits but maintain the status of an Episcopalian establishment. While status and glebes played some role in the debate, the controversy centred on education, marriage, and public offices.

In Saint John much of the bitterness over these debates was temporized by the intermediacy of the Grays and a number of evangelical Churchmen who continued and expanded their support of evangelical organizations. So influential a Churchman as Charles Simonds, long-time speaker of the House of Assembly, consistently supported the restructuring of King's College throughout the 1830s. Gray refused to support such specifically denominational organizations as the Church Society and argued with the High Churchmen in his own parish that the Madras School should be given a broader base of popular support.[46]

Colonial evangelicalism was sundered into two camps by the tensions of the 1830s. The moderates, led by the Grays, followed a more 'British' course, arguing for the necessity to maintain a British and Protestant establishment that would have the care of the state as its special mission. The radicals, by contrast, struck an increasingly American, free church, and liberal stance, arguing for disestablishment. But these views went much further than simply a question of politics. The radicals represented a purist and activist tradition that not only argued the necessity for the conversion of all men but also the creation of a society in which they would confront the least temptation to fail.

The dissenters' attacks on the Episcopal establishment precipitated the creation of The Chronicle in 1836. This organ of high church toryism espoused the traditional view of church establishment and the ideal of crown endowments to create a church glebe and to sustain a church schoolmaster in each parish, defended the prerogatives of the episcopacy against the parochialism of the local parish, and similarly defended the prerogatives of the crown against the political radicals, the temperance society, the Baptists, and all those who would tamper with the 'good old ways'. On occasion even the rector of Saint John felt the burn of The Chronicle's whip when he failed to defend the establishment. The Chronicle claimed to champion a return to the British principles and Reformation Protestantism – away from the licentiousness, factiousness, and liberality that marked the 'spirit of the Age.' It offered support to 'the constitutional principles which support a scriptural and unpersecuting church, also confirm in perfect liberty and security all the privileges of protestant dissenters,' and claimed that the interests of such a church and those of the Protestant dissenters would stand or fall together.[47]

This call for the preservation of the Loyalist order and the creation of a common front against the Roman Catholic enemy had a much greater appeal to the large and growing Irish Protestant population of the Saint John area than to the natives. It was among Irish Protestants that the Orange Order was gradually taking root in the 1830s. By the time it developed a mature institutional form in the early 1840s, its journal, *The Loyalist*, had joined *The Chronicle* as the principal defender of the Church of England establishment. *The Loyalist* argued for evangelical principles, a state church, and concerted action on the part of all Protestants in the face of the common enemy. In *The Loyalist* view the Orange Order was to become the secular equivalent of the Bible Society, providing the first line of defence for the common Protestant culture, while the Church of England establishment guaranteed control of the province's political institutions in Protestant hands. These arguments, with their assumption of a permanent British religious establishment, apparently had little impact on the leaders of the city's radical evangelicals. Moderates, too, viewed the source of the ideas with some suspicion, but evangelical Churchmen were soon caught up in a debate in which even the support of the Orange Order was welcomed.

The ideas of evangelicals at mid-century were shaped more than anything else by the arrival of Episcopalian and Roman bishops in the province. Both clerics encountered similar problems in the exercise of their new offices. There had never been a strong episcopal influence in the province, and parish life in both the Church of England and Roman Catholic traditions was marked by a pronounced congregationalism and lay control. In the long run, the Episcopal bishop, John Medley, offended evangelical sensibilities more deeply than did his Catholic counterpart – and deeply divided his own communion in the process. In the short run, both bishops seemed to confirm the worst fears of most evangelicals that in Saint John, as in England, there was a plot by a resurgent Catholicism in league with a fifth column within the establishment itself that planned to overthrow Protestant civilization and replace it with the anachronistic tyranny of mind that had characterized the Dark Ages. Added to these religious concerns were liberal fears – often held by the same people – of the resurrection of an unprogressive medievalism.

Dollard's problems, discussed in chapter 5, were minor compared to those faced by John Medley. As a partisan of the tractarian movement, which sought a deeper spiritual life in many of the traditions and liturgies that had been abandoned by the English Church in the sixteenth century, he was an object of controversy and suspicion almost from the time of his consecration. In 1846, he supported a tractarian Diocesan Church Society missionary who refused to bury in consecrated ground a young child who had been baptized by a Presbyterian minister.[48] The missionary took the position that Presbyterian sacraments were invalid because the sect did not possess a valid ministry. The issue offended liberal sensibilities and sparked anew the debate over legitimacy that had so troubled the city before 1819.

Despite the presence of a traditional high-church party in the city led by Chief Justice Ward Chipman, the bishop was able to make little headway against the influence of the Grays. They possessed the support of their vestry and most of their parishioners among whom were the editors of the two most influential newspapers in the province, Henry Chubb's *The Courier* and George Fenety's *The News*. Church expansion in the city was finally carried out under John Gray's direction and was accompanied by attempts on the part of the corporation of Trinity Church to ensure that the rights of presentation to the new parishes would be vested in the wardens and vestries.[49] John Gray, meanwhile, continued publicly to defend evangelicalism, condemning tractarian doctrines, extolling the Bible as the sole guide to faith and conduct, and maintaining solidarity with Protestant leaders in the Bible Society.[50] When St Mark's Church in the north end of the city was finally erected into a separate parish in 1852, the Loyalists' offspring who dominated the church corporation prepared a bill to restore to the lay members of the Church of England the presentation of ministers on the grounds that from the earliest settlement in the United States, 'lay members of the Church of England possessed the right of electing their own ministers.'[51] That bill did not survive the legislature, but Dr Gray did succeed in placing a Montreal evangelical in the parish who announced at his first sermon that he would 'preach only the Bible and only Jesus Christ and Him crucified.'[52] By 1850, Saint John had emerged as the centre of the evangelical church in the province, and John Gray was universally recognized as its champion.

Radical evangelicals viewed these developments with a growing sense of dismay. Despite the agitation of the 1830s, they had received few concessions on the issue of the establishment apart from the marriage issue. As early as 1842, *The Loyalist* was arguing that it was now necessary for the dissenters to accept their inferior status and support the Church of England establishment as the only bastion against the threat posed by Catholicism. By 1846 even the principal organ of political reform, *The News*, urged dissenters to abandon their quest for ecclesiastical equality and to place themselves in the hands of liberal Episcopalians who would attempt to accommodate them.[53]

The temptation to acquiesce to these pleas must have been great; in the English tradition, accommodations of these kinds had been the means through which religious dissent had managed to exercise a political influence out of all proportion to its numbers. Moreover Gray and Fenety were well-known and respected evangelicals. But Saint John was not

England, and the Church of England in New Brunswick and in Saint John was significantly smaller than the dissenting sects against which discrimination was practised. The social model to which the dissenters looked was New England, where the final collapse of the Congregational establishment had just occurred.

By 1845 leading dissenters had come to the conclusion that they could never participate in the common community on terms of equality while any kind of 'ecclesiastical ascendancy' was permitted to one denomination. This became their overriding concern, more significant even than their apprehensions over the rapidly growing strength of Catholicism and the dangers posed to the evangelical tradition in the Church of England by a Puseyite bishop. They voiced this concern through the same issues they had used a dozen years earlier: the Church of England's monopoly of King's College, the necessity of dissenting clergy to take the oath of allegiance and receive a licence in order to perform marriages, and the fact that most legislators and office holders in the province were Episcopalians. The first two were minor irritations, the outward manifestations of a system of social inequality. The third was more complex and provoked a demand that merit become the only test for appointment to the public service. In so doing, the radical evangelicals of Saint John drew very close to the English dissenters and to political liberals in both England and New England.

The issue of Episcopalian monopoly of public offices was at the heart of the debate. A community view – and one that was probably not inaccurate – held that three-quarters of the public offices of emolument or influence were held by Episcopalians, who also received at least three-quarters of the revenues of the province.[54] Speaking for the radical evangelicals in 1846, 'Humphrey Clinker' made the point: 'You make an Episcopal House of Assembly, this makes an Episcopal Council; an Episcopal Council makes an Episcopal Bench of Magistrates; this again makes an Episcopal Board of Education, this, in conjunction with the Episcopalian Rectors and Curates of the Province, makes Episcopal schoolmasters; hence almost every office becomes Episcopalian. The Chaplaincy of our Jail, our Penitentiary, etc., are Episcopalian.'[55]

Underlying all discussions of discrimination in the public life of the province was the claim by The Loyalist editor that if most office holders were Churchmen, it was because the Episcopal communion contained most of the qualified people possessing the intelligence and integrity to occupy those positions.[56] It was a contentious and damning statement – a final answer – which was never publicly debated in part because many perceived a grain of truth in it. Most professionals and most relatively well-educated people were Episcopalians; indeed that church had a veritable monopoly on certain high-status occupational groups in the province. The reason for this was seen by many dissenters in the church's monopoly of the educational system. King's College was the symbol, but more important were the grammar schools and other institutions of secondary education. Without full access to these, dissenters could never participate in the public service on equal terms with Churchmen. The point was made explicitly a few years later by the Free Will Baptist Conference as it prepared to create its own secondary schools: 'Our men must be prepared to fulfill positions of honour, trust and emolument or submit to being hewers of wood and drawers of water. Shall we open to them the highway of eminence or shall we bind on them the yoke of ignorance, or what is much more likely thrust them out from us to seek elsewhere, what we refuse to provide for them.'[57]

Despite the strength of the radical evangelicals in Saint John, the leadership of the movement was provided by British migrants. Disestablishment was a major issue in England and Scotland in the 1840s. The most vociferous critics of the established church were the supporters of the Anti-State Church Association. Formed in 1844, the association was dominated by the old dissenters – Congregationalists, Presbyterians, and Baptists – but contained some representation from the churches of England and Scotland, and had the support of the non-Wesleyan Methodists and most non-religious liberals. As its name implies, the organization advocated complete separation of church and state on the American model. Although it was never able to fully accomplish its purpose, it remained a powerful pressure group in British politics.

Among the 'more peaceful' non-conformists like the Wesleyan Methodists, the solutions offered by the Anti-State Church Association were viewed as too radical.[58] In England as in Saint John dissenters and Churchmen shared a common evangelicalism. Instead of an assault on the state church, they found common cause in the defence of evangelical Protestantism. At a convention in 1844 at the evangelical's great London preaching centre, Exeter Hall, they founded the Evangelical Alliance. The new union embraced all dissenters with the exception of the Unitarians, as well as the leading evangelical Churchmen. It was, in fact, an effort to effect a form of Christian unity on the model of the Bible and Tract societies. Implicit in its very organization was the assumption that the various denominations had a valid ministry and a true teaching and none possessed an inherent legitimacy or spiritual superiority over the others.[59]

Between 1842 and 1846, three British evangelicals moved from the complexities of their native environment to those of New Brunswick. There they assumed the leadership of the radical evangelical movement in

Saint John. The first and most articulate of these was W.T. Wishart, the scholarly Scottish minister of St Stephen's Church of Scotland. Wishart quickly became a popular and controversial figure and a leader in the activities of the Mechanics Institute. His writings and public lectures provided an intellectual framework for the local evangelicalism and provided a bridge between it and liberal philosophy of the period.[60] Wishart represented a prosperous and cultivated Scottish Presbyterianism.

The second British arrival was an Irish Presbyterian minister of the Ulster Synod, Robert Irvine, who was called in 1844 to the new St John's Church congregation that was formed following the disruption of St Andrew's Church of Scotland.[61] A dedicated evangelical and a powerful protagonist, Irvine came to his post with a missionary's zeal. He was followed a few years later by his brother, who occupied a second Free Church pulpit in the city.

Within months of Robert Irvine's arrival he was joined by an English Congregational clergyman, J.C. Gallaway. Gallaway's arrival provided the catalyst for the radical evangelical movement in the city. A natural leader with a strong commitment to the principles for which English Congregationalist leaders had been struggling, he found the Saint John situation with its large non-Episcopalian population a golden opportunity to introduce the strategies, approaches, and tactics his English confrères had been employing for years with indifferent success.

His first efforts were aimed at reviving the failing sense of evangelical unity in the city. He participated in the Bible Society but used the Mechanics Institute as the principal forum for his ideas. Working through the Institute, Gallaway proposed that the evangelicals of the city create a monitorial school based on the Lancastrian system that would provide religious but non-sectarian education for those of modest means. A public meeting in April 1845 established a committee to contact the British and Foreign School Society of London in an effort to secure a trained master for the city. The committee contained leading laymen from the Wesleyan, Church of Scotland, Free Presbyterian, and Baptist communions. By July they had secured their master, Edmund Duval, and in the autumn the British School opened in the Mechanics Institute.[62] The school was an immediate success, and by the winter of 1846 preparations were under way to turn it into a normal school for the training of Lancastrian teachers for service throughout the province.[63]

The activities at the Mechanics Institute were paralleled by an ecumenical activity among dissenters reminiscent of the 1820s. By late 1845, inter-denominational services were being held at the Congregational Church to help pay off the debt. In March 1846, a meeting of all the 'ministers and office holders of evangelical churches in Saint John,

Carleton and Portland' was convened in the Free Presbyterian Church for the purpose of forming the Evangelical Union of New Brunswick. As Gallaway explained a month later in a sermon at the Wesleyan Centenary Chapel, the union was sparked by the success of the Bible and Tract societies and by the 'effort of divines at Oxford to resume the dogmas of the Dark Ages and the extraordinary attempt of Rome to re-establish universal domination,'[64] which had led to the formation of the Evangelical Alliance in England the previous year. Some of them 'were longing to take a step in harmony with this movement at home' and organized a meeting out of which the union eventually emerged.

Gallaway's motives were probably pure but remembering the Wesleyan audience he was addressing he certainly put the best possible face on the similarities between the English and New Brunswick organizations. In fact they differed profoundly and the reasons for their difference had a great deal to do with those who were invited to – or at least who were *not* invited to – the organizational meeting. The most obvious omission were the clergy and office holders of the Church of England parishes of the metropolitan Saint John area. The St Andrew's Church representatives (Church of Scotland), if present, played little or no role in the deliberations. The participants were confined to the members of the free churches – Wesleyan, Free Presbyterian, Baptist, and Congregationalist. The meeting proceeded to accept the articles of faith held by the English Evangelical Alliance, but added to them the resolution that 'ecclesiastical ascendency and mere formalism is incompatible with enlightened and conscientious intercourse and fraternal feeling among the various sections of Christians which it is desirable to promote.'[65] In their enthusiasm to take a step 'in harmony with this movement at home' the organizers actually formed the New Brunswick Union three months before the Evangelical Alliance of Great Britain came into existence. But the model Gallaway followed was not so much that of the British Alliance as of Edward Miall, the British political radicals, and the Congregational Unions' 1842 proposal for an Evangelical Union of those opposing a religious establishment.[66] Catholicism might pose a continuous threat to the evangelical way, but in the short run, the Evangelical Union of New Brunswick under the leadership of British dissenters clearly viewed the established church of England as the enemy.

The formation of the union and the public declaration of its purpose shattered the community of Saint John. The more militant radical evangelicals attempted to put their program into effect. Two dissenters on the Commission for the Alms House attempted to open the institution to clergy of all denominations. They were defeated in this attempt and the subsequent public attacks on their characters led one of them to defend himself in the press claiming the attacks arose because of his membership in the 'much-abused, because much hated Evangelical Union.'[67] The outraged voice of New Brunswick Orangeism decried the organization as an imposter 'purporting to be founded upon the same principles as the British society ... they have – by their foolish departure from the Evangelical Union in England – made a division among Protestants, by virtually excluding *nine-tenths* (all evangelical churchmen) in the Province! Is it not true, then, that their principles are *false* and their representations ficticious?'[68]

Many evangelicals felt that pressure groups, petitions, and informal organizations would do little to achieve their cause. Ultimately, redress of their grievances could be achieved only through political action. In May 1846, a number of Evangelical Union members formed the New Brunswick Election Society, a party with the sole purpose of achieving equal rights and privileges for all religious groups.[69] In preparation for the 1846 elections, the society organized branches in Kings and Westmorland counties and then proceeded to select slates of appropriate candidates with a view to being able to create a parliamentary party if elected. In the city, the society selected three candidates – one each from the Wesleyans, the Free Presbyterians, and the Baptists.

Shortly before the election, the society announced its platform. Religious equality and the equitable sharing of public offices among the several denominations held pride of place. The social policies of the new party reflected its basically liberal orientation. It advocated a universal education system, efficient and cheap government, and the removal of government pensions.[70]

This attempt to create an evangelical political party failed in New Brunswick, as had similar efforts in the United States a few years earlier.[71] Its first effect was to divide the Evangelical Union. Distressed over the entanglement of the faith with a particular political interest, many of the more conservative dissenters insisted on a formal division between the Evangelical Union and the Election Society. Predictably, the Loyalist editor, fearful that the organization would divide the Orangemen along denominational lines, described the society as the bastard offspring of an 'unholy alliance,' a 'horrid depravity,' and its candidates as 'ultra radical.'[72] Even a responsible reformer of evangelical leanings like George Fenety, after a long period of silence, finally complained that the city was partitioned 'like ancient Greece,' into communities each attempting 'to promulgate its own views and fasten them on the Government as the rudder of the State.'[73] He opposed the Election Society on the grounds that many Episcopalians were liberals and they would attempt to meet the grievances of dissenters.

Despite these defections and criticisms, the strength of the radical evangelicals and the concern of dissenters over the issue were revealed in the 1846 balloting. The society's candidates failed to win election but one, John Owen, secured the support of nearly half the electorate in the city and county constituency, while 40 per cent voted for a second, William Jack, in the city constituency.[74] Both Owen and Jack received more votes than did the high tory candidate, John H. Gray, the grand master of the Orange Order, W.H. Needham, and the Catholic, Charles Watters.[75]

The electoral failure of the Election Society was seen by many enemies of the Evangelical Union as a failure of the union to command a significant public support. Comments to this effect produced a public response from the radical evangelical clergy. In an address to the 'friends of Evangelical truth, Christian unity and Religious freedom,' published a few days after the election, they repudiated the Election Society, professed their satisfaction with the candidates who had been elected, and then reasserted their position in purely theological terms denouncing Puseyism, the authority of tradition, the claim of any denomination to a monopoly of divine wisdom and sacramental efficacy, and the power of men to absolve sin.[76] Although they thought Catholicism to be in error, they repudiated any attempt to interfere with the civil and religious rights of Roman Catholics. Finally, they denied the existence of a legal religious establishment in the province, and solemnly warned of any attempt to maintain the religious establishment:

We know of nothing that could so soon and so easily throw our social institutions into fearful confusion, and endanger connexions which, at present, all truly loyal subjects in this country, so highly and so justly value as the accomplishment of an object which a certain party ... is eager to secure ... Whatever may be said of the *continuance* of this principle in old countries, where the inhabitants are familiar with its exercise, who that really understands our social and relative condition will calmly and openly advocate its introduction into this province? *Ecclesiastical ascendancy has never allied itself with vital Christianity – and is an impossible barrier in the way of general Christian union.*

Sam Robinson (1st Baptist)	Samuel Rice (Wesleyan)
Henry Daniel (Wesleyan)	Robert Irvine (Free Presbyterian)
F. Smallwood (Wesleyan)	James C. Gallaway (Congregationalist)
Ingram Sutcliffe (Wesleyan)	

This statement marked the end of any attempt to create a purely evangelical religious party. It also set the tone of the relationship between the Church of England and the dissenting denominations throughout the remainder of the colonial period. The Grays and numerous other evangelical episcopalians continued to participate in common evangelical concerns, but the growing strength of the Anglican tradition within the establishment, manifest in the hardening positions found in the columns of *The Chronicle*, led to claims and assumptions that challenged the very basis of the evangelical theology, made any institutional co-operation an impossibility, and severely limited the ability of the Church of England to act in an institutional capacity on any issue.[77]

At the same time the general aim of the Evangelical Union in creating an alliance of radical evangelicals seems to have been realized in the years after 1846. Inter-denominational tea parties, picnics, rallies, and special days of supplication joined the Bible Society as symbols of evangelical unity. By 1847, Free Presbyterian, Baptist, and Congregational clergy participated in the meetings of the Wesleyan Auxiliary Missionary Society.[78] Once again the movement was marked by the growth of broad co-operative institutions designed to create a culture nourished by evangelical values. The growth and ideology of the temperance movement that Robert Cooney applauded because it was strictly connectional in its motives provided an outlet for much of the energies of the radical evangelicals.[79] The temperance crusade and its curious marriage with the liberals in the 1850s reflected much of the evangelical sensibility. Perhaps the most direct descendant of the alliance was the British School, which Gallaway had been instrumental in founding in 1845. It continued to flourish in the late 1840s under evangelical patronage, and by 1849 acquired the status of a provincial normal school, becoming in the course of the 1850s the model upon which the public school system was built. As the issue of the religious establishment declined after 1846, Church of England evangelicals co-operated with dissenters in an effort to build a common culture. Together they built temperance institutions, struggled to create an educational system formed to their values, and formed a common Saint John Protestant Orphan Asylum and a Young Men's Christian Association.[80]

Zealous, articulate, and possessed of a keen sense of purpose, the Saint John evangelicals played a critical role in the remaking of the urban community. Between 1820 and 1850 they had grown from marginal pockets of social activity to a central element in the society of the city. Indeed, taking together all manifestations of the movement – moderates, radicals, dissenters, Churchmen, natives, Irish, English, and Scots – they certainly composed a majority of the Protestant population of the city and probably a majority of those capable of making the vital decisions that affected the nature of the common life of Saint John. The division between Churchmen and dissenters seriously weakened the movement and ultimately drove many radical evangelicals to seek their utopia in the arms of the liberals and of social pluralism, rather than in the effort to remake Saint John in the image of Geneva. Where evangelicals could agree, particularly on matters of faith, morals, charity, and public behaviour, they played a critical role in defining the urban community.

~7~

Temperance

Of all the institutional expressions of Saint John evangelicalism, none revealed so fully the program and problems of the culture as the temperance movement. The movement proceeded from a variety of motives and found its constituency across the whole spectrum of the social order. As in other cities, some employers used it as a means to improve the productivity of their employees. But the strength of the movement is understandable only in terms of the world-view of evangelicals and, to a lesser extent, of an uprooted Irish peasantry. The most radical temperance solutions originated among the most radical evangelicals and were often found among those most alienated from the dominant community norm. They were also overwhelmingly concentrated among the urban artisans and mechanics. A large proportion of temperance supporters were Irish, a fact that differentiates the Saint John movement from that of most American cities and seems to suggest that religion rather than ethnicity was at the heart of the movement. Saint John temperance began as a fairly modest proposal to redirect the drinking habits of the city's population from the consumption of ardent spirits to the use of ale and wine. Over two decades, it moved in ever more radical expressions from temperance through total abstinence to prohibition. Each successive wave built upon its predecessor, but the motivation and social basis of each differed in some important respects from the others. As it surged forward, each wave picked up support from different quarters and left behind many fellow travellers in the more conservative manifestations of the movement. The temperance movement may be seen as an attempt to assimilate workers to 'middle class' values,[1] but such a view requires either casting the 'middle class' in a curiously evangelical mould or arguing that the evangelicals in fact captured the urban 'middle class' of nineteenth-century Saint John and remade it in their cultural image.[2] Since a substantial part of the city's traditional bourgeoisie rejected most manifestations of the movement, neither of those propositions is entirely satisfactory. In Saint John, as in most North American cities, temperance was a complex movement that cannot be easily attributed to a single social group or motivation.[3]

A number of factors contributed to the development of the movement in Saint John.[4] The nature of the staples trade combined with a vital West Indies connection to provide the city's merchants with huge quantities of cheap liquor. The city's location as a major seaport, military garrison, and entrepôt for the frontier settlements of early nineteenth-century New Brunswick and Nova Scotia created a considerable demand for the drug. Finally, the city was home to a body of rootless and futureless men from the inland farm or Irish cottage to whom the city's numerous taverns served the function of club and social centre. This 'natural tendency' toward frequent use of alcoholic beverages was reinforced by tradition and by the urban condition. Although the evils of insobriety were frequently commented upon, the consumption of alcohol was not an issue before 1830. Traditionally an individual became a drunkard or disturbed the peace and was proscribed or punished for his act. Over-indulgence, like over-eating, was perceived as a sign of personal failing, a weakness that could be cured by self-will or, failing that, by a few days in the stocks or in gaol. The striking accomplishment of the temperance movement was to make a social and moral problem of a customary activity.

It is impossible to understand the movement that reshaped the behaviour of a substantial part of the population of Saint John without reference to the growing influence of evangelicalism. All evangelicals voiced similar concerns about those influences they perceived as promoting the cause of unrighteousness within the city. As their numbers and influences grew in the 1820s, so did their willingness to participate in the public concerns of the community. Campaigns were fought in 1828 and 1829 against theatres, drinking, and the decline of Sunday observance.[5] As early as 1828, in the columns of The Gazette, Alexander McLeod began his attack on the large number of tippling houses in the city – those 'haunts of vice' – and demanded that Common Council use its authority to set licence fees in an effort to reduce their numbers.[6] There was a substantial body of evangelical supporters in Saint John by 1829: they possessed some idea of the kind of city in which they wished to live, and they were prepared to use the secular institutions to secure that end.

Their worst fears seemed confirmed by the events of 1830. Prosperity, the attendant expansion of the timber trade, and a greatly increased number of sailors and immigrants in the city produced an unprecedented demand for liquor licences. It also produced a marked increase in incidents of social violence and disorderly conduct. Under city charter, the right to grant licences of all kinds was vested solely in the mayor. In 1830, he issued 206 tavern licences, in addition to 29 retail licences. One inhabitant in 50 held a liquor seller's licence, a far cry from the one in 132 that prevailed in Banbury, England, where the temperance movement began at about the same time, and a participation rate considerably higher than the one in 80 that prevailed in New York City.[7] All of the problems produced by a buoyant and uncontrolled commercial growth came to centre on the 'problem' of liquor.

In preparing their moral crusade, leading evangelicals followed the same strategy used in the organization of the Bible and Tract societies and in the Sunday School Union.[8] Temperance must not degenerate into a number of denominational groupings: it must become a broadly based movement that might fairly claim to command the support of a majority of the respectable citizens of the city.[9] Accordingly, the first organization became a coalition of interest groups containing individuals motivated by religious conviction, humanitarian concern, and fears of the threat posed to the social order.

The occasion for the organization of the society was a visit to the city in December 1830 of Dr Justin Edwards, one of the leading figures in American evangelicalism.[10] A meeting of clergymen at Dr Gray's rectory shortly afterward resulted in the formation of the St John Temperance Society with Gray as president, Dr Burns of St Andrew's Church of Scotland as vice-president, and Alex McLeod, the Wesleyan editor of *The Gazette*, as secretary. Its constitution was a half-way covenant of objectives. Members promised to abstain personally from ardent spirits and agreed to refuse to serve them to their friends and employees; beer, ale, cider, and wine were not included in the prohibition.

The influence of the society spread rapidly among most respectable orders in the city and its suburbs. Within a year of its founding, it had grown to 391 members and its ranks included a majority of the members of the Common Council. By this time, sister societies had been organized in the Carleton and Portland suburbs. In Carleton, which was largely populated by members of the shipbuildings trades, nearly 50 per cent of the entire population were members of the temperance societies as early as 1834. Virtually all the Protestant clergy in the city and its suburbs joined the society within a few weeks of its founding, as an example to their congregation.[11] Numbers of the great and near-great, including officers of the crown, justices of the peace, great merchants, and professionals – largely drawn from those with known evangelical sympathies – seem to have taken the pledge in 1832 and 1833. By 1834, there were more than 1400 members in good standing in the city and its suburbs in a total population of 18,000, accounting for nearly 20 per cent of the adult population of the area.[12]

The nature of the early movement is reflected in its three-part program, which emphasized personal abstinence, conversion through education, and control of liquor outlets. Conversion of the unsaved was undertaken in typical evangelical fashion. Quantities of tracts and books were secured from the London (later the British and Foreign) Temperance Society for general distribution within the community, a reflection of the strong Episcopalian influence in the movement.[13] Limiting the number and quality of taverns through use of the licence law was a more complex problem. Rallying the support of the grand jury and court of session, the Temperance Society in 1831 persuaded the Common Council to increase tavern licence fees from £5 to £10, the maximum permitted by law. As a result, the number of licences fell from 206 to 104. Yet this seeming triumph was probably viewed as a failure by most temperance advocates. Those forced out by the higher fees were undoubtedly the marginal figures in the trade, usually poor widows and others operating small hole-in-the-wall establishments.[14] The major offenders remained. With the support of Charles Simonds, the assembly Speaker, temperance advocates then attempted to achieve their ends by altering the statutes to give the Common Council and the magistrates much wider powers over the liquor trade. This failed in 1831, and again in 1832 and 1833.[15] None the less, year by year, the society continued its presentations to the assembly.[16]

The St John Temperance Society and its sister societies in Carleton and Portland represented the response of moderate and concerned evangelicals to a pressing social issue. Organized under the direction of prominent leaders of the provincial establishment, the society reflected an intelligent and humane concern for the interests of the broader Saint John population. Almost from the time of its creation, however, it was confronted with an alternative vehicle through which protest against the traffic might be channelled. This was a second manifestation of the temperance movement, one that offered a teetotal solution to the problem. Its leadership and its emphasis on abstinence and moral rejeneration of the fallen closely paralleled the Philadelphia experience.[17]

The St John Total Abstinence Society was formed on 25 May 1832 when thirty-one men formally assented to the 'long oath' in which they not only abjured all ardent spirits but also all wines, ales, beers, and other liquors.[18] In addition, they agreed neither to offer them to others nor to procure them for employees or for the entertainment of friends. Meeting quarterly at the Baptist Session Room, this society attracted little public notice in its first few years. By dint of careful recruitment, membership increased to 213 by 1835.[19]

In Saint John, as in England, evangelicals quickly came to realize that if any reformation of the fallen drunkard were to be accomplished, it could only be done in the context of total abstinence. The Baptist tradition fed from the same emotional sources as did those of Dr Edwards and New England Congregationalism and the similarity of their responses to the problems of intemperance is not surprising. The doctrine of total abstinence struck a responsive chord in the ethos of many radical evangelicals who undertook a campaign to persuade others of like beliefs and temperament to become associated with them in this new work.

The teetotallers are particularly interesting because of the socially radical position inherent in the 'long oath' that the society adopted. If the Temperance Society oaths set its members apart from the population at large, those of the teetotal organization utterly isolated its adherents. In a community where virtually every recreational activity centred on the tavern and the wide-spread use of alcohol beverages, and where liquour had become an integral part of the work culture, teetotallers were forbidden the use of any tavern and of many retail establishments. Moreover, their attendance at most social functions, including cotillions, weddings and funerals, public celebrations, and militia drills, turned these occasions into moments of great embarrassment for abstainers, partakers, guests, and hosts alike.

The creation of the Total Abstinence Society in 1832 might be perceived as a revolt against the inability of the temperance activists to achieve their ends through control of tavern licensing powers. A more plausible explanation is that groups of deeply committed radical evangelicals explicitly rejected many of the values of the larger society and deliberately defined their distinctiveness through this radical dietary prohibition. Had their belief not found root in the tendencies and doctrines of mainstream evangelicalism, teetotallers might well have remained, like the Quakers and Anabaptists of Saint John, a peculiar and unimportant sect existing on the fringes of the larger society. Instead, this small group set about to transform their values into those of the majority.

The social dimensions of the early organization are revealed in the occupations of the founders. Sixteen of the thirty-one were freemen of the city. Of these, two were minor merchants. The remainder consisted of an assortment of artisans, tradesmen, and labourers. The fourteen non-freemen either did not live in the city or, if they did, probably performed some unskilled function. Notable by their absence were clergy, doctors, lawyers, great merchants, and officers of the crown, precisely the groups that had provided leadership for the early temperance societies. The total-abstinence pioneers were not only leading evangelicals, they were people who were confronted daily with the problems of intemperance: tradesmen whose extended households included apprentices and other workmen, and artisans and labourers who lived in neighbourhoods surrounded by the problem.

The growth of the Abstinence Society in its early years contrasted sharply with that of its temperance rival. The spread of the latter had been a triumphal procession supported by the most respectable elements of society. Its typical vehicle had been the mass public meeting, and the altar call followed by a stampede to the membership rolls. Abstinence worked much more slowly. The society numbered 213 supporters in 1835, strikingly fewer than the 1400 claimed by the temperance societies a year earlier. There were, as well, significant differences in strategy between the two organizations. The teetotallers consolidated their numbers in a single central organization, making no effort to expand into neighbouring communities. They also worked outwards through extended families, friends, and employees. There was a conscious zealousness that seemed to mark the admission of abstainers, highlighted by the occasional corporate membership, such as that of N.S. Demill and Family and Company. Yet the slow process of personal conversion and organic growth made for a stable organization of highly committed individuals. In the three years before 1835, the group lost only ten members and this included backsliders, migrants, and those having the misfortune to die. Zealousness and stability were to remain the hallmarks of these new men and women.

After 1835, the organization began to play a more active role in the community at large. Its members were increasingly found in the ranks of those advocating legal control of the liquor trade. Significantly this date also marked the Temperance Society's change in emphasis from control of taverns to prohibition of ardent spirits, although whether this was done in reaction to the growing strength of the teetotallers or whether it represents the strength of the teetotallers within the Temperance Society cannot be determined. Between 1835 and 1840, the growth of the organization accelerated sharply. The number of recruits increased from 33 in 1836 to 99 in 1838 to 156 in 1840.[20] The Total Abstinence Society vigorously pressed its claims among the city's evangelicals, enrolling large numbers of church workers and officers in this period, including two young Portland Sunday school teachers from St Luke's Church, J.W. Lawrence and S.L. Tilley.

By 1840 membership had reached 758 members. The characteristics of this group reveal a good deal about the nature of the organization. Nearly

30 per cent were female, although this proportion fluctuated from 40 per cent of the pre-1835 membership to less than one-quarter of the recruits after that date. Of the male membership, only 2 per cent were unable to sign their names and only 2 per cent can be identified as Irish Catholics. Another 43 per cent were freemen of the city, and this group bore a striking occupational similarity to the 30 founders of the society. Of those for whom occupations can be identified, nearly two-thirds were domestic artisans and tradesmen, a striking fact when it is remembered that these groups accounted for only 23 per cent of the city's freemen. Among the artisans and tradesmen it is difficult to distinguish between masters and journeymen and small proprietors and wage-earners. About 60 per cent had been born in New Brunswick and another one-third were Irish. Finally, the Total Abstinence Society was a young men's organization: the median age of its members at enrolment was twenty-six.

Unfortunately, the detailed record of the society membership ends in 1840 just at the point when it had developed the impetus to overtake the Temperance Society and establish itself as the temperance movement in the city. Between 1840 and 1843, its membership rose from perhaps 700 to nearly 3000 members, of which 2194 were found in the east side of the city, 250 were in Carleton, and 500 in Portland.[21] The rapidity of this growth contrasted with the modest gains of the previous decade can only be explained through the disintegration of the temperance societies and the movement of most of their members into the Abstinence Society. The Carleton Temperance Society, with its heavy Baptist membership, was composed largely of abstainers by the late 1830s and the entire membership probably entered the Abstinence Society as one. However the transition was accomplished, the main teetotal organization by 1843 claimed the allegiance of perhaps one of every four adults in the city. Even more significant, if the tendencies found in the 1840 membership roll persisted, these certainly included an absolute majority of the tradesmen and artisans of the city.

An educational program was aimed at the young and those obviously in need of reform. Schools seemed to offer the greatest opportunity for the eventual victory of the movement and despite their abhorrence at the intemperance of many parish schoolmasters, abstinence leaders were pleased with their efforts to break older social habits through the medium of the educational system.[22] Gaols, almshouses, and the penitentiary provided captive audiences of what seemed to be the most obvious victims of the curse of insobriety. Tracts, books, and lecturers were provided at schools and public institutions across the province.[23] By 1845, the society determined on a broader educational program through publication of a weekly newspaper in which the temperance position on all issues could be elucidated on a regular basis. To this end, the legislature of the province was approached for a grant of £150–200 a year to permit publication of the *Temperance Telegraph*. With the foundation of their newspaper, the local temperance movement had reached its apogee.

The creation of the *Temperance Telegraph* suggests that temperance advocates had succeeded in sundering the Saint John community into two on a basic moral question. As early as 1833, a majority of the members of Common Council were supporters of the Temperance Society. At the time of the provincial election of 1834 four temperance supporters – Charles Simonds, J.M. Wilmot, Stephen Humbert, and L. Hatheway – were on the ticket and some temperance voters may have shared the sentiments of one *Observer* correspondent who complained that he was 'a temperance man' and that he and many others did 'not see the consistency of members of a Temperance Society voting for those who are opposed to that cause and who are practically encouraging the traffic in ardent spirits.'[24] *The Observer*'s support for temperance, as well as for the cause of triennial elections, control of government expenses, and the abolition of the militia, might well have evoked the suspicion that temperance had found its home with the supporters of radical causes. This suspicion could only be heightened by the vitriolic attacks on the 'radicals' by the *Chronicle*, the voice of the high tory Church of England, which crudely ridiculed the secretary of the Temperance Society, George Blatch ('Mr. Georgey'), his Baptist minister grandfather, and his temperance co-workers.[25]

Public demonstration of the distinctiveness of the temperance supporters was provided on the great public feast days of thanksgiving when the Common Council set up bread, meat, and ale in the city squares in preparation for the all-day celebrations, which usually concluded in general drunkenness. The temperance response to these affairs was to organize competing soirées, the first of which was held in 1838 to celebrate the Queen's coronation.[26] Although the event was organized by Mr Justice Parker and Dr Bayard of the Temperance Society, it was attended by abstainers. Significantly, all soirées featured only tea and coffee, despite the fact that many Temperance Society members had no scruples about using ale. The coronation gathering and a similar tea party held in 1840 to celebrate the royal marriage highlight two points: temperance and abstention had more in common with each other than with the habits of the rest of society, and two social groupings were forming within the city with the line between the two drawn not so much by economic or occupational class – although that certainly played some role – but by a view of the nature of men and women and their duties to other men and women.

In this sense the temperance movement was not so much a coming out from the world as the symbolic creation of a new world. Over the course of the 1840s, the soirée was to become a regular feature of temperance life in Saint John. Several were held every year in a manner reminiscent of the Sunday School Union celebrations. Despite these efforts to provide non-secular recreation for their followers, the leaders of the temperance movement never emulated the English movement in providing tea houses that might have served the social-club functions characteristic of the tippling room.

The triumph of total abstinence over temperance in the early 1840s undoubtedly sharpened these separatist tendencies. At the same time, as in Boston and other east-coast cities, many temperance supporters refused to follow their fellows into total abstinence. These included some of the most distinguished patricians of the movement, men like Charles Simonds who voted against the legislative grant to the *Temperance Telegraph* in 1845, and the rector of Saint John, John Gray, who as late as 1859 found himself under attack by the *Temperance Telegraph* for his defence of traditional temperance principles.[27]

The impact of the abstainers' pressure was first felt in those religious denominations most influenced by evangelicalism. From being a zealous minority within most of these churches in 1835, abstainers emerged a decade later as the dominant influence. Their influence varied in relationship to the strength of the denomination's evangelicalism: it was strongest in the Methodist and Baptist denominations, weaker but still powerful in the Church of England and Free Presbyterian, and weakest in the Church of Scotland. Many drinkers continued to play prominent roles in all denominations (Thomas Parks, a well-known Free Presbyterian layman, remained one of the city's leading liquor merchants and fought the smashers until the end of his life), but their influence was clearly dwindling and their dietary and recreational habits were increasingly objects of suspicion. The fathers of the Total Abstinence Society had built well. Their converts had been drawn from the 'rising generation' of young men of the 1830s and 1840s. They were drawn, as well, from among the stable artisan elements of the urban society who were most likely to mature the city's next generation. By the 1840s, young men were being received into the organization who had known no other tradition, who had been raised in temperance homes by temperance parents, and who very likely would marry into temperance families.

The third group in the Saint John temperance movement emerged from an altogether different tradition. On a Sunday morning early in February 1841, Father James Dunphy of St Malachi's Parish announced from his pulpit that he proposed to establish a temperance society in his parish on the following Sunday. This society was to be unique in that members were to be given the choice of taking either the long or the short oath. Seven hundred pledges were taken in the first week, and within a month membership exceeded 1400, of which all but 103 were total abstainers.[28] The temperance campaign within the Catholic communion continued throughout the spring and summer and by mid-October, association membership stood at 3500, embracing a clear majority of the permanent Catholic population of the city and its environs, although these figures are not comparable to those of the Total Abstinence Society because a large proportion consisted of young children.[29]

The immediate success of the new organization may in part be attributed to the economic benefits it offered. Father Dunphy extended the nature of the city's temperance movement by adding a mutual-benefit society to his association. The St John Roman Catholic Total Abstinence Relief Society provided three services to its members. In return for a small weekly fee, the society paid all the medical costs of its members, a weekly payment of 7s. 6d. during the period of illness, and burial expenses in the event the condition proved to be terminal.[30] Despite its name, the society accepted non-Catholics into its membership provided they had been abstainers for at least six months prior to admission.

The sudden success of Catholic temperance in Saint John had more to do with Ireland and the experiences of recent Irish migrants than with any compelling circumstances within the local environment.[31] The leading Catholic exponent of teetotalism in the early nineteenth century was Theobald Mathew, a Capuchin friar who served for more than two decades as pastor of the Capuchin parish in Cork. In 1838, at the urging of Quaker temperance advocates in the city, Mathew began a total abstinence crusade in Southern Ireland that enrolled some 2,000,000 members by 1840. Mathew's success was due in part to his personal piety and popularity and in even larger measure to the great Catholic revival of which he was a powerful symbol. To much of the Irish peasantry, Mathew became a living saint whose progress through the countryside was marked by throngs of thousands, and to whom was attributed a host of miraculous occurrences.[32]

Cork held a peculiar place in the minds of most Saint John Catholics. James Dunphy was the son of a prominent Cork family and had probably known the Capuchin as a young man. By 1840, Cork was the principal port from which Saint John immigrants were embarking. Some of them had been part of Father Mathew's parish; many more had already taken the long oath from his hands and wore his medal.[33] But their commitment of abstinence had been made in a Catholic context of self-denial and purity. It responded only to Dunphy's call for Catholic revival in Saint John. For quite different reasons, both Orangemen and older Irish patriots, Catholic as well as Protestant, viewed the movement with suspicion.

The organization of a temperance society along confessional lines pointed up the fragmentation of community within the city. The reasons for the failure of the early temperance society to acquire widespread support across the Catholic community are not difficult to find. Both organizations had been implicitly religious in their motives. While some more secular Catholics found no difficulty uniting with non-Catholics in the interest of the general well-being, most probably found the broader organization alien in rhetoric and potentially dangerous to the faith. The confessional organization also provided an opportunity for public demonstration of achievements by the faith and the culture. In March 1842 the society determined to publicly illustrate the change that abstinence had effected in the Catholic community. On St Patrick's Day, one thousand men in full regalia gathered for mass in the morning and, carrying high the banners of Father Mathew, St Michael, and St John, spent the afternoon parading the streets and square of the city. The performance evoked the praise of other temperance supporters but produced a storm of protest from Orange and tory leaders who saw sinister implications in this show of Catholic strength.[34]

Relations between the Catholic and the two other societies remained congenial. G.E. Fenety and *The News* applauded the Catholic society and remained its defender; leading members of the St John societies played prominent roles at every major gathering of the younger organization, and Wm. H. Needham served with T.W. Anglin in its vice-presidency.[35] Leading Catholic laymen such as Charles Doherty stressed the common ends of the two societies and argued that religious differences should be forgotten in the 'glorious reformation of one's fellow man.' Yet nothing could mask the fact that even in this common purpose, community could survive only as a rather precarious confederacy. The two abstinence societies in fact reflected two quite different cultural realities.

By 1847, then, a powerful and deep-rooted temperance tradition had developed in the city of Saint John and its suburbs. Centred on the respectable working classes and small proprietors, it none the less found supporters at each level of society; as it gained strength among the business and professional groups of the city in the 1840s, these high-status members were found in disproportionate numbers on the executive committees of the societies. The movement was essentially local in origin and organization, stressed personal total abstinence among most members, and pursued a policy of limited and supervised outlets for alcoholic beverages. It was at this point that the city came to host a new temperance phenomenon, the fraternal order.

The movement to fraternal orders seems to have been a natural development occurring independently in both the United Kingdom and the United States. Based on the most popular features of the Oddfellows and Masonic orders, fraternal temperance groups offered their members a combination of mystery, fellowship, hierarchical order, and economic security. Groups such as the English Rachebites and the American Sons of Temperance brought the newly initiated into the world of secret symbols and regalia and offered them entry through sacred oath into an order that was at once profoundly religious and profoundly secular. Like clerical postulants, new recruits bound themselves by oath to abstinence during their membership in the order. For those who were prepared to take their final vows and surrender self and resources to the cause for life, the Sons of Temperance offered an elite order – the Templars of Honour and Temperance. To mystery and excitement was added a full social life, including weekly meetings, parades, conventions, and outings. Finally, the brotherhood was cemented by mutual-aid benefits administered by the local divisions. Sons of Temperance paid 25¢ a month and received sick benefits of $4 a week and a death benefit of $30.

The Order of the Sons of Temperance was organized in New York City in 1842 and spread concentrically from there throughout the eastern United States and British North America, then to the United Kingdom, and finally to Australasia. By 1855, it contained more than 134,000 members organized into 3500 subordinate divisions.[36] The order's movement northeast from New York followed the coastline. The Grand Division of Maine was organized in 1844, and two years later the order formed its first New Brunswick division at St Stephen, on the Maine border.

The entry of the Sons of Temperance into Saint John in 1847 was in the nature of a triumphal army moving into an already conquered bastion. Plans for the arrival had been laid well in advance by some leaders of the St John Total Abstinence Society. A party of over 100 Sons from the St Stephen, St Andrews, and Eastport, Maine, divisions arrived by steamboat in the city. They were met by N.S. Demill and other members of the Total Abstinence Society, and were escorted through the city by the Mechanics Institute Band. That evening, before an impressive gathering, a number of young men from the Total Abstinence Society were initiated into the Sons of Temperance.[37] The order grew rapidly. Within a year it had formed ten divisions in the Saint John area. When the American patriarch of the order visited the city in May 1848, he was greeted by a procession of more than 1200 men in full regalia. Preceded by a marching band, the Sons paraded the streets, gathered in Queen Square for an address by the patriarch, and ended the ceremonies with an impressive torchlight procession.[38]

The initial success of the Sons of Temperance reflected the strength and

work of the total-abstinence and temperance societies. Given the membership of the New Brunswick Temperance, the St John Total Abstinence, the
Ladies Total Abstinence, and the Roman Catholic Total Abstinence
societies, it is questionable whether the Sons of Temperance added any
numbers to the temperance cause. The old St John Total Abstinence
Society, which continued to coexist with the Sons, reported a membership
of more than 4500 in 1852, drawn entirely from the city and its suburbs.[39]
Since most of this membership would have come from the evangelicals
among the 10,000 males over sixteen in Saint John and Portland, it seems
inconceivable that any significant number of Sons were not already
members of the Total Abstinence Society.[40]

The organization of the city had occurred quickly and while the Sons
continued to expand there after 1848, their major efforts were directed to
the task of evangelizing the province. From their Saint John centre, the
order's leaders proceeded to establish outposts in every village and rural
settlement in southern New Brunswick.[41]

Fired by such zeal and nourished by the evangelical culture, the order
expanded rapidly. The membership was 2500 in 1848; another 1370 were
added the following year.[42] By 1852, there were 4500 members in 70
divisions, about 40 per cent of whom were found in Saint John and its
suburbs.[43] By this time, the order had formed women's and children's
auxiliaries and the Cadets of Temperance and the Cold Water Army added
to the numbers and influence of the organization.[44] It was an aggressive-
ness and an unwillingness to accept a place on the margin of society that
most sharply differentiated the Sons from the Total Abstinence Society.
The Sons had abandoned both pietism and compromise. As the principal
vehicle through which the evangelical spirit was secularized, they
brought the zeal and the self-righteousness of that tradition to the task of
remaking the community in their image. The Sons of Temperance were an
American phenomenon. Their domination of the Saint John temperance
movement was paralleled by the eclipse of British evangelical influence.

The transition from British to American leadership was accompanied by
the growth of a more uncompromising attitude on the liquor issue.
Massachusetts and Maine prohibitionists succeeded in imposing prohibition in their states by 1852.[45] Through close links with the New England
movement, New Brunswick leaders came to expect that a system of legal
prohibition could become a reality. But the move to prohibition was not an
easy one. Many abstainers would not support the prohibitionist position
of the Sons.[46] Many fellow travellers from the Temperance Society, those
who had never actually taken the long oath but who supported the
movement as the 'great engine of moral reform,' drew back at the coercive
elements inherent in the proposal. Earlier proposals for a legal prohibition

of the import, manufacture, and sale of all alcoholic beverages by the Ladies Total Abstinence Society had gone largely unnoticed in the city.[47] When the newly organized Saint John Sons of Temperance, comprising nearly 1000 adult males, announced its prohibitionist policy in a widely distributed pamphlet, the issue polarized the city. Conservatives and interests that had been prepared to tolerate the idiosyncrasies of abstainers provided they kept to their own part of town counter-attacked in some alarm. The editor of *The Loyalist*, who had always taken a neutral position on the issue of temperance, attacked the new 'secret society' and its 'sanctimonious' adherents and condemned the prohibition proposals as 'insane, tyrannic and blasphemous.'[48] The knowledge that the Sons were directed from the American states added considerable fuel to his fire. Other temperance supporters, such as Henry Chubb of *The Courier* and Charles Simonds, maintained a discreet but noticeable silence on the objectives of the new order.

Having stated its faith in prohibition, the order proceeded to treat it as an ideal that could be accomplished at some future time. Instead, the years 1847 to 1850 were devoted to the organizational tasks of public relations and building a strong leadership. Analysis of the social origins of the 1850 officers of four city divisions reveals a leadership marked both by its respectability and its lack of distinction. While the officers were drawn from an occupational spectrum ranging from merchants to mechanics, they were virtually all freemen or freeholders of the city. Together they composed perhaps 3 per cent of the city electorate. The group was divided almost equally between business men and artisans. Nearly 60 per cent employed live-in servants. Nearly 60 per cent had been born in New Brunswick; most of the remainder were English or Scots.

Despite the respectability and high status suggested by these categories, it would be erroneous to assume that the leadership represented the socially prominent elements of Saint John society. The leaders were minor merchants with purely local interests, small master craftsmen, and minor civic functionaries. The Carleton leadership consisted of shipbuilders and shipwrights. In all, it was an artisan/merchant movement, drawn from the traditional craft groups, and headed by a petite bourgeoisie of evangelical origins. Patricians, great merchants, major functionaries, lawyers – in short, the traditional leaders of the Saint John community – were almost entirely absent from the leadership of the Sons of Temperance.

The temperance strategy pursued by this leadership between 1847 and 1850 was an imitation of that developed a decade earlier by the Massachusetts groups and employed in a more limited way by the old St John Temperance Society. Through use of the licensing law, the sale of alcohol was to be restricted on a parish-to-parish and ward-to-ward basis. To this end, considerable lobbying was carried out among the county magistrates and efforts were made to secure the election to Common Council of those sympathetic to the temperance cause. In April 1849, by a vote of 18 to 3, the magistrates of the county of St John decided not to license any sellers of liquor for the coming year.[49] This act effectively cut off the legal supply of liquor in the rural parishes of the county but did not affect the parishes of St John and Carleton where the grant of licences lay in the gift of the mayor. In May, the Common Council received petitions from 235 men and 100 women of Carleton asking for the 'utter suppression' of taverns in the parish. The council unanimously supported the recommendation and the mayor agreed not to grant tavern licences for the two west-side wards.[50] This left only the four wards on the east side of the harbour with legal liquor outlets. Finally, following the great riot of 1849, the grand jury of Saint John supported a proposal to prohibit all alcoholic beverages on the grounds that it was the only effective way to combat crime, pauperism, and misery.[51]

Despite these successes, the leaders of the Sons hesitated to undertake a campaign for total provincial prohibition. The event that sparked the move to prohibition on the part of the order was the formation of the New Brunswick Colonial Association in 1849. The association was a broadly based political alliance of mildly reformist interests that proposed to remake a more secure provincial economy from the uncertainties created when the British abandoned their traditional mercantilist policies. Among the organizers of the new coalition were two prominent prohibitionists, S.L. Tilley, and the city attorney, W.R.M. Burtis. Their participation linked temperance to a political movement with liberal overtones. In the provincial election of 1850, the Colonial Association produced a seven-point platform of political, administrative, and financial reforms. Slates of candidates supporting the platform were endorsed in most constituencies.[52] The platform contained no reference to temperance and many leaders of the association were clearly unsympathetic to the temperance movement.[53]

Despite this, temperance became a part of the general mythology of political reform; indeed, in many constituencies the prohibitionists undoubtedly formed the backbone of the party. And even an old temperance supporter and Colonial Association founder such as Charles Simonds, who had abandoned the movement in its prohibitionist phase, found it expedient to carry the cause of prohibition onto the floor of the House of Assembly.[54] Some reformers felt less than comfortable with their new bedmates, but most spokesmen eventually accepted them as partners in a moral revolution. On the prohibitionist side, the *Temperance Telegraph*

Samuel Leonard Tilley, c. 1864 (NBM)

printed all the records of the Colonial Association and threw its support behind the party in the election of 1850.[55] So completely had the movement become indentified with political reform that the grand patriarch for New Brunswick, James Johnson, noted in 1852 that he looked upon 'the prosperity or failure of our institution as identical with the rise or fall of our great Provincial interests.'[56]

The exact relationship between the Colonial Association and the Sons of Temperance is unclear, but the demand for an uncompromising legal prohibition began in Saint John with the legislative session of 1851. Headed by Thomas Harding, the first locally elected mayor of Saint John, the magistrates of the sessions of the county of St John petitioned for an act to prevent the traffic of intoxicating liquors. This was followed a few months later by the 'Great Petition,' a single scroll bearing more than 20,000 signatures, which was placed before the assembly by Charles Simonds. Many of the signatories were female and many were drawn from York, Sunbury, Queens, Kings, Charlotte, and Westmorland counties, but by far the largest group of supporters were male residents of Saint John City.[57]

Opposition to the prohibitionists emerged from three quarters. Saint John Catholic leaders, like those of Boston, viewed the abuses arising from the use of alcohol as a personal rather than a social evil.[58] They co-operated with the Total Abstinence Society but not with prohibitionists. The liquor interest itself was active in every petition. The most effective opposition was that of the conservatives, drawn notably from the merchant, professional, and functionary aristocracy of the city. This group quite rightly perceived the prohibitionists as spear carriers for a more broadly based movement of political reform. The debate was fought through pamphlets, newspapers, advertisements, and petitions.

By and large the tenor of the discussion, although sometimes shrill, was of a good quality. The argument centred on three issues: the capacity of human nature to be modified by environmental factors, the right of the state to determine for the subject what he should eat and drink, and the effects prohibition would produce on the revenues of the province and the city. Prohibitionists argued that while personal resolve was ideal, weaker natures could be prevented from falling if they were not exposed to evil, and that all Christians had a moral obligation to create a social environment that would be most conducive to proper behaviour. Underlying this position was the traditional evangelical view that the Christian was guilty of the sin of omission if he tolerated an impediment that might cause his brother to fall. Prohibitionist opponents responded that human nature was intractable, that if people were unwilling or unable to moderate their passions, any effort to save them from their own nature was doomed to failure, since the weak character enslaved to his own desires would persist until he had found the source of his own destruction.[59] Ultimately morality could not be legislated, since law could only attempt to contain but never change human nature. The political argument followed much the same lines, with the anti-prohibitionists posing as defenders of the rights of the subject, while the prohibitionists, a little uncomfortable in the position, argued for the prerogative right of government to constrain the freedom of the individual for the welfare of the whole society.[60]

In terms of the population as a whole, the prohibitionists were a minority, albeit an articulate and committed minority. But the view of a small group imposing its wishes on an inchoate majority is inaccurate. The core of their strength lay in the 1860 active resident Sons of Temperance living in the city and its suburbs in 1854, nearly 1000 of whom were enrolled in the five divisions on the east side of the city.[61] Beyond this core were the other elements of the movement, notably the St John Total Abstinence Society, which numbered between 4500 and 5000, many of whom were adult males who were not members of the Sons of Temperance. The numerical strength of the movement was further demonstrated in the licence petition presented to the county sessions in 1853 and signed by more than 5700 people.[62] Since the total number of eligible freemen and freeholders did not exceed 2000, the prohibitionists must have had in every election a reasonable possibility of enforcing their will upon the city.

The problem was not one of numbers but of the underlying disunity among temperance supporters over the issue of legal coercion. Since the 1830s, temperance supporters had periodically controlled the Common Council. Although they had restrained the liquor trade, they had never moved decisively toward its eradication. Until 1850, the council had been faced with appointed mayors, most of whom opposed the goals of the temperance movement. In 1851, however, the provincial government assented to the election of the mayor by the Common Council. The first mayor under the new regime was Thomas Harding, master tanner, prominent Calvinist Baptist, and vice-president of the St John Total Abstinence Society. Harding's term of office was marked by its moderation: tavern licences were restricted to those areas of the city where strong temperance elements were not to be found. Harding's theology permitted to each person the free choice of going to hell in his or her own particular fashion.

The organization, the rhetoric, and the public debate peaked at the time of the provincial election of 1854. Following the Maine and Massachusetts example, the Sons of Temperance were prepared to fashion their own

Eden out of this contest. At the quarterly session of the Grand Division in January 1854, the grand patriarch expounded a vision of the new world order ripe with the views of American millenialists and perfectionists.[63] He saw 'indications of mighty change in the moral and social conditions of the World ... New and constantly diversifying elements and activities ... to some grand display of Almighty Goodness and Wisdom as the World never witnessed before ... and this continent would appear to be the Theatre on which an important part of the great design is to acted out.'[64] He called upon his brethren to play their role in this design at the polls.

Without doubt, the prohibitionists played a decisive role in the Liberal victory of 1854. W.S. MacNutt has described the victory as that of the smashers over the rummies.[65] Yet the Liberal party on paper remained one of economic and political reform; its program contained no prohibition pledge. The continued ambiguity of the party leadership toward its principal group of supporters was demonstrated in the manner by which the prohibition legislation was introduced into the House. It was brought forward as a private member's bill; although passed by reformers' votes with the aid of a few loose fish, it was never treated as a government measure.[66]

Having achieved their aims so rapidly and so completely, the prohibitionists were virtually at a loss as to how to deal with the practical problems of enforcement. Nowhere was the problem more complicated than in the city of Saint John, the prohibitionist centre and the key to the movement's success in the province as a whole. The polarization of opinion that occurred throughout the province after 1851 was replicated in the city. A minority among the members of the 1852 Common Council, the temperance advocates succeeded in electing a clear majority the following year. The successful temperance candidates included a variety of prohibitionists, abstainers, and temperance supporters, including the president and two vice-presidents of the Total Abstinence Society (N.S. Demill and Joseph Fairweather), elected from the heavily Irish Catholic Kings Ward, and W.H.A. Keans from Wellington Ward, which had been carved out of the residential areas of Kings. They completed their victory by securing the election of a temperance candidate as mayor.

The 1854 civic elections, coming within weeks of the provincial contest, provoked a straight race for the mayoralty between prohibitionist and anti-prohibitionist factions. The contest, the first city-wide election for mayor, provided a useful test of strength between the two factions. Running on behalf of the anti-prohibitionists was the wholesale druggist W.O. Smith. The prohibitionists were represented by the incumbent mayor, James Olive, a Carleton shipbuilder of Methodist persuasion. Olive won the election by a vote of 1108 to 768, carrying every ward with the exceptions of Kings and Sydney, in a victory that paralleled that of the Liberals in the city a few weeks later.[67] The committed rummies were reduced to three on the thirteen-member council.

The temperance forces thus controlled the Common Council from 1853. With Olive in the mayor's chair, they could have achieved a large part of the prohibitionists program at any time by simply denying tavern and retail liquor licences to anyone in the city. Yet despite this fact, the council did not act through 1853. Nowhere was the understanding of the limitations of power more clearly revealed than on this issue at this time. Council could regulate but it could not prohibit.[68]

In the end it was Olive who took the initiative on the issue. Following his city-wide election in April 1854, he announced that he would accept the council's advice on whether or not to grant tavern and wholesale liquor licences in the coming year. After a prolonged and spirited debate, a resolution not to issue any liquor licences to freemen or freeholders of the city passed on a 10 to 3 vote. The council's decision and the passage of the provincial prohibitory act, which was to come into effect on 1 January 1856 – just three years following the passage of the Massachusetts act – created a situation in the city akin to a civil war. As tensions mounted, a motion by Nowlin to rescind the resolution on the tavern licences was carried by a one-vote majority when three temperance advocates broke ranks and voted with the anti-prohibitionists.[69] The temperance advocates had stuck to their compromise: there would be liquor provided for consumption in regulated public places, but none for private consumption.

When total prohibition descended, the already tense situation deteriorated rapidly. The law was condemned and flouted not only by the transient, but also by most of the prominent citizenry of Saint John. Led by *The Courier* editor, Henry Chubb, its opponents included the police magistrate and most of the leading merchants, lawyers, functionaries, and Roman Catholics.[70] In the face of open defiance of the law by a substantial part of the community, including those functionaries sworn to uphold the law, James Olive found his principal task one of enforcement. Since the bureaucracies charged with that function could not be trusted, Olive turned to those who possessed an ideological commitment toward the destruction of the liquor traffic. The employment of the Sons of Temperance and other prohibitionists to enforce the act set half the city spying on the other half. The more effective the prohibitionists were in this task, the more bitterly divided the city became. The *Temperance Telegraph* defended the practice. T.W. Anglin replied in the Catholic *Morning Freemen*, 'but when the advocates of a mighty moral reformation attempt to make the character of the informer and spy, an honourable one ... and insist that we should submit to this horrid loathsome system with thankfulness it is time to express the horror and indignation such conduct always excites.'[71]

The debate over what constituted social improvement and the means that should be employed to accomplish it came to an abrupt end in the special session of the New Brunswick Legislature called in the summer of 1856 for the express purpose of repealing the prohibitory act. Whatever the virtue of the great experiment, its effects on the Sons of Temperance were disastrous in the short run. The animosities created by the effort to impose prohibition and the potential for social violence revealed during the dry period stunned many prohibitionists. For many, the commitment required to remain in such a controversial organization outweighed any social benefits it might bring. Membership losses between 1854 and 1856 were heavy. The Saint John area divisions lost about 400 of their 1800 members, although most of the decline was in Portland where membership was halved.[72] A more gradual decline continued into the early 1860s when Saint John membership bottomed out at 1000 before beginning to rise again. In 1854, the city contained nearly 40 per cent of the provincial membership; this proportion declined to one-third in the late 1850s. Even so, the temperance movement remained urbanly based; Saint John at mid-century accounted for about 15 per cent of the provincial population.[73]

By 1857, the movement had recovered from the crises of prohibition. In his address to the Grand Division in 1857, the grand scribe of the order, W.H.A. Keans, described those who remained as 'a band of sons ... for the sole purpose of advancing the true and with real interest in the work of reform ... to persevere to the end in the sacred cause of human progress ... *The good must eventually triumph*. The God, in whom we rely, will turn and overturn until this destructive foe of our race shall meet with a doom proportional to his deserts.'[74] Keans's statement is probably a reasonable reflection of the attitudes of those who had persevered in the conflict. If the changes in the leadership of the Saint John order were any reflection of the rank and file membership, then Keans's evaluation was probably accurate. It is notable that among the twenty-seven new officers who can be identified, there is a small proportion of men from high-status and white-collar occupations and a corresponding rise of those of lower socio-economic origins. If, as is almost certain, the 1850 leadership was not characteristic of the social background of the typical prohibitionist, then it seems likely that many of the higher-status members had withdrawn from positions of leadership and their places had been taken by the more steadfast rank and file. Certainly the high proportion of non-native born, particularly the presence of a substantial number of Irish Protestants among the later group, would seem to confirm this hypothesis.

By 1857, the equilibrium of 1852 had been restored. Smashers and rummies continued to stare at each other over a psychological and cultural chasm and to mutter calumnies about the evils and weaknesses inherent in the other's position. Prohibitionists, by and large, contented themselves with the tactics of the earlier period: to minimize access to alcohol and to drive the taverns into clearly defined districts. Not that their hope for the final moral victory and the subsequent rise of a Brave New World was forsaken, but the idea developed the more intangible quality of an idea whose time had not yet come.

The North American temperance movement was the liveliest child of early nineteenth-century evangelicalism. As such, temperance supporters were generally the spear carriers of a broad evangelical culture. Each of its three manifestations reflected tendencies within the parent movement. The early Temperance Society was a mildly meliorist expression of the traditional paternalistic concerns of the establishment for the well-being of the community. By contrast, Protestant and Catholic abstainers shared a common pietism and a determination to create viable cultures within the framework of the traditional community; their approach came closest to creating a genuine pluralism within the city. Prohibition was a genuinely radical movement. Its social ideal was the unitary comprehensive community that its followers proposed to remake within the framework of their own culture. The derivative nature of the temperance issue was reflected in the reaction of Catholic abstainers to the prohibitionist proposal. They quite correctly recognized the move as part of a program arising out of evangelical sensibilities and assumptions. None of this denies the role of utilitarian motives or the self-interest of employers who saw in the temperance movement the means of securing order within the city and greater efficiency among their journeymen. There were certainly individuals within all of the temperance organizations motivated by these views. But they do not provide an adequate explanation for the emergence, the strength, and the persistence of the movement. That must be seen in terms of the ideological world-view provided by evangelicalism. And that world-view was one that redefined the very notion of respectability – replacing status, position, or class with attitude and behaviour. In the same way, total abstinence and the organizational and behavioural patterns associated with it conferred respectability on large numbers of Irish Catholic labourers whose station in life remained unchanged.[75]

~8~

Education

Education, like temperance, was one of the movements for betterment that characterized the nineteenth century in most English-speaking societies. Both movements contributed in significant ways to the debate over community in Saint John because they placed activities previously viewed as matters of private discretion into the public sphere. The nurture of the young at the beginning of the century was a private undertaking carried out at the discretion of parents or guardians. Over the next half-century, no educational system emerged but parents were offered a number of options for their children, almost all of them subsidized in some fashion by the provincial government. The Saint John experience before 1860, like that of New York, emulated developments in England where a variety of private institutions coexisted with Sunday schools, subsidized monitorial schools, and a number of sectarian institutions.[1] This pluralism was a mark of the urban condition in New Brunswick: only the city contained the concentration of population and interests that could sustain such an exotic variety of educational experiences. Since the nurture of the young was an expression of a culture and essential to its survival, the creation of public educational institutions became a central concern to leaders of all cultural traditions. Their attempts to define what was essential to the well-being of the child, and what role the state should play in the child's formation, did much to remake and extend community in Saint John. Because of their broader and less complex program, evangelicals were most easily able to shape the new order to produce a system both utilitarian and biblical in emphasis. In these activities they came closest to expressing the needs and interests of the artisans and small freeholders who composed such a large part of their constituency.

Financial provision for the education of the New Brunswick young before 1802 was limited to the schoolmasters that the Society for the Propagation of the Gospel provided to each missionary. The only public regulation of the educational process was through the requirements that those proposing to teach be licensed by the governor, and the statute binding apprentices to their masters. The Parish Schools Act of 1802 provided £10 a year for one teacher in each parish.[2]

The most important act, under which the city's public schools functioned until the 1850s, was the one of 1816. This provided three parish trustees for the east-side parish of St John and three for the west-side parish of Carleton, all appointed by the quarter sessions. Each of these groups of trustees was permitted to grant £20 a year to each of three teachers maintaining schools within their parish boundaries. In 1833 the act was amended to provide grants for up to eight teachers in each parish when the parents raised £30 in fees for each teacher. Although a number of administrative changes occurred in the next twenty years, this was, for all practical purposes, the city's public common school system.[3]

The unconcern demonstrated by the provincial government for the elementary education of its citizenry was never evident when it came to deal with the education of the small élite that desired a secondary education. The Saint John Grammar School was founded as a private corporation in 1805. Its administration was entrusted to a self-perpetuating board of directors chaired by the rector of Saint John. The provincial government made an annual grant of £100 toward the salary of the master.[4] The Saint John Grammar School was the principal college preparatory school in the province and, with the Fredericton Collegiate School, provided most of the student body of King's College. With few exceptions, its students were drawn from prominent families within the city and surrounding suburbs.

Apart from this limited external intervention, the educational services of Saint John were generated within the city by a number of private entrepreneurs. The services they offered were essentially a reflection of the social status and expectations of those clients they hoped to attract. A handful of business men and professionals maintained private tutors or governesses who lived with the family.[5] Other high-status families sent their sons to fashionable residential schools. For young ladies of prosperous or ambitious parents, there were late-afternoon classes in music, French, needlework, and dancing offered by respectable single ladies proclaiming Old World backgrounds.[6]

Many highly respectable families of modest means and some expectations found the financial burdens of such instruction onerous. They, along with many master craftsmen and some artisans, mechanics, and labourers, turned to the numerous private masters who offered a wide variety of programs for a price, usually accepting students from small children to adolescents.[7] For most artisan families and for many ambitious labourers, literacy was simply the first step to an apprenticeship in an appropriate trade or as a merchant's clerk. These arrangements were usually made between the ages of twelve and fourteen and young men wishing to improve their skills were invited to Mr Wilson's evening classes in globe and geography or to Mr Gibb's 'evening classes for young gentlemen' in English, bookkeeping, maps, and trigonometry.[8] The schools were a market activity in which independent teachers offered their reputations and a variety of curricular wares in an effort to attract and hold the patronage of city parents who could or would spend £2 or £3 a year for the instruction of each child. In most cases, concerned parents of even modest means probably got the kind of training they desired for their children.

It is impossible to determine the number of parents who provided these opportunities for their children or the proportion of city children receiving some formal instruction before 1820. It is unlikely that any of the children of the institutionalized poor, the seasonably employed urban proletariat of the port, or the black population received any kind of formal education. Even the parish schools required fees that were substantial in terms of the 1s. 5d. to 2s. a day wage earned by a labourer of the period. Parish school teachers received their £20 grants only when parents of the 30 or 40 children in the school had contributed £30. Even where 60 children enrolled with each teacher, a day labourer would have to pay tuition fees equivalent to six days' wages for each child.

The earliest concerns expressed for children of such families were from the evangelicals of the city and their concerns were coached not in economic but in religious terms: knowledge and interpretation of scripture was fundamental to the process of salvation. Like their English and American counterparts, Saint John evangelicals turned to the Sunday school as a means of providing a basic literacy to the young. While the original English schools had been established to impose social discipline, they had increasingly passed into the control of dedicated evangelicals, many of working background, whose motives were primarily religious.[9] In accordance with their basic purpose, Sunday schools emphasized reading in preference to other skills and the primary vehicles of instruction were the scriptures and catechisms. While the schools doubtless became means of proselytizing among the poor, they were first developed on behalf of the children of poorer families within the congregation and were seen as a form of benevolence. The first Sunday school in the city was organized as early as 1809 in conjunction with the

Wesleyan Methodist Chapel several years after a series of revivals had brought hundreds of converts into that denomination, many of them from the poorer elements of the city's population. It was sustained for many years through public subscription. Presbyterians, Episcopalians, and Baptists followed suit after 1815; by the early 1820s the Sunday school had become a significant element in the education of Saint John youth.[10]

The movement was given an impetus in 1818 when the established church, under the patronage of the lieutenant-governor, determined to exercise its mandate to provide for the spiritual welfare of the city as a whole by introducing the national school system. The National or Madras School was one of two monitorial charity systems established in England in the early nineteenth century to provide an education for the children of the less affluent. The systems were claimed to be both cheap and effective. A single teacher could instruct a hundred or more students through the use of monitors. The first of the monitorial systems was the Royal Lancastrian Society (later the British and Foreign School Society) founded by Joseph Lancaster in 1808. Lancaster was a Quaker who created a school designed to accommodate the broadest spectrum of English people. The Bible was the moral centre of his curriculum and inculcation of its teaching became the distinctive characteristic of the system. Because of its efficiency and liberality, the Lancastrian system received the strong support of Wilberforce, Bentham, Mill, and the utilitarians, as well as most English non-conformists. The support of these groups raised the suspicions of English conservatives who saw in this, as in the Sunday-school movement, the hand of French Jacobins stirring the lower orders of society for some sinister purpose. In 1811, an Episcopal clergyman created the National School Society in opposition to the Lancastrian. Although the two systems were very similar in method, the curriculum of the National Society centred on the Book of Common Prayer and the catechism of the Church of England. With the full support of the established church, the National School rapidly became by far the largest of the two systems. Until mid-century, monitorial schools remained at the centre of the English educational system.[11]

The National School was brought into Halifax in 1816. The following year Major General George Stracey-Smythe encountered it when he was serving in Halifax as colonel-in-chief of British forces. On his appointment as lieutenant-governor of New Brunswick in 1818, Stracey-Smythe led the move to establish the schools in New Brunswick. With the assistance of the National Educational Society of England and the Society for the Propagation of the Gospel, the Central Madras School was opened in Saint John in 1818.[12] The following year came a royal charter, financial assistance from the public purse of New Brunswick, and a Saint John girls' school.[13]

Growth from that point on was rapid. In 1820, the legislature granted £1000 to the trustees of the new institution and new schools were created in a number of communities across the southern part of the province including a school for 'coloureds' at Saint John.[14] By 1822 the system had enrolled 2761 students including 953 in Saint John, 131 of them in the coloureds' school.[15] It seems possible that half the children of Saint John were affected in some measure by the Madras schools in the early 1820s, and among those 6–10 years old, the proportion was probably even higher.

The reason for the popularity of the schools is not difficult to find. With the substantial grants received from the province and the Society for the Propagation of the Gospel, the trustees were able to offer full-time schooling at very small prices. Initially parents paid 10s. to £2 a year, depending on their ability to pay.[16] Those who declared themselves paupers might have their children admitted free. There were 37 free scholars out of 224 in 1820 but the proportion of poor students rose rapidly as the system expanded.[17] A fourth Saint John school – Carleton – was opened in 1827.[18] By 1830, more than 80 per cent of the student body consisted of free students, including all of the students in the African (black) and Carleton schools and about two-thirds of those in the east-side boys' and girls' schools.[19]

The provision of an organized new school system under trained teachers at bargain prices caused a movement into the schools of children from non-Episcopal families and created a growing anxiety on the part of many dissenters that the schools were devised to proselytize dissenters. The secretary of the trustees, E.J. Jarvis, tried to allay these fears by pointing out that such children were sent to their own churches on Sunday.[20] In his reply, Jarvis either missed or deliberately ignored the point of the debate. The Madras schools had been established explicitly for the purpose of teaching the 'principles of religion' as imparted by the established church, and the transmission of useful knowledge.[21] An hour on Sunday was scarcely an antidote for six days of careful Episcopal indoctrination.

The Madras School was one of the principal issues in the 'Holy War' that so soured relations between Episcopalians and Presbyterians between 1817 and 1830. The Madras system and the grammar school gave the Church of England a virtual monopoly on cheap, publicly supported education in the decade after 1818, and there is little doubt that dissenters perceived the Madras system and the creation of King's College by royal charter in 1829 as part of a tory plan to create a fully developed state church in the province and the city.[22]

But the dissenters' fears did not materialize. The reasons would seem to be the hostility of the dissenters and the failure of the Madras system itself. That failure was in part the result of the initial success that the system enjoyed. In 1819, two teachers instructed 200 Saint John students. Within three years nearly 1000 children were taught by three teachers. The ratio was reduced in later years, but 250 students to a teacher stretched even the capacities if the flexible monitorial system.[23] Moreover, in the boom of the 1820s many teachers sought employment in the timber trade and were replaced by poor untrained Irish teachers. The decline in esteem in which the school was held was reflected in the declining enrolment of the late 1820s and particularly in the flight of children from more prosperous families. The province reduced its support for the system in 1829 and by 1830 enrolment in the schools had fallen to 520, over 80 per cent of whom were free students.[24] The costs of this schooling totalled £400 a year – about 15s. a pupil – of which the province paid £240 and the Society for the Propagation of the Gospel, £105. The provincial grants at that time were exactly four times the amount available to the parish schools.

The objections of Protestant dissenters to the Episcopalian monopoly of the urban charity schools were seconded in the growing Roman Catholic community. There is no evidence of any private Roman Catholic schools before 1827. Prosperous Catholics apparently enrolled their children in the parish schools or in the variety of specialized private schools available. Children from poorer Catholic families either received no formal education or, after 1818, attended the Madras schools.

Early in 1827, the pastor of St Malachi's, John Carroll, organized a free school for the education of children from poor Catholic families. Operating on subscriptions raised within the Catholic parish, the school employed two teachers and enrolled 87 boys and 97 girls. The economic downturn of 1828 made it impossible to collect many of the subscriptions and the parish finished the year with a debt. In the winter of 1828–29, Carroll petitioned the legislature for a grant to cover the debt. The grant was refused but the executive council apparently promised that if the school acquired licensed teachers, they would be eligible for the common school grants of £20 for each teacher. On the strength of this promise, Carroll acquired two licensed teachers and continued to operate the school at a deficit. Unfortunately, the county magistrates failed to appoint school trustees in 1829 and the expected grants were not forthcoming. Early in 1830, the Catholics again petitioned for a grant of £178 from the public funds of the province to cover the greater part of two years' expense.[25] In an unprecedented move, the executive council assented to this request. As a result of this decision there were in 1830 approximately 620 free students in Saint John schools – 420 in the Madras and 200 in the

Catholic. A rough calculation using the 1824 and 1834 Census data suggests that perhaps one child in four between the ages of six and fourteen was enrolled in a free school during 1829–30. If teacher/student ratios are any indication of quality, the education received in both of these systems was not very good. Given the size of its classes – roughly 100 students in each – the Catholic school must have operated on a modified monitorial system. Both systems were plagued by wildly fluctuating levels of attendance: only half as many students appeared in winter as in summer and average daily attendance was only a fraction of total enrolment. Even so, a child exposed irregularly to several years of such experience acquired a rote knowledge of fundamental Episcopalian or Roman Catholic doctrine and the basic skills necessary to read simple passages, do sums, and even write a few words.

Still, the lot of the free Catholic school was not an easy one. The provincial grant was not statutory. The parish was required to petition the assembly each year and was dependent on the goodwill of the Committee on Supply, which alone possessed the authority to insert the grant into the budget. The school ceased operation in the early 1830s and was revived in 1836 by James Dunphy, who argued that 300 Catholic children were growing up in ignorance because of the poverty of their parents.[26] He petitioned for support for his seminary and there is some evidence that, in most years, grants were made to the Catholic free school. *The Courier* reported in 1842 that the quarter sessions had examined the 'Free School not in connection with the Madras School' and that provincial grants had been forthcoming for the support of its two teachers. These provided nearly nine-tenths of the school's income.[27]

Following the consecration of Bishop Dollard in 1843, the position of the schools vis-à-vis the government improved immensely. The annual grants for all Catholic schools were generally handled as a patronage between the bishop and a member of the provincial executive council.[28] Following the entente between the governor and the bishop in 1846, the Roman Catholic Free School allowance was given each year without hindrance and the grants were extended to permit the creation of Catholic schools in Portland and Carleton. By 1860, the Saint John and Carleton schools provided an elementary education for 557 students, all of whom studied Christian doctrine, while a majority studied spelling, reading, singing, writing, and needlework, and small numbers attempted grammar, geography, history, philosophy, and composition.[29]

Only the Protestant dissenters failed to achieve denominational free schools before 1840. The only group of Protestant dissenters that had attempted to establish publicly supported sectarian schools of its own was the Calvinist Baptist. The children of dissenters attended private schools or parish schools, if their parent could afford the fees; if they could not, the options were the Sunday schools, the Madras School, or no school at all.[30] Surprisingly, apart from the Presbyterian protests, there was little effort made to rectify this state of affairs. The size and activity of the dissenters' Sunday schools and of the Sunday School Union, which they formed in the early 1820s, would seem to indicate that this part-time institution serviced by voluntary workers played an important role among the city poor. The lack of protest over the Madras School probably reflected the unwillingness of the most numerous body of dissenters, the Wesleyans, to challenge the position of the Church of England. The Wesleyans possessed the constituency, the respectable though socially modest leadership, and the children of poorer families that stood to be drawn into the Episcopalian tradition. Yet there is no evidence that the denomination responded to this threat at any point before 1830.

Despite the divisiveness of the education issue, evangelicals within and without the established church continued to co-operate in a number of educational and charitable activities after the arrival of Dr B.G. Gray as rector of Saint John in 1825. Episcopalians, Presbyterians, and Methodists established the Infant School of Saint John through private subscription. Opened in 1834, the school taught moral and religious principles and inculcated 'kindliness of feelings' to about forty children aged three to six from poor families who paid a penny a week.[31] In 1853 the evangelicals established two Ragged schools in Saint John. The Ragged schools had been founded in southern England in 1844 by Lord Shaftsbury and other prominent evangelicals as a means of providing for street urchins and those abandoned by their parents. Using voluntary teachers, the schools attempted to convert 'incipient criminals to Christianity.'[32] The Saint John schools were more broadly based than their English counterparts and accepted children from any family of limited means. They were attached to St James Church and functioned under the direction of its rector. About one-third of the students were admitted free; the remainder paid 7s. 6d. a year. From 1854 onwards the province made an annual grant of £50 to the committee.[33]

Evangelicals also took considerable interest in the education of the city's black population. The Madras system had originally maintained a school for black children. The school was never popular with the Madras trustees who in 1823 threatened to cut it if their funds were not increased.[34] By 1840, despite some efforts of the Carleton school trustees, there were no school facilities for blacks anywhere in the city with the exception of the Sunday schools.[35] In the autumn of 1840, a number of evangelicals established a school for blacks on the east side, using the facilities of the new Baptist Chapel. The school was the centre of a public controversy from the start, with charges by many townspeople that it was a common nuisance.[36] The issue came to a head when the blacks of Carleton petitioned Common Council to allow their children free use of the ferry to attend the east-side school.[37] Despite support from prominent evangelicals, the motion was defeated on the grounds that such a move would be unfair to poor white children. The blacks of Carleton subsequently applied to the legislature for school support, which was granted while supporters of the east-side school tried to have it designated a normal school for teacher training so that it would be eligible for grants.[38] The latter was not forthcoming and the schools continued a precarious existence under the leadership of ad hoc African School committees, which generally succeeded in acquiring annual grants from the province and in raising sufficient funds to maintain a free school.[39]

Through voluntary Sunday schools and special schools for infants, blacks, and ragged children, evangelicals could provide educational services for limited numbers of children through personal benevolence. After 1840, Protestant dissenters gradually developed common evangelical alternatives to the sectarianism of the Madras system. In accordance with their almost mystical faith in the efficacy of scripture, this new way took the form of an education that was at one and the same time profoundly religious, yet strictly non-sectarian.

The evangelical emphasis on non-sectarian charity schools was replaced after 1840 by a demand for a public, subsidized, useful education designed to prepare young men for specific trades. In the countryside this was generally perceived as training in agriculture, following a basic primary education. In Saint John it was seen as training in the application of scientific principles to technical problems encountered in the mechanical trades. These scientific utilitarians brought several new and important emphases to the debate over education. Their influence reflected the growth of the technical trade, particularly those relating to metals technology during the 1830s. The principal promoters of useful education were drawn from the city's physicians, merchants, and master mechanics. Their program was aimed at the creation of a skilled work-force. Although it offered a training from basic literacy to adult education, the program was designed as an alternative to the classical education of the grammar school.

The first concrete proposals for practical education were brought forward by the master founder Robert Foulis. Foulis was born in Scotland and studied at the University of Glasgow and the Andersonian Institution.[40] In 1838, he proposed to teach evening classes in natural philosophy, chemistry, and mechanics for the benefit of the junior mechanics of the city.[41] Foulis received a grant from the provincial legislature to procure 'philosophical apparatus' and opened his academy in August 1838. He offered three-month specialized courses to artisans at 5d. each and admitted forty-seven free students through a system by which employers were able to recommend deserving young men for the course.[42]

The success of the evening classes led Foulis and his backers to petition for a second grant in 1839 in order to mount another set of lectures on natural philosophy and chemistry to which all mechanics and apprentices were invited to attend free once a week. The interest created by these courses contributed to the decision to create the Mechanics Institute, and the institute reciprocated by forming an academy of arts in autumn 1839 that offered evening classes for apprentices. The academy provided arithmetic, mensuration, land surveying and navigation, penmanship, drafting, French and English, and Latin and Greek at fees of 7s. 6d. a quarter.[43]

The Mechanics Institute took final form in 1841 with the erection of a building containing eight classrooms and a hall capable of seating 800.[44] Here were established a day school for children to supplement the evening classes, a library, and a collection of scientific apparatus for use in experiment. In addition, from the time of its formation, the institute provided a series of evening lectures for the membership at large. These covered a wide variety of subjects relating to natural science, technology, and political economy. The speakers of these series ranged from the provincial geologist, Abraham Gesner, to the botanist Asa Gray, to Foulis, to the father of modern geology, Charles Lyell, to the theologian and economist Rev. W.T. Wishart. Gesner, who participated in the exploitation of the province's mineral resources in the 1830s and 1840s, played a leading role in the organization of the St John Athenaeum for the promotion of useful knowledge and the application of science in 1841. The following year he hired an apartment and opened one of the first museums in British North America.[45]

The great public interest in useful scientific knowledge received a sudden setback in the prolonged depression of the early 1840s, when nearly half its membership abandoned the organization forcing it to discontinue its day school and leaving nearly 100 boys without schooling.[46] As the city began to recover after 1844, the educational plans of the institute leaders began to merge with those of the radical evangelicals. This development was not surprising. Every religious denomination is a social as well as religious reality. While Methodist, Baptist, and Free Presbyterian membership was found in all economic and occupational groups, their leadership was clustered in the artisan community. Relationships were particularly close between the institute and the Presbyterian clergy, most of whom showed a keen interest in scientific studies. In his much publicized lectures on political economy over the winter of 1844–45, W.T. Wishart argued for a provincial system of practical education that would comprehend a central school board as well as local trustees, and a strong single college of literature and science 'uncontaminated by the pollution of sect.'[47] The Bible would be presented and moral precepts taught as part of a curriculum emphasizing objective knowledge. In this he was reiterating appeals made by Saint John Presbyterian laity in the 1830s.[48]

Wishart's addresses occurred the same autumn as the arrival of the English Congregational Union minister J.C. Galloway. In March 1845, Galloway, in a public letter, proposed the creation of a British and Foreign School Society in Saint John.[49] This society employed the Lancastrian monitorial teaching system, the traditional non-sectarian rival of the Madras system. Although largely confined to the dissenters in England, the smaller British and Foreign School Society had rapidly spread into much of the continent of Europe and into the United States where its religious but non-sectarian tenets made it popular in the denominational pluralism of that society. At the time of their arrival in Saint John, the Lancastrian schools were the major publicly supported schools in the city of New York.[50]

The idea to create a non-sectarian monitorial school had obviously been earlier broached with the city's evangelical leadership, for within two weeks a public meeting was held at the Mechanics Institute at which resolutions favouring the undertaking were passed and a subscription list opened.[51] A 'sound, practical and useful English education' was offered to potential patrons, one in which the Bible would be read daily and its fundamental truths impressed on students. The meeting elected a committee containing representatives of each of the principal Protestant denominations in the city. By summer the committee had engaged E.H. Duval, a Bristol schoolmaster of the British School Society.[52] The school opened in September in the Mechanics Institute. Classes were held from nine to twelve and from two until four each day. Mechanics Institute members were permitted to enrol one child for 5s. a quarter. Second and third children from the same family were admitted at reduced rates. The children of non-members paid twice the fees charged to members.[53]

The new school quickly developed a reputation as the best in the city, a distinction enhanced by the fact that its members' fees were only half those charged by the parish schools. Within six months of its founding the school contained 140 day students and 50 apprentices in its evening course. On petition, the 'British School in St. John' was granted £100 by the legislature in 1846. It became the first charity school granted to the city's Protestant dissenters. A second master was sent for to assist Duval and on his arrival the school committee planned to turn the school into a normal school for the training of masters for service in British schools across the province. The provincial grant was repeated in 1847 and 1848.[54]

The grant of provincial funds for the British School characterized the shift in political influence in the province between 1836 and 1846. Gone was an executive and legislative council representing a clear sense of purpose and a single consistent policy. Instead influence had shifted to the more malleable assembly in which a variety of interests contended. This latitudinarianism permitted the government to simultaneously sustain policies and positions advocated by high church, radical evangelical, and Roman Catholic partisans in respect to education, public institutions, and Episcopal establishment.

Official interest in the British school system also reflected a growing crisis in the parish and grammar schools of the province. Concern with the quality of instruction led the assembly in 1844 to appoint a committee to investigate the situation. The committee's report indicted the grammar schools for gross inefficiency, sparing only those of Saint John and Northumberland.[55] Similar concerns with the lack of system or standards in the parish schools led to a new Parish Schools Act in 1847 that provided for training and model schools offering a basic three-month training course for all teachers.[56] The executive council selected the British School of Saint John to be the model school for the new system and Duval instructed forty parish school teachers from southern New Brunswick during the first year of the new order.[57] As a consequence, the British School was adopted into the parish school system and its annual grants were paid by the Board of Education. The following year, the Fredericton training school burned and the British School became the normal school for the province. Duval trained all the new teachers and granted all of the first- and second-class licences until 1859 when he was appointed one of the four provincial inspectors responsible for supervising the parish school system.[58]

The integration of the British School into the parish school system was followed in 1851 by the creation of another private school based on modified Lancastrian ideas whose promoters reflected many of the influences of the Massachusetts school reformers of the same period.[59] The Commercial School was designed to offer 'a sound, cheap and suitable education' to the 'middle class' children of mechanics and shopkeepers. Aiming at older children, the founders of the school deprecated the 'expensive and limited advantages of the Grammar School' and offered instead a syllabus that included history, mensuration, land surveying, navigation, bookkeeping, trigonometry, geometry, algebra, astronomy, natural philosophy, logic, chemistry, Latin, and French, in addition to the elementary subjects. This wide variety of subjects was taught by five teachers who divided the 200 students into departments each superintended by a teacher and each providing a 'state of study' through which a student progressed. All of this closely resembled the monitorial system. The Commercial School differed sharply from them in an important respect: teaching was conducted entirely through the inductive method and duty was 'morally enforced' without the use of corporal punishment. Parents of children in the school petitioned for and received a provincial grant of £150 in 1852 and 1853. With its broad array of specialized useful education, its austere teaching of 'moral values' and Bible reading, and its modest cost, the school won strong support from virtually all evangelicals including the Episcopalian clergy. By 1854, Henry Chubb and a number of others were petitioning that it be raised to the status of a public grammar school.[60] This was not done, but the Commercial School remained an important element in the education of the children of the city's artisan community. Following Duval's resignation in 1859, the master of the Commercial School became the master of the Normal Training School and the Commercial School became the new model school for the system.

By 1860, the Lancastrian ideal had come to shape the parish school system. The reasons for this development were not difficult to find. The strength of the radical evangelicals in the villages and rural areas of the province was irresistible. They composed a majority of the population of most rural parishes of the province by 1860 and could probably determine, in a clear majority of cases, who would sit in the House of Assembly.[61] The principal rival traditions were heavily concentrated in Saint John and in the large towns of Fredericton, St Andrews, and Chatham. The Madras system reflected this cultural reality in withdrawing from the villages and concentrating in the urban centres. Distinctive Roman Catholic charity schools only developed in these same areas.

Saint John did not conform to the provincial society. In addition to the statutory parish and grammar schools, the province gave substantial and sustained support to Church of England and Roman Catholic charity schools and to inter-denominational British and commercial schools. The government's open policy in fact spurred a resurgence of denominationalism after 1850. For many denominational leaders, the possibility of establishing denominational schools offered an opportunity to meet the rising social expectations of young men in their churches. The schools they created reflected a determination to create a system in which they could produce their own business and professional leaders. The moves were also an implicit rejection of the Episcopalian-controlled grammar school.

There was a growing number of upwardly mobile men within the dissenting denominations. There had always been a few small business men among the Wesleyans, but by 1850 there were a number of modestly prominent self-made merchants, grocers, and master artisans in the communion seeking educational opportunities for their sons. Typical of the group was Mark Varley, who began his career as a carpenter and died a merchant in 1852. Varley left a sum of money to be used for the creation of a denominational Methodist school in the city. The following year the city circuit established the Varley School, which Robert Cooney described as 'strictly and legally Wesleyan under the trustees of the St John chapels.'[62] The school received the £100 provincial grant during the first year of operation and that grant was continued without interruption for the next twenty years.[63] By 1860, its male and female departments were taught by two first-class licensed teachers and it had an enrolment of 164 students of whom 30 were free scholars.[64]

In 1847, the Irish Presbyterians of St John's Church under the leadership of Rev. Robert Irvine established the Presbyterian Seminary directed by two teachers, one a graduate of Glasgow, the other of Dublin.[65] The new institution offered instruction to students from age eight to twenty-one in a variety of subjects including the classics, natural philosophy, mathematics, logic, and grammar. Arguing that the Episcopalian, Roman, Methodist, and Baptist schools all received provincial assistance, the Presbyterians requested support as well. The school grant of £100 was made in 1848, rejected by the Legislative Council in 1849, and made again in 1850.[66] The Presbyterian Seminary does not appear to have survived the early 1850s. In the 1850s, the Free Will Baptist Conference debated the educational issue several times and finally agreed on the necessity to control their own secondary education in order to provide for the young men of their community. There is no indication that the Saint John school they authorized was ever actually established.[67] Finally, in 1860, the Calvinist Baptists brought the former principal of Horton Academy to the city and founded the Saint John High School. Offering full English and classical courses, the school was home to 147 students in 1861. Despite the support of every Baptist minister and leading laymen in the city, the school did not receive a government grant until after 1866.[68]

Despite the patchwork nature of the city's educational systems and the frequent ominous reports of public education officials about the illiterates to be found on all sides, there seems to be little doubt that by 1851 most Saint John children – and certainly all of those whose parents had any concern for the matter – were receiving the elements of a basic primary education. In their discussions of the rate of child participation in the education system, professional educators always ignored the non-parish schools and provided a misleading and sometimes grossly distorted picture of the educational services offered in the city. In fact, it is probable that the rate of participation in organized schools by children aged six to fourteen had been steadily rising throughout the 1840s, after declining sharply under the impact of rapid growth and heavy immigration in the 1830s.

The 1851 Census revealed that more than 60 per cent of all children six to fourteen were attending school for some part of the year, a far cry from the 12 per cent of six-to-sixteen-year-olds cited by provincial educational authorities in 1858,[69] and a proportion that compared favourably to that of New York City where a similar variety of school systems existed.[70] There was, of course, considerable variation in participation rates among classes and between sexes. The occupation of the family head did play some role in determining whether or not children attended school. Grocers were more likely to send their children to school than were labourers and the instruction was probably of a higher quality. The difference between white-collar workers and unskilled labourers was not so much that the children of the latter did not participate in the schools, but that they were more likely to participate selectively. In most families, however, there seems to have been little distinction between the education of the young male and young female. Unfortunately, the census question was so broad that it is impossible to determine the number of years of schooling each child had or whether this was taken in the parish or charity schools or in one of the denominational or inter-denominational institutions. Qualitative evidence and the grammar school record would seem to indicate that sexual distinctions in education did not begin until the completion of elementary instruction. It is doubtful if any young woman studied beyond the basic English course. Children who did not attend school were overwhelmingly concentrated in families headed by women, by relatives other than parents, or by fathers who were lodgers.

The expansion of a plural ad hoc educational system in the city led to a growing demand for its rationalization. Spokesmen for this position were usually laissez-faire liberals who argued their case in terms of equality, economic utility, and the necessity to have a single academically strong system that would reflect and serve the community.[71] This theme was most persistent in the writings of Presbyterian leaders who argued that all knowledge was of God and that the state had a duty to create a properly educated citizenry that could think and work and vote.

A similar theme characterized the position of Henry Chubb and *The Courier*. Chubb represented the utilitarian opinion that had opposed King's College in the 1830s and supported the Mechanics Institute and the British School in the 1840s. By the early 1850s, Chubb was particularly anxious to establish a strong parish school network. In 1851 he advocated the creation of a free parish school in each ward, maintained by public assessment on the whole population of the ward. Two years later he proposed the creation of a single large public academy for the city. Arguing that many parents paid for sectarian or foreign schools, but that what was needed was a 'good' domestic seminary, Chubb suggested that a commission drawn from all denominations should nationalize the Grammar School and use it as the basis of a non-sectarian public academy employing several good teachers and offering a variety of useful courses.[72]

The Liberal electoral triumph in 1856 was hailed by both evangelicals and utilitarians as the beginning of the new era when the old shibboleths and antiquated forms and institutions would be swept away. The creation of an adequate educational system to enable the province to function in the new world was clearly one of the principal purposes of the reformers. The debate over the proper nature of education was fought on several fronts and embraced interrelated issues. The first was the question of the nature of the parish schools: should they be sectarian, religious, or non-religious? The second concerned the non-parish schools: should they continue to be supported by the state, or integrated into the parish schools, or left as private schools? A third concerned the problem of access for children from poorer homes.

In all of this, *The Courier*'s position was clear. It was the duty of the state to put a secular education within reach of every member of the community since 'self-maintenance requires a competent education.' Moreover, in any true meritocracy, there must be equality of opportunity and this could only be provided by common education. To accomplish this there must be universal assessment, compulsory attendance, and a common secular curriculum. To accomplish the latter, even the Bible must be banned from the class-room, since it was a denominational book in the eyes of the Roman Catholics.[73] As the organ of the Reform party, *The Courier* acted as a lightning-rod drawing the attacks of all opposing parties. By the end of 1857, *The Courier* was at war with the Catholic *Freeman* whose editor, T.W. Anglin, assailed the idea of non-religious education as atheism and the proposal for assessment for state schools as a scheme to provide incomes for an army of Smasher placemen.[74] *The Freeman*, instead, demanded that a distinctive Roman Catholic school system be assured.[75] The Episcopalian *Church Witness*, not surprisingly, advocated the retention of the Madras schools and supported the evangelical position in demanding that the scriptures and moral training based on Christian ideals be an integral part of the parish schools. The Free Will Baptist Conference declared a common school was possible only if the Bible was required and the government through them, 'fearlessly sustain the Protestant Character of our nationality and institutions.[76]

Baptists and Methodists had been perennial non-conformists. Their mistrust of government and the authority it wielded ran deep. In the final analysis, while the Free Will Baptists were prepared to accept compulsory common schools under certain circumstances, they felt that the absolute equality of denominations and the education 'most satisfactory and safe for the religious character of youth' could be best assured by giving each denomination the appropriate educational institutions. Clearly Roman Catholics and Free Will Baptists agreed that in the 'rendering,' children were of the category that belonged to God not to Caesar. The bishop and more than 1700 Saint John Catholic parishioners petitioned the legislature requesting that, if the new school law provided for general taxation for school purposes, Catholics be permitted to establish separate schools in the districts where this tax was levied.[77]

The response to both the utilitarians and the Roman Catholics was delivered by the city's leading evangelicals. In two petitions, containing the same signatures, they asked that no school law be enacted that did not require that the scriptures be used in tax-supported schools, and that the law be preserved from all sectarian provisions.[79] The extent of the evangelical consensus by 1858 is revealed by the fact that a document that claimed that all sectarian provisions were distasteful to the Protestants of the country was signed by every Church of England clergyman in the city and its suburbs. In fact, both petitions were headed by virtually all the Protestant clergy in the city. Apart from the clergy, the petitions were of as much interest for those who did not sign as those who did. The core signatures were evangelicals active in other arenas. The petitions contained a sprinkling of evangelical merchants, but the great mass of the signatures were drawn from the artisans, mechanics, grocers, and labourers of the city. Notable by their absence were virtually all of the great merchants of the city and most of its leading functionaries and lawyers.

In the end the evangelicals achieved their ends in the 1858 School Act. Despite the opposition of utilitarians, they succeeded in imposing a religious but non-sectarian philosophy on the common school system.[80] At the same time, the denominational charity schools remained and continued to draw public funds at the suffrance of the legislature.

By 1860 the city of Saint John possessed a mixed public/private educational system that was largely denominational in nature; Old England rather than New was its model. Reflecting the maturity and strength of their cultures, Episcopalians, Catholics, and evangelicals all maintained separate school systems, the latter often in conjunction with utilitarian liberals. In addition, the evangelicals, whose religious demands on any educational system were more ecumenical, had succeeded in imposing their program upon the common schools. The efforts to create denominational or inter-denominational schools tell a good deal about the social aspirations of denominational leaders and their determination to create a society in which each significant culture group would possess the means both to form its members and to allow them to participate in the larger community of the city.

~9~

The Anatomy of
Political Reform

Temperance and education were two of the great urban reform movements of mid-nineteenth-century Saint John. The third was that of the civic political institutions. The demand for reform of public institutions had become endemic throughout the empire by mid-century, and the passage of the English Municipal Reform Act in 1835 made the notion of municipal reform not only possible but even respectable.[1] The conditions that precipitated the English act – the growing urban network, the claims of corruption, and the perceived inadequacies of ancient charter and custom – were present in Saint John.[2] To the demands of interest, class, and culture were added the problem of providing the basic services and infrastructure needed to create a safe and orderly environment. By 1850, the idea of reform – the concept that the human condition could and should be improved – had become part of the world-view of a substantial part of the Saint John citizenry. Yet when municipal reform occurred within the city, it was a product of the needs and tensions of the several local interests and cultures. The rhetoric of the English utilitarians and liberals was used as justification for change but in practice the result often reversed the trends prevailing in the mother country. While the reforms frequently permitted a more rational and liberal administration, they also aimed at restricting the franchise, enhancing the influence of freeholders, and curtailing the powers of the Common Council.

Reformers' comments revealed, more than anything else, the changing standards of public morality. Just as the temperance forces accomplished their greatest victory in changing public views of dietary proscriptions, so too reformers – often temperance supporters as well – proscribed much of the traditional behaviour of the Common Council.

This process was abetted by the sometimes questionable behaviour of the more cavalier aldermen who sought personal advantage from their office and from the opportunities afforded by the city's expansion. The first indication of these changing views of what was publicly permissible arose in connection with the issue of conflict of interest on the part of individual councillors.

Criticisms were heard in 1835 in connection with the lease of corporation lands.[3] The city held ownership of several hundred lots of land on the two peninsulas, along the waterfront and on the Carleton Flats, most of which were rented on twenty-one-year leases. Critics charged that many leases had been granted at a private auction. While this was a somewhat unusual practice, the lease of corporation lots in each ward had been considered one of the traditional prerogatives of the aldermen and assistants from the wards. The criticism seemed to suggest that the patronage that was in the gift of a legally elected alderman was not his to grant as he chose. The protests apparently produced some effect, for after 1835 auctions of public lands were frequently held and the committee responsible for making the leases always contained councillors from outside the ward concerned. Even so, the Common Council never surrendered its prerogative to lease the public lands and public works in any manner it chose. Arrangements were often made privately between the land committees and potential lessees, particularly where some form of development was expected. In 1836, Alderman Van Horne of Sydney was awarded a lease on two Sydney water lots by a committee of which he was a member. Three years later, Alderman Coram of Guys was given a thirty-five-year lease on Guys land by the council without benefit of public auction and was later given a lease of the municipal steam ferry. The following year and again in 1844, Alderman Bond of Brooks received leases on land in his ward despite the fact that, in the first instance, he was a member of the committee making the award.[4]

Critics further argued that a number of councillors were law-breakers. In several cases this was demonstrably true. Perhaps the most persistent offender against the ethics of political purity was Alderman Van Horne. His public experiences were frequently an embarrassment to council and doubtless played a role in shaping the view of the council held by a substantial part of respectable public opinion. Van Horne was an inveterate trespasser on corporation lands. In 1835, a committee consisting of aldermen Porter and Lockhart had recommended that Van Horne either pay rental on five lots on which he had squatted or that they be sold at public auction. Their recommendation was apparently ignored, for by 1841 Van Horne occupied fifteen lots comprising 700 feet of prime river-front land. As a reward for his pains, when the council decided to create the office of police clerk at £100 a year in 1836, Van Horne was appointed to fill the office.[5]

Van Horne was also an inveterate manipulator of elections. Having secured election to the aldermanic office in 1833, Van Horne resorted to a number of questionable devices in order to secure his re-election in 1834. This, combined with Van Horne's unpopularity among the more respectable citizens, produced a storm of protest. In response to this pressure, council proceeded to remove both Van Horne and the assistant elected with him.[6] Five days later Van Horne submitted the opinion of the solicitor general that the Common Council had no legal authority to remove a councillor except on conviction of a crime.

Faced with this argument the council acquiesced.[7] The citizenry at large did not. The Sydney election scandal became the basis for the first mass protest of the citizenry against the prerogatives of the Common Council. A petition signed by 361 of the most respectable citizens was prepared for the 1835 sitting of the legislasture.[8] In earlier discussions of the franchise, the law officers of the crown had offered the opinion that the intention of the charter was to restrict the freedom of the city to the offspring of the original grantees and to protect the political and economic rights of those who were already freemen. The petition reflected this position and demanded that the freedom of the city be restricted to sons of freemen who had served an apprenticeship in the city. Newcomers who were British subjects might be admitted as freemen on payment of £25 instead of the £2–5 charged at the time, a change that would bring Saint John practice into conformity with that of most British cities. Although the petitioners argued that this was their purpose – and the petition did appear within a few years of the English Municipal Corporations Act – the views expressed by the petition clearly reflected the fears of both freeholders (that political power could become a monopoly of the propertyless) and natives (that they would be subsumed by the incoming migrants). The signatories to the petition made up perhaps one-third of the city's freemen in 1835, including not only the great merchants, functionaries, and patricians, but a broad cross-section drawn from every element of the native population – artisans, tradesmen, and Wesleyans being liberally represented among their number. The proposals were rejected in a 5 to 4 vote for Common Council through the efforts of a populist majority on council led by Stanton, Harding, and Van Horne.[9]

The efforts of the petitioners were opposed by a counter-petition led by Harding and Van Horne and supported by 127 petitioners drawn largely from among Irish-Protestant and Catholic freemen. About 40 per cent of the signatories to the counter-petition can be identified as Sons of Erin.[10]

Given the resistance of the Common Council, the legislature did not act on the requested reforms of 1835. The 1835 petition was the earliest and most impressive indication of public dissatisfaction with the council; it was by no means the only one. If many citizens perceived the old vices as unacceptable, they still demanded the old virtues of their representatives. Traditionally the councillors had paid for their authority with free service. As the scope of those services broadened, councillors asked the same remuneration that other office holders under the city received for public services. In 1838 they voted themselves per diem salaries of 7s. 6d. for time actually spent in Common Council – perhaps £10 a year – a move that provoked unfavourable comment from the high tory press.[11] A council decision in 1841 to pay each councillor a flat annual fee of £50 occasioned an even stronger outburst on the part of the editor of the *New Brunswicker*.[12] The issue divided the council itself, with the merchant-councillors generally opposing the grant while the master- and artisan-councillors favoured it.[13]

The public debate over the behaviour and responsibilities of councillors was replicated in the council itself. If some councillors took advantage of the charter for their own purposes, their strongest opposition after 1835 was found within the council. Indeed, throughout the 1830s there was a growing and vocal element on the council expressing dissatisfaction with the worst abuses of the system. The group lost more struggles than it won, but its presence on the board provided a considerable impetus to change. While its personnel changed over time, the consistency of the voting patterns of its leading members gave it the quality of a party which, by drawing a few loose fish, could sometimes win important votes. Its leading spokesman was the Guys alderman, Robert Salter, a Wesleyan circuit steward and prohibitionist. Its other principal supporters were the Kings aldermen and assistant, Henry Porter and Joseph Fairweather, and the Queens alderman and assistant, John Humbert and Robert Ray. Faithweather, Salter, and their followers argued that functions such as the harbour steam-ferry service should be operated by private enterprise under lease rather than by the council itself (they lost the ferry issue on a 7 to 5 vote), proposed that no councillor should hold a position of employment under the Common Council (they succeeded in this 8 to 3), supported efforts to widen the streets of the Burnt District (lost 7 to 5), opposed the leasing of corporation lands to councillors (failed 7 to 5), were prepared to tax the city at large to assist the water company in completing its system (failed 7 to 6), and supported the city chamberlain in his battle with its critics over financial policy (succeeded 6 to 5). Their positions on most issues emphasized purity in public life coupled with a belief in progress and efficiency. As a group, these puritans and liberal magistrates were small merchants and masters of native origins. Most of

them had strong temperance connections and perhaps half were Wesleyans. They were the councillors of the two largest and most complex
wards.

Their opponents were the supporters of the old way. On important
issues, the conservatives were as consistent and identifiable as the
puritan liberals. Their core members were the long-term aldermen and
assistants from Dukes and Sydney wards: Thomas Harding, Gregory Van
Horne, William Hagarty, and Ewan Cameron. Together with the support
they could gather in Carleton, the traditionalists were the dominant
element in the council before 1849. It was this group that successfully
defied the provincial government in 1839, arguing for the inviolability of
the charter on the street-widening issue. The conservatives had a lower
status in the community than did their opponents, numbering carpenters,
fishermen, and tanners in their ranks. While their leaders were native
born, virtually all the Irish councillors supported the traditionalist
position. Conservatives were as prepared to engage in development
strategies as were liberals; they differed from them in the means through
which that end would be accomplished and in their willingness to use the
charter powers to protect the economic interests of the city's freemen.
Finally, the conservatives were not necessarily tory in philosophy –
indeed, there is a good deal of evidence to suggest that most of the city's
leading tories (supporters of an established Church of England) placed
their trust only in the provincial executive council. Harding, for example,
was a prominent Baptist and a leader of the Total Abstinence Society. Far
from being élitists, the traditionalists jealously guarded the popular
nature of their mandate. They were, in fact, populist conservatives.

Despite the multi-motivated criticisms of its personnel and activities,
the record of the Common Council in the critical years between 1825 and
1841 is impressive. Using the resources at hand and the organizational
structure of the traditional town, the council made the adjustment from
the role of conservator to that of developer with considerable ease. The
infrastructure needed for expansion of harbour and streets was formed.
Two steam ferries were built, and substantial public buildings, major
marketing facilities, a cholera hospital, a poor house, and a pest house
were erected; development of a water system and sewerage facilities was
encouraged; roads and fire equipment were upgraded; public squares and
gardens built; scavenger service and street lighting expanded; and a
permanent night-watch put in place.

The Common Council's ability to play such a dynamic role in the city's
development after 1830 was largely a function of its financial policies. The
financing of the city before 1820 was simple. Revenues were raised from
the sale of licences and freedoms, from the rent of corporation revenues

(largely harbour revenues such as wharfage and anchorage), and from the rent of corporation lands. In addition, taxes for particular purposes could be levied on the population at large by statute, although these levies were usually limited to specific sums. As for most nineteenth-century municipalities, Saint John's financial resources were absurdly small.[14] Until 1830 the city's cash flow generally remained under £4000 a year.[15]

In the early 1820s, financial difficulties began to emerge. Traditionally, capital costs were treated as part of the current account and the liability was carried in the form of promissory notes drawn on the city corporation and payable on demand. These were issued in the form of small notes and of corporation notes. Small notes had their origins in 1820 when there was a severe shortage of circulating medium in the colony. At that time, the Common Council issued several thousands of promissory notes in small denominations (6d., 1s., 2s., 2s. 6d.), which were accepted as currency by the city's business men. By 1835 more than 40,000 small notes valued at £5000 had been issued, and by increasing their number or by calling them in and burning them, the Common Council was able to exercise at least a minor moderating effect in the local economy.[16] The small notes permitted the chamberlain to meet short-term obligations through payment of city notes, which the recipient could use as currency within the city. Watchmen, lampmen, and road workers, none of whom were involved in the external economy, could be paid in small notes.

By far the most important element in municipal finance in the 1820s was the corporation note made payable to a single individual. Since the corporation was the most stable entity in the colony, the notes worked entirely to the advantage of the creditor. They yielded 5–8 per cent, well above British or New England securities, and the note holder could demand payment on thirty days' notice. By 1830 these notes totalled £10,000 held by twenty prominent citizens.[17]

Such instruments, while useful in carrying short-term debt, were simply not adequate to the city's long-term needs. To procure the social capital needed for its development, the city required a secure and growing source of revenue out of which it could amortize the interest on any debt and build up a sinking fund. The strategy was planned and implemented by the chamberlain, John R. Partelow, perhaps the leading financial authority in the colony. In 1830, Partelow reorganized the financial structure of the city, creating a permanent funded debt composed of city bonds issued for three, six, nine, or twelve years.[18] The costs of the scheme were to be met from the rental of several hundred corporation lots, the value of which rose sharply as pressure on limited urban land increased.[19]

The capital so raised permitted the orderly development of urban facilities. Between 1830 and 1840 the city's debt rose from £10,000 to £70,000, and as expansion reached its peak in 1841, two-thirds of the city's £34,000 expenditure was raised from borrowings. By 1842 the funded debt stood at £106,000. In addition, a private water company had invested more than £20,000 in the construction of a pumping station and reservoir and several miles of pipes.[20]

Partelow's strategy of debt management was a sound one but it did require a considerable expenditure of capital in order to raise capital. The expansion of the city into undeveloped areas enabled the Common Council to negotiate profitable leases on unused lots, but the most valuable parts of the corporation lands, the lots and water privileges in the city centre and along the waterfront, were already in leasehold. When these leases expired, the city had a choice of either renewing the lease at a rent agreeable to the lessee or purchasing the improvements on the land and leasing to another tenant. The latter was ultimately the key to the strategy, but it was a costly procedure.

The development of the Carleton waterfront proved particularly profitable. In October 1836 alone, the Common Council leased 164 of the corporation's Carleton flat lots at an annual rental of £1032. In all, between 1828 and 1842, revenues from land rentals rose from £905 to £3473. By 1840, rental revenues alone were sufficient to carry the city's debt. As late as 1842, Partelow calculated the current value of the corporation's leasehold at £140,000 and argued that the city could carry that amount of debt without difficulty. The strategy seemed vindicated.[21]

What Partelow and his Common Council masters could not foresee were the twin disasters of fire, which in 1841 destroyed a large part of the harbour area, and the collapse of the carrying trade a few months later. In order to meet the city's capital requirements, the chamberlain was at first forced to negotiate high-interest loans with Boston and Halifax financial interests, and finally to set about the painful process of hawking bonds at discount among even the meanest capitalists in the city.[22]

The economic stagnation continued into the spring and summer of 1842. Artisans, masters, grocers, and even merchants joined the poorer elements of society in the common ruin. Even the city corporation could not long escape the consequences of such a general and prolonged depression. By the autumn of 1841, council revenues were dramatically reduced by the inability of a large part of the population to pay its assessments and hundreds of city leaseholds had fallen into arrears as business men were unable to fulfil their contracts. In November, the chamberlain reported that only £400 of £5000 owed the city by lessees of corporation lands and renters of corporation revenues had been collected.[23] Efforts to secure bank support were futile. The provincial government, in even more desperate straits, had already entered the money market and its borrowings, together with the problems of a number of financially embarrassed merchant customers, had effectively reduced the circulation of the city banks from £360,000 to £50,000.[24]

Instead of assisting the beleaguered city, the banks demanded repayment of current loans. Several bond holders refused to renew their bonds when they fell due in the summer of 1841. Desperate, the chamberlain borrowed in Halifax, Boston, and Fredericton on an almost non-existent capital market, paying high-interest rates and selling the notes to the lenders at substantial discounts on their face value.[25] By the beginning of 1842 even these efforts proved fruitless and the city was unable to make interest payments on its bonds, much less redeem £5000 in bonds held by the New Brunswick Marine Insurance Company, which fell due early in 1842. The company proceeded to institute proceedings in the Supreme Court against the city for collection of its capital. The company's appeal was successful and in February 1842 the high sheriff of Saint John seized the property of the city under a Supreme Court writ. The action was symbolic rather than real; having established its prior claim to corporation assets, the company agreed to take a mortgage on certain city property.[26]

The suit and the subsequent judgment provided the enemies of the Common Council with a long-sought opportunity. Following several attacks on the council by the editor of *The New Brunswicker*, the high sheriff called a public meeting at the Court House on 18 February. Public meetings served as a forum for the views of the most prominent elements in Saint John society in much the same way as the grand jury reflected the views of the middling orders. The meeting drew a large audience and was addressed by a substantial part of the legal fraternity. Early in the meeting it became obvious that the goal of the organizers was to secure the suspension of the charter and to replace the Common Council with commissioners appointed by the lieutenant-governor in council. During the prolonged debate, the Common Council was condemned as a corrupt body, but a majority of those present drew back at the prospect of a 'root and branch' solution to the problem and contented themselves with a resolution to 'turf out the rascals' in the April elections.[27]

The crisis was resolved in September when thirty-three bond holders agreed to a Common Council proposal to create a trust, held by a committee of bond holders, which would receive a mortgage on all city real-estate and corporation rents and revenues.[28] The trust deed was effective for one year. Under its terms, the chamberlain was to pay to the trustees the rents and revenues from city assets. From this money, a 3 per cent dividend would be paid to the bond holders; another 3 per cent interest would be added to the capital value of the bonds and interest paid on it. On 22

September the mortgage was turned over to the trustees. In the meantime, the Common Council sought the aid of the lieutenant-governor in their efforts to secure a £100,000 loan on the English money market.[29] This move failed and after the first year, the trust deed was renewed regularly until 1850 with 5 per cent annual dividends paid to the bond holders and another 1 per cent added to the capital sum held by bond holders.[30]

The respite thus earned was a costly victory. The trustees were harsh task masters: the chamberlain was hounded and sued for making financial agreements that allowed bonuses and high-interest rates to many bond holders, the city was forced to pay 6 per cent interest on many bonds bearing only 5 per cent interest rates, and the Common Council was forbidden to borrow further until the entire debt had been repaid.[31] The last was a serious and unreasonable restriction. Under ordinary circumstances, the city was quite capable of carrying a substantial debt. Indeed much of the reason for the city's financial embarrassment was the failure of a number of merchants, some of them bond holders, to pay the rentals they owed the corporation. The restriction also seriously diminished the capacity of the Common Council to intervene in any significant way in the local economy or to participate in the urban development of the period. This, in the view of its patrician and great-merchant opponents, was all to the good. It provided economy in government and limited the opportunities for corruption and maladministration on the part of the venial councillors.

In the long run, however, it was a grave and costly error. The political and social instincts of the petite bourgeoisie that dominated the civic administration were more correct than were those of their opponents. Council expenditures fell from £32,000 in 1841 to £6000 in 1843 – roughly back to their 1830 levels – and public spending did not rise significantly until the 1850s.[32] This crippling of the Common Council was certainly a contributing factor to the collapse of the old order and to the social violence that began to plague the community late in 1842.

The bond holders, to whose will the council became largely captive, represented a broad cross-section of the city's social establishment. The largest – each holding between £4000 and £12,000 in city bonds – were the Bank of British North America, the chamberlain John Partelow, the merchant Nehemiah Merritt, the priest James Dunphy, the Bank of New Brunswick, the Marine Insurance Company, and the Saint John Savings Bank. Beyond these were three broad groups of individuals each holding between £100 and £3000 in bonds. The largest of these groups were the great merchant families, including the Blisses and Johnstons, the Lawtons and Leavitts, the Merritts and Wiggenses, the Jarvises and Robertsons. The second was a group of rentiers drawn heavily from widows and daughters of prominent families and from the legal functionaries. Finally, there were a few outsiders, such as J.B. Uniacke of Halifax and the firm of Dana, Fenno and Hershaw of Boston.[33]

The most important of these bond holders were the great merchants, not only because of the size of their personal holdings but because they dominated the directorates of the financial institutions. Their participation in the process is informative because a number of them, including at least one of the five trustees, the Honourable John Robertson, had been among those embarrassed leaseholders of the city who had several months earlier declared their inability to make payment on their leases. Robertson's position is particularly instructive in this connection. As mayor of the city during the expansionary years 1836–38 and owner of a large Carleton sawmill, he had taken long-term leases on 93 corporations lots in the Carleton town plot and later acquired an additional 48 lots on the Carleton Flats.[34] The rents on these remained unpaid and by 1843 totalled £744. Robertson later refused to surrender his share of the trust deed until the city forgave him some £600 that he owed on leased city lots and agreed to release him from unprofitable leases he held on 146 corporation lots.[35] A second trustee, William Wright, retained possession of corporation lots on which the rents had not been paid, on the advice of the recorder. Fearful of Wright's influence, the Common Council decided to drop the suit of ejectment that had been started.[36]

Ironically the attacks on the council system resulted, by 1843, in the retirement or defeat of most of the puritan liberals who had been most critical of the old council system, including Henry Porter, Robert Salter, and Robert Ray. The determination of the public meeting of February 1842 to oust 'the rascals' resulted in patricians and prominent merchants running against and securing the overthrow of several incumbent councillors. Two great merchants and a distinguished lawyer carried the banner into the civic elections. B.L. Peters secured election as alderman for Queens in 1841, defeating John Humbert, and the following year John Thurger succeeded Porter in Kings. Even *The Courier* mourned the loss of Porter, noting that 'no other councillor will be as honest as he had been.'[37] However, the newcomers had no success against the populist conservatives. Robert Crookshank's run against Van Horne in Sydney resulted in a rout for the notables, and they did not even make an attempt against Harding in Dukes. By 1843, Peters, Thurger, and Crookshank had disappeared from the civic scene. Battered and modified, the old council system survived.

In the minds of many the problem lay in the franchise. *The New Brunswicker* argued that the lowness of the franchise 'throws the preponderance of elected power into the hands of a class of men, little gifted with reflection and forethought and exceedingly open to election-eering *influence* and the interests of patronage, generally causes the election of civic representatives to fall, not on men *best qualified* to discharge the duty, but on those whom the *office* and station are most needful and important.'[38]

Within the Common Council, pressure mounted for reform of the charter itself. Salter's proposal that the charter was defective gained sufficient support that in 1842 a committee of council was created to study ways of meeting the objections of charter critics. Salter had a good deal of support in the city. Early in 1843 a group of 113 leading Saint John business men, most of whom were known for their progressive senti-ments, simultaneously petitioned the Common Council and legislature for a thorough reform of the 'defective' provisions of the charter. Their three-point proposal provides a useful insight into the nature of the puritan liberal view of the city and its constitution. In an effort to restrict the franchise to the most responsible elements within the city, the petitioners asked that the vote be restricted to freeholders and freemen who were tenants or owners of tenements of a yearly value of £15 and whose taxes were paid. Freemen who met these conditions would be permitted to vote for councillors but membership in the Common Council itself would be restricted to freeholders. The petitioners further asked for the abrogation of the judicial authority of the mayor and aldermen and their replacement by a permanent stipendary magistrate and a well-organized police force. Finally, they proposed to abandon the protection afforded freemen of the city ('a Policy so illiberal and exclusive appears ... calculated to banish to other quarters much of the capital industry skill and science which might otherwise flow in from abroad') by authorizing the mayor and Common Council to grant licences at an annual fee to non-freedmen.[39]

Predictably the electoral proposals created a public furore. A hundred freemen from modest circumstances, representing both Irish and native born, hastily prepared a counter-petition to Common Council in which they condemned the franchise proposal 'as measures calculated to create uncalled for distinction in the community, by rendering the industrious tax paying and really more useful portion of the people subservient to the advancement of a comparatively small number of wealthy individuals.'[40] The Common Council, reflecting the influence of the élite members elected in 1841–42, responded favourably to the reformers. After considerable discussion, the council rejected the proposals of a £15 tenancy for electors and stipendiary magistrate. It accepted all of the other recommendations and suggested that non-freemen British subjects be permitted to practise their vocations in the city on payment of an annual fee of £5; aliens would pay £20 for the same privilege. In addition, civic elections should be conducted by election commissioners in each ward. Finally, in a move obviously designed to entrench the position of the native population, council proposed that fees of £25 be charged for all freemen except those who were sons of freemen and had served a six-year apprenticeship in the city. These recommendations were accepted and forwarded to Fredericton with the prayer that they be made into law.[41]

The council's amendments only further fuelled the public debate on the franchise. The editor of *The Loyalist* sardonically observed that he did not opposed the £25 fee provided that it was applied to everyone and that it was applied retroactively.[42] The debate continued in the legislature, which finally incorporated all the Common Council proposals into a statute excepting the one relating to the franchise which was effectively left as it had been.[43] The new licence law permitted the licensing of non-freemen artisans at £1 a year, business men at £2, and aliens at £25 for all purposes.[44] In its first nine months of operation, sixteen non-freemen artisans and two alien merchants were licensed under the law.[45]

The legislation of 1843 was designed to cure a number of ills. The limiting of the council itself to freeholders, although not going nearly as far to restrict the electorate as many liberals had hoped, at least was expected to produce candidates of better quality. To control the incomes of council officers, the new law permitted the council to place all of its officers on salary and require them to turn over their fees to the chamberlain for the benefit of the general revenue. That privilege was only gradually exercised largely because, under the straitened circumstances of 1843, it was to the council's advantage to leave the traditional structure in place. The chamberlain had already been placed on salary and the harbour master, sheriff, and coroner soon followed, but the recorder and clerk cloaked themselves in the charter and refused to be bound by the law; it was not until 1845 that the duties and emoluments of these officers were finally fixed.[46]

The 1843 settlement was only a truce between the liberal puritans and the conservative populist factions on council. On the latter side, neither Harding nor Van Horne was effected by the new regulations and their positions on the franchise question made them even more popular among the artisans and labourers who composed the great majority of their electorates. Their capacity to assist that constituency had been limited by the events of 1841–43, but so too was the capacity of the liberal remnant to continue its task of building a great city. After the initial wave of enthusiasm that had brought the élite into the political arena had subsided – certainly by 1844 – leadership of the council quickly reverted to the government of small merchants and masters who had traditionally dominated its proceedings. In the main its policies were conservative, displaying at one and the same time the traditional veneration of authority coupled with a contemptuous deference to those in positions of wealth and authority.

The 1843 Act provided Fredericton with an effective veto over most council activities. All by-laws and regulations passed by Common Council were subject to the approval of the lieutenant-governor in council. The restricted funds available to the council meant that constant appeals for authority to tax had to be made to Fredericton for even the meanest undertaking. Most serious was the council's inability to deal with the peculiar problems of social violence that dominated and soured so much of the life of the city between 1842 and 1849. The growing dissatisfaction with the charter was manifest in the attacks on it by liberals like George Fenety, who perceived it as an anachronism surviving from an unenlightened age of despotism, an authority that permitted magistrates 'to do as they pleased' without restriction.[47] Like most liberals, Fenety was scandalized by the union of powers that permitted aldermen, who functioned as lawmakers and administrators, to also sit on the judiciary despite the fact that they possessed neither the detachment nor the professional qualifications to hold such an office.

The impasse between puritan liberals and populist conservatives was broken in 1848 with the entry of William Henry Needham into the political arena. An attorney and a Baptist of Loyalist origins, Needham had devoted his early career to the reconciliation of native, Protestant-Irish, and Catholic-Irish elements within the city. He had served both as provincial grand master of the Orange Order and as a vice-president of the St John Catholic Temperance Society. As the incidence of violence between the Irish factions rose in the middle 1840s, Needham seems to have withdrawn from a position of leadership within the Orange Order but still retained a considerable following among Irish Protestants. In contrast, despite his native origins, he was never entirely acceptable to much of the native population. None the less, in the context of the disintegrating community of the late 1840s, Needham seemed to offer the best opportunity for creating a consensus around which community could be re-created.

Needham's first step was to create a political program comprehending elements of both populist-conservative and puritan-liberal philosophies, designed to attract native and Irish Protestant and Catholic freemen of modest but respectable circumstance. The 1841 Common Council was attacked as oppressive, and the necessity for a root-and-branch reform of the city charter designed to produce a more representative and egalitarian government was emphasized. Needham was supported by a number of reform-minded council candidates, notably the small merchant, evangelical, and leading prohibitionist George A. Lockhart; the English-born prohibitionist William Keans; the Irish-Protestant minor merchant Thomas McAvity; and the Irish-Catholic storekeeper John Murphy. In the 1848 civic elections, Needham succeeded in defeating Henry Porter in Kings, Lockhart won the Queens aldermanic office from W.O. Smith, and Keans and McAvity secured election as assistants in Queens and Sydney. Murphy was defeated in his effort to overturn the puritan liberal Joseph Fairweather as assistant in Kings.

The Kings Ward election of 1848 is of particular interest because Needham and Murphy ran as a ticket in an effort to appeal to all major interests in the ward apart from the patrician and great-merchant élite. Murphy won in the initial vote but on protest by his opponent, 73 of his votes were found to be invalid and the election was awarded to Joseph Fairweather. The voting patterns in this contest provide a useful insight into the strength of ethnic, religious, and occupational loyalties. The great majority of Irish Catholics voted a Needham/Murphy ticket. The correlation was high, although less obvious, among Irish Protestants. The Fairwether/Murphy fight was largely decided on ethnic grounds, although Murphy drew more heavily among artisans and Fairweather among labourers and merchants.

In contrast to his running mate, Needham built up such a sizeable plurality over his opponents that even the disallowance of a number of his votes in no way threatened his position. He took only one-third of the business and professional votes, but captured nearly 60 per cent of the artisan vote and more than two-thirds of the votes of the semi-skilled and unskilled. In Queens Ward the same voting pattern was evident in the victories of Lockhart and Keans, except that the presence of the two evangelicals on the ticket did not provoke the religious division that cost Murphy his seat.

The newcomers wasted no time in establishing their purpose. On 22 April they persuaded Common Council to establish a committee to study possible charter changes. In some respects the task force resembled a committee of the whole council as care was taken to ensure that every point of view was adequately represented on the committee. In the end it contained not only Needham, Lockhart, and Keans but also Harding, Van Horne, and Bond from the populist conservatives and Fairweather from the remnants of the old reformers.

On 15 July the committee made its first report. After 'thorough investigation,' they had satisfied themselves that the charter was 'wholly inconsistent with the spirit of the times' and that in order 'to keep pace with the age' it was essential that the city should have a new constitution.[48] The new charter would emphasize rather than restrict the local democracy. Among tentative proposals was the annual election of the mayor from among the council members, the appointment of all charter officers by the Common Council rather than the lieutenant-governor in council, and the extension of the franchise. Only on the issue of the judiciary did they turn to the traditional liberal position: the alderman should surrender their authority as police magistrates to a stipendiary magistrate appointed by the Common Council. Three weeks later the committee brought in the remainder of its revisions. Kings Ward, because of its great population, should be divided into two wards, distinctions between aldermen and assistants should be abolished, aldermen should not be required to live in the ward they represented, the secret ballot should be instituted to ensure 'free unbiased returns,' two election commissioners and a voters register should be established for each ward, attachment should be abolished as a means of summoning persons to court, the authority of the city court should be extended to £10, the prohibition against 'coloured' persons acquiring their freedom – 'a relic of ancient barbarism, unfit even for the times when the charter was granted' – should be removed.[49]

The proposals split the council. When a resolution that the committee continue its deliberations was introduced at the 3 August meeting, Fairweather joined the four new reformers to split the council and permit the mayor to save the committee's life. Despite Fairweather's move, the Needham party had destroyed the political dichotomy of the council. Needham argued for a liberalism of the propertyless, one that would somehow combine personal and public integrity with efficiency, cheap government, and a form of participatory democracy in which power would be shared by all groups within the community. It was a potent brew, one that produced a considerable impact not only on the respectable poor but also on those radical evangelicals and Irish Roman Catholics who for so long had perceived themselves as victims of a powerful establishment. In effect Needham combined the concerns of liberals like Fenety with a demand for a more popularly based electorate to produce a form of populist liberalism.

The popularity of the new program was demonstrated in the early winter of 1848–49. On 3 November the charter committee announced that it had incorporated its proposals into a bill that would provide the city with a new charter. The following month, Needham presented Common Council with the petition of 785 men, claiming to be freemen and freeholders, and praying that the legislature would pass the bill.[50] On a straight 8 to 4 vote in a full council, the new reformers were defeated in their efforts to get council concurrence with the prayer of the petition.

Instead, the conservative majority on council decided to deal with the report on a section-by-section basis. Debate began on 21 December and continued at the sittings of 4, 16, 26, 29, and 30 January 1849. The debates were marred by great bitterness and the mayor was frequently unable to maintain order. Gradually, however, sufficient compromises were made in specific parts of the report to enable their passage. The keys to the issue were assistants Fairweather and Dunham, the last remaining representatives of the old puritan liberal reformers, who could give the populist liberals a bare majority. The hope that the aldermanic office would again be opened to all freemen was doomed; Fairweather and Dunham would agree to any liberalization in the nature or function of the office but were adamant that the property qualifications were necessary for election.[51] With compromises, most of the remainder of the bill was passed in a series of 6 to 5 votes. The new law reflected the curious combinations of compromises effected by the puritan and populist liberals. It did not extend the franchise or eliminate the property qualification for councillors, as its populist sponsors had hoped. It did legally prevent councillors from having positions of profit under the city, provided for an elected mayor and the appointment of all officers by the council, and created the city's first stipendiary magistrate and police force. In substance it represented more of a triumph for the puritan liberal ideal than that of Needham's populist liberalism.

Conservatives, on the council and off, attacked the bill with a blind fury. At three council meetings in February the conservative minority, led by Van Horne, attempted to prepare a bill that would withdraw the charter amendments sent to Fredericton. These efforts ended in failure when the reformers withdrew leaving the council without a quorum.[52] Failing in these efforts, the five dissidents, with the support of the mayor, prepared a petition to the legislature under the seal of the corporation asking that the bill not be assented to. The reformers responded to this action by calling a public meeting that passed resolutions of support for Needham and condemnation of the mayor, and sent them in petition to the legislature.[53]

The passage of the charter reforms in no way deterred the activities of the conservatives. With the defeat of Joseph Dunham in the April election, they once again controlled the council and sought to have the Queen disallow the provincial legislation.[54] The Great Riot of 1849, occurring just nine days after their request, assured the victory of the Needham party on the issue of separation of the legislative and judicial functions in municipal government. The symbol of the new way occurred in the early summer when the lieutenant-governor in council appointed B.L. Peters as police magistrate and control of the city watch passed into the hands of this provincial appointee and former puritan liberal aldermen.[55]

Needham and his followers had gained only part of their program in the 1849 legislation. They were never again able to mount so sustained an effort at charter reform or to face so sympathetic a council. The conservatives controlled the council from 1849 to 1851. Efforts by Needham to have apprentices admitted as freemen and to have freemen's fees reduced were turned back by one-vote majorities. Attempts to remove the business and trades monopoly held by freemen, to provide Americans equality with British subjects, and to offer the freedom of the city to black males over twenty-one who had been born in the city all went down to defeat.[56]

Most other concerns were at least partially accepted. Needham got general agreement in 1851 for the abolition of statute labour and its replacement by a street tax graduated to require from each taxpayer a payment of from 2s. 6d. to £3.15.0, depending on his wealth. The admission of Americans to the business life of the city on the same terms as British subjects who were not freemen was accomplished as the conservative strength began to ebb following the 1850 elections. The proposal for an elected mayor required two steps before the liberals attained their goal: in 1851, council agreed to petition for legislation permitting the electors of Saint John to elect their mayor from among the councillors; two years later, they agreed to ask for election at large.[57]

Needham retired from the council in 1852. By this time, however, the concerns of the populist liberals had been caught up in the image of the brave new world offered by the prohibitionists. A combination of all elements on council finally forced through the resolutions on the secret ballot and attempted to secure something approaching proportional representation on council by dividing Kings Ward into Kings and Wellington over the opposition of the small band of populist conservatives left on council by the autumn of 1852.[58] The creation of Wellington Ward, although designed to provide a more democratic system of representation, was perceived by many Carleton freemen as a threat to their influence in the government of the city. It provided the catalyst for an active west-side separatist movement that repeatedly attempted to create a town of Carleton in the late 1850s.

Defence of the ancient charter effectively ended by 1853. The new order was essentially liberal. Improvement and efficiency were its watchwords. The liberal system would emphasize water and sewage systems, professional fire and police departments. There was unity on little else. Issues of equality as opposed to responsibility were constant sources of debate throughout the remainder of the decade. Debate centred on the practical issues of whether or not to broaden the franchise, grant the vote to those freemen whose taxes had not been paid, and place a large part of the tax burden in the poll tax. But of all issues, the one that most divided council in the 1850s and in fact remade the alliance around which that body functioned was the prohibition question. From 1853 onward this amalgam of reformers, comprising elements from both the old puritan and populist traditions, remained dominant in the Common Council.

The symbol of the passing of an age occurred in two events in 1854 and 1855. On 11 April 1854, the Common Council decided to attend in a body the funeral of the thirty-times alderman of Dukes and first locally selected mayor of Saint John, Thomas Harding. Fifteen months later, his long-time ally, Alderman Gregory Van Horne of Sydney, died. The character and the institutions of the city in which they had grown up and sat as governors for so many years had been profoundly altered between 1840 and 1853. Equally distressing from their perspective were the changes in attitude and morality that accompanied and, in some cases, precipitated the changes. The most obvious victim of the changes was the view of the city as a confederation of wards united under the mayor. The informal relationships that bound the councillors to their electors and provided the basis of their personal authority were seriously eroded. So, too, was much of the extensive system of patronage through which so many activities of the ward were carried out and through which an informal social control had been exercised. The new civic administration was more comprehensive, less personal, better organized, less arbitrary but more capable of imposing its will on a broader front.

That change drew from several sources. External forces were important. The Irish migration of the 1840s and the determination of successive lieutenant-governors to impose English municipal practice in this British colony contributed to the change. Even more critical was the 1841–42 commercial crisis that left the traditional civic system helpless and at the mercy of its enemies. Much of the stress was internal. The traditional homogeneous village community could not be maintained in the face of a rapidly growing urban landscape densely settled by strangers. Traditional social controls failed but so did the physical amenities that had served the villages. The growth and subsequent pressure on limited civic resources exacerbated tensions among social groups within the city. The proportion of freeholders among the city's family heads certainly fell dramatically; the proportion of freemen probably did so as well. Many natives feared they would lose control of their city to the British migrants and moved to ensure their own control. Patricians and the well-to-do conspired to ensure their position against the claims of all propertyless freemen.

The political community changed significantly in the heat generated from this cauldron. The city-wide election of mayor and the proposed

city-wide election of aldermen, together with the professionalization of
the civic work-force, weakened the sense of ward identity. By the end of
the 1850s – as many leading merchants and professionals began to build
large homes in the suburbs – non-resident freeholders and freemen were
permitted to vote in the local aldermanic contests and attempts were made
to allow freeholders to vote in each ward in which they held property.[59]
At the same time, the poorest freemen effectively lost the provincial
franchise in 1855 when their traditional privilege of voting for the two city
members was replaced by a uniform provincial requirement.[60] The shift
from the ward to the city and from the aldermen to the civic professionals
was accompanied by a much greater uniformity of practice and discipline
within the city. The issue of which values and whose culture would
provide the basis of that uniformity became the burning question in civic
politics after 1840.

The Hon. John Robertson, c. 1860 (NBM)

~10~

Private Capital and
Public Purposes

All nineteenth-century cities were woefully underfinanced.[1] As the discussion in the preceding chapter has demonstrated, the Saint John council was forced to borrow heavily to provide the public works required in the expanding city. The city fathers of Saint John, like those of most British and British North American cities, did not attempt the development of public resources such as utilities and harbours.[2] Merchant ownership of the harbour wharves, the most valuable resource in any port, is used by Edward Pessen to demonstrate élite control of the city,[3] and the fact that the question never became an issue in Saint John lends credence to the position of the élitists.[4] Yet, while the place of the merchant as principal commercialist was never challenged, the relationship between the merchant élite and the regulating public trustees was more complex than the model suggests. Utilities posed still another problem. Water systems were treated as private enterprises in Toronto and in most English cities until after 1870.[5] Most were costly, provided modest returns unless regulated by legislation, and lacked a monopoly of the market. Saint John had one of the first fully developed public water utilities in British North America but the coercive implications of the development created the same debate that marked the prohibition and later the public-education issue. And the relationship between the citizens and the private utility strongly reflected the social tensions of the mid-century.

The distinction between private and public activities was only dimly drawn in early nineteenth-century Saint John. British eighteenth-century practice assumed that public offices were private benefices with which the crown endowed their occupants and this tradition was transmitted to the Loyalist city.

The blurring of distinctions between private and public activities was extended to the city as a corporation. In law, Saint John was a proprietorship holding the harbour and substantial land as tenant-in-chief from the crown. The charter defined the inalienable rights of property holders within the city and the primary responsibility of Common Council to ensure the protection of that property and the welfare of its owners. The corporation was, then, in the curious position of being a proprietor, frequently in economic competition with the major property holders within the city, and at the same time the public guardian charged with the protection of their property and the advancement of their welfare. Since the councillors were annual trustees of the corporation on behalf of the freemen and freeholders, it was possible for some prominent freeholders to secure election to the Common Council with a view to arranging the corporation resources in ways that were most advantageous to their interests. Since the Common Council was essentially only a broker in the organization and use of its own resources, it was wholly dependent on the private entrepreneur to utilize the land and harbour in such a way that would yield a revenue. There was at no time any suggestion that the corporation itself might make use of its own lands. The corporation confined itself to the provision of public market houses and non-profit institutions such as gaols, workhouses, hospitals, court houses, and poor houses. In the harbour the Common Council played a more active role constructing north and south market wharves and providing a ferry service between the two parts of the city. But even these facilities and services were normally leased at annual public auctions transferring the administration to private farmers.

As conservator of the harbour, the Common Council could regulate all uses to which it was put. The minimum improvement needed was the provision of piers and wharves. The core of the harbour was the waterfront of Kings and Queens wards on the north end of the eastern peninsula. At the time of the city's foundation the corporation had erected the North Market Wharf at the foot of King Street and the South Market Wharf in Queens, thus creating the market slip that became the centre of the city's commercial activity. Through this slip flowed the foodstuffs, fuel, and other material essential for the city's survival.

As the commerce of the port expanded in the late eighteenth century, the need for further wharving facilities became acute. This posed a problem, for while the corporation owned the water lots of the harbour, the land adjacent to them belonged to the city's leading merchants. Moreover, the capital cost of the structures was something the council was ill-prepared to pay, while the merchants eagerly sought this opportunity to enhance both the value of their property and its potential revenues by creating what one observer called 'the safest and most satisfactory investment in the province.'[6] Some owners of harbour-front lots in Kings and Queens were granted perpetual leases of water lots on the payment of annual rentals that varied depending on their size and location in the harbour.[7] In return they were required to build and maintain wharves to city specifications.[8] In all, 33 perpetual wharf leases were granted to Saint John merchants before 1820, 10 before 1800 and 23 after.[9] Once granted, wharf leases became part of the personal estates of the lessees – sometimes being sold to other business men, more often being passed on to sons or nephews on the demise of the lessee. By 1842 the Johnstone, Thurgar, Jarvis, Barlow, Leavitt, Tisdale, Gilbert, Wiggins, and Ward proprietorships all represented second-generation firms. While most great merchants possessed a wharf lease, several, like High Johnston Jr, David Hatfield, and Ezekiel Barlow, had acquired two. The rentals accruing to the city from these thrity-three lessees totalled just over £440 a year in 1842, a sum that greatly underrepresented their value under any reasonably prosperous circumstances.

By 1815 the harbour front of Kings and Queens wards was peppered with the wharves of the city's great merchants extending to the limits of their water lots. Those limits had been set at the low-water mark of the harbour in an effort to keep the main channel of the harbour clear and to prevent the accumulation of sediment on the harbour floor. The newer, larger timber ships that became a common feature of Saint John shipping after 1810 found the narrow slips and twice-daily beachings less convenient than did the smaller coasting vessels. The problem was exacerbated because of the one-to-three-week loading time required by these large vessels. A number of wharf owners lobbied for the privilege of extending their wharves below low water. The first to receive permission was C.I. Peters in 1815, and he was followed by David Hatfield in 1819. By 1822 a total of seven extended wharf leases had been granted. Typical of the lessees was Noah Disbrow who in 1820, while member of Common Council, received permission to extend his wharf eighty feet beyond its existing length. None the less, Common Council was acutely aware of the dangers of these installations and followed a policy of deliberately limiting their numbers. By 1842 only ten leases had been granted, nine of them in Queens Ward and one to Robert Rankine, entering the harbour from Portland.[10]

As the centre of the timber trade shifted from timber to deals in the 1830s, the Carleton sawmilling industry came to play an increasingly important role in the city economy. That decade witnessed a mad scramble on the part of the city's merchants to initiate development of the wharfing facilities on the Carleton harbour front. Here, however, a different situation prevailed. The corporation not only owned the water lots but also the tidal flats on which they fronted. Under the circumstances, the Common Council – now acutely aware of the potential value of its harbour resources – proposed a quite different form of wharf ownership for the west harbour than prevailed on the east side. When Craven Calverly petitioned to erect a wharf on the slip at the foot of Main Street, council agreed on the condition that the completed wharf would become city property on which the city would collect shippage and wharfage from all but Calverly and his heirs. A similar principle was extended to the construction of wharves on lots facing the Rodney, Wellington, and Nelson slips.[11] Here the lots were to be auctioned on thirty-five-year leases on condition that each lessee build a wharf within three years. These contracts required the corporation to buy the wharves at the end of thirty-five years, but relieved the city of the embarrassment of perpetual leases. On the north side of the Rodney Slip, thirty-five-year leases were granted on condition that a forty-foot-wide wharf be built and delivered up to the corporation for public use. Even so, the Carleton policy does not seem to have been aimed at giving the wharves to the city. Rather it provided the corporation with the opportunity of reassessing rental rates at regular intervals.

Even in the halcyon days of the 1830s, the council made no effort to expand the public presence. In fact, its policies seemed designed to strengthen the role of private interests in the harbour. In the face of demands for substantial harbour improvements, the corporation proceeded to seek alternative private sources of capital and enterprise. When the breakwater reached a state of disintegration in 1837, the Common Council decided to divide and lease it and the surrounding land. The lessee was given a provincial grant of £1000 toward the building of a 200-foot wharf at the breakwater and was to supervise the discharge of all ballast. Similarly, when in 1854 the need for deep-water wharves to accomodate the rapidly increasing number of first-class ships in port became imperative, the corporation – while admitting that these should be constructed by the city – declined to do so. Instead, John Robertson and David Waterbury were offered the opportunity to extend their wharves and were offered perpetual leases on the adjacent corporation land as an incentive.[12] Robertson's wharf lay next to the North Market Wharf and that, together with the corporation lands he would receive, would make him effective master of the upper harbour.

It was only in their efforts to establish adequate steamship facilities in the port that Common Council finally admitted defeat and went to the provincial legislature for permission to borrow the necessary capital. The steamship crisis was precipitated in 1848 with the proposal by Boston entrepreneurs to establish a regular ocean-going steamship service between Saint John and Boston. Neither Boston nor Saint John business men were prepared to invest in a facility that seemed to have such a small hope of showing profit. Finally in 1857, Common Council itself completed plans for the terminal.[13] The legislature was approached to grant the city authority to sell debentures to finance the enterprise and to assess the city £360 a year as a guarantee of the interest.

The problem of raising capital was perhaps the most important consideration behind the council's willingness to turn the administration of the harbour facilities over to private interests. As the possibilities of revenue growth from these facilities became more apparent after 1820, the council became increasingly reluctant to permanently alienate harbour resources through perpetual leases. Yet even if the council had possessed the power to abrogate the leases, there was little it could have done to achieve ownership of the facilities. Ideally, control of the harbour would also involve ownership of the harbour front lots in Kings and Queens. This constituted the most expensive real estate in the province. Many of these lots could demand £3000 exclusive of buildings or improvements. But even without the waterfront, the purchase of wharves and improvements on the water lots would have been far beyond the city's means. The corporation estimated the capital cost of the market wharves at £8000 in 1842.[14] While this cost would certainly exceed that of any of the forty-one private east-side wharves in that same year, an average value of half this sum would yield more than £160,000 – and many of the private wharves contained improvements and structures that added substantially to their value.

No issue created greater tensions within this closed circle than the question of extended wharves. The welfare of the harbour clearly required that the number of wharves extending below low water be limited and strictly controlled. At the same time, the advantages they offered were such that they would draw the trade of the largest and most profitable vessels leaving the less-profitable coasting trade to the smaller wharves. Charles Simonds was almost certainly correct in his assessment at the height of the harbour debate in 1833 that some merchants had used their influence with the Common Council to obtain the privilege of extending their wharves, and a few had even gone to the extent of securing election to council in order to ensure their lease. Others, such as the Johnstons, the Hatfields, the Peterses, undoubtedly used their considerable provincial influence to secure the right.[15] A number of other owners, lacking access to political influence, proceeded to build in defiance of council.

The running war between Common Council and its recalcitrant tenants is instructive of the uneven odds against the public authority operating in a system in which there was no strong, cohesive, and continuous executive authority. Common Council had two avenues of recourse. One was persuasion, a method in which councillors or officers of council pointed out to the culprit the illegal nature of the activity and the consequences that might flow from it. The other was an appeal to the Supreme Court – a long, arduous, and costly undertaking. If council was prepared to pursue the case to its conclusion, it could usually win, but the annual elections so rapidly changed the personnel and interests of council that only rarely did such an eventuality occur. As early as 1823, the council began proceedings against several owners who had illegally extended their wharves. One such case involved William Jarvis, who offered to give part of his land to facilitate entrance to the public slip if he were allowed to extend his wharf. Jarvis encountered a committee, composed of Peters, Ansley, and Robertson, that branded such compromises as blackmail and refused the offer. When Jarvis persisted in his efforts and proceeded to erect his wharf, the committee first ordered him to stop on pain of prosecution and finally retained the attorney general to proceed with the charge before the Supreme Court.[16] By the time the case was heard, the renovations had been completed. Yet few of these prosecutions seem to have been continued to their conclusion, and by 1832 the Common Council defended its stewardship of the harbour by arguing that, while there were many wharves extending below low water, only nine had been authorized by the council and the remainder represented encroachments by private individuals. Finally in 1839, in a remarkable declaration, the Common Council conceded the reality of the situation and ordered all of those who had extended wharves without permission to pay an annual fee. This concession only provoked a second wave of wharf extensions, including one by the former and future mayor, Lauchlan Donaldson, followed by the inevitable council resolution to protect the rights of the corporation. In 1853, the reform-dominated harbour committee noted bitterly that the resolution had never been enforced largely because of the council's weakened position after 1841.[17]

Another device used successfully by the great merchants against the Common Council was bluff. During a recession in 1839, those merchants who had signed leases to construct wharves on Rodney Slip announced that they could not fulfil their contracts. John Robertson simply declared that he would neither complete his wharf nor pay his rents on city lots. Faced with the collapse of the whole harbour development program or a lengthy and costly legal battle, the council acquiesced and relieved the lessees of all rents on the Rodney Slip lots for seven years.[18]

Despite the concerns expressed by the Common Council for the harbour, the issue of public as opposed to private operation was of small moment to the bulk of the civic electorate. So long as the harbour costs remained competitive with those in the surrounding estuaries, most towns-people were not prepared to challenge the wharf owners and merchants for its control. Indeed, the striking fact before 1860 was the small role the harbour played in the business of the Common Council. The myth of corporation sovereignty was maintained, but the interests of corporation and great merchant were so interwoven as to be almost indistinguishable in the popular mind.

Of much greater concern was the construction and operation of public works and utilities needed to service a growing urban population. Streets and steam ferries were clearly public undertakings. A few services were joint undertakings carried out by private and public resources. Most public works were purely the result of private initiatives. Among the latter were the Reversing Falls suspension bridge, the Portland Mills and Tunnel Company, and the gaslight enterprise.[19] The most successful of these was the gaslight company. In 1839, Abraham Gesner first proposed to make gas from New Brunswick coal. A joint stock company was finally organized by a group of great merchants in 1845.[20] After Common Council permitted the company to lay pipes through the city streets, the promoters acquired the contract to provide the city street lights. With this revenue guarantee, construction of the works was rapidly completed. In the autumn of 1846, gas-lit lamps came into service on the major city thoroughfares.[21] The company was an instant financial success. By 1850 it was providing gas to 140 street lamps and to 750 private homes and businesses through twenty-one miles of pipes; ten years later the number of customers had doubled.[22]

By far the most vital and controversial of the public services required by the city was the provision of water and sewerage. This more than any other single factor altered the quality of life in ways that made the European and North American nineteenth-century city a natural human habitat, the population of which could regenerate itself without a continual infusion of farm and village youth. In mid-nineteenth century Saint John, the presence of the water-and-sewer system divided the city into two distinct social groups just as effectively as the freedom divided it into political groups.

One of the earliest signs of the transition of Saint John from town to city was the impossibility of the private well and private waste disposal. The well-to-do who possessed their own systems continued to maintain them, but only at considerable risk as water contamination became a growing problem. The outhouse or privy had always been a luxury afforded only by the freeholder or house renter. For many city dwellers, the accumulation of human waste in pails and its disposal as 'night soil' in the streets or the harbour had been the common practice.

As the density of population increased, the disposal of excrement and other wastes became a medical and aesthetic problem of enormous proportions. These concerns were first expressed by neighbourhood groups seeking a collective solution through the technology of the common sewer. While the council had constructed common sewers as early as 1817, the neighbourhood proposals emerged as the city expanded in the late 1820s and continued through the next decade. The Union Street freeholders petitioned in 1827; the Germaine and Duke Street inhabitants in 1828; those of Brussels Street in 1835; of Germaine Street again in 1830; Duke Street (again), Dock Street, Colburg Street, and Dorchester Street in 1836.[23] Common Council was generally sympathetic to the plight of the petitioners but chary about the financial implications of the proposals. There was no question that collective action involved the public interest: any main sewer would have to run through the streets and empty into some common land.

In these circumstances, the city only gradually assumed responsibility for the undertakings. The Union Street group asked that Common Council cut a common sewer through the street. Council took no action. A year later, when the petitioners offered to raise part of the capital cost of the project, Common Council agreed to the undertaking on the condition that the work be completed for no more than £30 and that no person run a drain from his home to the sewer without payment of a £5 entry fee.[24] Under these terms it was impossible for council not to finish with a handsome profit on the arrangement. In fact, the Union Street contract was finally let for £63, a figure that enabled the city to obtain possession of the completed common sewer at no public expense. The Union Street sewer became a model of others in the city: council would view with favour any petition from a neighbourhood in which there was promise of a number of 'subscriptions' toward the cost of the sewer and the guarantee of a number of householders willing to pay from £5 to £17.10.0 for the privilege of entering drains into the common sewer. Generally, the sewers were contiguous and formed and intersected pattern using the inclines on each side of the peninsula to produce a simple gravity system, although isolated sewers, such as the one on Charlotte Street, functioned independently of the larger system. Where convenient, householders on certain streets adjacent to existing streets containing sewers were invited to participate in this service.

The wooden sewer system that emerged in the 1830s was centred on the west watershed of the eastern peninsula through certain main thoroughfares of Kings, Queens, and Dukes wards. Only at a few points did it penetrate the densely populated tenements of York Point. Yet even in the neighbourhood through which it passed, only a minority of householders and tenants at first availed themseves of the service. The entry fee was enough to discourage most householders of limited means and most tenants had little choice in the matter. After 1840, there was a small but constant stream of householders and proprietors living in streets long served by common sewers paying their £5 and £17.10.0 fees for the privilege of entering the common sewers.[25] By mid-century most of the core city streets contained sewers, and in 1851 the Common Council petitioned for and received authority to assess householders for the cost of putting common sewers through the remainder of the city.[26] Even so, as late as 1857, the Board of Health discovered 548 households in Saint John and Portland in which all excrement was still disposed of by the process of spreading it on the streets.[27]

By comparison with the sewers, the city water system was a primitive affair combining elements of both private and public enterprise. Many early city freeholders maintained private wells and continued to use them well into the ninteenth century. The mass of the population was dependent upon the municipal wells maintained in each ward for the general use of the populace. Supplementary to these was a small army of water-carriers that had emerged to serve the needs of businesses and prosperous families unable to maintain their own wells.[28] By the early 1830s the opportunities offered by those prepared to pay for a continuous supply of fresh country water, coupled with the city's desperate need for massive quantities of water for street cleaning and fire-fighting purposes, persuaded a number of local capitalists, merchants, and patricians alike that the situation provided fertile ground for a profitable venture. Early in 1832 they approached the legislature for incorporation as a joint stock company for the purpose of building a piped water system in the city.

The initial success of the water-company proposal was a function of the cholera epidemic of 1832. That epidemic, more than any other event in the early nineteenth century, produced a tendency toward change. The epidemic undoubtedly strengthened the resolve of the water-company promoters and added to the profit motive the satisfaction of creating an important benefit for the city. The proposal's success rested upon obtaining the Common Council's consent to its objectives, since the main thoroughfares of the city would have to be dug up in order to install the water mains. Perhaps stunned by the crisis and thankful that no attempt was made to involve them in the project, the Common Council agreed to the company's first proposal. As a gesture of support and a guarantee of council participation in the company's deliberations, the city agreed to purchase 200 shares in the new concern.[29] As the cholera hysteria passed, in the winter of 1832–33, so too did the initial enthusiasm for water systems. The idea languished until 1835 when, under the leadership of the mayor, Lauchlan Donaldson, the promoters reorganized the company and set off in earnest. The city participated in the new venture with the purchase of twenty-two shares, sufficient to give it at least a nominal voice in the election of directors. None the less, although the council did not oppose the incorporation of the company, neither would it permit itself to be drawn into the financial web the company was attempting to construct. In the autumn, the mayor proposed that the council buy up the considerable block of unsubscribed stock. The council refused.[30] Despite the presence of the mayor and recorder on the company directorate, common councils throughout the 1830s treated the company as a wholly private undertaking, the interests of which were frequently inimical to the public interest of the city. Despite serious financial difficulties, the company made considerable progress during its first three years. Lily Lake was secured as a water-supply; water was piped from the lake to a reservoir at the Abideau and from there by iron pipe to a reservoir near the Block House in the city.[31] Pumps and engines were installed and by July 1837 the company was able to deliver 'a constant stream of pure water' from their engine house to the Abideau reservoir.[32] The following month the company installed the first fire-plugs in the city.

With the completion of the main line from the lakes to their city reservoirs, the company began the task of laying pipe through the streets of the city itself.[33] Still, despite irritations over street repairs, an uneasy partnership between the company and the council developed in the late 1830s, stimulated in large measure by the growing strength of the utilitarian liberals on the council and in part by the essential role played by the company in the city's defence against fire. When the company encountered a financial crisis, in autumn 1838, the Common Council borrowed £500 on its own credit in order to protect its embarrassed client. Increasingly the proposal was made by George Fenety and by liberals among the councillors that the Common Council should purchase the utility in the public interest. The company officers encouraged the idea by demonstrating their indispensability in the fire of 1839 and again in the winter of 1839–40 when they offered to open a fire-plug for an hour each day for the benefit of the poor.[34]

The company's willingness to participate in its own demise was not surprising. By 1840 its directors had invested £18,000, of which £13,000 represented shareholders' capital. In five years no dividends had been paid and with the debt of the provincial loan, there was no chance of the work yielding a profit in the forseeable future. Most discouraging, the utility was only half finished: the laying of pipe through the major thoroughfares was essential to generate the income to make the utility appear an attractive speculation. On 30 January 1840, the Water Committee of Common Council recommended that the Water Company surrender its rights to the city. Two weeks later, the council forwarded a petition to Fredericton asking for authority to acquire the company's assets. In June the stockholders agreed to surrender their stock to the city in return for city bonds to the value of the actual paid-up capital, an offer the Common Council agreed to accept.[35]

The rapid progress toward agreement came to an abrupt halt when councillors supporting the interests of the Water Company shareholders proposed that the city not only pay the capital cost of the stock but also allow the shareholders a sum sufficient to cover five years' dividends on their investment.[36] The proposal provoked a storm of resentment among those opposing the transfer. Nevertheless, following the defeat of two of the anti-company councillors in the April civic elections, the city conceded the principle of interest payment to the shareholders.[37]

When the next sitting of the legislature opened in January 1842, the Common Council announced its willingness to assume responsibility for the 'dirty, expensive job' of building a water system in order to overcome the danger of fires.[38] The enabling legislation was passed in April and a re-evaluation of the company ordered. By the spring of 1842 this was a purely academic exercise. The city was on the verge of bankruptcy and within a month of the evaluation the bond holders moved to set into motion the commission that curtailed the council's activities and destroyed its capacity to borrow. What had begun as a privately controlled utility constructed in the public interest and had moved to a partnership with the Common Council in the late 1830s now became a purely private corporation as a result of the 1842 crisis.[39]

At this point, in addition to the works and engines, the company had constructed mains in a long line extending the full length of the east-side peninsula from the barracks to Lily Lake. In a desperate attempt to reach a greater market, the company quickly moved to open Mill Street, west Duke Street, and North Street. The following year the mains were laid through the Market Square and in 1844 through Brussels Street, Germaine Street, part of Prince William Street, York Point to the North Slip, and into Union Street.[40]

By 1845 the mains formed an erratic pattern radiating from the harbour front through the major business district to the mills and through the most prosperous neighbourhoods of the city. Essentially the firm went hunting for customers and moved from the great mains in the direction in which they were to be found. Unlike the public sewer facility, the private water company laid branch pipes right to the houses of paying customers.[41] By the end of 1843 the company had spent over £27,000 on its installations, which included 850 rods of pipes and 23 fire-plugs within the city.[42] In the straitened circumstances of 1842–43, the company explored every avenue seeking capital to maintain the expansion. It approached the legislature for a new act to enable it to accomplish its purpose of supplying the city with water. The principal element in the bill was a provision permitting the company to raise up to £1000 a year through an assessment of 4*d*. a foot on buildings within 600 feet of a fire-plug. The city was to assess and collect this tax in return for free water.[43] The taxing proposal provoked a furious debate in council, one that pitted puritan liberals against populist conservatives. It culminated in a motion to permit taxation of up to £500 on the company's behalf, but even this passed only with the deciding vote of the chairman.[44] However this bill failed to achieve passage at the 1843 sitting of the legislature. The following year the company again approached the legislature for the taxing authority.

This company proposal fared even less . well at the hands of the Common Council than had the one presented the previous year. The 1844 elections had strengthened the hands of the populist conservatives and council forwarded to Fredericton a petition opposing any assessment.[45] None the less, with the support of the lieutenant-governor, the bill received a favourable hearing in the House, which finally enacted a statute permitting an annual assessment of £300.[46] Even this concession led Common Council to consider a petition to the queen requesting disallowance. In the end, council contented itself with refusing to assess the sum permitted by the legislation.[47]

The Water Company assessment rapidly developed into one of the most acrimonious discussions in the council's history. The debate had both social and political implications. The populist conservative majority on the Common Council saw the company as the instrument of prosperous merchants who had used it for their own benefit. The mains of the company, with their promise of a plentiful supply of pure water, ran from Lily Lake straight to the businesses and homes of the company shareholders and their friends. The company was a commercial venture the profits from which would not have been shared with ratepayers; why, asked the council in petitioning for repeal of the assessment act, should the losses?[48] Essentially a lower middle class of small ratepayers resisted what they perceived as the demands of the mighty.

The response to this argument was given by George Fenety, who argued that the Water Company was the most useful corporation ever formed in Saint John. It had been most shabbily treated by private property owners, Common Council, and the province. Saint John should follow the example of New York and buy the company, close all municipal wells, and offer Lily Lake water to all people regardless of their capacity to pay.[49] If the city could not purchase the company, then at least the council should move to protect it from financial embarrassment.

Meanwhile, the debate between the Common Council and the company accelerated. The council refused the assessments provided for in the

1844 legislation. The company, however, had powerful friends in the provincial legislature. The following year, in an effort to tie the city's hands, the promoters of the Water Company interests in the legislature combined the water assessment with a city-sponsored bill for assessment in support of the fire department.[50] An angry council protested this act, and when the company returned from the 1846 sitting with an act to authorize assessment of 4d. a foot on all property fronting streets with mains regardless of whether or not they received any benefit from the facility, the council flatly refused to collect the tax, an action that led the company to appoint its own collectors.[51]

There the situation stood at the time of arrival of Needham and the populist liberals in 1848. The Water Company had become a publicly subsidized privately owned concern that seemed to justify the worst fears of the populist conservatives on the 1845 Common Council. Water was being delivered to reservoirs and to those businesses and private households willing and able to pay for it. The company was returning a dividend on the original investment, but its directors demonstrated a notable reluctance to extend the mains into areas of the city where financial returns were less certain and per-unit costs consequently higher. Moreover, virtually all the expansion undertaken was being financed by taxes levied on buildings near existing mains.

It was the 1849 Common Council which proposed a resolution of the dilemma. Needham preferred that the city acquire the works. Most of his followers, fearful of the financial costs inherent in such a solution, proposed a policy of gradualism: the Common Council would acquire control of the enterprise in piecemeal fashion and simultaneously provide the company with the additional capital to undertake its new works and avoid the detested tax for the benefit of a private concern. At the 1850 sitting of the legislature, the Common Council requested and received authority to become a shareholder in the Water Company and to assess city inhabitants to meet the costs of interest and amortization of the principal over a number of years.[52] Following passage of the enabling legislation, the populist liberals (with the support of the puritans) used their majority to force a resolution through Common Council authorizing purchase of £3000 of Water Company stock, the capital to be raised by the sale of corporation debentures that were guaranteed as to capital and interest by a special annual assessment of £250. The proposal met with a good response in the local money market and the entire issue, which was over-subscribed, was sold to two merchants at 5.5 per cent.[53] The city already held 200 shares with a par value of £1000; its new acquisition made it by far the largest stockholder in the company.

The new infusion of capital permitted completion of the new works in

1851, and throughout 1851 and 1852 there was a growing public sentiment favouring the city take-over of the company and its transformation into a public utility.[54] Early in 1853, the Common Council made its bid to obtain effective control of a private corporation without actually acquiring its assets. Council offered to acquire another £3000 in new Water Company stock on condition that the company issue new stock to a par value of £5000. As a condition of the purchase, the city demanded the prerogative of naming the streets through which the new mains would be laid, of setting the water-rates that would be charged, of having the privilege of free water with which to wash the streets, and the right to appoint two of the five company directors.[55] Those terms would have placed the direction of the company's development strategy in the realm of public policy. The company balked at these terms.[56] *The Courier* editor proposed that the council buy out the company and complete the task of 'piping' the city: the solution to the problem was simple to all right-thinking men.[57]

Unfortunately it was not nearly so simple to aldermen who had 'the fear of their constituents before their eyes.'[58] In the previous decade the fire hydrant had replaced the public well, and it now ranked with the public market as one of the focal points of urban convenience and well-being. City hydrants served a variety of functions. From the time of their installation the Common Council and the Board of Health had made a practice of opening a number of hydrants at certain times of the day in order to provide a water-supply to poor families. As the mains expanded, so too had the number of hydrants and their accessibility. What had begun as an act of charity soon became the basic source of water for most families within the city. Those who were well-to-do or lived in some degree of refinement or perceived themselves as having or hoping to have a certain stature in the community paid the annual charges and piped water into their houses and businesses. They were a small minority of the population. Piped water was deemed a luxury, even an extravagance, and those on outdoor and indoor relief were joined at the hydrants not only by the city's labourers, but also by its artisans, grocers, and the servants of its master tradesmen.

In 1854 the whole debate became academic. In that year an all-consuming catastrophe – the second cholera epidemic – reduced all other consideration to insignificance. As in 1832, its progress through the known world became a morbid preoccupation of city newspapers. As in 1832, its entry into the city was seen as a forgone conclusion, and the Board of Health moved to mobilize the city and its resources against the common plague. Yet nothing, not the 1832 visitation, not even the 1847 famine migration, prepared the citizenry for the plague that struck the city in the summer of 1854. By the time the three-month visitation had ended, more than 1500 of the population of just over 30,000 had perished in the city and its suburbs. Municipal strategies to contain disease were no longer perceived as political games.

At a public meeting called by the sheriff at the demand of a number of thoroughly frightened leading citizens, resolutions were passed asking that commissioners of sewers and water be appointed to provide a water-supply for the city and Portland. A committee was appointed to prepare a proposal for the provincial government.[59] In mid-October at another public meeting, the committee submitted a comprehensive plan for the consideration of the provincial government and the Common Council. The proposal argued the necessity for an integrated system of fresh piped water and waste disposal employing water as its agent. Since the city contained seventeen miles of streets and Portland had two, the cost of laying sewer mains over that distance would exceed £54,000. Matching water mains would add £71,000. With additional equipment, the total cost would be just over £137,000, a sum considerably greater than the city's total indebtedness.[60] Revenues for the sewers would be raised by an assessment of 20s. on each house and 5s. for each vacant lot. Water-rates would be paid on a family rather than building basis and would be assessed on a graduated scale ranging from 60s. to 15s. a year, depending on family income. Manufacturing enterprises, ships, and steamers would be assessed separately. These assessments would raise £14,000 a year, providing a 6 per cent interest on the needed capital and a 3 per cent sinking fund.

The bill to incorporate the commissioners of water and sewerage and invest them with authority to regulate the provision of these services came before the special session of the legislature in late October. The Common Council, after a marathon debate, consented to the proposal on a 7 to 5 vote, a motion effectively carried by the prohibitionists.[61] The act came into effect in November and the commissioners took control of water distribution and policy within the city.

At the winter sitting of the legislature, they presented a bill to deal with the now vexing problem of a privately owned public utility. In this proposal, the city would purchase all Water Company stock in private hands, offering its owners full interest as an added incentive. The commissioners would the extend the water-and-sewerage systems throughout east Saint John and Portland, raising capital by assessment.[62] In reply, the Common Council accepted the principle that the system should be expanded but rejected the idea of purchase of the company. Instead, with the fear of their constituents still before their eyes, the councillors offered to purchase £20,000 of new stock if the company would extend its pipes throughout the city as provided for in the 1850 legislation. The issue split the prohibitionists with the merchants – Fairweather and Demill – voting for take-over and the others for retention of the mixed corporation regulated by public authority but operated by private entrepreneurs.[63]

A strong provincial executive – which had just finally wrested control of the province's financial life from an obstreperous assembly the previous year – moved, where the Common Council would not, to create a universal public utility. Under the terms of the new act, the commissioners were permitted to issue water debentures to a value of £75,000 (raised to £100,000 in 1858), the interest on which was guaranteed by an assessment on the property of every householder and tenant in the city.[64] Shareholders in the Water Company received the first £25,000 worth of debentures in return for the surrender of their stock: ironically the Common Council, with £4000 of stock, began as a principal creditor of the utility.[65] As a sop to local autonomy, the legislation vested appointment of two commissioners in the Common Council and the third in the county sessions. Commissioners were empowered to assess every owner or leaseholder in east Saint John and Portland for full water service once the water main passed his building. They were further given control of all private privies, cesspools, and sewers. That same year the province created a Board of Health that transferred public-health concerns from the Common Council to five provincially appointed commissioners.[66]

Thus ended the twenty-five-year marriage of private and public initiative in this critical area of urban policy. The commissioners of sewers and water worked rapidly to fulfil their mandate. By the autumn of 1857, they had issued the remainder of the £75,000 debentures, laid a 24-inch main the five miles from the reservoir to the Marsh Bridge, and laid pipe through virtually every street in the city. The Board of Health found more than 500 households without adequate sewerage facilities in the summer of 1857, but these constituted a small and clearly declining fraction of the households in the metropolitan area and represented the last hard-core areas of destitution.[67] In contrast to the east-side experience, a movement on the part of Carleton inhabitants in 1845 to create a water system resulted in the creation of a public utility constructed and operated by public commissioners appointed under legislative authority; the system was in the final stages of completion by 1860.[68]

The transition of the piped water system from a largely private to purely public function was unique among the urban activities of Saint John. So long as public safety permitted, no single system held a monopoly of the urban water-supply. The choices of private or public well, fire hydrant, or personal supply of piped water all remained alternatives from which householders might choose as late as 1850. The pressure of urban reformers and the cholera disaster forced a solution that required the creation of a water-and-sewer monopoly in which all householders had to participate for the common good. The solution was no more radical than those proposed by prohibitionists and common-school advocates, but in process the traditional rights of both the Water Company shareholders and the householders were ignored. Equally significant was the implied shift in the nature of the political community. If the late-nineteenth-century city could be measured in terms of the area swept by its street-cars, the mid-century city could be defined in terms of its water system.

But if public capital superseded private in the water utility, private capital benefited in the process. The borrowed capital used to purchase and complete the water-and-sewer system was largely raised from among city capitalists who received returns well above that paid to British investors of the period.

The growth of public influence in the urban utilities was paralleled by its decline in the development of the harbour resource. The Common Council's responsibility as regulator, conservator, and landlord of the harbour continued to be recognized. The partnership between public authority and private capital in the exploitation of public resources remained theoretically intact, but the capacity of council to control its powerful tenants was restricted by the events of the early 1840s. In the face of the development needs of the 1850s, council's restricted ability to borrow and the necessity to maintain the goodwill of the corporation bond holders left it to deal on less-than-equal terms with great capitalists like John Robertson. The mistrust of the popularly elected Common Council on the part of patricians and great merchants remained a common motif in the Saint John community.

The wharves, in fact, represent the high point of the influence of Saint John's merchant élite; their ability to control the harbour was never effectively challenged in the first half of the nineteenth century. In no other public activity were they able to achieve so obvious a victory. The hostility they engendered among many of the lesser freemen and freeholders is reflected in the long struggle for the water company. Ultimately they never succeeded in achieving their ends in this enterprise; the salvaging of the water company through the creation of a universal public water system occurred only when the prohibitionists – a significant element among the city's freemen – embraced the concept as part of their program.

~11~

Policing the City

Public order was a primary mandate of the Common Council. Those responsible for its maintenance were the link between the formal urban structures and the informal activities of citizens.[1] As the city evolved, the ward-based administration gave way to a city-wide system increasingly directed by professional barristers and policemen. The question of what values should or could be imposed on the city came to the fore, as did debate over the benefits received by the different elements of the urban society. Social control was certainly a central part of the constabulary's function, but it is not altogether clear that any single group within the society possessed a monopoly of the policing function. Despite their considerable influence, patricians and merchants were a minority within a body of freemen and a council dominated by artisans, small business men, and masters whose interests were those of small freeholders, religious dissenters, and neighbourhood politicians. The constables, and later the police, were drawn largely from artisans' ranks.

The evolution of the Saint John police bore a striking resemblance to that of the English police system, notably that of London, and undoubtedly reflects the presence of politically active lieutenant-governors using English models.[2] By 1848, Saint John possessed a fully functioning police system and the following year control of the force passed to a provincially appointed magistrate.[3]

The maintenance of order in early-neneteenth-century Saint John was essentially a function of the ward. Every year at the April elections the freemen and freeholders of the ward met to elect their magistrate and their constable. Responsibility for keeping the peace rested with the alderman who was given considerable discretionary authority to intervene either personally or through a warrant issued to his constable. This highly personal method of law enforcement based upon the concept of the extended neighbourhood remained the centre of the criminal justice system for more than half a century after the city's founding.[4] The relationship between the alderman and his constable tended to be symbiotic. The former normally chose the latter to be part of his ticket in the annual contests and since the constable could act only on the direction of a magistrate, his economic welfare rested in large measure on the alderman's willingness to use him. The constable was in no sense a 'peace' officer. Essentially he was an officer of the court acting only after the commission of a felony or a misdemeanor in response to a court order. Like most public activities, the policing function of the constables was episodic and paid for by a user fee charged either to the complainant or to the Common Council. In addition to the servicing of warrants and the arrest of felons, miscreants, and debtors, constables earned extra fees for the delivery of prisoners, attendance at court, and the seizure of goods. In the small city of the 1820s, the office often yielded such a trivial income that it was sometimes necessary to keep the people's choice in his office by threats of fine. After 1830, however, the increased activities and larger fees made the office increasingly attractive to individuals who were willing to ignore the dangers and unpopularity that accompanied the job.[5] The only other law officer in Saint John was the city marshal appointed by the Common Council. The marshal served the city and the mayor as the constables did the ward and the aldermen. The marshal was the officer normally used to deal with more serious felonies.

The protection of citizens from violence by day was never taken as seriously as the protection of property from fire by night. In summer 1812, the Common Council ordered the creation of a night-watch of eighteen men – twelve for the east side and six for the west – to be formed from volunteers drawn from among the freemen and freeholders of the city. This attempt at a voluntary protective organization proved a failure and nothing more was done until the war's end. A second attempt was made in 1814 to enact a law conscripting all white males twenty-one and over into the night-watch.[6] The watch thus joined the militia and statute labour as a public duty. The new watch began on 2 December but was less than successful. The supremely unpleasant task of maintaining a vigil through the long and bitterly cold winter nights was left in large measure to men who either had no stake in protecting the property of the city or would have conceived the duty as far beneath them. To maintain a nightly patrol of 18 men would require the services of 540 men a month, no mean task in a community with a total population of perhaps 6000. Finally, in autumn 1815, the Common Council conceded the impossibility of a mass enrolment and instead proposed to petition Fredericton for authority to assess £250 a year for a permanent watch. In the meantime, the council proceeded to hire watchmen and pay them from public funds.[7] With the passage of the enabling legislation, the council acquired the services of a full-time east-side watch consisting of three men and a sergeant.

The night-watch system was a medieval concept used in virtually every North American urban centre in the eighteenth and nineteenth centuries. It achieved only limited success in most towns because the watchmen were perceived and treated as a species of part-time labourer.[8] The meagre wages they received tended to attract the feeble and the unstable. These complaints did not apply to the early watchmen of Saint John. Although the force was small and confined to the east side, its members received larger wages – about £60 a year – than did their successors thirty years later.[9] If the record of complaints is any indicator of effectiveness, the watch was highly effective in its first fifteen years of operation. The superintendence of the watch was in the hands of a Common Council committee. Groups of two or three watchmen paraded the city every night between ten and seven o'clock. While their first purpose was the detection of fires, they constituted as well the city's first peace officers. They were commissioned to enforce the curfew, to demand knowledge of anyone abroad after midnight, to keep the peace, and to bring to the gaol anyone infringing an ordinance or unable to give an account of himself.

As the commerce of the city expanded, so too did its transient population, the amenities needed to provide for their comfort and entertainment, and the need for control. And control was an increasing problem. Saint John had a peacetime garrison of upward of 700 single men, several hundred transient seamen on shore at any given moment from April to November, as many as a thousand British immigrants in a good spring month, a small army of lively late-teenage 'prentices,' a substantial force of single ship labourers, and a growing flood of unskilled young men and women from the provincial countryside – all in town to make their fortune. Together they combined to produce a growing threat to the public peace. In the course of the 1820s and 1830s, the primary function of the watch slowly, subtly, but significantly shifted from the protection of property from fire and vandals to the protection of persons. The erection of the watch house in 1827 was the first clear sign of the shift. This provided a centre in which a watchman could be left to maintain the care of incoming prisoners and a base from which the captain could oversee the activities of his little garrison. The most significant symbol of the shift occurred in 1836 with the creation of the permanent office of police clerk – a post given to Aldermen Van Horne – which effectively provided a single police magistrate who would both oversee the watch and every morning render judgment on problems of the previous night.[10]

Public debate over the watch in the 1830s centred on the question of who should bear the cost. Watchmen were paid from an assessment on all taxpayers regardless of the benefit that accrued to them. It was this issue of benefit that precipitated debate over who should bear the costs. Because the early watch had been perceived essentially as a fire-detection service, the major beneficiaries from its services were freeholders, but even among freeholders those with warehouses and business property not normally occupied at night were seen as having a far greater stake in the watch than the small householder living with his tenant. Yet the enabling legislation required that the tax burden for the service be borne with some equality throughout the community.[11] Hence successive councils, representing essentially small freeholders and unpropertied freemen, were exceedingly reluctant to impose greater taxes on these constituencies in order to subsidize protection for the property of the well-to-do. As the city grew in population, there was a slower growth in the size of the watch. The four men of 1816 only grew to six in 1835, to nine in 1839, and perhaps to eleven or twelve in 1841. In the face of the 1841–42 financial crisis, the watch was reduced to nine, where it remained until the late 1840s when it was increased to eleven.[12]

A related but even more serious problem was the depreciation of labour that began in the late 1820s primarily as a result of the influx of large numbers of Irish migrants willing to work for wages well below those paid to native labourers. The Common Council took full advantage of this situation to acquire a larger force for less money. The £60 annual wage of a watchman in 1816 fell to only £39.6.0 by 1835[13] and remained there for the next fourteen years. With it went poverty and loss of status. From the savings, the Common Council was able to increase the force from four to six members. It was a false economy. The more able men disappeared and their places were taken by those unable to find employment elsewhere. The most notable effect – among watchmen as among teachers – was the flight of natives into other occupations that retained a more reasonable renumeration and a higher status, and their replacement by Irish-Protestant migrants.[14] To supplement their meagre incomes and, incidentally, to facilitate their power to make arrests, most watchmen were also sworn as special constables. Like the elected constabulary, they were permitted to take fees for serving legal documents and carrying out arrests under the direction of a magistrate – that is, if they were able to muster the strength after working their seven-day weeks.[15]

As ethnic tensions mounted after 1836, the watch found itself understaffed, badly paid, and lacking the respect of the rest of the community. To add to the situation, most watchmen were Irish Protestants while most of the disorderly elements complained about were Irish Catholics. The council's solution to the growing disorder was to increase the size of the watch. Once again councillors were not prepared to devote the general revenues of the city to this purpose; once again they argued that those who benefited most from the protection offered by the watch – the great property holders – should be made to bear the largest part of the tax. In 1838, they asked for authority to increase the watch tax assessment on the inhabitants of the east side of the city as a whole and to raise the maximum assessment on any individual from £5 to £7.10.0. When the legislature refused this request, the council redoubled its efforts at the 1839 sitting, arguing that watch and light services cost the city £1000, of which only £500 could be raised by assessment on the properties of those benefiting from the services.[16] The act passed and resulted in a 20s. a month increase in wages and an addition of two watchmen to the force.[17]

The urgency of the situation was heightened a few days later with the great fire of 1839 that devastated much of the city's central business district and left the merchandise and possessions of hundreds of business men and other citizens exposed to the elements and human depredation. In the emergency, the mayor summoned 128 members of leading families to his office and swore them in as special constables with authority to protect property exposed by the fire.[18]

These efforts may have controlled but could not stem the rising tide of violence. In September, George Fenety complained in *The Commercial News* of 'disorderly and evil disposed persons who prowl about our city in the dead hour of the night' and advocated an expansion of the watch. By February, he was arguing that 'every corner of our city ... is infested with vagabonds of the very worst order, and if some steps are not soon taken to arrest their career, we will not give much for the morality that has hitherto been the characteristic mark of the community and that it was no longer safe to leave one's door unbarred in the city.'[19] Fenety's perception and assessment was essentially correct. What he complained of was not a criminal act, in the legal sense of the word, but a pattern of behaviour that threatened the peace of the city and the accepted cultural norms of its dominant citizenry. As this form of group violence became endemic in the winter and spring of 1840, the watch came under stronger public criticism and the Common Council sought ways to find a more 'efficient' police.[20]

The previous problems of the night-watch paled into insignificance in the late summer when the latent ethnic violence, which had been confined to minor street fights, suddenly broke loose in the city's first major daytime riot. The 'riot' was a highly organized ritual directed against a known Orangeman and his Irish-Protestant neighbours.[21] The reason for the vendetta against this particular Orangeman did not emerge, but it was obviously part of a much larger long-standing feud. Against such violence the city had no defence. The mob was only dispersed when the mayor entered the area with elements of the 33rd Regiment. The military had been used several times before to battle and maintain order in the midst of the conflagrations that periodically swept the city, but this was the first time it had been used against the civilian population.

The city was just recovering from this violence when, on the evening of 4 November, one of the city's leading physicians, Dr George Peters, scion of a distinguished Loyalist family, was assaulted near his home by Irish labourers.[22] At the trial that followed a few weeks later, the defence attorney argued that the public outrage was not a result of the nature of the crime as much as the quality of the victim. His contention was entirely correct. Despite the brutality of the attack, the crime was no more serious than dozens of similar incidents that had occurred in the previous months. But the Peters incident was the first in which Irish hooliganism directly threatened the native population.

The assault led to demands for more effective law enforcement. The Common Council responded by adding six men to the watch for a brief time. The strengthening of the watch at this time was fortunate. Almost as if by signal, the Peters incident precipitated a crime wave that turned the night streets of the city into a battleground. The editors of both *The News* and *The Courier* suggested that since no part of the city was safe after 8:00 pm, every citizen going out after nightfall should carry weapons in the New Orleans manner.[23]

The reaction of the respectable populace was predictable. The grand jury had presented the police of both Saint John and Portland in 1840 'as being lamentably inefficient either for the preservation of good order or the prevention of crime.' At the suggestion of Mr Justice Parker, it had recommended the appointment of a stipendiary police magistrate and a permanent constabulary in each of the two communities. At the 28 January sitting of the Supreme Court, the grand jury again presented the police force as a public nuisance and then went on to attack the magistracy itself declaring that 'two of our elected police magistrates either embezzled or otherwise improperly withheld' the fines accruing from the courts.[24] In the petition it prepared for the legislature, it set forth the freeholders' fears of an elected magistracy:

Such a[n appointed] magistracy being unbound by a dependence on the popular voice for their appointment ... would be enabled much better and more effectively to preserve the peace of this community ... than can ever be expected of Magistrates who rely upon an annual vote of the very people they are to rule over, but to whose will and pleasure they must be submissive in order to ensure their election to office.[25]

G.E. Fenety, c. 1875 (PANB)

View of the Great Conflagration ... [of January 1839]
(after Thomas Hanford Wentworth [1781–1849], lithograph, 39.7 cm × 64.2 cm,
Beaverbrook Art Gallery, Fredericton, NB)

The jury represented a broad cross-section of cultural interests from the business and professional community, including noted Episcopalians like the merchant Edward Jarvis and the editor G.E. Fenety, prominent Catholic business men like F. McDermott and William McCannon, the Wesleyan merchants D.L. McLaughlin, John and B. Ansley, and J.V. Troop, and the Independent lawyer Moses Perley. The suggestion of the grand jury that the citizenry should arm itself was taken a step further a few weeks later when a correspondent in *The News* proposed that 'the young men' – presumably the trustworthy young men – 'of Saint John shall be called with a view to forming a *Nightly Watch* for the protection of the inhabitants and their property,' a proposal hailed by the editor.[26]

The idea of citizen participation in such an activity was first tested during circus riots in June 1841. On the second night of the circus, Aldermen Peters had been severely beaten by an unruly mob of young men. The next evening the mayor attended, accompanied by 113 respectable citizens whom he had sworn in as special constables, and the evening passed without incident.[27] The autumn was plagued by incendiaries.[28] On 1 December, George Fenety brought forward again his proposal that 'the citizens who created' the Common Council – presumably the freemen and freeholders – form a patrol body to take upon themselves the guardianship of the city to guard against the thief, the assassin, and the incendiary. Two days later, at a meeting called for the purpose, 300 men formed the 'Saint John Mutual Protection Association.' With the support and encouragement of the Common Council, they organized themselves into companies, each under the direction of a manager, and proceeded to patrol the city as special constables.[29] Virtually all the 400 or more who eventually enrolled in the association were freeholders or sons of freeholders.

The following week, the managers of the association arranged a meeting with the mayor to take steps for the organization of an efficient police.[30] The debate that followed found the association divided on a solution, although a majority favoured a stipendiary magistrate and the creation of a police responsible to the executive council of the province. The meeting appointed a committee to draw up a petition to the legislature proposing a stipendiary police magistrate for Saint John and Portland. The lead in this action was taken by the lawyers with Moses Perley and W.J. Ritchie arguing the most radical position and George Blatch seeking the co-operation of the Common Council.

In a spirited defence of the council and the watch, Alderman Henry Porter argued that almost every crime committed since November had been solved and the criminals jailed through the instrumentality of the alderman and the watch. He further noted that although the lieutenant-governor in council appointed nearly thirty justices of the peace in the city, virtually all the active investigation of criminal activity was undertaken by the six elected magistrates. In response to the jury's attack on the integrity of the magistrates, Porter pointed to the hundreds of hours he had served on the bench during the previous six years and vehemently denied that he was unfit or unqualified to act in that capacity.[31] The choice of Porter to respond to the grand jury was a shrewd one: even the most severe critics of the council acknowledged him to be able, conscientious, and scrupulous.

Given the bitterness of the situation and the radical nature of the grand jury solution, the legislature chose not to act on the petition. The Common Council was left in command of the police but without the resources to undertake the job adequately. Having repelled the attacks on its privileges, the Common Council sought to re-create a police establishment under council control that would meet the objections of liberal critics. The proposals made by councillors at this time clearly represent a shift to a quite different perception of police function. In September, a committee was appointed to prepare a general proposal for policing the city.[32] It prepared a new police ordinance providing for the creation of a police force of fifteen men combining the responsibilities and authority of the watch and the constabulary. The force would be formed into three divisions each containing five men, headed by a captain. The divisions would rotate so that two would serve each night as a night police while the third would provide the city with its first day police, functioning directly on the orders of the police magistrate. All watchmen would wear police badges and the day division on Sunday would walk the streets to apprehend sabbath violators.[33]

The plan met a mixed reaction in Common Council. All councillors accepted the necessity of a day-and-night police with expanded powers. On the issue of the police magistracy, they split into three clear positions. Generally the populist conservatives favoured the existing system of rotating aldermen, although they accepted the necessity to conscript magistrates from the county sessions to deal with the increased responsibilities implied in the new arrangement. Puritan liberals were prepared to accept the annual appointment of an alderman to the stipendiary position of police magistrate. Finally, Alderman Peters insisted on the necessity for the division of powers and argued for a stipendiary magistrate holding his appointment independent of the Common Council. The initial petition asked for the revenues from all fines and auction duties to help defray the costs of a day-and-night police force, and for authority to use the justices of the peace of the county sessions as rotating police magistrates.[34] On 26 January council forwarded to Fredericton an amendment requesting the appointment of a single alderman as police magistrate. This amendment passed on a 7 to 5 vote with the support of Peters and most of the puritan liberals.[35] Once again the legislature refused to act.[36]

Meanwhile, for a short time in December and January, the city had nightly patrols of thirty volunteers and as many as eleven watchmen: public nuisance, arson, and assault were practically eliminated – apart from confrontations between the volunteers and the professionals. This state of affairs was short-lived: the cold, the tedium, and the constancy of the undertaking soon cooled the ardour of the young citizenry and by February the effective volunteer strength was down to twelve men a night.[37] The affairs of the professional watch were in even more desperate straits. By February 1842, the city was on the verge of bankruptcy. The watch did not long escape the financial crisis. Wages were cut to £4 a month and in June the watch was reduced to nine men.[38] Those chosen to remain found it a dubious honour. For the next year, the watch pay was perpetually in arrears, sometimes as much as three months. At the best of times the small pay forced the watchmen to live hand to mouth and to work at other jobs to supplement their meagre incomes; when the city failed to pay at all, their families were reduced to the verge of starvation.[39]

The condition of the watchmen reflected that of the community at large. Thousands were reduced to destitution and the gaol and work house became places mainly for debtors.[40] In June, the deputy emigrant agent reported to the provincial secretary the arrival of 5000 immigrants, more than half of whom joined a resident labouring population 'already steeped in the deepest poverty and for some time past suffering the extremest privations in every shape.'[41] In the midst of these difficulties, on 12 July, there occurred a second ethnic riot.[42] This troubling event was followed by a third the following July.

The initiative to restore public order was taken by Lieutenant-Governor Colebrook who summoned the Common Council and the sessions to discuss the possibility of creating a police establishment on the new English model. Despite Colebrook's concerns about the dangers posed by the religious divisions introduced by recent migrants, no progress was made. Led by the Honourable John Robertson, the appointed members of the sessions argued for a police force directed by a stipendiary magistrate responsible to the executive council. They further proposed that the assessment of the police tax on the city be made by appointed magistrates of the session rather than the elected Common Council because, as Robertson noted, the judgment of the Common Council was not to be trusted, nor would one dare place such a large tax under its direction. In the face of this provocation, the aldermen reiterated their traditional stand: they were prepared to establish a police force at a cost of £2000 a year, but only if it were under the control of the Common Council.[43] On that note the conference ended.

Colebrook's prophecies were soon fulfilled. On 7 March, in a scenario that was already becoming a tradition, a band of ribbonmen (Irish Catholics) attempted to seal off the major thoroughfares through the Irish Catholic centre at York Point. They were opposed by a group of Portland Orangemen led by Squire Manks. In the mêlée that followed, Manks fired on the ribbonmen, wounding a Catholic youth. Manks returned to his house in Portland, which was soon surrounded by an outraged mob of Catholics. Mayor Donaldson, accompanied by his constables and several 'respectable citizens,' proceeded to Portland, arrested Manks, and with difficulty returned to the city with his prisoner.[44] Donaldson described the growth of groups of Orangemen and ribbonmen as a recent phenomenon and pointed out one critical fact: even if the city funds were adequate to double or triple the watch, 'such additional members must be drawn from classes whose feelings, sympathies and prejudices all make them partisans on the one side or the other, and so increase in place of putting down the agitation.' Donaldson should have added that the city itself was becoming so polarized that it was becoming increasingly difficult to form a jury free from the same feelings, sympathies, and prejudices.

The capacity of city authorities to deal with the accelerating ethnic violence was seriously weakened by the proximity of the completely unpoliced parish of Portland in which the urban areas were simply given over to crowds of partisans and hooligans once darkness descended. Bands from Portland joined by city partisans frequently made incursions into the city. Throughout 1844 the situation in the city streets at night rapidly deteriorated toward the state that had existed in 1841. The disorder culminated in late December and early January. On Christmas Eve, two watchmen were fired on and then severely beaten by a mob. The next evening, a gang of 200 men armed with clubs seized and held the Portland Bridge at York Point in an effort to intercept several enemies. Every night throughout the following week the same group reassembled and effectively cut off the main thoroughfare between Saint John and Portland.[45] On New Year's Eve, the mayor and several magistrates finally got control of York Point by using two companies of the 33rd Regiment, which cleared the area with fixed bayonets.[46]

Again the usual scene was replayed. The lieutenant-governor requested a report on means to prevent disturbances and arrived in the city in early January to discuss solutions to the problems with the Common Council. The editor of The News suggested that martial law was preferable to civil rule under such circumstances, and The Courier proposed that even taxation was to be preferred![47] Two hundred prominent freeholders petitioned the Common Council for a stipendiary magistrate and a police controlled by three or four provincially appointed commissioners.[48] The session petitioned the legislature for a law to provide police.[49] The Common Council, again, pointed out to the lieutenant-governor the necessity of creating a day-and-night police, maintaining the administrative and juducial supremacy of the council, and forming a Portland police. This proposal was followed, again, by a petition to the legislature asking for authority to assess for a day-and-night police.[50]

Under these circumstances, the citizens of Saint John awaited the next Irish feast-day with considerable trepidation. There was a general fear that St Patrick's Day would turn into a blood-bath. On 15 March, Mayor Donaldson issued a proclamation prohibiting processions. The proclamation held until the evening of the 17th when groups of Orange and ribbonmen began to form in Portland. Donaldson went to the Portland Catholic magistrate, James Gallagher, and to Father Dunphy in an effort to have them persuade the rival factions to go home. These efforts were to no avail. Following a tavern incident, a riot speedily developed with large mobs gathered on both sides armed with muskets. The special constables were unable either to control the crowd or to arrest the offenders. The first encounter was a bloody one with several casualties, two of them serious.[51] Gallagher sent for the mayor who arrived with the military. But even the presence of the military did not dissuade many of the rioters who defied the soldiers from a distance and assaulted Drs William and Samuel Bayard as they attended the wounded. An Irish Protestant later died from gunshot wounds.[52]

The Portland riots produced still another flurry of policing proposals. In January 1846, the appointed magistrates once again attempted to gain control of the city's police powers through a bill proposing to create Portland and the east side of Saint John City into a single police district under a stipendiary magistrate. In the subsequent debate in the legislature, the attack on the city court and police system was led by two assemblymen from the city and county, Isaac Woodward and W.J. Ritchie.[53] Ritchie promised the mayor that if the aldermen consented to the surrender of their police court authority to a stipendiary magistrate they could dictate the other terms of the police bill. The proposal had a great appeal to the liberal puritans on the Common Council, but in the end the legislature failed to deal with it. There was little ethnic disturbance throughout 1846 and despite considerable problems of discipline and morale with the watchmen – whose pay had been cut to £3.10.0 a month – the traditional system continued to function amidst chaos and confusion.[54]

It was a short reprieve. Ethnic violence between the two Irelands broke out afresh in 1847 and saw the death of a Saint John Catholic on 12 July. This was the beginning of a series of violent confrontations resulting in several killings and culminating in the brutal murder of a Portland youth who was returning from a temperance meeting.[55] The motive for this shooting is unclear – whether it was a case of mistaken identity, or robbery, or simply a grudge – but the victim, like Dr Peters a few years earlier, was the son of a native family, a Sunday school teacher and choir member at St Luke's Episcopal Church. The pressures for protection again became intense. This time the lieutenant-governor in council moved decisively. The session was empowered to create a parish police. One of the parish's four magistrates, Jacob Allan, directed the organization of the force.[56] Within a month, the £500 needed to maintain the force for six months was borrowed from the Commercial Bank and by early November an 'efficient force of 10 good Protestants' was sworn in.[57]

In late winter, the legislature was confronted with opposing petitions from Portland respecting the future of the force. One, headed by the clergy, the shipbuilders, Allen, and the Honourable Charles Simonds, urged the creation of a permanent police under a stipendiary magistrate; the other, supported largely by Irish householders and the other two parish magistrates, opposed the proposal on the grounds that the costs would be oppressive.[58] They proposed instead that a number of house-holders in each neighbourhood be armed and sworn in as special constables.[59] The legislature, at government urging, supported the prayer of the first petition and in early April the session obtained the statutory authority to assess for police and for the installation of gas lights to light the streets of inner Portland.[60] The police attained a statutory existence and serious breaches of the peace all but disappeared from the parish throughout 1848.[61]

The presence of a multitude of unemployed and masterless immigrants, the public outrage at the Portland murder, and the growing fear that the government might secure the peace under general legislation following the widespread summer riots persuaded even the traditionalists of the need for a strong police force. Led by Harding and Van Horne, the council proceeded to organize a full day-and-night police.[62] On 2 November, the watch was increased from 11 to 21 men to provide two 10-man shifts. Each police officer was provided with uniform, great coat, and rifle and bayonet from the Saint John ordinance stores.[63] The six aldermen rotated daily as police magistrates, a particularly arduous undertaking since the office effectively combined the functions of magistrate and police director. The decision to implement the plan symbolized the collapse of the old order. Stripped of much of the financial superstructure that provided the basis of their patronage, faced with the breakdown of the ward systems in which they had traditionally functioned, the aldermen admitted the impossibility of their traditional tasks. In the process, the maintenance of the peace became a city function performed by a professional structured bureaucracy.

The decision finally to create a stipendiary magistrate was an internal one taken by the populist liberals under Needham, with the support of the remaining puritan liberals, as part of their program for major charter reform. These reforms, including the appointment of a stipendiary police magistrate with responsibility for the administration of the police force, were incorporated into law at the 1849 sitting of the legislature. The act also provided the Common Council with the authority to assess the population of the east side. In the settlement, the aldermen of the city retained their judicial jurisdiction over civil cases, although in the interests of efficiency the new act required weekly sittings of the city court.

Ironically, the new police order was instituted at almost the same time as the most frightening and widespread breakdown of order in the city's history. On 12 July occurred the last and most brutal of the confrontations between Irish Catholics and Irish Protestants in New Brunswick. The riot was one of the best-planned events in the city's history. In preparation, most of the aldermen and appointed magistrates made a point of absenting themselves from the city, and the York Point Catholics erected their barriers and prepared their roof-top ammunition drops.

The events of 12 July were not calculated to endear either the Common Council or the sessions in the eyes of the lieutenant-governor; in particular they destroyed altogether any hope the populist conservatives had of suspending the charter amendment and returning control of the police to the council. With London's consent, Sir Edmund Head created the first stipendiary magistrate, who was also given authority as director of police. The appointment of B.L. Peters to this office may have been an effort to placate the Common Council for the loss of its prerogatives.[64] If so, the attempt failed. Council accepted its loss of the magistracy; it never accepted the loss of control of the police.

Inevitably, disputes over the whole matter of the maintenance of the peace flared on the issue of costs. The magistrate's stipend was stipulated at £25 a month by order in council. In addition, his clerk (Peters appointed his son to that office) was to receive £150 a year. Peters further proposed to employ a police superintendent for £150 and to pay his constables £60 each, a return to the wages paid the watchmen in 1816 and a substantial increase from the £42 they were receiving.[65] The council objected to the salaries and Peters appealed to the provincial secretary who began an action in the Supreme Court to force the mayor to pay.[66] By early 1850, Peters had succeeded in increasing the number of police to twenty-five and requesting an annual budget of £2195 for their support, up from £900 the previous year. Council again balked and another effort was made, this time led by Needham, to cut the wages of the police establishment.[67]

Despite these disputes, Peters got along well with Common Council and his three-year tenure of office was marked by few difficulties, either with the council or the police. The salary adjustments gave the police status they had never enjoyed before and allowed Peters to acquire capable men. The uniformed day-and-night police were armed with pistols on a permanent basis.[68] Operating with fifteen men at night and eleven on day duty, the force continued to be effective in controlling the city streets and maintaining the peace under ordinary circumstances.[69] Peter's retirement from the magisterial office in 1852 and his replacement by John Johnston quickly brought to the fore unresolved financial problems of police administration.[70] Johnston was the son of Saint John's premier Scottish merchant and brother of a former member of the executive council of the province. An able man, he possessed neither the tact nor the patience of his predecessor.

The debate prompted the council to seek still another reorganization of the police administration. Borrowing the arguments of their former opponents, the councillors claimed that the judicial authority of the magistrates was not compatible with administrative control of the police. In its place the council proposed that the appointment, discipline, and dismissal of the police should be entrusted to an inspector on the model of the educational system.[71] The inspector, like the magistrate, would hold office at royal pleasure, thus ensuring his independence, but the financial decisions of wages and numbers of policemen would remain with the Common Council, which had to raise the revenues for their support.

The debate between Johnston and the council was at least partly political. Johnston was an appointee of the old order; by 1854, the council was firmly in the hands of the liberal-prohibitionist smashers, a fact dramatically illustrated by the debates between the mayor and magistrate over the liquor issue in 1854–56. The general breakdown of public order in the prohibition experiment reflected as much as anything a determination on the part of an anti-prohibitionist magistrate to undermine a statute that he deemed to be unenforceable.[72] The trial of strength between the magistrate and the council continued throughout the whole of Johnston's term of office. It finally culminated in 1856 when a smasher's government acceded to the repeated prayer of the council and placed control of the police force under a chief. In the new arrangement, the Common Council achieved most of its goals; the chief held office at royal pleasure, but the council set the numbers and wages of the policemen and had to give assent to all police regulations.[73]

There were few public complaints of the effectiveness or composition of the force. Although the great majority of officers were Protestants, the Saint John police leadership was always astute enough to recognize the new community by including Catholics on the force. By contrast, the Portland police, which remained a Protestant monopoly, was the subject of persistent public debate.

By 1860, the peace of Saint John and its suburbs was maintained by three separate police districts, each reflecting a particular form of development. The Carleton wards had their own police committee and retained the traditional constabulary functioning under the authority of their aldermen. In the parish of Portland, the small police establishment functioned under the direction of a stipendiary magistrate. Finally, within the parish of Saint John existed a police force and criminal justice system reflecting the complex relationship of local and central authority and influences.

The transition of the criminal justice system of Saint John between 1816 and 1856 reflected the remaking of the urban community. Public order in the early part of the century was maintained as part of a highly personal relationship between the aldermen and their extended neighbourhood. Its epitome was the image of the alderman strolling the streets of his ward on a Sunday afternoon warning potential sabbath violators that they might be charged and directing his constable to bring the recalcitrants before him for summary conviction. The shift from this village order to a professional bureaucracy of peace officers patrolling the city at large under central direction reflects both the centralizing tendency of the urban order and the influence of the new utilitarian and evangelical ideas of order, progress, efficiency, and equality. The public order of 1856 prized consistency of treatment, sobriety, quiet passage, and authority based on contract rather than birthright. The further impulse to direction of the peace-keeping forces and defence of the social order by external agencies, though dear to the hearts of much of the city's social and economic élite, was perceived by both traditionalists and liberals as something to be resisted. All recognized the vital role of the military in preserving the public order as the older forms of community disintegrated, and most accepted the necessity of an external Caesar's role as final arbiter, but the tradition of local autonomy remained deeply ingrained.

~12~

The People of a
Loyalist City

The population of Saint John was the product of a half-dozen major groups of people. Pre-Loyalist and Loyalist Americans, trickles of Scots and English, rural New Brunswickers and Nova Scotians, and more than 100,000 Irishmen moved in successive waves into port. Most continued on within a few years. The minority that remained constituted powerful islands of stability in the midst of the general transiency that characterized most North American nineteenth-century societies, and contributed to the stratification within a social system where, by mid-century, third-generation Loyalists and Scots interacted with famine-Irish migrants.

The dimensions of that stratification are revealed in the 1851 Census manuscript, the only one of the colonial census and assessment records to survive. More than 30,000 people resided in the three connected urban parishes of St John, Portland, and Carleton, nearly two-thirds of whom resided in the four wards composing the east-side parish of St John. The city contained over 2000 houses occupied by 4200 families, mostly in the east-side wards. The manuscript census of the households of these wards is extant and provides a picture of the mature urban society.[1] The following analysis is based on a 20 per cent simple systematic sample of the households of Kings, Queens, Dukes, and Sydney wards using every fifth household from the census manuscript. Since the census was recorded on a street-to-street basis, the sample is reasonably representative of the whole population of the parish.[2] The analysis assumes that the household was the basic social unit around which urban life was organized and that household heads played the most significant roles in forming communal values.

To explore the structure of this urban society, two variables – ethnicity and occupation – have been established against which other social characteristics of the household are measured (see details in the appendix). Since the household head is assumed to have been the central figure in each little commonwealth, ethnicity was assigned in terms of the birth-place of the family head. For purposes of this study, the following 'ethnic' categories have been established: native (New Brunswick-born), Nova Scotian, American, English, Scottish, Irish. In addition, since the Irish constituted such a large and complex group, they have been divided into two groups based upon their length of residency in New Brunswick. Those Irish heads who arrived before 1840 have been classified as early Irish and the more recent arrivals as recent Irish.

The occupational analysis has been based on that of the household head. With some modification, it employs the standard categories developed and used in a number of North American and British nineteenth-century urban studies.[3] In this system, most occupations are assigned to one of five status groups. The first contains high-status positions, such as merchant wholesalers, leading officials, and prominent professional groups. The second is essentially a white-collar group including grocers, clerks, and teachers. Group three consists of artisans, mechanics, and other skilled labour. The fourth includes such semi-skilled groups as teamsters. All unskilled common labour is assigned to the fifth group. For some purposes, three additional categories have been added. The sixth includes those whose status is unclear; the seventh is used to indicate households headed by women; and the eighth comprises female servants. Since the census rarely identified women by occupation, the last two categories are useful only in the analysis of household structure.

The census sample produced 732 households. The most striking social reality revealed in the census is provided by the birthplace – and the cultural formation that assumes – of the family heads. Mid-nineteenth-century Saint John was, above all, a British city. Nearly three of every four family heads had been born in the British Isles, a striking com-ment on the impact that post-Napoleonic migration had produced in this Loyalist centre. Native New Brunswickers – rural migrants to the city, as well as children and grandchildren of the Loyalist and pre-Loyalist founders – headed only one-quarter of the households. The dominant ethnic group was the Irish. Nearly three of every five household heads had been born in Ireland. In part this Irish dominance is attributable to the famine migration that spawned the movement of more than 30,000 people to Saint John between 1845 and 1849. Yet it is quite clear that it was the pre-1840 arrivals who tended to remain in the city. In 1851 they still constituted a large majority of the Irish heads. Given the rate of attrition found among urban residents in other nineteenth-century cities, it is reasonable to assume that recent Irish migrants should have greatly outnumbered the earlier Irish arrivals. The fact that this was not so strongly suggests that occupational and cultural factors were far more important than time of arrival in determining immigrant continuity. By 1851, Saint John was distinguished by the presence of three large groups, representing two ethnic groups (early Irish, recent Irish, natives), two small ethnic groups (English and Scots), and a sprinkling of Nova Scotians, Americans, Germans, and West Indians too small in number to form any distinctive presence.

The occupational distribution of family heads revealed the city's dual economic purpose as commercial and manufacturing centre. More than one-third of the male heads were artisans. Those engaged in high-status and white-collar occupations composed another one-quarter and together outnumbered the urban labourers. Indeed, the strength of the artisan and commercial elements lends a rather bourgeois and prosperous quality to the civic society reflected in the census.

That perception is sharply modified when the occupation of the household heads is correlated with their birthplace. The striking feature of this analysis is the high correlation between the native, English, and Scots born and high-status occupations on the one hand, and the Irish born and low-status occupations on the other.[4] Only among artisans were the ethnic groups found in numbers approximating their part of the total population. The occupational pattern of the native heads of household is particularly interesting because, together with the Scots, they contained the remnants of the pre-1820 civic population. That earlier population had certainly contained a substantial number of day labourers. Yet by 1851 only 3 per cent of the natives and 2 per cent of the Scots identified themselves as labourers. Two conclusions are possible from this. Either the labourers of the earlier period abandoned the city or they or their children acquired the skills or capital that permitted them to become something other than a labourer. Evidence suggests that the latter actually happened in a number of cases, although probably the former more often occurred. By 1851, no more than twenty native household heads made a living as day labourers, a fact made even more remarkable because a substantial part of the native born were migrants to the city from New Brunswick villages and rural communities. Native-born heads were concentrated among the artisans, women, and the commercial and professional groups.

The native occupational pattern was paralleled among English- and Scottish-born heads of household. Almost half the Scots were found in high-status and white-collar occupations, as were two of every five

Englishmen. Taken together natives, English, and Scots composed four-fifths of those in high-status and half of those in white-collar occupations.

At the other end of the social scale, the Irish born accounted for more than 90 per cent of the household heads who made their living as labourers. There were, however, marked differences between the two Irish groups: the earlier Irish arrivals were only somewhat overrepresented among the labourers (39 per cent of the labourers and 30 per cent of the heads), while the smaller group of recent Irish composed a clear majority of the unskilled. When all working males are included in the analysis, the occupational differences among these ethnic groups become even more pronounced. Such an occupational distribution from native born to early Irish to recent Irish strongly suggests that each successive wave of newcomers had seriously depressed the labour market and forced earlier workers either up or out. The pattern of occupations among earlier Irish arrivals differed from that of the recent Irish in other important ways. Although few Irish were found in high-status occupations, the early Irish were markedly stronger in the middling orders – white collar, artisan, and semi-skilled – than were the later arrivals, a phenomenon that may be explained in terms of a period of time required for immigrant adaptation or, as Donald Akenson has argued, as a result of social and economic differences between the pre-1845 and later-arriving migrants.[5]

About one Saint John household in seven was headed by a woman. The census takers listed no occupations for any women in the city, apart from servants, but it seems clear that female-headed households spanned the full range of the social and ethnic spectrum. The largest group of female heads consisted of natives; qualitative evidence indicates that it ranged from the widows and daughters of patrician and great-merchant families down to small households containing one or two children living with one or two women whom the census taker did not designate as widows. A number were freeholders. Overall, the households headed by native-born women seemed to reflect a comparatively high level of prosperity. By contrast, the other large group of households with women heads was found among the recent Irish arrivals, and there is every reason to believe that most of these were victims of the famine who either were shovelled out of Ireland together with their children, or whose husbands had died or deserted them shortly after their arrival.

The households of Saint John averaged 5.4 people in 1851, but ranged in size from a single man or woman to extensive lodging houses where as many as eighteen children, lodgers, and servants were to be found under the administration of a single head. The characteristic city household was a single nuclear family consisting of a parent or parents, their children, and, in one case in five, a servant. About 70 per cent of all households were organized in this fashion. The only other significant household structure was one consisting of the nuclear family and lodgers together with any live-in servants. This form accounted for another 20 per cent of all households. The remainder contained either apprentices or members of the extended family. It is possible, then, to speak of the city as a private community in which children grew up and lived in close proximity with a narrow range of people to whom they were closely related by blood. What is striking in the situation was the uniformity of structure across all major occupational and ethnic groups: about seven in ten families in each major element of society were nuclear in structure. Where structural differences did exist, they demonstrate that nuclear families were more common in lower-status households. Households headed by great merchants or professionals were just as likely as those headed by labourers to have lodgers, and were twice as likely to have members of the extended family in the household.[6] Similarly, female-headed households were less likely to have lodgers than households headed by any category of males. Far from creating a situation where the poor built up warrens of boarders and extended families, poverty in Saint John seems to have produced simple, lean households.

The characteristic that sharply distinguished higher-status households from lower ones and those with native, English, and Scottish-born heads from those with Irish-born heads was the presence of servants. Servants were the ineffable household convenience of the nineteenth century. They were cheap, plentiful, and (since they lived in) constantly on call. Almost all families of patricians and leading business and professional men employed at least one – and sometimes as many as four or five – and even families headed by grocers, teachers, and clerks employed them more often than not. They were a common sight in the homes of artisans and women heads and were occasionally found in those of labourers. Given the ethnic distribution of household heads, it comes as no surprise that servants were found in over one-third of households with native-born heads. That record was matched or exceeded in American-, Scottish-, and English-headed households. Trailing behind were early Irish households, although in terms of absolute numbers, there were more servants working in those homes than in those of any ethnic group other than natives. The distribution of servants and masters had significant social implications. Four of every five servants were Irish born; seven of every ten masters were not. For nearly one-third of all native households this was the nature of the personal relationship that existed with the recent Irish arrivals.[7]

The households of Saint John were formed either as a result of marriage

or from the determination of a single man or woman to set up a home. Few
married couples lived as part of an extended family. The typical resident
lived in a household having a married couple as its nucleus. That
description fitted nearly four households in five containing almost 90 per
cent of the city's population in 1851. The choice of marriage partner in a
pluralistic society was undoubtedly the most important cultural decision
made by any individual. It set the pattern of the little commonwealth
created by the union. Ultimately the marriage decisions of several
thousand individuals who formed the households of Saint John played an
important role in determining the shape and nature of the cultures that
would flourish within the city. Unfortunately, the data for assessing the
status of each partner at the time of each marriage do not exist. What the
census manuscript does permit is an examination of the extent to which
intermarriage occurred among members of the city's several 'ethnic'
groups. The results reconfirm the confluence of status and ethnicity to
create a lower-status group of Irish origins and a higher-status group of
natives.

The most noticeable feature of this structure was the manner in which
ethnic groups maintained a form of ethnic or cultural identity through the
marriage bond. The lowest level of ethnic intermarriage might have been
expected of those immigrant men over forty who had arrived in New
Brunswick after 1839. Most of these would have been past thirty at the
time of migration and would have taken British brides. This, in fact,
happened. Within the sample, 48 of 49 Irish and all 6 of the Scottish
husbands married in their native lands. Those men under forty who had
arrived in New Brunswick between 1840 and 1851, and those who were
over forty and who had been in the province since before 1840, might be
expected to have taken brides in either the United Kingdom or New
Brunswick, depending upon the time of their arrival. This expectation
was fulfilled by the English and Scots migrants, about half of whom
married outside their own ethnic group. It did not occur among the Irish,
90 per cent of whom took Irish brides. Finally and most significantly, the
young men who were under forty in 1851 and who had come to the
province before 1840 could reasonably be assumed to have taken wives
from ethnic backgrounds that conformed in some rough proportion to the
women available in Saint John County in the previous decade. In fact, this
did not occur among any of the major ethnic groups. Even the English,
who traditionally had demonstrated little discrimination, chose native
brides and carefully excluded the Irish, who must have composed more
than half the population of potential brides in the 1840s. The Scots
followed the same pattern. While some intermarriage occurred between
younger Irish heads and native women – in about one case in seven – it

was relatively infrequent, even though many of the native women over the age of twenty in the late 1840s would have been daughters of Irish migrants.

The marriage practices of native females seem positively liberal in comparison with those of native males. Only 4 of 64 native males under forty selected Irish brides. When added to the lone male over forty who was married to an Irish woman, it seems that just 5 of the 141 native-born household heads in the sample had Irish wives after nearly thirty-five years of Irish settlement in the city, a pattern conforming to the one Donald Cole found in Lawrence, Massachusetts.[8] Put another way, native males married more Scottish than Irish brides, despite the fact that Irish women were at least eight times as numerous as Scots. The sense of caste that is inherent in these figures is strengthened by the fact that native women who married Irish men tended to do so at the higher-status levels. Thus half the Irish-born heads found in high-status occupations took native wives. Whatever the reasons, the exclusion of the Irish population was socially significant. Religion undoubtedly played an important role in preventing intermarriage between many Irish and most other groups – all of which would have been largely Protestant – but it is not a sufficient explanation of the extent of the separation. A substantial part of the Irish population was Protestant and while it is probable that most intermarriage between natives and Irish involved a common protestantism, the census provides little evidence to suggest that Irish Protestants and native Protestants intermarried with that same casualness that characterized the English or Scots and the natives.

Having selected a wife, the young Saint John husband came to the trying matter of finding a place to live. Like most early-nineteenth-century cities, Saint John was a walking city. Time and the state of transportation technology dictated that everyone whose work was centred in the city must live within easy walking distance of the basic amenities of life. These would include, in particular, proximity to work place and market. The shape of the land mass on which the city was constructed severely limited the available territory for settlement and necessitated a succession of long, narrow lots and even narrower wooden buildings as the standard housing for the city. It necessitated, as well, very compact neighbourhoods in which the affluent and the very poor frequently lived within a block of each other. It encouraged the construction of three-storey buildings through much of the harbour area which were, in time, renovated for use as tenements. This in turn gave rise to a myth of a city of tenements, a myth seemingly confirmed by the numerous illustrations of the times. In fact, there were neighbourhoods of affluence and high status on the one hand, and of labourers on the other. In this, as in many other situations, the social cement holding the city together was the ubiquitous artisans, who were found in all neighbourhoods in every corner of the city.

The distribution and nature of housing reinforced other social patterns that characterized city life. The typical Saint John household was found in a rented duplex, although the range extended from single-family dwellings to sixteen-family tenements. Only one household in ten was found in a building containing more than five families. Nearly one-third of all households lived in single-family dwellings and nearly six in ten in either one- or two-family buildings. The quality of housing a family used was largely a matter of social position and ethnicity. The move from the houses of those engaged in high-status occupations to those of artisans to those of labourers was like stair steps: 70 per cent of merchants, 25 per cent of artisans, and 8 per cent of labourers lived in single-family dwellings; 14 per cent of labourers, 4 per cent of artisans, and no merchants lived in five-family dwellings. The accomodations enjoyed by families headed by women corresponded very closely to those of artisans. The same differences were found among ethnic groups. The median dwelling place of the family headed by an Englishman was a single-family dwelling; that of the native, Scot, and American, a two-family dwelling; while the early Irish arrival lived in a three-family dwelling and the recent Irishman in a four-family dwelling. The result was a concentration of the non-Irish in the business areas and the residential areas on the Courtenay Bay side of the peninsula. Later Irish migrants were concentrated in multi-family dwellings, particularly in Kings and Sydney wards, where large, socially undifferentiated Irish ghettos were formed.

The principal purpose of the Saint John household seems to have been the raising of children. Nearly half the population in 1851 was under the age of 17. Families within the sample averaged 2.29 children under 17 living at home; households averaged 2.36 including, in addition to their own children, a collection of nieces, nephews, younger brothers and sisters, servants, apprentices, clerks, and boarders. The most characteristic relationship, however, was children living at home. Until the age of ten, virtually all children lived with their parents.

Examination of the children at three-year intervals – ages 3, 6, and 9 – provides an insight into the social environment of these young children and into the nature of urban society at mid-century. Both occupational status and ethnicity were factors in family size. Not unexpectedly, households headed by women had the smallest number of children, a reflection of the large number of elderly widows included in the sample. By contrast, labourers headed 20 per cent of Saint John households and accounted for 27 per cent of the city's children. The families headed by natives were slightly underrepresented among the city's children – a possible reflection of the greater average age of the native heads – while the households with Irish-born heads, who accounted for 57 per cent of the households, provided 63 per cent of the children aged 3, 6, and 9. Perhaps the most striking fact to emerge from this examination was the selective-sieve effect of the Irish migration. Few of the great numbers of 'famine Irish' of the 1845–49 period stayed in the city. Of the 97 six-year-olds in the sample, only 16 had been born in Ireland. At the same time, 62 of the 97 fathers of these children had been born in Ireland. The same ratios characterized the city's nine-year-old children. These data suggest that three-quarters of the Irish in the child-bearing years remaining in the city were pre-famine arrivals.[9]

The relationship between children and parents became less permanent as the children entered the teen years. The process of coming of age in Saint John began as early as 11 years for a few children and was well under way for most by the age of 16. It continued for some until the age of 30. The process was influenced as much by the sex of the child as by the status and ethnicity of the parents. After the age of 12, the upbringing of a girl broke entirely from that of her brother. The most important decision in the life of a Saint John adolescent girl was to go into service. One twelve-year-old in fourteen was a live-in servant in 1851. The proportion grew rapidly after that age. By 16 it was one in four. At the height of the movement to service – at age 20 – approximately 42 per cent of all Saint John women cleaned, cooked, washed, and waited in the homes of their betters. Thereafter, as they married, the proportion of servants slowly declined, falling back to one in four at age 25 and to one in seven at age 29.[10]

The decision to enter service had important implications for a young woman. Whether 12 or 20, a servant moved from her father's household and authority to the household and authority of her employer. The critical determinants in deciding which girls became servants were the ethnicity and occupational status of their household head. The highest correlation was between those who remained at home and father's ethnicity.

Native-born women stayed home longer than females born elsewhere; and among natives, those with native fathers stayed home longer than those with Irish-, Scottish-, or English-born fathers. Among girls 3, 6, 9, and 12 years of age living at home, the proportion of Irish fathers to native fathers was nearly three to one; at ages 15 and 18 it fell to one and one-half to one; and by 24 was one to two in favour of the native fathers. Some servants were certainly recruited from among the country girls who flocked to the city seeking their fortunes – they may have accounted for the relatively large number of native-born servants in the city – but the high proportion of very young Irish-born servants who had recently arrived in the city suggests that most were either fatherless or the daughters of urban labourers. About four of five servants were Irish born and nearly four-fifths of these were recent Irish arrivals. A majority of fourteen-year-old Irish girls who had arrived in New Brunswick after 1839 were servants; by age 20 the proportion of servants among this group had risen to three in four. The native/Irish dichotomy, so obvious in the occupational status of household heads, was the striking feature of this analysis. Among twenty-year-old native-born women, two-thirds lived at home and one in seven was in service. Among their Irish-born counterparts, one in nine lived at home and more than two-thirds were servants.[11]

The final act in the rites of passage to adulthood for a woman was marriage. Few women took this step before the age of 20 and it was only at 26 that a clear majority of women were married in 1851. Some may have continued as live-out servants after marriage, but as all but a handful went on to form their household after marriage, it is impossible to identify them. The late age of marriage stands in striking contrast to early departure from the parental household. At age 20, when most women were just beginning to think of the possibility of marriage, more than three in five were living away from home.

Fundamental to any understanding of the male coming of age in mid-century Saint John was the basic demographic balance between males and females in the 16–30 age range. A rough numerical equality between the sexes was maintained up to the age of 12. After that, the number of females rose slightly – doubtless reflecting a migration of country girls to the city – and the number of males fell sharply. In 1851, adult Saint John was essentially a city of women. The census sample revealed 41 eighteen-year-old women for every 28 men. Among twenty-four-year-olds, the differential rose to 44 females for every 17 males. The evidence suggests that the number of young men in the city fell by about one-third between the ages of 15 and 21. The 'missing third' was to have important long-range effects on the composition of the population. Among several social factors that can be measured, the highest correlation exists between retention and fathers' occupation. Among children living at home aged 3, 6, and 9 years, about 28 per cent were offspring of labourers and other unskilled workers. The proportion fell to only 6 per cent among eighteen-year-olds and finally to nothing among the twenty-year-olds in the sample. Virtually all labourers' sons left home sometime between 15 and 18 years and since few of them can be found boarding elsewhere as labourers, it is probable that they were either boarding as artisans or clerks or had left the city, thus accounting for most of the diminished numbers of males in the 16–30 age group.

The young men who remained in the city seem to have lived at home until the time of their marriage. Those who did not live at home between 14 and 18 were largely apprentices living with their masters. After that age there was a growing minority of young men of the city: among twenty-two-year-old men, for example, 80 per cent lived at home. It was not until the age of 25 that boarders outnumbered those living with their parents, but by this time nearly 40 per cent of the male population was married. In fact, the age of 25 seems to have been a marital watershed for young men who had been raised in the city. Few married before the age of 25; by 26 a majority had made that commitment.[12]

The young men who remained at home after the age of 15 were concentrated in the families of white-collar workers, artisans, and the semi-skilled. Artisans' sons alone composed well over half of all the twenty-one-year-old males living at home in 1851. Their numbers remained undiminished from ages 15 to 21, while those from households headed by women and by men of other occupational statuses declined significantly. Seemingly, the artisans provided the most stable and tightly knit group of families in the city.

Most young men who lived at home after the age of 18 were engaged in some gainful employment. Typically, they were artisans and either Irish-born or native-born sons of Irish artisans who had come to New Brunswick before 1840. The longer the Irish household head had been in the province, the more likely was his son to be an artisan. A minority of working sons – about one in five – were sons of native household heads, and all of these were either artisans or clerks. Regardless of background, however, the great majority of working sons lived with and were the sons and brothers of artisans. And their presence in their father's household, together with the similarities in trades practised by father and son, strongly suggests that they acquired marketable skills from their fathers.

Working sons and brothers of household heads were part of a larger group of working lodgers found in the households of Saint John. Gainfully employed males who were not household heads constituted about one-fifth of the city's male work-force. About one-third of these were related to the household head. As a group they were part of a workers' élite possessing, on average, a level of skill above that of the work-force at large.

The conjunction of occupational status and ethnicity that produced such notable differences among household heads was repeated among the working lodgers. Two distinct elements are obvious within the group. One consisted of young, recent Irish migrants who had arrived alone in the city between 1847 and 1851. They composed about a quarter of all lodgers and were divided almost equally between artisans and labourers.

The second, larger, group of lodgers consisted of those either born or raised in the province.[13] They were younger than the recent Irish arrivals and were engaged in significantly higher-status occupations. A few were employed at semi-skilled tasks, but almost all were clerks and artisans. Even within this group, there was a sharp difference in status between the early Irish arrivals on the one hand and the native, English, and Scots born on the other: the former were concentrated among the artisanal occupations, while a majority of the latter were found in clerical occupations.

Just as lodgers in general reflected a higher occupational status than did family heads, so, too, did lodgers of each origin possess a higher status than did the family heads of that origin. That fact was particularly significant for the native- and English-born lodgers. Native-born workers who remained at home were overwhelmingly artisans. Those who became lodgers in the homes of other people apparently did so to procure advancement. Most became clerks in the city's larger mercantile establishments. If social mobility was occurring in the city at mid-century, this was almost certainly the means through which the sons of artisans and semi-skilled workers moved through white-collar employment toward the goal of commercial proprietorship. The monopoly that the natives, English, and Scots had established in this nursery of entrepreneurship was remarkable: while they constituted only 42 per cent of the city's lodgers, they held 88 per cent of the critical white-collar positions. Most of the remaining native, English, and Scottish lodgers were artisans. With the exception of a single Scot, there were no labourers or semi-skilled workers in the group.

Unlike those of Hamilton, Saint John lodgers seem to have lived in households where the heads possessed an occupational status comparable to their own.[14] More than half the white-collar workers lived in households with men of high social standing. More than 80 per cent of artisan lodgers lived in artisan households, and nearly the same proportion of labourers lived in labourer-headed households. The identity of occupational interests between household heads and lodgers was also characteristic of ethnicity. The universal landlords of the city were the early Irish who accommodated natives, early Irish, and late Irish in about equal numbers. But this constituted the greatest degree of integration that occurred among the city's lodgers. The high correlation between native, English, and Scottish birthplace and high-status occupation meant that native-born workers were found among the clerks and artisans and boarded with native clerks and artisans. Similarly, early and recent Irish lodgers were mostly artisans and labourers and boarded with artisans and labourers. As a result, most Irish workers lived with recent Irish landlords, early Irish workers with early Irish landlords, and native lodgers with native landlords. Conversely, recent Irish landlords rarely had non-Irish lodgers while native, English, and Scottish landlords confined themselves to native, English, and Scottish lodgers.

The high correlation between the occupational status of lodger and landlord in the first three occupational ranks listed earlier can be explained through the fact that most Saint John lodgers had either familial or occupational connection with their landlords. Saint John was a commercial pre-industrial city. Merchants' buildings were often mercantile establishments in which the clerks lived with their employers, and the presence of fourteen-year-old lodger-clerks strongly suggests an apprentice/master relationship. Workshop manufacture remained a prominent feature of the city's economic life in 1851. Explicit legal apprenticeships still continued and hundreds of journeymen artisans, including some married men, lived with their masters. While it is impossible to determine with any degree of accuracy which lodgers were actually employees of household heads, the frequency with which groups of two, three, or four clerks lived with prominent merchants, shoe-makers lived with master shoe-makers, and builders lived with master builders strongly suggests an employee/employer relationship between lodger and household heads in a clear majority of cases. In most cases, these live-in arrangements were marked by a high correlation of ethnic background for employer and employee. Whether this was a policy of deliberate discrimination on the part of employers or resulted from a tendency to employ or apprentice acquaintances, the effect was the same. Native heads had mainly native employees living in their homes, English heads had mostly English, Scots heads had largely natives, and late Irish had largely late Irish. Only among the early Irish household heads was the pattern broken. They selected employees from among natives, and both early and recent Irish arrivals, although, since some of the native clerks and artisans were sons of Irish migrants, the diversity may not have been as great as it appears. In all, given the number of working sons and brothers living at home and the number of employees and apprentices living in their masters' households, it seems that a large majority of Saint John's population of permanent lodgers were an integral part of the household in which they lived. The pattern reflects both the homogeneity of the household and the unintegrated character of the city as a whole.

Taken together, gainfully employed male heads of households and lodgers constituted the permanent male work force of the city. Within the sample, they totalled 782 individuals and averaged slightly more than one per household. The ethnic structure of that work force corresponded very closely to that of the household heads. The occupational structure differed from the latter in that the artisans assumed a much more important place, composing nearly two-fifths the entire work-force, while white-collar workers were somewhat more significant.

The remainder of the urban work force consisted of women. Unfortunately, although it is certain that many women performed tasks outside the management of the household, the census records occupation only for those women who were live-in servants. This record is of limited value since it omits such obvious groups as women teachers and women labourers, both of which were to be found in the city. Even this record, however, reveals something of the extent and significance of female participation in the urban work force. There were 194 live-in female servants in the sample, indicating a total of about 1000 in the east-side city. And this figure omits all day servants. This figure suggests that servants made up by far the most numerous occupational group in the city, easily outnumbering all male labourers. In this respect, the labour force of Saint John at mid-century bore a curious resemblance to that of England in the same period, where servants outnumbered the factory workers who played such important roles in the work life of the period.

At mid-century, then, the structures of household, work force, and demography combined with social origins, status, and length of residence in the city to produce clearly identifiable cultural patterns having considerable potential significance for the kind of community that might develop. The social status of the keepers of the Loyalist tradition, the tendency of certain groups to remain in the city while others left, the strongly upwardly mobile tendency among young natives, Scots, and English born, coupled with the stark social division between Irish and non-Irish households and families, contained many of the elements of a caste system. The conjunction of ethnicity, occupational position, and political influence suggests a dominant minority and a low-status majority, which played only a small role in determining the nature of the community.

Conclusion

Between 1815 and 1860, Saint John made the transition from town to city. By the latter date, it was already into what in retrospect would be viewed as a 'golden age' of affluence and prestige. The transformation occurred very quickly; the adjustments that the people and institutions of this small port made, or were forced to make, provide some insight into the process of nineteenth-century urban growth and into the problem of maintaining community in the face of that process. A number of questions arise in connection with this transformation. How does a traditional society hold together as it rapidly increases in size and complexity? Is it through a process of integration, accommodation, or social conflict? What are the sources of urban growth? To what extent are these sources internally or externally generated, and to what extent do they strengthen existing relationships within the community? In Saint John, as in all cities, the urban process was characterized by growing economic inequality, ethnic diversity, new transport, banking, and industrial institutions, mass-based popular movements, and new social institutions. The process is best understood through the changes it wrought in the town during the period of this study.

The native returning to Saint John in 1860 after a half-century's absence would be most struck by changes in its physical appearance. Not that these were dramatic: Saint John remained a walking city and the urban concentration did not extend much more than a mile and a half in any direction from the market wharf. Within that area, the small market villages clustered around the harbour had fairly well filled in the east-side peninsula; the high promontories at the centre had been cut down and the main thoroughfares widened. Streets now extended in a grid pattern throughout the peninsula and linked with those of neighbouring Portland. Most streets on the harbour side were lighted by gas lamps and the streets themselves were constantly broken to permit gas and sewerage-and-water lines to run from mains to the edge of each property. The military installations remained in the south end, but otherwise the harbour side of the peninsula was scarcely recognizable. At either end, but particularly at York Point in the north, were thick clusters of three- and four-storey buildings in narrow streets housing the poorest elements in the city's population. Between them, occupying most of the harbour side, were warehouses, stores, workshops, modest homes, and the more opulent homes of the wealthy – an area in which neighbourhoods of identifiable social groups might be no more than one-half block in size. The most striking feature of this area was the King Square–Market Wharf–Prince William commercial centre where the increasing use of brick and even stone (in reaction to the recurring holocausts of the mid-century) created buildings standing in sharp contrast to the wooden structures that dominated the city and its suburbs.

The back half of the peninsula, which in 1815 had been largely meadow, was mainly occupied by the modest narrow one- and two-family dwellings of artisans, shopkeepers, and the most prosperous labourers, and the shops of small producers. And this sweep of wooden structures continued backward into Portland. In the north, near the Portland border, were found many of the larger industrial enterprises. Much of the east-side harbour structure would be recognizable to the 1815 resident, but there were more wharves and even the older had in many cases been widened and extended. The west-side harbour would have been unrecognizable. The mill-pond, which occupied much of the peninsula, had been drained. The extensive system of terminals (developed to accommodate the lumber industry) and the large steam-powered sawmills in Carleton and Portland were all new emplacements. Even the larger timber ships in the summer harbour – often exceeding 1500 tons – would have seemed to dwarf the harbour in comparison with the much smaller ships of the Napoleonic period. Finally, the shipyards lining the shores of Carleton, Portland, and Courtenay Bay would not have changed much, but there were many more of them and they were designed to permit construction of much larger vessels.

The urban site in 1860 was not substantially different from that of 1815. The distinction was in the concentration of activity. Many more activities were carried out in the same area by many more people using many more tools. The effect was to produce a congestion in public places that provoked images of disorder. The noise, particularly in the harbour areas, would often be intense and the smells emanating from many activities often distressing.

Physical change in the city was largely the result of population and commercial growth and changes in modes of production. The 1815 town had been a distribution centre for the St John River valley and a port for export of timber to the United Kingdom. These activities gradually changed. Until 1830 the timber trade remained the principal engine of economic growth. After 1830 the economy diversified, with sawn lumber and other wood products playing increasingly important roles. The exploitation of timber resources and interior settlement created many urban opportunities for both entrepreneurs and producers, and the extensive merchant marine offered easy access to both British migrants and American skilled labour. The flood of unskilled British labour and the growing demands of the port combined both to depress wages and to create a large body of unskilled urban labourers whose habitations and work centred on the harbour.

The most significant development after 1830 was the growth of an extensive network of enterprises capable of making a variety of commodities ranging from shoes to ships to steam engines for both local and overseas markets. It was manifest structurally through a large number of small proprietorships, many of which housed journeymen and apprentices and provided opportunity for upward or lateral mobility for many native and incoming artisans. Gradually a number of these businesses had evolved into sizeable firms, notably foundries, employing numbers of highly skilled mechanics. By mid-century, the urban economy contained elements of traditional, mercantile, handcraft, and industrial systems, but commerce and workshop manufacturing remained the dominant forms of enterprise.

As the economy expanded and became more diversified, it produced a more stratified society – one in which the extremes of great wealth and abject poverty became increasingly obvious. This trend was particularly noticeable in the old timber trade sector, which produced both the great merchants (by far the wealthiest men within the province) and the ship labourers who toiled on their docks. While the urban expansion provided increased opportunities for many small proprietors and artisans, the stratification itself posed a threat to artisans without sources of capital or influence. Yet despite social diversity and the growth of a powerful producers' interest, there was at no time any questioning of the assumption that property rights were inalienable and absolute. While the influence of the old functioning élite diminished, the social prestige and influence of the great merchant remained a potent force in the political life of the city, although this group played a less direct role in the decision-making process. The crisis of the timber trade after 1840 produced a long period of disorder, tension, and sometimes confrontation between supporters of that interest and those whose concerns were more local. Occasionally, too, there were episodes of resistance on the part of some workers, notably ship labourers, to wages and terms laid down by employers.

Ethnic and religious complexity added to the stratification of the emerging city. Ethnic complexity was provided primarily by the Irish migrants, consisting of powerful and assertive groups of Roman Catholics and Protestants. The integration of this large immigrant population was further complicated by a virtual Irish monopoly of the unskilled labour of the port and the concentration of a large part of the Roman Catholic population in the low-cost housing of York Point. Attempts by Catholic leaders to create a distinctive sub-community after 1830 were initially met with violence and finally, through a series of accommodations, the tacit recognition of certain group rights. The Catholic struggle for recognition was only the most spectacular sign of the growing religious complexity of the city. The old Episcopalian-Wesleyan accommodation of the eighteenth-century town was broken with the emergence of Presbyterian and Baptist traditions in the city. This was accompanied by bitter conflict between defenders of the traditional order and supporters of the migrant tradition. The most successful integrative influence in this case was evangelicalism, which had arisen for many of the same reasons and to accomplish the same ends as the Catholic revival. In its efforts to save and reform the community, evangelicalism gave rise to a variety of voluntary associations. Although it challenged the old high-church position and was viewed with suspicion by much of the old élite, it cut across denominational structures and ethnic traditions. It was particularly strong within the producers' interest.

These were all manifestations of the urban process. Their effects generally were to alter the social structure of the community and to introduce traditions and institutions that threatened its stability. That destabilization of the community did not occur easily. The durability of the community and the ability of its leaders to make adjustments when necessary are striking. The Catholic accommodation has already been mentioned. The accommodative tradition was most obvious in the matter of education of the young. Before 1830 this had been an Episcopal monopoly. After that, each tradition of any influence within the city was eventually permitted to maintain its school. By 1860 a genuine pluralism was evident in this area. Another attempt to forge a common bond within the city was the temperance movement, which began as an élitist society, expanded to embrace all major traditions in the city, and in its later manifestations emerged as a popular but proscriptive movement.

Most of the burden of urban adjustment was borne in the common life and public institutions of the city. The common life of the town had centred on a village market ward, headed by an alderman and assistant, and involving a large proportion of the resident males in fulfilling the functions necessary to the community. Population growth and subsequent demands for services and facilities led to the professionalization of the common life. Increasingly a brokerage of public servants mediated the city to its citizens and other residents. The breakdown of the old ward and patronage-based system was long in coming and its demise after 1850 saw the integration of the public life not only of the city but, for certain services, of the urban periphery. The pressure on land and the growing number of less-affluent migrants led to a growing group of propertyless freemen and potential freemen, and to demands to 'modernize' what was perceived as the archaic structures of the common life by eliminating the traditional entitlements to economic protection and to the franchise. Citizenship was to be equated to possession of physical property rather than possession of skills. The old way proved to be particularly resilient and it was only when faced with the urban catastrophes of group violence and massive fire damage that the structures of community were fundamentally altered.

A prominent feature of public life after 1830 was the development of several broadly based movements for reform. Drawing from several motives and social groups, they all in some fashion aimed at the improvement of the urban environment, although their solutions were sometimes contradictory. Supporters of temperance, education, religious equality, police and charter reforms, and, after 1850, public health, all demonstrated a need to organize and integrate all elements of the community, usually in the interests of some ideology or social group. The changes that occurred or did not occur, however, had a good deal to do with those individuals and groups that were able to exercise power within the city. Throughout most of the transition period, the active leadership of the city remained in the hands of small proprietors and leading artisans. The economic élite could intrude under certain conditions – as they did decisively in the collapse of 1842 – to achieve a particular end, but even in the era of the reformed charter, leadership of the principal public institutions was an arduous undertaking and those who made most public decisions were those who devoted a great deal of time and effort to cultivating the constituency. Indeed the growing artisanal presence and its strong influence in the major social and religious movements of the period provide one of the most distinctive features of urban society of the colonial period. The innovation and urban growth that altered all other segments of Saint John society necessarily affected the artisan as well. The most successful masters were in the process of becoming mill owners and the traditional artisan formation weakened under the impact of steam power. None the less, the interest provided a nexus around which many of the newer visions of urban community coalesced.

Many of the most critical decisions involving the welfare of Saint John were made through external agencies. The imposition of the preference for colonial timber and its removal were imperial decisions. An imperial garrison provided the final solution to any problem of urban disorder, and an imperial governor in Fredericton could intervene to impose a stipendiary magistrate. Equally important, those who considered the urban condition of Saint John did so in terms of English models, and the city's municipal institutions at mid-century reflected more than anything else that early nineteenth-century English experience. Despite the imperial influence, the autonomy of the city, like that of the province of which it was the metropolitan city, actually increased during the period. Saint John banks carried the provincial debt and provided the principal circulating medium throughout much of New Brunswick, Nova Scotia, and Maine. Saint John firms dominated the commercial and industrial life of the Bay of Fundy watershed. Saint John was the publishing and administrative centre that generated and informed so much of the religious, educational, journalistic, and popular life of the region. And as the imperial influence diminished at mid-century, the city increasingly became the final reference point of its urban élites.

The community of 1860 was a much more abstract and centralized ideal than the one that existed earlier in the century. The ward and the neighbourhood had all but disappeared as anything other than electoral districts and with them had disappeared the integrative force of the older ideal where alderman, supervisor, and resident had met in a series of personal relationships. Also gone was the unity of a formal social hierarchy implied in the charter and the imperial establishment. Instead, Saint John citizens defined themselves not only in terms of a city increasingly interpreted through impersonal institutions staffed by professionals, but also in terms of sub-communities based on culture and interest. This limited pluralism, coupled with changing definitions of respectability and a fair degree of social mobility engendered by urban growth, gave the impression of a city in flux, in which one thing was becoming another. The sources of this change were complex, embracing changing economic circumstances, ideological viewpoints, the intrusion of new social and ethnic groups into the urban environment, and the impact of an English urban model.

Appendix

The occupational-status categories appearing in some of the following tables are discussed in chapter 12.

1 high-status positions (merchant wholesalers, leading officials, prominent professional groups)
2 white-collar group (grocers, clerks, and teachers)
3 skilled labour (artisans, mechanics, and other skilled workers)
4 semi-skilled workers (the teamsters, for example)
5 unskilled workers
6 status unclear
7 female-headed households

TABLE 1
Population of Saint John 1785–1861

	East side		West side		City		Portland		Urban Saint John
1785					3,500*				
1810					4,500*				
1824					8,488	+	1,813	=	10,301
1834	12,073	+	812	=	12,885	+	3,215	=	16,100
1840	19,281	+	1,435	=	20,716	+	6,207	=	26,923
1851					22,745	+	8,429	=	31,174
1861					27,317	+	11,500	=	38,817

*Estimates based on the constables' census of 1785 and militia counts of 1808–09–10

TABLE 2
Shipbuilding in New Brunswick and Saint John in five-year averages

	New New Brunswick vessels built		New Saint John vessels built	
	Total tons	Tons per vessel	Total tons	Tons per vessel
1820–24			1,899	288
1825–29	21,160	216	3,314	388
1830–34	11,465	229	4,087	426
1835–39	25,500	221	11,564	521
1840–44	21,609	323	9,698	630
1845–49	25,601	366	12,715	714
1850–54	43,737	554	27,621	939
1855–59	46,636	569	21,805	832

SOURCES: Keith Matthews, 'The Shipping Industry of Atlantic Canada: Themes and Problems,' *Ships and Ship Building in the North Atlantic Region* (St John's 1978); E.C. Wright, *Saint John Ships and Their Builders* (Wolfville 1976); New Brunswick, *Journals of the House of Assembly*, customs house reports

TABLE 3

Freeman admissions in Saint John 1785–1859

		Percentage by occupational status*						
	Number	High	White collar	Artisan	Semi-skilled	Unskilled	Unknown	Total
1785	499	15	19	48	7	1	9	100
1786–99	496	14	5	32	16	15	18	100
1800–09	355	11	2	38	13	21	15	100
1810–19	757	11	4	37	10	31	8	100
1820–29	943	9	11	30	8	42	1	100
1830–39	1,216	15	11	34	8	26	6	100
1840–49	1,041	15	11	39	7	22	4	100
1850–59	1,690	12	19	36	13	4	16	100

*For a breakdown of the five occupational groups used here see chapter 12.
SOURCE: Freeman's Rolls

TABLE 4

Occupational status of Saint John aldermen and
assistant aldermen 1815–19, 1835–39, 1854–58

	Aldermen		Assistant aldermen	
Status	Number (%)	Terms (%)	Number (%)	Terms (%)
Gentlemen/lawyers	5	6	2	2
Great merchants	15	15	2	2
Millowners	2	5		
Minor merchants	29	35	4	2
Clerical/teachers	15	11	11	12
Major artisans*	12	14	11	15
Minor artisans	7	6	39	45
Mariners	2	2	4	4
Labourers	2	1	13	8
Unkown	10	5	13	10
TOTAL	100	100	100	100
TOTAL NUMBER	41	96	45	96

*Tanners, printers, shipbuilding trades

TABLE 5
Comparison of daily wages at Saint John
by craft 1831, 1841, 1846

Craft	Daily wage (in pence)		
	1831	1841	1846
Master carpenter and joiner	108		
Millwright		90	75
Plasterer		90	
Carpenter and joiner	90	85	66
Shipwright		84	60
Cabinet-maker	80	79	66
Tailor		79	54
Painter		79	60
Quarryman		72	
Blacksmith		68	60
Butcher	64	66	54
Sail maker			66
Mason		66	
Tanner			66
Cooper	60	60	60
Cartman		60	48
Sawyer			60
Shoe-maker		57	42
Gardener		54	
Watchman (police)		40	
Baker	33	32	43
Wheelwright		30	66
Labourer*	36	30	30
Groom		20	
Cook	9	12	
Maid		8	

*Based on wages paid to road workers by the city corporation
SOURCE: CO 188/41, 306. Campbell to Goderich, Rates of Wages
at Saint John. Prepared by L. Donaldson, 10 October 1831. CO
188/75, Colebrook to Stanley, 26 February 1842, Return of
Average Wages in Saint John. Prepared by A. Wedderburn. New
Brunswick, *Journals of the House of Assembly* (1847), appendix,
report of the emigrant agent

TABLE 6

Comparison of consumer prices of food, fuel, and clothing
at Saint John 1831, 1841, 1846

	Price (in pence)		
Commodity	1831	1841	1846
Bacon (lb)		9	
Salt beef (lb)		6	3½
Fresh pork (lb)		6	3½
Salt pork (lb)			4
Mutton (lb)		5	
Lamb (lb)		5	
Herring (lb)	½		
Salt fish (lb)	1	1	⅘
Butter (lb)		13	9
Cheese (lb)		8	6
Eggs (doz)		11	10
Oatmeal (lb)		3	1½
Flour (lb)	2		1⅓
Wheat bread (lb)	3½	2	1¾
Potatoes (lb)	⅓	½	½
Tea (lb)		48	24
Brown sugar (lb)		6	4
Milk (gal)		20	12
Beer (gal)		18	15
Firewood (cord)		240	216
Coal (chald)		420	240
Candles (lb)		12	8
Soap (lb)		6	
Men's work shoes		120	72
Women's work shoes		105	54
Flannel shirt		69	40
Smock frocks		39	
Coat cloth (yd)		108	
Cotton cloth (yd)		9	
Fustian cloth (yd)		12	

SOURCE: See table 5

TABLE 7
Religious distribution of Irish
population in Saint John region, 1871 Census*

Ward	Population	Irish origins	Catholic Irish (%)	Protestant Irish (%)	Total (%)
Prince	4,976	2,988	51	49	100
Wellington	4,008	2,057	48	52	100
Kings	3,785	2,767	81	19	100
Queens	4,985	2,354	50	50	100
Dukes	4,253	2,088	51	49	100
Sydney	2,265	1,320	70	30	100
Brooks	1,332	765	52	48	100
Albert	1,219	679	59	41	100
Guys	1,982	587	46	54	100
City	28,805	15,605	58	42	100
St John County (outside city)	23,315	14,515	48	52	100
Charlotte County	25,882	10,154	35	65	100
Kings County	24,593	10,841	30	70	100
Queens County	13,847	5,469	22	78	100

*The figures in this table are based on the assumption that 90 per cent of the Roman Catholic population in the region were of Irish origin.

TABLE 8
Social characteristics of the members of the Saint John
Total Abstinence Society 1832–40*

Number in sample		124
Number in sample who were freemen		54
Occupational status		
high status	12%	
white collar	4%	
artisans	72%	
semi-skilled	4%	
unskilled	10%	
TOTAL	100%	
Number in sample for whom age identified		51
Under 15	8%	
15–19	22%	
20–24	18%	
25–29	12%	
30–34	12%	
35–39	12%	
40 and over	16%	
TOTAL	100%	
Average age at admission		25.9
Median age at admission		26
Number in sample for whom birthplace identified		22
New Brunswick	54%	
Ireland	32%	
England	10%	
Scotland	4%	
TOTAL	100%	

*Based on a 20 per cent systematic sample of male membership

TABLE 9

School attendance in Saint John (1851) by
ethnic origin and occupation of family head

	Number	Percentage attending school
Total of children 6–16 in 1851 Census sample*	876	
Total attending school	526	
Children of high-status family heads	83	84
Children of white-collar family heads	115	73
Children of artisans	259	63
Children of semi-skilled workers	53	58
Children of unskilled workers	248	54
All other children	118	29
Children of native-born heads of household	200	66
Children of Irish immigrants before 1840	332	68
Children of Irish immigrants after 1839	190	43
Children of English heads of household	61	67
Children of Scots heads of household	45	60

*See chapter 12 for a definition of the sample.

TABLE 10
Saint John school enrolment c. 1860

School	Enrolment	Percentage of city enrolment	Annual provincial grant (£)	Number of schools 1861
Common schools (1859)*	1555	45	500	16
Private schools	1868†	55	1085	42†
Church of England Madras schools (1859)	731		400	
Roman Catholic free schools (1863)	557		210	
Wesleyan Varley School (1860)	164		100	
Saint John High School (Baptist) (1861)	147			
Inter-denominational Commercial School (1860)	131		100	
Saint John Grammar School (1815)	47		150	
Inter-denominational Ragged schools (1860)	91		50	
Inter-denominational African schools (1857)	–		75	
TOTAL	3423†	100		58†

*The 1858 Schools Act doubled the number of students in the common schools. In 1857 there were only 775 students.

†This is not a final figure. There were, in addition, a number of small private schools that did not receive government support.

SOURCES: New Brunswick, *Assembly Journals* (1859), 39th Report of Madras School, app. DC/xiv–v; New Brunswick, *Assembly Journals* (1862), Report of the Public Schools 1861, 64, REX/PA, vol. 44, 7/33, 7/34, 7/35, 7/36; REX/PA, vol. 43, 7/25; REX/PA vol. 41, 6/25, PANB

TABLE 11
Sources of electoral support for aldermanic candidates in the Kings Ward election 1848
(number of votes cast: 517; number of voters identified: 266)

		Origin of voter			
	Status	Native	Irish	Other	Total
	1 and 2	40*	30	15	85
	3	32	53	12	97
	4 and 5	10	63	11	84
	TOTAL	82	146	38	266

Porter			Needham			Ansley		
Native	Irish	Other	Native	Irish	Other	Native	Irish	Other
33*	43	40	25*	53	33	42*	4	26
31	26	17	44	64	66	25	10	17
10	25	27	40	67	64	50	5	9

*The numbers in the bottom part of the table are percentages of the numbers in the same cells of the top part. Thus 33% of the 40 status 1 and 2 natives voted for Porter.

TABLE 12
Occupational status and ethnicity of household heads,
Saint John 1851 Census sample

				Ethnicity (in per cent)						
Occupational status	All heads	Early Irish	Late Irish	Native	English	Scots	NS	US	Other	Number
1	9	2	2	17	21	21	7	13	–	66
2	14	12	8	18	19	23	13	13	–	99
3	30	30	24	31	35	42	40	33	–	222
4	10	15	9	8	12	4	7	7	–	74
5	20	26	40	3	4	2	7	13	–	150
6	3	2	1	4	6	2	13	–	–	20
7*	14	12	16	19	2	6	13	20	3	101
TOTAL	100†	100	100	100	100	100	100	100	100	100
NUMBER	732	220	198	182	48	48	15	15	6	732

*Female-headed households. No occupation specified.
†Rounding figures may sometimes produce totals of 99 or 101.

TABLE 13
Ethnic variations in occupational distribution of
household heads, Saint John 1851 Census sample

Ethnicity	All heads	Occupational distribution (in per cent)							Number
		1	2	3	4	5	6	7*	
Early Irish	30	9	26	30	43	39	25	30	220
Late Irish	27	5	17	21	24	53	10	31	198
Native	25	48	32	26	19	3	35	35	182
English	7	15	9	8	8	1	15	1	48
Scots	7	15	11	9	3	1	5	3	48
Nova Scotian	2	1	2	3	1	1	10	2	15
American	2	3	2	2	1	1	–	3	15
Other	1	3	–	2	–	1	–	–	6
TOTAL	100†	100	100	100	100	100	100	100	100
NUMBER	732	66	99	222	74	150	20	101	732

*Female-headed households; no occupation specified
†Rounding figure may sometimes produce totals of 99 or 101.

TABLE 14
Ethnicity and intermarriage,
Saint John 1851 Census sample (percentage)

Husband–Wife	All husbands	In New Brunswick before 1840		To New Brunswick 1840–51	
		Under 40	40+	Under 40	40+
Irish × Irish	88	81	90	89	94
Irish × Native	8	14	6	9	2
Irish × English	2	3	2	1	–
Irish × Scots	1	–	2	1	–
Irish × other	2	3	1	–	4
TOTAL	100	100	100	100	100
NUMBER	331	72	109	99	51
Native × Native	86	82	89	–	–
Native × Scots	4	3	6	–	–
Native × Irish	3	5	1	–	–
Native × English	3	3	3	–	–
Native × other	4	6	1	–	–
TOTAL	100	100	100	–	–
NUMBER	140	69	71	–	–
English × English	45	10	60	40	70
English × Native	30	50	22	40	10
English × Irish	17	–	18	20	20
English × Scots	4	20	–	–	–
English × other	4	20	–	–	–
TOTAL	100	100	100	100	100
NUMBER	47	10	17	10	10
Scots × Scots	51	13	58	38	100
Scots × Natives	36	62	24	63	–
Scots × English	8	25	6	–	–
Scots × Irish	3	–	6	–	–
Scots × other	3	–	6	–	–
TOTAL	100	100	100	100	100
NUMBER	39	8	17	8	6

TABLE 15
Coming of age:
women 12–29,
Saint John 1851 Census sample

Age	Number	Unmarried living with parents (%)	Servants (%)	Lodgers (%)	Married (%)	Total (%)
12	46	93	7	–	–	100
14	52	77	21	2	–	100
15	39	77	15	8	–	100
16	45	66	27	4	2	100
17	45	64	33	2	2	100
18	40	53	41	5	–	100
19	42	48	38	2	12	100
20	65	45	38	3	14	100
21	30	50	23	3	23	100
22	40	40	33	2	25	100
23	35	9	3	11	57	100
24	44	23	27	5	45	100
25	41	10	24	15	51	100
26	31	10	19	–	71	100
27	27	11	15	7	67	100
28	23	4	4	4	88	100
29	14	14	14	–	71	100

TABLE 16
Coming of age:
men 12–29,
Saint John 1851 Census sample

Age	Number	Unmarried living with parents (%)	Servants (%)	Apprentices (%)	Lodgers (%)	Married (%)	Total (%)
12	38	100	–	–	–	–	100
14	31	84	4	6	6	–	100
15	34	82	–	–	18	–	100
16	35	83	3	6	8	–	100
17	32	59	3	29	9	–	100
18	28	71	–	11	18	–	100
19	27	74	–	7	19	–	100
20	28	57	–	11	32	–	100
21	23	61	4	–	26	8	100
22	27	70	–	7	19	4	100
23	14	50	–	–	50	–	100
24	17	53	6	–	35	6	100
25	34	21	3	–	38	38	100
26	28	14	–	–	29	57	100
27	14	7	–	–	22	71	100
28	26	8	–	–	27	65	100
29	15	20	13	–	–	67	100

Comparison of occupational status and ethnicity of gainfully
employed male household heads, relatives of household heads, and lodgers,
Saint John 1851 Census sample

	Household heads (%)	Relatives (%)	Lodgers (%)
Occupational status			
1	10	–	5
2	16	20	28
3	35	54	45
4	12	13	–
5	24	14	21
6	3	–	2
TOTAL	100	100	100
NUMBER	631	56	95
Ethnicity			
Early Irish	31	25	13
Recent Irish	26	14	40
Native	23	45	28
English	7	7	8
Scots	7	–	6
Other	6	9	–
TOTAL	100	100	100
NUMBER	631	56	95

Notes

CHR	*Canadian Historical Review*
CO	Colonial Office (British)
mfm	microfilm
MSJ	Saint John Manuscripts
NBM	New Brunswick Museum
PANB	Provincial Archives of New Brunswick
pe	petition
RE	Report
REX, MG9	Records of the Executive Council, Public Archives of Canada
REX/PA	Records of the Executive Council, Provincial Archives Collection
RG	Record Group
RJU	Records of the Supreme Court
RLE	Records of the Legislative Assembly
RMU	Municipal Records
RS	Record Series
SJCH	Saint John City Hall
UNBA	University of New Brunswick Archives

INTRODUCTION

1 These are estimates based on the figures found in Warren Kalback and
Wayne W. McVey, *The Demographic Bases of Canadian Society* (Toronto 1971),
17. The following regional distribution is estimated between 1791 and 1860
(in thousands):

	Upper Canada (West)	Lower Canada (East)	Maritimes
1791	20	160	60
1815	100	350	140
1840	430	650	400
1860	1390	1110	660

2 The most useful overview of settlement and land policy remains Norman Macdonald's two-volume study, particularly volume I, *Canada 1763–1841 Immigration and Settlement: The Administration of the Imperial Land Regulations* (London 1939).
3 Discussion of this development and assessments of its significance are found in W.T. Easterbrook and H.G.J. Aitken, *Canadian Economic History* (Toronto 1956), chs IX, XI; A.R.M. Lower, *The North American Assault on the Canadian Forest* (Toronto 1938); W.S. MacNutt, *New Brunswick: A History: 1784–1867* (Toronto 1963); Graeme Wynn, *Timber Colony: A Historical Geography of Early Nineteenth Century New Brunswick* (Toronto 1981).
4 There is an extensive literature on this subject. See P.A.M. Taylor, *The Distant Magnet* (New York 1972); Helen I. Cowan, *British Emigration to North America: The First Hundred Years* (Toronto 1967); W.S. Shepperson, *British Emigration to North America* (Minneapolis 1957); Brinley Thomas, *Migration and Economic Growth: A Study of Great Britain and the Atlantic Economy* (Cambridge 1954); H.J.M. Johnston, *British Emigration Policy 1815–1830: Shovelling out Paupers* (Oxford 1972).
5 Cowan, *British Emigration to North America*, appendix B
6 Metropolitanism has been the dominant tradition in Canadian historical writing on the colonial period. Its principal philosopher has been J.M.S. Careless but it pervades most major work in the field. See Careless, 'Frontierism, Metropolitanism and Canadian History,' CHR xxxv (March 1954): 1–21, and his *Brown of the Globe* (Toronto 1959, 1963).
7 These trends are detailed in G.M. Craig, *Upper Canada: The Formative Years 1784–1841* (Toronto 1963); J.M.S. Careless, *The Union of the Canadas: The Growth of Canadian Institutions, 1841–1857* (Toronto 1967); MacNutt, *New Brunswick*; H.C. Pentland, *Labour and Capital in Canada 1650–1860* (Toronto 1981); J.S. Moir, *The Church in the British Era* (Toronto 1972); G.J.J. Tulchinsky, *The River Barons: Montreal Businessmen and the Growth of Industry and Transportation 1837–1853* (Toronto 1977); Bryan Palmer, *Working-Class Experience: The Rise and Reconstitution of Canadian Labour 1800–1980* (Toronto 1983).
8 G.A. Stelter, 'The City Building Process in Canada,' in G.A. Stelter and A.F.J. Artibise, eds, *Shaping the Urban Landscape* (Ottawa 1982), 5–10
9 J.M.S. Careless, 'Metropolis and Region: Interplay between City and Region in Canadian History before 1914,' *Urban History Review* (Feb. 1979): 99–118
10 A state Stelter denotes as a commercial town (Stelter, 'City Building Process,' 10)
11 There is an abundance of recent American literature discussing the formation of community and detailing the process of becoming urban. See, for example, Michael Frisch, *Town into City: Springfield Massachusetts and the Meaning of Community 1840–1880* (Cambridge, Mass. 1972), and D.H. Doyle, *The Social Order of a Frontier Community: Jacksonville, Illinois 1825–70* (Chicago 1983).
12 See Wynn, *Timber Colony*, and MacNutt's *New Brunswick* and his 'Politics of the Timber Trade in Colonial New Brunswick,' CHR xxx (March 1949): 47–65.
13 S.M. Blumin, *The Urban Threshold: Growth and Change in a Nineteenth-Century American Community* (Chicago 1976), 223–6
14 See, for example, Doyle *The Social Order of a Frontier Community*, 12–15. The

issue is implicit in the work of Frisch and Doyle, and in Blumin's *The Urban Threshold*.

15 This seems to have been true in Springfield, Mass., Kingston, NY and Jacksonville, Ill. See Blumin, *Urban Threshold*; Doyle, *Social Order*; and Frisch, *Town into City*.

16 This is argued for New York and Boston by Edward Pessen in 'Who Governed the Nation's Cities in the "Era of the Common Man"?' *Political Science Quarterly* LXXXVII (1972), and in Frisch, *Town into City*, 40.

17 In *The Social Organization of Early Industrial Capitalism* (Cambridge, Mass. 1982), Michael Katz argues that all inhabitants of every nineteenth-century North American city were members of either the business class or the working class, depending on whether or not they or their providers owned the means of production or worked for wages. By Katz's definition, part of this producers' interest was clearly business class, much was working class, and the working masters (small working artisans who owned their own shops) were the final vestige of an ancient class of no significance. In his earlier work on Hamilton, Katz argued for the existence of a three-class social system that seems to have more closely corresponded to the class structure of Saint John. See Katz, *The People of Canada East: Family and Class in a Mid-Nineteenth Century City* (Cambridge, Mass. 1975), ch. 4.

18 Discussions of the social instability of these groups and of the difficulty of classifying them in the nineteenth century are found in Geoffrey Crossick, 'Urban Society and the Petty Bourgeoisie in Nineteenth Century Britain,' in Derek Fraser and Anthony Sutcliffe, eds, *The Pursuit of Urban History* (London 1983), 306–25; Derek Fraser, *An Artisan Elite in Victorian Society: Kentish London 1840–1880* (London 1978); Susan Hirsch, *The Industrialization of Crafts in Newark 1800–1860* (Philadelphia 1978), esp. ch. 5; Bruce Laurie, *The Working People of Philadelphia 1800–1850* (Philadelphia 1980).

19 Some sense of the power of this tradition is found in Oscar Handlin, *Boston's Immigrants: A Study in Acculturation* (Boston 1941); Robert Ernst, *Immigrant Life in New York City 1825–1863* (New York 1949); M.W. Nicholson, 'The Catholic Church and the Irish in Victorian Toronto' (PHD thesis, University of Guelph 1980).

20 Frisch found a similar situation in Springfield, Massachusetts (see *Town into City*, 47–9).

21 A point made most forcefully by Blumin in *The Urban Threshold*.

CHAPTER 1

1 G.A. Stelter, 'The Political Economy of the City Building Process: Early Canadian Urban Development,' in Derek Fraser and Anthony Sutcliffe, eds, *The Pursuit of Urban History* (London 1983), 171

2 A detailed examination of trading patterns is found in F.B. MacMillan, 'The Trade of New Brunswick with Great Britain, the United States and the Caribbean 1784–1818' (unpublished MA thesis, University of New Brunswick 1954), particularly chs 2–4. A constables' census taken in 1785 showed 1121 males between the ages of 16 and 60 in the city. This group constituted about a quarter of a normally distributed population, but Loyalist returns reveal that the proportion of adult males was higher than normal.

See J.S. MacKinnon, 'The Development of Local Government in the City of Saint John 1785–1795' (unpublished MA thesis, University of New Brunswick 1968), 11–13, 44. The 1810 figure is derived from the militia rolls of 1809 that indicate a male population 16–60 about equal to that present in 1785.

3 Graeme Wynn, *Timber Colony: A Historical Geography of Early Nineteenth Century New Brunswick* (Toronto 1981), ch. 1, and J.H. Clapham, *An Economic History of Modern Britain: The Early Railways Age 1820–1850* (Cambridge 1964), 238

4 P.D. McClelland, 'The New Brunswick Economy in the Nineteenth Century' (unpublished PH D thesis, Harvard University 1966)

5 Arthur Lower, *The Assault on the Canadian Forest* (Toronto 1938), 66

6 The system is best described by Wynn in *Timber Colony*, ch. 5.

7 The 900-ton *Avon* required 390.5 man-days of labour for loading; by extrapolation the loading of 200,000 tons in a year would require the services of 500 men each working 200 days. See List of Labourers Loading the *Avon*, Ward Papers, packet 5, NBM. See also Judith Fingard, 'The Decline of the Sailor as a Ship Labourer in Nineteenth-Century Timber Ports,' *Labour/Le Travailleur* II (1977): 35–73.

8 *The New Brunswick Courier* (hereafter *The Courier*), 10 June 1837

9 Nathan Rosenberg, 'America's Rise to Woodworking Leadership,' in Brook Hirdle, ed., *America's Wooden Age: Aspects of Its Early Technology* (Tarrytown, NY 1975), 46

10 The figures for the value and weight of ton timber and deals are found in the annual customs house reports published in the New Brunswick *Journals of the House of Assembly.*

11 *The Courier*, 27 February 1836; *The Chronicle*, 12 July 1839; *The Commercial News* (hereafter *The News*), 23 April 1841; *The Courier*, 22 June 1839

12 RLE/836, pe. 91; RLE/837, pe. 78, PANB. By 1838 the company had erected 8 mills at a cost of £15,000; RLE/836, pe. 65, PANB; RLE/836, bill 65, PANB; RLE/839, pe. 43, PANB; *The Chronicle*, 12 July 1839.

13 New Brunswick, *Journals of the House of Assembly* (1852), population returns, appendix, xxiii

14 McClelland, 'The New Brunswick Economy,' 3, 4, A8

15 A detailed examination of the composition and changing nature of the Saint John fleet is found in Lewis R. Fischer, 'From Barques to Barges: The Shipping Industry of Saint John, New Brunswick 1820–1914' (paper presented to the Atlantic Canada Studies Conference, Fredericton, April 1978). The early history of the city's shipbuilding industry is traced in E.C. Wright, *Saint John Ships and Their Builders* (Wolfville, NS 1976), 5, 8, 40.

16 New Brunswick, *Journals of the House of Assembly* (1824–26, 1839–41, 1855–7), appendix, customs house returns

17 See the discussion of wealth and social position in chapter 4.

18 New Brunswick, *Journals of the House of Assembly* (1839, 1850, 1855), appendix, customs house returns

19 See the Chamber of Commerce report in *The Courier*, 2 February 1842.

20 The best study of evolution of the industry is Richard Rice, 'Shipbuilding in British America, 1787–1890: An Introductory Study' (unpublished PH D thesis, University of Liverpool 1977). Rice demonstrates that almost half the provincial tonnage of new vessels in 1865 was built in Saint John.

21 H.Y. Hind, et al., *Eighty Years Progress of British North America* (Toronto 1863), 599.

22 There was a total of 62 marine tradesmen in the 1851 Census sample figures that indicate 300 tradesmen. However, the shipyards of Carleton and Portland were more extensive than were those of the east-side city. It is reasonable to assume that two-thirds or more of the marine tradesmen lived outside the east side.

23 This figure is based on Perley's figures that New Brunswick shipping was worth about £8 a ton in 1854.

24 The difference between this figure and Perley's £8 reflects the cost of nails, copper and ship iron chain, sail, and rope that went into the construction.

25 See the discussion in Acheson, 'Saint John Merchants and Economic Development in Mid-Nineteenth Century,' *Acadiensis* (Autumn 1979): 3–24.

26 New Brunswick, *Journals of the House of Assembly* (1842), appendix, shipping returns

27 New Brunswick, *Journals of the House of Assembly* (1827, 1841, 1854), appendix, customs house returns

28 For the development after 1860, see the work of Lewis R. Fischer and Keith Matthews in David Alexander and Rosemary Ommer, eds, *Volumes Not Values* (St John's 1979), 117–56, 195–244.

29 *The St. John Gazette* (hereafter *The Gazette*), 14 June 1820

30 *The Observer*, 11 November 1834

31 New Brunswick, *Journals of the House of Assembly* (1839), returns of banks; Bank of New Brunswick ledger 1828–38, 1 April 1837–31 March 1838, NBM. Total bills at discount in the year totalled £483,433.7.4 of which £94,000 had been carried forward from the previous year. The £2.3 million figure assumes that all banks had roughly the same ratio of daily and yearly discounts.

32 As of November 1837. See the 'Returns of the Banks' in the 1838 Assembly Journal.

33 Bank of New Brunswick Ledger, 1 April 1837–31 March 1838, NBM.

34 RLE/831, pe. 79, PANB

35 RLE/845, pe. 1, PANB; *The Courier*, 19 April 1845

36 New Brunswick, *Journals of the House of Assembly* (1852), returns of insurance companies

37 The value of the province's commodity trade in 1851 was £1,627,000 borne in vessels totalling 854,000 tons. Even at only £3 a ton, the total risks of this shipping would amount to over £2,500,000, exclusive of cargo.

38 Timber and deal exports exceeded 400,000 tons in 1825. Only in 1846 did export tonnage rival that of 1825.

39 Rough estimates of output based on the 1861 Census and customs reports suggest product output was worth about £1,400,000, agricultural output about £1,700,000, and non-wood manufactures about £800,000.

40 The only other option is that most of the 1839 imports were brought for re-export.

41 Canada, *Census of 1871* IV, 129, 226–8, 336–43. By 1861 farmers produced about 90 per cent of the meat consumed in the province, virtually all of the potatoes, oats, buckwheat, butter, and about 20 per cent of the wheat

flour. These commodities contributed about £1.7 million to the provincial economy, about 60 per cent more than the value of all timber and lumber exports.

42 New Brunswick, *Journals of the House of Assembly* (1852), appendix, Census of 1851
43 Ibid. (1852), population returns 1851, appendix, xxiv–xxv
44 Ibid. (1862), 'Census of the Province of New Brunswick 1861,' 95
45 Gordon Bertram, 'Historical Statistics on Growth and Structure in Manufacturing in Canada 1870–1957,' Canadian Political Science Association Conference on Statistics 1962 and 1963, *Report*, 122. The figures were Ontario $69.60, Quebec $62.00, New Brunswick $59.80, Nova Scotia $30.70.
46 Canada, *Census of 1871* III, tables XXII, XXIII, XXIV, XXXI
47 There is no evidence that any New Brunswick cloth was exported. In 1871, the Saint John mills produced cotton cloth to a value of £40,000 and woollen cloth worth £24,000. That same year, the clothing trades consumed £120,000 worth of materials.

CHAPTER 2

1 J.S. MacKinnon, 'The Development of Local Government in the City of Saint John 1785–1795' (unpublished MA thesis, University of New Brunswick 1968), 27–30
2 The charter is printed in E.L. Teed, *Canada's First City, Saint John* (Saint John 1962)
3 In the original civic charters it was assumed that freemen and freeholders would participate directly in the legislative process. The New England town meeting was a survival of this older tradition.
4 They were Gabriel Ludlow (1785–95), William Campbell (1795–1816), John Robinson (1816–28), and William Black (1828–29, 1832–33, 1840–43).
5 Brief biographies of these men are found in J.W. Lawrence, *The Judges of New Brunswick and Their Times* (Saint John 1907), chs IX, XI, XIII, XIV, XVIII. Terms of office: Ward Chipman, Sr 1785–1809; Ward Chipman, Jr 1815–22; Edward Jarvis 1822–24; Robert Parker 1824–30.
6 Freemans Rolls, city of Saint John, 1785–1865, NBM
7 Common Council minutes VII, 21 August and 29 October 1829, Saint John City Hall. These include the opinions of Peters and Parker, who agree that the charter, following English civic practice, was designed to be exclusive.
8 The scale for fees of admission to the freedom of the city in 1829 is found in *The Gazette*, 13 May 1829.
9 This has been computed by determining the number of freemen and freeholders in the 1851 Census sample. The figure may be slightly higher since the sample does not include residents of the Carleton wards. The 1856 freeholders list suggests that the proportion of freeholders on the west side was higher than on the east. However, since more than 80 per cent of the population lived on the east side in 1851, this difference would not significantly alter the conclusion that a greater number of male heads and one-fifth of all adult males held the franchise.
10 E.P. Hennock, *Fit and Proper Persons: Ideal and Reality in Nineteenth-Century Urban Government* (Montreal 1973), 12

11 See Edward Pessen, 'Who Governed the Nation's Cities in the Era of the Common Man?' *Political Science Quarterly* LXXXVII (1972): 601, and 'A Social and Economic Portrait of Jacksonian Brooklyn: Inequality, Social Immobility and Class Distinction in the Nation's Seventh City,' *New York Historical Society Quarterly* LV (1971): 348–9.

12 Kings Ward Poll Book, Queens Ward Poll Book, supporting papers of the Common Council of the city of Saint John, vol. 17, 22 April 1848, PANB

13 Freemen elected two members to the Legislative Assembly of New Brunswick for the city of Saint John. Freeholders could also vote for the four members elected for the county of St John.

14 The exceptions were Moah Disbrow and John M. Wilmot.

15 See Hennock, *Fit and Proper Person*, 27; Derek Fraser, *Urban Politics in Victorian England* (Leicester 1970), 133; and John Garrard, *Leadership and Power in Victorian Industrial Towns 1830–80* (Manchester 1983), 14, 16, 20, for the occupational structure of the councils of Leeds, Manchester, Salford, Boulton, and Rochdale. Only the Manchester council resembled that of Saint John.

16 One simple method of measuring social mobility is to compare the occupations of freemen at the time of their admission to the freedom of the city with those they reported in the 1851 Census.

17 This generalization is approximately true. The origins of some councillors is not known and those may include one or two Irish Catholics or Scots Presbyterians. However, no notable member of either of those communities served on the council in this period.

18 A very useful discussion of the place of this group in nineteenth-century English society is found in Geoffrey Crossick, 'Urban Society and the Petty Bourgeoisie in the Nineteenth Century,' Derek Fraser and Anthony Sutcliffe, eds, *The Pursuit of Urban History* (London 1983), 306–25.

19 This collective portrait is drawn from a range of sources including, notably, the minutes and papers of the Common Council, the wills and probate court records, the freemen rolls, and the manuscript Census of 1851.

20 Garrard, *Leadership and Power*, 69. The competing views of the way in which power is exercised within communities – often designated as pluralist and élitist – are explored by Raymond E. Wolfinger in 'Non-decisions and the Study of Local Politics' and in Frederick Frey 'Comment: On Issues and Non-issues in the Study of Power,' *The American Political Science Review* 65 (1971): 1063–1104.

21 See R.W. Greaves, *The Corporation of Leicester 1689–1836*, 2nd ed. (Leicester 1970), 22.

22 Common Council minutes, vol. xx, October 1841; vol. xx, 21 August 1851 SJCH

23 Actual assessed days exceeded 10,000 but those assessed paid only 2s. 6d. for each day commuted while labourers were normally paid 3s.

24 Common Council minutes, vol. xv, 19 April 1842, SJCH.

25 For example see Common Council minutes, vol. xi, 27 November and 4 December 1835; vol. xix 7, December 1848; vol. viii, 5 May and 17 November 1827; 4 June 1829; vol. viii, 28 May 1830; vol. ix, 4 May 1831, SJCH.

26 See for example constable accounts, Common Council supporting papers, vol. 6, 17 May 1843, PANB; RLE/842, rept 6, PANB

27 See Common Council supporting papers, 26 July 1843, PANB.

28 *The City Gazette*, 18 June and 28 November 1848
29 Common Council minutes, vol XIII, 28 May 1839, SJCH.
30 Common Council minutes, vol VI, 20 October 1824; vol. XV, 24 November 1841, SJCH
31 RLE/830, pe. 38; RLE/850, pe. 373; RLW/852, pe. 38, PANB
32 Common Council minutes, vol. V, 28 January, 11 February, and 8 November 1822; vol. XI, 5 and 28 November 1834, 5 January, 7 March, and 27 April 1835; vol. XIX, 19 February, 3 August, 3 July, and 22 November 1848; vol. XX, 30 October, 6 November 1850, 29 January, 22 April, and 30 July 1851; vol. XXII, 19 July 1852, SJCH
33 Common Council minutes, vol. IX, 21 January 1832; vol. X, 9 July 1833; RLE/834, pe. 134, SJCH
34 See, for example, RLE/816, pe. 40, PANB; Common Council minutes, vol. XI, 20 May 1834; RLE/841, pe. 199, RLE/860, pe. 3, PANB. Common Council minutes, vol. XV, 22 and 26 January 1842, SJCH
35 J.R. Partelow to Hazen, 2 February, 25 February, 5 March, 10 March 1839, R.F. Hazen, Mayor's Correspondence, packet 3, NBM
36 RLE/834, pe. 834; RLE/841, pe. 233; RLE/858, pe. 52, PANB
37 Common Council minutes, vol. XIV, 14 October 1839, SJCH
38 Ibid., 7 November 1839
39 G.I. Harvey to deputation of Common Council, 9 November 1839, CO 188/66, Common Council minutes, vol. XIV, 21 November 1839, SJCH
40 Common Council minutes, vol. XV, 17 March 1841, SJCH

CHAPTER 3

1 D.G. Creighton, *The Commercial Empire of the St. Lawrence 1760–1850* (Toronto 1937)
2 Gerald Tulchinsky, *The River Barons: Montreal Businessmen and the Growth of Industry and Transportation 1837–1853* (Toronto 1977)
3 David Sutherland, 'The Merchants of Halifax 1815–1850: A Class in Pursuit of Metropolitan Status' (PH D thesis, University of Toronto 1975)
4 A.G. Frank, 'The Development of Underdevelopment,' in Robert Rhodes, ed., *Imperialism and Underdevelopment* (New York 1970), 4–17
5 These figures are tabulated from the Roll of Freemen, 1785–1859.
6 Although Michael Katz has argued that all North American clerks were part of the business class and hence owners or managers of the means of production. See M.B. Katz, M.J. Doucet, and M.J. Stern, *Social Organization of Early Industrial Capitalism* (Cambridge, Mass. 1982), 44–5.
7 These figures are tabulated from the 1851 Census manuscripts for the east-side wards of Saint John.
8 T.W. Acheson, 'The Great Merchant and Economic Development in Colonial Saint John,' *Acadiensis* IX (Spring 1979): 3–27. The list includes Isaac Bedell, Robert W. Crookshank, Noah Disbrow Jr, L.H. Deveber, Thomas Barlow, Ezekiel Barlow Jr, Lauchlan Donaldson, John Duncan, Henry Gilbert, James T. Hanford, John Hammond, David Hatfield, James Hendricks, Ralph Jarvis, Hugh Johnston Sr, Hugh Johnston Jr, John H. Kinnear, James Kirk, Thomas Leavitt, Wm. H. Leavitt, Nehemiah Merritt, Thomas Millidge, William Parks, John Pollok, Robert Rankin, E.D.W. Ratchford, John Robertson, W.H. Scovil, Charles Simonds, Walter Tisdale, John V.

Thurgar, John Walker, John Ward Jr, Charles Ward, Stephen Wiggins, John M. Wilmot, R.D. Wilmot, John Wishart.
9 The origins and composition of this group are discussed in W.S. MacNutt, *New Brunswick A History: 1784–1867* (Toronto 1963), chs 2–6.
10 Mary Caroline Boyd to Master James William Boyd, Malta, Jarvis Papers, 1 February 1825, NBM, *The Courier*, 26 December 1840
11 *The Courier*, 9 January 1841. John McGregor spoke of the assemblies as drawing the social line of demarcation and exciting 'the angry bile of those who are excluded.' McGregor, *British America* (Edinburgh 1832), 356
12 *The Courier*, 28 February 1843, 4 March 1848, 17 February 1849
13 Ibid., 5 February 1853
14 Court of Probate, City and County of Saint John, book G, 131ff. mfm, PANB
15 Perley to Mother, 3 June 1832. Moses Perley letters (typescript) NBM. John McGregor spoke of 'some building their pretensions on their families being of the number of the first Loyalist settlers; others measuring their respectability by the length of their purses.' McGregor, *British America*, 234
16 Appointments 2/1 and 2/2. Commissions of the Peace for the County and City of Saint John, REX/PA, PANB
17 Ibid., appointments 2/1, magistrates, Saint John. The phenomenon was particularly noticeable among the Ward, the Johnston, and the Jarvis families.
18 Petition of J.T. Hanford, 20 July 1843, petition of E.D.W. Ratchford, 25 July 1843, and E.D.W. Ratchford to private secretary to the lieutenant-governor, 19 June 1843, REX, MG9, A1, vol. 98, PANB
19 Account book, 5–10, Hugh Johnston Papers
20 John Robertson to Common Council, Common Council supporting papers, vol. 20, 10 October 1849, PANB. Schedule of Real Estate Owned by the City of Saint John 1842, REX/PA, miscellaneous, PANB
21 Saint John County, book G, 131ff, probate records, mfm, PANB
22 Stephen Wiggins, 1863, RG7, RS71, PANB
23 County of Saint John, book G, 131ff, probate records, mfm, PANB
24 Account book I, 100–07, Johnston Papers, NBM
25 Daybook and journal 1814–34; extract of cash received for land sold 1814–21, Hon. Wm F. Hazen Papers, NBM
26 New Brunswick, *Journals of the House of Assembly* (1841), customs house report – shipping owned by port of Saint John
27 Schedule of real estate belonging to Saint John and annual income, January 1842, REX/PA, miscellaneous Saint John, PANB
28 Common Council supplementary papers, vol. VI, 7/8, 12/13 September 1842, PANB
29 The charge was frequently made publicly that this was the case. Hugh Johnston alone held 8 per cent of the bank's share capital in 1826. Johnston account book, 58
30 New Brunswick, *Journals of the House of Assembly* (1842), appendix, return of insurance companies, New Brunswick Maine Insurance Company
31 A practice identical with that found by Pessen in New York. See Edward Pessen, 'Who Governed the Nation's Cities in the Era of the Comman Man?' *Political Science Quarterly* LXXXVII (1972): 605.
32 MacNutt, *New Brunswick*, 256–7

33 John Gerrard, *Leadership and Power in Victorian Industrial Towns 1830–80* (Manchester 1983), 5
34 RLE/829, pe. 2, 23, PANB
35 RLE/828, pe. 42, 43, 44; RLE/840, pe. 122. Among the dissenters were N. Merritt, R. Rankin, J. Walker, D. Wilmot, I. Bedell, and W. Parks; RLE/ 829, Bill 6.
36 RLE/834, pe. 15
37 RLE/832, bill 15, PANB
38 *The Courier*, 14 December 1833
39 RLE/834, pe. 15, 43, 66, 67, 68, PANB
40 *The Courier*, 22 March 1834
41 For discussions of these activities see D.S. Macmillan, 'The "New Men" in Action ...,' in Macmillan, ed., *Canadian Business History; Selected Studies, 1497–1971* (Toronto 1972), 44–103; David Sutherland, 'Halifax Merchants and the Pursuit of Development 1783–1850, CHR LIX, no. 1 (March 1978): 1–17; Creighton, *Empire of the St. Lawrence*; Tulchinsky, *The River Barons*.
42 Statements of this view by the most respected editors in the city are found in *The News*, 10 September 1839, and *The Courier*, 10 February 1843. They are explicit statements of a viewpoint implicit in almost every public discussion of the city's economy.
43 See, for example, *The Courier*, 1 May 1830.
44 Ibid., 14 November 1835
45 The debate over the crown lands is dealt with by W.S. MacNutt in 'Politics of the Timber Trade in Colonial New Brunswick 1825–40,' CHR XXX (1949): 47–65, and by Graeme Wynn in 'Administration in Adversity: The Deputy Surveyors and Control of New Brunswick Crown Lands before 1844,' *Acadiensis* VII (Autumn 1977): 49–65, and in his *Timber Colony: A Historical Geography of Early Nineteenth Century New Brunswick* (Toronto 1981).
46 RLE/823, pe. 13; RLE/824, pe. 6; RLE/831, pe. 10; RLE/839, pe. 80
47 CO 188/49, 169–71
48 *The Courier*, 6 and 13 December 1834
49 See Harvey to Stanley, 18 May 1838, CO 188/59; Harvey to Russell, 8 September 1840, CO 188/69; RLE/835, pe. 124; RLE/833, pe. 102; RLE/842, pe. 214, 237 PANB; *The Courier*, 4 February 1843.
50 *The Courier*, 1 May 1830; RLE/832, pe. 18
51 John Boyd to E. Jarvis, 18 June 1825, Jarvis Papers, NBM
52 RLE/831, pe. 36; *The Courier*, 7 and 29 January 1832
53 *The Observer*, 4 and 11 August 1835
54 CO 188/45, 115–20; CO 188/56, 125–31
55 RLE/834, pe. 15, PANB
56 RLE/834, pe. 41; RLE/839, pe.43
57 *The Courier*, 13 August 1836; RLE/837, pe. 10
58 *The Observer*, 27 October 1835
59 RLE/836, pe. 81
60 Some sense of the extent of the collapse is found in the bankruptcies noted in *The Courier*, 4 March, 3 June, 15 July, 7 October, 18 and 25 November 1843.
61 *The Courier*, 4 February 1843
62 Ibid., 10 February 1844
63 RLE/843, pe. 143; RLE/850, pe. 416

64 *The Courier*, 10 February 1843; 25 February 1850
65 Noah Disbrow, 1853, RG7, RS71, PANB; William Jarvis, 1856, RG7, RS71, PANB
66 Partnership agreement, William Parks Papers, FNO. 3, NBM. This figure does not include Park's estate.
67 Stephen Wiggins, 1863, RG7, RS71, PANB. This figure does not include Wiggins's estate.
68 RLE/856, pe. 110, PANB
69 See New Brunswick, 7 Victoria c. 1 and New Brunswick, *Journals of the House of Assembly* (1844), 152–7.
70 See the letter from 'Merchant' in *The News*, 17 March 1845.
71 *The News*, 2 and 16 April; 6 and 7 May 1845, 25 February 1846
72 *The Courier*, 28 June and 4 August 1849
73 Ibid., 15 September 1849 and 8 June 1850
74 See Acheson, 'The Great Merchant'
75 Carl Wallace, 'Saint John Boosters and the Railroads in the Mid-Nineteenth Century,' *Acadiensis* VI (Autumn 1976): 74–6. Of the eight primary leaders in the railway movement, only John Robertson was a leading merchant.
76 RLE/853, pe. 263; RLE/854, pe. 385, PANB

CHAPTER 4

1 See M.B. Katz, *The People of Hamilton, Canada West* (Cambridge, Mass. 1975), 27, 311, and with M.J. Doucet and M.J. Stern, *The Social Organization of Early Industrial Capitalism* (Cambridge, Mass. 1982), ch. 1. In his second work, Katz argues that all nineteenth-century urban societies were divided into a business class and a working class and these corresponded to those who owned the means of production and those who sold their labour in return for money. Membership in the class, then, has nothing to do with class consciousness or class awareness; one is a member of a class because of one's relationship to the means of production. It is difficult to quarrel with any objective statement of classification. However, Katz destroys the objectivity of his model by insisting that the business class contains not only 'those individuals who owned the means of production' but also 'those whose interests and aspirations identified them with the owners' (p44). Using this definition Katz assigns entire categories of men to the business class: all professionals and even the meanest clerk or school teacher become a capitalist. It is not improbable that a majority of members of the business class did not own the means of production unless it is defined in terms of skills or hand tools. Leaving aside the question of how the historian measures the aspirations of each member of a society – a concept that, in any event, seems very akin to class consciousness – why does Katz assume that no artisan or labourer possessed any aspiration to become a proprietor or at least to better his material lot in life? And if that possibility is admitted, is it possible to assign artisans en masse to the working class?
2 Susan Hirsch, *Roots of the American Working Class: The Industrialization of Crafts in Newark 1800–1860* (Philadelphia 1978), 8, 11, 12, 41; Bryan Palmer, 'Kingston Mechanics and the Rise of the Penitentiary, 1833–1836,' *Histoire Sociale/Social History* (May 1980): 7–32
3 See, for example, Robert Gray, *The Labour Aristocracy in Victorian Edinburgh*

(Oxford 1976), and Geoffrey Crossick, *An Artisan Elite in Victorian Society: Kentish London 1840–1880* (London 1978). For useful discussions of the nineteenth-century petite bourgeoisie see Crossick, 'Urban Society and the Petty Bourgeoisie in Nineteenth-Century Britain,' in Derek Fraser and Anthony Sutcliffe, eds., *The Pursuit of Urban History* (London 1983), 306–25.

4 J.S. MacKinnon, 'The Development of Local Government in the City of Saint John 1785–1795' (unpublished MA thesis, University of New Brunswick 1968) 21–4; W.S. MacNutt, *New Brunswick: A History 1783–1867* (Toronto 1963), 60–2; James Hannay, *History of New Brunswick* I (Saint John 1909), 154–6

5 Biographical details of these clergy groups may be found in E.A. Betts, *Bishop Black and His Preachers* (Sackville 1976), appendix II; A.W.H. Eaton, *The Church of England in Nova Scotia and the Tory Clergy of the Revolution* (New York 1891); G. Herbert Lee, *Historical Sketches of the First Fifty Years of the Church of England in the Province of New Brunswick, 1782–1833* (Saint John 1880).

6 Freemen's roll of the city of Saint John 1785–1862, NBM

7 A point made by Hirsch in her study of Newark. Palmer, however, sees it as an exploitative arrangement after 1800. See Hirsch, *Roots*, 6, and Bryan A. Palmer, *Working-Class Experience: The Rise and Reconstitution of Canadian Labour 1800–1980* (Toronto 1983), 28–9.

8 Indenture of Henry Chubb, Chubb Family Papers, NBM

9 See, for example, the firecracker ordinance of 1819 that provided a 20s. fine against the master of the offender (*City Gazette*, 11 August 1819).

10 *The Courier*, 15 January 1817

11 See, for example, *The Courier*, 18 January, 25 September, and 15 November 1817.

12 Ibid., 12 June 1841

13 Despite Katz's contention that few nineteenth-century journeymen became masters, Bruce Laurie has demonstrated that over half the Methodist and Presbyterian journeymen in 1830 were masters or small retailers by 1850. Hirsch found that most Newark artisans over the age of forty were masters. See Bruce Laurie, *The Working People of Philadelphia 1850–1880* (Philadelphia 1980), 48.

14 See the Mechanics Institute School in *The Courier*, 28 December 1839 and the petition of Peter Cougle for release from his apprenticeship after 3 years, 9 months of service with H. Littlehale, a house joiner. Common Council supplementary papers, vol. 4, 30 June 1842, PANB.

15 These examples are drawn from the Roll of Freemen.

16 *The Courier*, 28 October 1858

17 These data are drawn from the 1851 Census manuscript sample. See chapter 12.

18 On the relative strength of the artisan group in other British North American cities see Palmer, *Working-Class Experience*, 31, and Katz, *The People of Hamilton*, 70.

19 Based on CO 188/41, 306; CO 188/75; New Brunswick, *Journals of the House of Assembly* (1847).

20 See Palmer, *Working-Class Experience*, 22.

21 CO 188/41, 306

22 Katz has argued that journeymen and master artisans should be in different classes because the differences between them are greater than the differences among either journeymen or masters. This conclusion was reached on the basis of the Hamilton assessment records.
23 An experience common to Newark as well. See Hirsch, 'Roots', 47.
24 Saint John 1851 Census manuscript, Kings Ward, 238, PANB
25 As was the case in Newark. See Hirsch, 'Roots', 8.
26 Ibid., ch 2
27 RLE/834, pe. 91; RLE/845, pe. 208; PANB
28 RLE/828, pe. 42, 43; RLE/840, pe. 122; RLE/850, 418; *The Chronicle*, 22 March 1839
29 *St. John and Its Business: A History of St. John* (Saint John 1875), 124, 128–9
30 Ibid., 125–6
31 RLE/851, pe. 412, PANB
32 *St. John and Its Business*, 101, 103, 105, 137
33 This is what Katz assumed in his work on Hamilton and Buffalo. Crossick, too, has reservations about the closeness of small masters and men in mid-nineteenth-century Birmingham. Hirsch, however, found that small masters in Newark paid fairer wages and kept their firms operating longer in times of adversity than did larger operations. See Crossick, 'Urban Society and the Petite Bourgeoisie,' 322, and Hirsch, *Roots*, 89–90.
34 A useful comparison and discussion of work place forms is found in Bruce Laurie, *Working People of Philadelphia 1800–1850* (Philadelphia 1980), ch. 1.
35 J.R. Rice, 'A History of Organized Labour in Saint John, N.B., 1815–1890' (MA thesis, University of New Brunswick 1968), ch. I. Rice suggests that collective action by shipwrights and carpenters may have begun in 1799, but it is probable that the 'principal shipwrights' who composed the organization were the masters, not the journeymen. The earliest active unions were among shop clerks, the semi-skilled and unskilled sawyers, and ship labourers. The first documented instance of artisans taking action against masters occurred in 1864 when the caulkers struck for several months. (ch. II).
36 *The Courier*, 29 May 1830. Tailors were usually paid half in board and half in cash; *The News*, 17 May 1841.
37 *The Courier*, 20 December 1856
38 Eugene Forsey found evidence of organizations among sawyers, ship carpenters, carpenters and joiners, tailors, and cabinet-makers between 1835 and 1849. Yet there is no indication of any activity directed against their employers. See Forsey, *The Trade Unions in Canada* (Toronto 1982), 9–10.
39 RLE/835, 2nd session, pe. 1
40 New Brunswick, *Journals of the House of Assembly* (1838), appendix 1, Mechanics Whale Fishing Company
41 *The Courier*, 4 March 1837
42 See the merchants' letters in *The Courier*, 26 December 1840.
43 Details on operations of the company between 1838 and 1847, including financial statements and lists of shareholders and directors, may be found in the *Journals of the House of Assembly*.
44 The Saint John development closely paralleled the English. See Mabel Tylecote, *The Mechanics Institutes of Lancashire and Yorkshire* (Manchester 1957), chs 1, 2, and 8. The Halifax Mechanics Institute pre-dated that of Saint John

and suffered from many of the same early problems. See Patrick Keene, 'A Study in Early Problems and Policies in Adult Education: The Halifax Mechanics' Institute,' *Histoire Sociale/Social History* no. 16 (November 1975), 255–74.

45 *The Courier*, 5 November 1836
46 Ibid., 1 December 1838; 2 March 1839
47 Ibid., 20 April 1839; 17 May 1851
48 See, for example, the letter from 'Mechanic' in *The Chronicle*, 28 December 1838.
49 A similar debate conducted among artisans, white-collar workers, and the gentry occurred within the London mechanics institutes at mid-century. See Crossick, *An Artisan Elite*, 137–9.
50 *The Chronicle*, 28 December 1838
51 See the correspondence from A.R. Truro in *The Courier*, 2 March 1839, and from 'Mechanic' and 'Member of the Water Company' in *The Chronicle*, 4 and 18 January, 8 March 1839. The motion to give control of institute funds to the executive committee had apparently been passed at a meeting attended by fourteen members.
52 See 'Member of Mechanics Institute' in *The News*, 26 November 1841.
53 *The Courier*, 16 April 1842
54 E.P. Costello, 'A Report on the Saint John Mechanics Institute 1838–1890' (unpublished MA report, University of New Brunswick 1974), 9–10
55 *The Courier*, 5 May 1855
56 Ibid., 30 May 1840. These parades were similar to the craftsmen's independence day parades in Newark before the community divisions of the 1830s. See Hirsch, *Roots*, 6.
57 Ibid., 25 July 1840
58 *The Courier* account of 25 July makes this point clear: 'The members of the Mechanics Institute assembled in the following order: carpenters, *members not in the trades*, riggers, shoemakers, ...'
59 See *The News*, 24 April 1841 and *The Courier*, 6 November 1841. The president of the Mechanics Institute, a 34-year-old Irish-born joiner, John Wilson, was also vice-president of the Chamber of Trades.
60 *The Courier*, 2 February 1839. Hirsch noted the same problem among Newark masters in the 1840s. See Hirsch, *Roots*, 92.
61 RLE/839, pe. 203, PANB.
62 New Brunswick, *Journals of the Legislative Assembly* (1839), 330, 434
63 RLE/849, pe. 295, PANB
64 New Brunswick, *Journals of the Legislative Assembly* (1849), 35, 61–62; New Brunswick, *Journals of the Legislative Council* (1849), 428
65 RLE/850, pe. 103, PANB; New Brunswick, *Journals of the House of Assembly* (1850), 120; New Brunswick, *Journals of the Legislative Council* (1850), 725
66 Rice, 'A History of Organized Labour in Saint John,' 4, 6
67 City inspector's report, 25 July and 8 August 1838, R.L. Hazen Papers, folder 2, NBM
68 *The Courier*, 9 November 1839
69 Ibid., 18 July 1840
70 *The News*, 9 April 1841
71 'Hobshot' to the editor in *The News*, 5 May 1841
72 *The Courier*, 16 May 1840

73 Bryan Palmer argues that in Upper Canada such protest involved an alliance of manufacturers and merchants. Hirsch notes that any distinctions among masters and journeymen in the early nineteenth century were overridden by their commitment in keeping prices up and markets stocked. See Palmer, *Working-Class Experience*, 57, and Hirsch, *Roots*, 8.

74 RLE/827, pe. 117; RLE/834, pe. 1

75 RLE/828, pe. 142; RLE/840, pe. 122; RLE/835, pe. 124

76 Duties on American manufacturers averaged 10 per cent in 1842. New Brunswick, *Journals of the Legislative Assembly* (1842), appendix ccxxix

77 RLE/844, pe. 163; RLE/844, pe. 84; RLE/842, pe. 84

78 Colebrook to Stanley, 29 March 1842, CO 188/76; Colebrook to Stanley, 27 September 1842, CO 188/79; *The Courier*, 22 December 1842

79 *The Courier*, 15 April 1843

80 RLE/843, pe. 143, 149, PANB

81 *The Courier*, 20 January 1844

82 Ibid., 10 February 1844; RLE/844, pe. 239, PANB

83 New Brunswick, *Journals of the House of Assembly* (1844), 152–7

84 *The News*, 19, 24 April 1841

85 *The Courier*, 10 February 1843

86 *The News*, 4 April 1845; *The Courier*, 5 April 1845

87 *The News*, 9 April 1845

88 RLE/844, pe. 84, PANB; RLE/846, pe. 208; RLE/847, pe. 367

89 *The News*, 15 March 1847, 'Debates on the Tariff' (by electric telegraph); RLE/844, pe. 155, 163, 168, PANB; RLE/845, pe. 298; RLE/848, pe. 178, 310, 378; RLE/850, pe. 343, 357, 358, 414, 415; RLE/851, pe. 412

90 *The Courier*, 23 February 1850; *The Observer*, 19 February 1850; RLE/850, pe. 416, PANB

91 *The Courier*, 22 February 1851

92 The data upon which these generalizations were drawn were produced by computer analysis of the city freemen with the signatories to 106 petitions and other documents that played some significant role in the life of the community between 1830 and 1860. Common names (i.e. John Smith), names held by two or more freemen of different occupations, and names that could not be clearly identified as belonging to a particular freeman were eliminated. This process removed about half those who were probably freemen. The remainder – those who can be clearly identified as freemen who signed some public document between 1820 and 1860 – included 207 merchants and 581 artisans. It is this group that forms the basis for these statements.

CHAPTER 5

1 Sam Bass Warner, Jr, *The Private City: Philadelphia in Three Periods of Its Growth* (Philadelphia 1968); Allen Davis and Mark H. Haller, *The People of Philadelphia: A History of Ethnic Groups and Lower-Class Life 1790–1940*; Michael Feldberg, *The Philadelphia Riots of 1844: A Study of Ethnic Conflict* (Westport, Conn. 1975); David Montgomery, 'The Shuttle and the Cross,' *Journal of Social History* 5 (Summer 1972): 411–46; Bruce Laurie, *The Working People of Philadelphia 1800–1850* (Philadelphia 1980); Dennis Clark, *The Irish in Philadelphia: Ten Generations of Urban Experience* (Philadelphia 1973)

2 See Oscar Handlin, *Boston's Immigrants: A Study in Acculturation* (Boston 1941; New York 1988); Robert Ernst, *Immigrant Life in New York City 1825–1863* (New York 1949); Paul Kleppner, *The Cross of Culture; A Social Analysis of Mid-Western Politics, 1850–1900* (New York 1970).

3 See, for example, Laurie, *Working People of Philadelphia*, ch. 6.

4 In the 1820s, fares from British ports to Saint John and Quebec were frequently half those charged for transportation to American ports. The differences in fares began to narrow in the next decade but remained significant as late as 1855. See W.F. Adams, *Ireland and Irish Migration to the New World from 1815 to the Famine* (New York 1932); R.D. Edwards and T.D. Williams, eds, *The Great Famine: Studies in Irish History 1845–52* (New York 1957).

5 The most recent study of the Canadian Irish of the same period strongly makes the point that the great majority of Irish moved into rural settlements. See Donald Akenson, 'Ontario: Whatever Happened to the Irish?' in Donald Akenson, ed., *Canadian Papers in Rural History* III (Gananoque 1982):204–56; see 'Report of Government Agent,' New Brunswick, *Journals of the House of Assembly* (1845, 1849, 1853); Helen I. Cowan, *British Emigration to British North America* (Toronto 1961), 195.

6 St John sessions, 7 September 1827 RMU, PANB. New Brunswick, *Journals of the Legislative Assembly* (1946), xxi; New Brunswick, *Journals of the Legislative Assembly*, (1849), xcxi–xcxii

7 St John sessions, 4 September 1827. RMU, PANB

8 *The Courier*, 31 December 1831

9 Partelow to executive council, 16 July 1831. REX, MG9 A1, vol. 31, PANB

10 RLE/837, pe. 116, PANB

11 *The Courier*, 19 June 1830

12 RLE/839, pe. 42, PANB

13 *The Courier*, 19 June 1830

14 RLE/833, pe. 116, PANB

15 Patient lists for the hospital are found in the annual reports published in the assembly journals of the late 1840s.

16 *The Courier*, 3 January 1846

17 James F.W. Johnston, *Notes on North America: Agricultural, Economical and Social* II (Edinburgh 1851), 128–9

18 Agricultural wages in St John County were £19.6.0 in 1851 as compared with £24 in York. A total of 17,074 British immigrants arrived in New Brunswick in 1847; Cowan, *British Emigration to British North America*, 192–3.

19 Report of the Committee to Enquire into the State of Emigrants on Partridge Island, Common Council supporting papers, vol. 16, 9 October 1847, PANB; vol. 16, 2 November 1847; vol. 16 and 10 November 1847; vol. 16, 14 January 1848; minutes of the Common Council of the City of St John, 2 November 1847, SJCH

20 The xenophobia of native Philadelphians was aimed only Irish Catholics. Germans and other Catholic minorities were largely ignored. See Feldberg, *The Philadelphia Riots*, 20.

21 *The Courier*, 2 April 1831. This point was frequently made in connection with the Upper Canadian experience. See, for example, Kenneth Duncan, 'The Irish Famine Migration and the Social Structure of Canada West,' in

Michiel Horn and Ronald Sabourian, eds, *Studies in Canadian Social History* (Toronto 1974), 19–40.

22 *The Courier*, 31 December 1831; RLE/835, pe. 133, PANB

23 See Handlin, *Boston's Immigrants*, 151, 154

24 London Catholicism remained largely unorganized until 1850; Toronto Catholicism until 1842. See Lynn Holler Lees, *Exiles of Erin: Irish Migrants in Victorian London* (Ithaca 1979), 172; Murray W. Nicholson, 'Ecclesiastical Metropolitanism and the Evolution of the Catholic Archdiocese of Toronto,' *Histoire Sociale/Social History*, no. 21 (May 1982): 134.

25 *The Courier*, 22 July 1820

26 The Saint John experience was similar to that of Toronto. See Nicholson, 'Ecclesiastical Metropolitanism,' 130–4.

27 Desmond Bowen, *The Protestant Crusade in Ireland 1800–1870* (Montreal 1978), 62, 68

28 *The Observer*, 13 October 1835

29 Bowen, *Protestant Crusade*, 31–3

30 *The Courier*, 8 and 28 June 1842; 15 and 19 October 1842

31 Parks to Dr Cooke, 19 June 1844, 22 February 1845, Parks Papers, NBM

32 *The Courier*, 17 June 1848

33 As was the case in Philadelphia. See Clark, *The Irish in Philadelphia*, 82

34 Thirty-seven members of the organization can be identified and detailed information is available on twenty-five of them.

35 RLE/832, pe. 40, PANB; RLE/835, pe. 18, PANB

36 RLE/836, pe. 49, PANB

37 *The Courier*, 24 July 1830

38 The debate began with an attack on the society by the temperance advocates, who argued, 'It is enough that the inhabitants of the province whether born here or in any part of the Empire, should consider themselves as *one people* whose true interest is to conduct themselves ... as sober Christians and faithful British subjects.' See *The Courier*, 2 April 1831.

39 *The Chronicle*, 26 April 1839; *The Courier*, 17 November 1842; End to Baillie, 3 November 1842 in *The News*, 18 November 1842, and Baillie to End, 9 November 1842, ibid.

40 At least 167 members can be identified and detailed information is available on 55. The average age of members was 29 years; that of the St Patrick's Society membership was 36.

41 *The Courier*, 23 March 1832

42 RLE/835, pe. 133, PANB

43 *The Observer*, 2 December 1834

44 Bowan, *Protestant Crusade*, 31–2, 143–56

45 The London clubs alone numbered more than 80,000. See Lee's *Exiles of Erin*, 225; Feldberg, *The Philadelphia Riots*, 29; Handlin, *Boston's Immigrants*, 174.

46 *The News*, 11 February 1841

47 *The Courier*, 27 November 1841

48 Ibid., 23 July and 6 August 1842

49 See Lees, *Exiles of Erin*, 180–1

50 See Nicholson, 'Ecclesiastical Metropolitanism,' 134–6, and H.C. Pentland, *Labour and Capital in Canada 1650–1860* (Toronto 1981), 108.

51 See Perley to Mother, 30 June 1832, Moses Perley letters (typescript) NBM.

52 Letter of Francis McDermott in *The Courier*, 28 June 1841
53 Members of this group included John Dooley, Nugent Creighton, Thomas Corkery, James Gallagher, Michael McGuirk, Philip Kehoe, Terence McGirr, Hugh Sharkey.
54 *The Courier*, 3 July 1841; minutes of meeting of contributors, *The Courier*, 17 July 1841; see Edward Koche, writing in *The Courier*, 24 July 1841.
55 Tim Collins, Wm. Doherty, John Dougherty, Joseph Gill, J. White
56 *The Courier*, 13 February 1841. Feldberg argues that Catholic temperance was organized in Philadelphia only to conciliate the native Protestant population. See Feldberg, *The Philadelphia Riots of 1844*, 27.
57 D.C.F. Collins, J. Ward, D. Collins, J. Finn to Dollard, 9 February 1845, Dollard correspondence no. 584, Chancellory of the Diocese of Saint John
58 Wm. McDonald to Dollard, 5 September 1843; Wm. Moran to Dollard, 14 October 1843; Wm. Moran to Dollard, 10 November 1843; Dollard Correspondence, no. 515, 517, 518; *The Courier*, 4 and 10 November 1843, 24 February, 18 and 25 May 1844, 10 February 1845; Parishioners of St John to Dollard, 25 November 1843, Dollard correspondence, no. 520, Chancellory of the Diocese of Saint John
59 Charles Watters to Dollard, 27 November 1843, Chancellory of the Diocese of Saint John, Dollard correspondence, no. 519
60 Committee of twenty parishioners to Dollard, 7 October 1844, Dollard correspondence, no. 535, Chancellory of the Diocese of Saint John
61 Thomas Watters, Wm. Doherty, Thos. McCullough, John Campbell, Charles Matters, Francis Clais, among others
62 The parish priest at Chatham, John Shanahan, indicated that there were three parties in Saint John in 1844. See Shanahan to Dollard 19 December 1844, Dollard correspondence, Chancellory of the Diocese of Saint John.
63 Colebrook to Dollard, 11 April 1845. Dollard correspondence, no. 560, Chancellory of the Diocese of Saint John. The lieutenant-governor noted: 'By a little steadiness and patience I think the factions which have threatened to disturb the Province ... will be effectively subdued.'
64 The Toronto case is discussed in Nicholson, 'Ecclesiastical Metropolitanism,' 134, 141.
65 J. Cunard to Dollard, 15 April 1845, Dollard correspondence, no. 562, Chancellory of the Diocese of Saint John
66 'Old Pewholder' in the *The Courier*, 4 February 1846
67 James Quinn to Dollard, 18 and 28 May 1846. Dollard correspondence, nos. 632, 633, Chancellory of the Diocese of Saint John.
68 But see also Duncan's argument that the arrival of the famine Irish destroyed Irish unity because Protestants tried to distance themselves from the new arrivals. Duncan, 'The Irish Famine Migration,' 147
69 Doherty to Dollard, 11 September 1846, Dollard correspondence, Chancellory of the Diocese of Saint John
70 *The Courier*, 24 June 1845
71 Ibid., 19 August 1848. The speakers at the meeting were James Gallagher, J.P. Dennis Coll, Wm. Doherty, James Finn, G.J. Campbell, P. McCourt, John Doherty, Alexander McTavish, John McCorkeny, and Peter Brogan. Of these, only Wm. Doherty remained of the Catholic leaders of 1841.
72 Norman, *History of Modern Ireland*, 93. A detailed discussion of the suppres-

sion is found in Hereward Senior, *Orangeism in Ireland and Britain 1795–1836* (London 1966), chs x, xi.

73 There is an extensive literature on the Orange Order and its place in nineteenth-century Canada. Hereward Senior's *Orangeism: The Canadian Phase* (Toronto 1972) remains the standard work, but assessments of the movement figure in virtually every survey of nineteenth-century Canada. See, for example, Gerald Craig, *Upper Canada: The Formative Years 1791–1841* (Toronto 1964), and J.M.S. Careless, *The Union of the Canadas* (Toronto 1967). A promising recent approach to the subject is found in Gregory Kealey, 'The Orange Order in Toronto: Religious Riot and the Working Class,' in G.S. Kealey and Peter Warrian, eds, *Essays in Canadian Working Class History* (Toronto 1976), 13–35.

74 Cecil Houston and William J. Smyth, *The Sash Canada Wore: A Historical Geography of the Orange Order in Canada* (Toronto 1980), 40.

75 Ibid., 69

76 Joseph Brown to Robert Hazen, 11 July 1837, Robert F. Hazen collection, mayor's correspondence, 1837–40, packet 1, no. 36, NBM

77 'An Irish Roman Catholic' to Hazen, 19 June 1838, ibid., no. 18

78 *The Chronicle*, 13 July 1838

79 *The Courier*, 18 July 1840

80 Ibid., 25 July 1840

81 *The Loyalist*, 9 October 1846

82 *The Courier*, 26 March 1842

83 Ibid., 27 April 1842

84 Irish Episcopalians were concentrated in border counties of Ulster, which contained large Catholic populations. It was in these areas that the threat to Protestant tenants was greatest. See W.E. Vaughan and A.J. Fitzpatrick, *Irish Historical Statistics Population 1821–1971* (Dublin 1978), 51–3. More than 96 per cent of Ireland's 523,000 Presbyterians were found in the province of Ulster in 1861. In one large territory, comprising Antrim, North Down, and Eastern Londonderry, they constituted a substantial majority of the population; Bowen, *Protestant Ireland*, 30.

85 The 1871 Census provides the first opportunity to compare ethnicity and religion from the printed census summary. See Gordon Darroch and Michael Ornstein, 'Ethnicity and Occupational Structure in Canada in 1871: The Vertical Mosaic in Historical Perspective,' CHR LXI (September 1980): 326–7.

86 *The Loyalist*, 9 July 1846

87 *The Loyalist*, 13 and 17 October, 3 and 17 November, and 12 December 1842

88 Ibid., 17 November 1842

89 Indictment, depositions of James Downie, Gresham Clark, John Hall, Thomas McBride, affidavits of Pat Reilly, Edward Kelly, Terence McManus, Supreme Court records, S841, 29, PANB; *The Courier*, 28 November 1840. Indictment for assault against Patrick Gallagher, labourer and John Devine, labourer, Supreme Court records, S841, 29; indictment, testimony of George Busteed, Wm. Powers, John Powers, John Nixon, Charles Godsoe, Supreme Court records, S843, 2 (5), trial for rioters of 12 July 1842. There was general agreement on the details of the riot. Disagreements in the testimony concerned the motivations that inspired the principals; report on trial for riot, 3 October 1843, REX/PA, crime I, PANB. Thomas Hill, editor of

The Loyalist, later claimed that Robert Blair witnessed the blow that killed Allingham but dared not testify because of threats to his life. Thomas Hill to the attorney general, 6 February 1845, REX/PA, crime I, PANB; Supreme Court records, s844, 2 (1)

90 *The Loyalist,* 16 July 1846
91 Wellington Orange Lodge minute book, 1844–1867, NBM
92 *The Courier,* 17 February 1843
93 RLE/844, pe. 257, PANB
94 RLE/844, pe. 258
95 L. Donaldson to A. Reade, 8 March 1844, REX/PA, vol. 120, PANB
96 Major F.W. Whingate to officer commanding 33rd Regiment, 20 March 1845, REX/PA, vol. 122
97 *The News,* 30 December 1844, 3 January 1845; *The Courier,* 4 and 18 January 1845; petition of grand jury of St John, March 1845, REX/MG9, vol. 122, PANB
98 For a stimulating view of the riot see Scott See, 'The Orange Order and Social Violence in Mid-Nineteenth Century Saint John,' *Acadiensis* XIII (Autumn 1983): 68–92. Influenced by the literature of American urban experience, See views the riot as a confrontation between natives and immigrants. He argues that the Orangemen had come to represent nativist traditions and that a majority of identifiable Orangemen were not born in Ireland. From this position he contends that the authorities, including presumably the officers of the British garrison, were determined to support the Orangemen and suppress the Catholics. The present study suggests some modifications of these positions.
99 Information of Jacob Allen regarding the riot, REX/PA, vol. 98
100 Head to Gray, 15 July 1849, CO 188/110; evidence before the coroners court and before B. Peters, JP, W.H. Needham, JP, and G.A. Lockhart, JP. The information of Jacob Allan, JP, REX/PA, vol. 98, PANB; *The Courier,* 14, 21, and 28 July 1849
101 A contention supported by See, 'The Orange Order and Social Violence in Saint John,' 90
102 Head to Grey, 15 July 1849, CO 188/110
103 For example, John C. Crookshank was enrolled as an Orangeman in 1842. He was the son of the great merchant, Robert, and a nephew of John McGill, the receiver general of Upper Canada. Crookshank Family Papers, shelf 104, box 4, packet 3, NBM
104 See RLE/85, pe. 94–101, 139–50, 186–94, 204–11, 282–93, 356–66, 424–7, 459–60, PANB. Scott See puts the figure at about 10,000; See, 'The Orange Order and Social Violence in Saint John,' 88–92.
105 The conference declared that 'Therefore we, whom the Holy Ghost has made overseers of the flock which he has purchased with his own Blood and who watch for souls as they that must give account in the exercise of that affection and care which we have Entreat them to come out of their Lodges and be Separate. And further we feel bound though with pain and sorrow to instruct out Churches to withdraw fellowship from those brethern who willfully reject our counsel and care, and the labour of the Church in this particular.' Report of Ad Hoc Committee on the Orange Order, Minutes of the General Conference of the Free Christian Baptist Church of New Brunswick 1850–1873, General Conference of 1857,

UNBA. The decision was taken without opposition. McLeod was also editor of *The Religious Intelligence.*
106 Of the signatories of the 1844 petition, 30 per cent held high or white-collar occupations; only 16 per cent of the 1854 signatories were found in these groups.
107 Johnston, *Notes on North America* II, 155–6
108 Ibid., 176
109 Colebrook to Stanley, 14 May 1842, CO 188/77
110 Colebrook to Grey, 31 July 1847, enclosure CO 188/101
111 Quoted in *The Morning Freeman*, 6 July 1858
112 Records of the court of probate for the county of Saint John, book E, 198–200, Saint John County Court House
113 These ideas are discussed in Feldberg, *The Philadelphia Riots*, 23.
114 Clark argues for Philadelphia that by 1850 a 'Victorian Compromise' had been reached in which the Irish would remain in the social framework they had created for themselves and leave the native leadership in unchallenged possession of the larger society and its institutions. See Clark, *The Irish in Philadelphia*, 35, 126; Handlin *Boston's Immigrants*, 176; Nicholson, 'Ecclesiastical Metropolitanism.'

CHAPTER 6

1 Historians have generally found it difficult to distinguish religious content from its ethnic form. Katz refers to them as one in his Hamilton study, Feldberg posits Irish Roman Catholicism against native evangelicalism in Philadelphia, and S.D. Clark creates a dichotomy between the British church and the frontier sect which is clearly identified with evangelicism. See Michael Katz, *The People of Hamilton: Canada West* (Cambridge, Mass. 1975); Michael Feldberg, *The Philadelphia Riots of 1844: A Study of Ethnic Conflict* (Westport, Conn. 1975); S.D. Clark, *Church and Sect in Canada* (Toronto 1948), particularly chs II, IV, V.
2 The effect of this leadership development is dealt with by Paul Boyar in *Urban Masses and Moral Order in America, 1820–1920* (Cambridge, Mass. 1978), esp. part one.
3 Although, as Roger Martin has pointed out, the theological distinctions between Calvinists and Arminians were not easily bridged. Even moderate Calvinists maintained a healthy suspicion of Pelagian tendencies, which they perceived in Wesleyanism, and their interpretation of the nature of the atonement differed markedly from that of the Methodists. See Martin, *Evangelicals United: Ecumenical Stirrings in Pre-Victorian Britain 1795–1830* (Methchen, NJ 1983), ch. I.
4 There is a considerable literature on English evangelicalism. A useful recent study of the movement's effect is Ian C. Bradley, *The Call to Seriousness: The Evangelical Impact on the Victorians* (London 1976). The most useful statement on Canadian evangelicalism is Goldwin French, 'The Evangelical Creed in Canada,' in W.L. Morton, ed., *The Shield of Achilles: Aspects of Canada in the Victorian Age* (Toronto 1968), 15–35. Case studies of the activities of individual British North American evangelicals include W.P.J. Miller, 'The Remarkable Thaddeus Osgood: A Study in the Evangelical Spirit in the Canadas,' *Histoire Sociale/Social History*, no. 19 (May 1977):59–76.
5 J.H. Overton, *The Evangelical Revival in the Eighteenth Century* (London 1886),

154; T.L. Smith, *Revivalism and Social Reform in Mid-Nineteenth-Century America* (Nashville 1957), 29–30

6 Charles I. Foster, *An Errand of Mercy* (Chapel Hill, NC 1960), 81, 93, 99

7 The movement of mainstream Congregationalism from unyielding Calvinism to evangelicalism and from defence of the standing order to a recognition of all orthodox Protestant denominations is examined by Stephen E. Berk in *Calvinism vs. Democracy: Timothy Dwight and the Origins of American Evangelical Orthodoxy* (Hamden, Conn. 1974). The most useful general study of the ante-bellum movement remains Smith, *Revivalism and Social Reform*. Smith emphasizes the urban nature of nineteenth-century evangelicalism.

8 For example the 1400 attending Methodist services in 1835 grew to about 6000 in 1846, meeting with 4 ministers and 9 local preachers in 7 chapels and 13 other preaching places. Devout Methodists living within walking distance of the chapels would have attended two services each Sunday. Even when this is accounted for the figures suggest that attendance rose from perhaps 1000 individuals in 1835 to between 3000 and 4000 eleven years later. By 1846 there were about 6000 attending Catholic services, 2000 at Baptist services, and 1000 at those of the Church of Scotland. REX/PA, ret. and stats., 1, 2, 3, 6, 7, PANB

9 George A. Henderson, *Early Saint John Methodism and History of Centenary Methodist Church, Saint John, N.B.* (Saint John 1890), 23

10 Bumsted argues that it was well in decline in the region by this time. See J.M. Bumsted, 'Church and State in Maritime Canada, 1749–1807,' in Bumsted, ed., *Canadian History before Confederation* (Georgetown, Ont. 1979), 179–95.

11 Henderson, *Early Saint John Methodism*, 23–5

12 Robert Cooney, *Autobiography of a Wesleyan Methodist Missionary* (Montreal 1856), 147, 149

13 The closest comparisons are for 1829 when Episcopalian attendance averaged 800 each Sunday and 1833 when 1600 Methodists were in chapel. REX/PA, ret. and stats. 1, 2, 7, PANB

14 There is no way to establish the social background of the majority of pre-1840 Methodist members. That has to be done negatively. Most recognized leaders were artisans and the most socially prominent were minor businessmen and a single physician.

15 RLE/814, pe. 16, PANB

16 See *The City Gazette*, 24 February 1817 and *The Courier*, 19 June, 10 and 17 July 1817, for examples of the debates. By 1850 there were five Presbyterian congregations: St Andrew's and St Stephen's Church of Scotland, St John's and St David's Free Church of Scotland, and the Irish Covenenter's Church.

17 I.E. Bill, *The Baptists of Saint John: Two Sermons* (Saint John 1863), 5. Local families included the Hardings, the Lovatts (Leavitts), and the Blakslees. Among the rural emigrants were two prominent merchants: Thomas Pettingill and John M. Wilmot.

18 For an example of the public attacks on the Baptists, see *The City Gazette*, 28 November 1828

19 The Wilmots did this and so, too, did W.B. Kinnear, N.S. Demill, and Joshua Barnes. See, for example, Joshua N. Barnes, *Lights and Shadows of Eighty Years* (Saint John 1911). For an Episcopal view of Baptists at mid-century,

see William M. Jarvis to Mrs Frederick Brecken, 27 August 1860, Jarvis Papers, NBM. For the Halifax experience, see Clark, *Church and Sect in Canada*, 250–2.

20 Minutes of the Free Christian Baptist Church of New Brunswick 1850–73, preface, UNBA

21 A comprehensive elaboration of this idea is found in R.F. Wearmouth, *Methodism and the Common People of the Eighteenth Century*. There are a number of New Brunswick autobiographies and diaries that attest to the strength of the tradition in the early nineteenth century.

22 See, for example, the letters from 'Churchman,' 'Archippus,' 'Locius,' 'Wattie Strang,' and 'Scoto-Britannicus' in *The Courier*, 10, 19 and 26 July 1819.

23 *The Courier*, 28 November 1818

24 RLE/829, pe. 16, PANB

25 See *The City Gazette*, 31 March 1819; 22 March and 17 April 1822.

26 *The City Gazette*, 1 and 18 October 1820

27 J.W.P. Gray, at Trinity Church, in Saint John, in December 1865, *Sermons upon the Second Advent of Our Lord Preached in Saint John, 1865*, UNBA; see also Wm. M. Jarvis to Mrs Helen Brecken, 15 September 1859, Jarvis Papers, NBM

28 Judith Fingard, ' "Grapes in the Wilderness": The Bible Society in British North America in the Early Nineteenth Century,' *Histoire Sociale/Social History*, no. 9 (April 1972): 16–20

29 *The City Gazette*, 28 May 1819

30 Ibid., 5 March 1828. The Aprocrypha Controversy is dealt with in Martin, *Evangelicals United*, 123–31.

31 *The Courier*, 17 March 1832

32 *The Observer*, 12 April 1836

33 *The Courier*, 1 January and 18 December 1820

34 *The City Gazette*, 22 June 1822

35 Ibid., 8 May 1822

36 *The Courier*, 9 August 1823; *The City Gazette*, 29 April 1824. Charles Simonds was its president in 1823.

37 At one such general rally of the Church and Methodist Sunday Schools *The Courier* editor, a prominent Churchman, referred to the two groups as 'different battalions of the Christian army.' *The Courier*, 5 October 1823

38 *The City Gazette*, 22 March and 17 April 1822

39 Ibid., 26 March, 18 June 1828

40 Ibid., 22 and 29 April, 10 June 1828

41 Charles Cole, *The Social Ideas of the Northern Evangelists* (New York 1954), 118–21

42 *The City Gazette*, 8 June 1830

43 Mary Caroline Boyd to Mrs E. Jarvis, 31 January 1831, Jarvis Papers, NBM. Most clergy, she argued, joined the society to set an example for the community.

44 *The Observer*, 20 January and 23 August 1835; *The Courier*, 26 July, 2 and 9 August 1830

45 The differences are perhaps best illustrated in the spirited public debate between 'D' and 'G' in *The Courier* in 1829: 'D' opposed not only dancing, flirting, ostentatiousness of dress, and the waste of time and money that

could better have been devoted to good works, but also membership in and loyalty to national societies such as St George's and St Patrick's. See *The Courier*, 26 December 1829; 9 January 1830. See also the letter from 'Y' in the issue of 2 April 1831.

46 *The Chronicle*, 3 and 17 February 1837; *City Gazette*, 18 February 1837
47 *The Chronicle*, 6 and 30 September; 2, 14, 21 and 28 October; 4 and 11 November 1836; 3 and 17 February 1837; *The Loyalist*, 17 November 1842
48 *The News*, 6 November 1846; *The Loyalist*, 29 January 1847
49 Trinity Vestry minutes, vol III, 1 November 1847, mfm, PANB
50 *The Observer*, 19 April 1848; *The Courier*, 22 January 1848; 5 January 1850
51 RLE/854, pe. 3. 480, PANB
52 *The Courier*, 18 December 1852
53 *The News*, 5 October 1846
54 See, for example, 'Correspondent' in *The News*, 26 May 1846.
55 *The News*, 16 September 1846
56 *The Loyalist*, 25 September 1846
57 Minute book of General Conference of the Free Christian Baptist Church, 1856, Education Committee report, UNBA
58 H. MacKintosh, *Disestablishment and Liberation* (London 1972), 28–35
59 J.B.A. Kessler, *A Study of the Evangelical Alliance in Great Britain* (Goes, Netherlands 1968), ch. VI
60 See W.T. Wishart, *Extracts of Lectures on Political Economy* (Saint John 1845).
61 Irvine to William Parks, 19 January 1844. Parks Papers F, no. 5, NBM
62 *The Courier*, 29 March 1845, 2 August, and 13 September 1845
63 RLE/846, pe. 46, PANB
64 *The News*, 12 January and 9 May 1846
65 Ibid., 28 March 1846
66 R.W. Dale, *History of English Congregationalism* (London 1907), 637–44; MacKintosh, *Disestablishment*, 11–13, 23–25
67 James Dunn writing in *The Courier*, 25 July 1846
68 *The Loyalist*, 22 September 1846
69 *The Courier*, 23 May 1846
70 *The News*, 23 September 1846
71 On the failure of religious political parties in the U.S., see Charles Foster, *An Errand of Mercy* (Chapel Hill 1960); and C.C. Cole, *Social Ideas of the Northern Evangelists 1826–60* (New York 1954).
72 *The Loyalist and Conservative*, 25 September and 8 October 1846
73 *The News*, 5 October 1846
74 *The Loyalist*, 13 October 1847; *The Courier*, 13 October 1847; *The News*, 7 October 1842
75 Since each voter in the county and city constituency could vote for up to four candidates, it was possible for a man to secure the support of more than half the electors and not win election. Unusually popular candidates sometimes received support of 80 per cent of the electorate.
76 *The Courier*, 11 October 1846
77 *The Chronicle* editor argued that apostolic succession was the essential mark of a church. Having destroyed the legitimacy of the non-episcopal Protestant denominations, the paper went on to demonstrate that, since the Roman Catholic Church had embraced false doctrine, the only gate to salva-

tion was to be found in the Church of England. Much of the public debate on the issue is summarized in *The News*, 21, 26, and 30 October, 6 November 1846.

78 *The Courier*, 23 January 1847

79 Robert Cooney, *The Autobiography of a Wesleyan Methodist Missionary* (Montreal 1856), 390–1

80 The unity of the movement is reflected in the act creating the orphanage. See Statutes of New Brunswick, 18 Victoria, c. 70.

CHAPTER 7

1 Joseph R. Gusfield, for example, argues that lower-status native-born Americans sought out the temperance movement in an effort to achieve middle class and to distinguish themselves from the immigrant population. See *Symbolic Crusade: Status Politics and the American Temperance Movement* (Urbana, Ill. 1965), 5.

2 For a provocative exposition of this view, see Paul E. Johnson, *A Shopkeepers' Millennium: Society and Revivals in Rochester, New York 1815–1837* (New York 1978).

3 See, for example, Bruce Laurie, *The Working People of Philadelphia 1800–1850*, 120–1.

4 There is only a small literature on the British North American phase of the movement. While W.S. MacNutt, in *New Brunswick: A History: 1784–1867* (Toronto 1964), indicates the political implications of the New Brunswick movement, the most useful study is J.K. Chapman, 'The Mid-Nineteenth Century Temperance Movement in New Brunswick and Maine,' CHR XXXV (March 1954): 43–60. The only general survey of Canadian temperance remains Ruth E. Spence, *Prohibition in Canada: A Memorial to Francis Stephen Spence* (Toronto 1919).

5 *The City Gazette*, 26 March and 30 April 1828; 10 June 1829; 9 March 1831. Common Council minutes, IX, 24 September 1830

6 *The City Gazette*, 30 April 1828

7 Brian Harrison and Barrie Tinder, *Drink and Sobriety in an Early Victorian Country Town: Banbury 1830–1860* (London 1978), 2

8 Charles I. Foster, *An Errand of Mercy* (Chapel Hill 1960), 137

9 See, for example, the correspondent to *The Gazette*, 3 June 1831, who argued that it would produce a religious revival.

10 Edwards was a founder of both the American Tract Society and the American Temperance Society. He served for many years as secretary of the latter organization.

11 *The Observer*, 21 October 1834. See also the letter of Robert Salter in the issue of 28 October.

12 *The Courier*, 3 May 1834. Comparison of known Temperance and Abstinence Society members with the freemen's rolls of the city indicates that the number of members under 18 was probably small. The typical member was a male between 30 and 40 years of age.

13 *The Courier*, 14 July 1832

14 RLE/831, pe. 35, PANB

15 *The Courier*, 19 March 1831; the 1833 bill actually became law but its wording challenged the Common Council's charter rights. *The Courier*, 22 March 1833

16 See, for example, RLE/832, pe. 2, PANB; RLE/835, pe. 149; RLE/839, pe. 149
17 See Laurie, *Working People of Philadelphia*, 120–1. Laurie describes the older American Temperance Society as élitist.
18 *The Courier*, 30 June 1830
19 St John Total Abstinence Society membership rolls 1832–1840, NBM
20 Recruiting efforts in the period included the creation of committees 'to commune' with each of the city's clergymen. The move succeeded in recruiting the soon-to-be-retired rector of Saint John.
21 *The Courier*, 23 December 1843
22 See George Fenety's editorial in *The News*, 3 January 1842.
23 RLE/845, pe. 318
24 *The Observer*, 2 December 1834
25 *The Chronicle*, 24 March 1837
26 *The Courier*, 30 June 1838
27 W.M. Jarvis to Lt Col. Edward Boyd, June 1859, Jarvis Papers, NBM
28 *The News*, 5 February 1841; *The Courier*, 13 February and 13 March 1841
29 Ibid., 23 October 1841
30 Ibid., 30 October 1841
31 Although Dennis Clark argues that Philadelphia Catholic temperance societies were designed to displace rowdyism and nationalist secret societies. See *The Irish in Philadelphia: Ten Generations of Urban Experience* (Philadelphia 1973) 103–4.
32 Edward Norman, *A History of Modern Ireland* (London 1977), 74–5
33 *The Courier*, 9 April 1842
34 Discussions of the parade and its significance are found in *The Courier*, 1 March 1842; *The News*, 16 March 1842; and *The Loyalist*, 12 October 1842.
35 *The News*, 5 February 1841; *The Courier*, 9 April 1842
36 W.H. Daniels, *The Temperance Reform and Its Great Reformers* (New York 1878), 197
37 *The Courier*, 22 May 1847
38 *The Observer*, 23 May 1848; Common Council minutes vol. XIX, 12 May 1848
39 *The Courier*, 3 April 1852. The figure for the Sons and the Total Abstinence Society (TAS) are not strictly comparable, since the TAS admitted some women to membership.
40 *Journals of the House of Assembly of New Brunswick* (1852), Appendix, Census of 1851, St John County
41 *The Temperance Telegraph*, 4 April 1850. In one four-day tour, S.L. Tilley held a division meeting at Norton and organized divisions 52, 53, and 54 at Norton, Sussex Valley, and Sussex.
42 *Journal of the Fourth Annual Session of the Sons of Temperance*, Grand Division of New Brunswick (1850), 89, UNBA
43 *Quarterly Session, Grand Division, Sons of Temperance* (July 1852), 294, UNBA
44 *The Temperance Telegraph*, 6 June 1850
45 G.F. Clark, *History of the Temperance Reform in Massachusetts 1813–1883* (Boston 1888), 80–7, 90–4.
46 Membership in the Total Abstinence Society was always at least twice as large as that of the Sons of Temperance. The leadership of the two organizations remained quite separate throughout the 1850s.
47 RLE/47, pe. 465, PANB
48 *The Loyalist*, 23 December 1847
49 *The Courier*, 7 April 1849

50 Common Council supplementary paper 20, 22 May 1849; Common Council, vol. XIX, 22 May 1849
51 *The Courier*, 22 December 1849
52 *The Courier*, 8 June 1850
53 W.M. Baker, *Timothy Warren Anglin, 1822–96: Irish Catholic Canadian* (Toronto 1977), 32
54 RLE/52, pe. 406
55 For example, see the issue of 6 June 1850.
56 *Journal of the Quarterly Session of the Grand Division, New Brunswick Sons of Temperance* (28 July 1852), 293
57 RLE/52, pe. 406
58 Oscar Handlin, *Boston's Immigrants: A Study in Acculturation* (New York 1971), 134
59 For example, see the petition headed by six justices of the peace, RLE/852, pe. 264, and the petition of Henry Chubb and 1763 others, RLE/854, pe. 385.
60 See J. Bliss in *Journal of the Grand Division, New Brunswick Sons of Temperance* (30 April 1856), 140.
61 *Journal of the Grand Division, New Brunswick Sons of Temperance* (25 October 1854), membership reports. The figures of the Granite Rock Division are taken from the January report.
62 *The Courier*, 19 May 1853
63 T.L. Smith, *Revivalism and Social Reform in Mid-Nineteenth Century America* (Nashville 1957), ch. x
64 *Journal of the Grand Division, New Brunswick Sons of Temperance* (25 January 1854), 414–5
65 MacNutt, *New Brunswick*, ch. 14
66 James Hannay, *History of New Brunswick* II, 173–81; MacNutt, *New Brunswick*
67 Common Council minutes, vol. XXII, 2 May 1854
68 Motions by two militant prohibitionists, Fairweather and Demill, to prevent the grant of licences were lost from lack of a quorum. See Common Council minutes, vol. XXI, 27 April 1853.
69 Common Council minutes, vol. XXII, 8 May, 30 June, and 5 July 1854. The dissidents were Mercer, Beattey, and Wilson.
70 See RLE/53, pe. 265; RLE/54, pe. 385, PANB; Common Council supplementary papers, 32, 27 July 1854
71 *The Morning Freeman*, 24 July 1855
72 *Journal of the Grand Division, New Brunswick Sons of Temperance* (25 January 1854), membership reports (30 April 1856)
73 Saint John-Portland had a population of 38,000 in 1861 out of a provincial total of 252,000.
74 *Journal of the Grand Division* (October 1857), 270
75 See Clark, *The Irish in Philadelphia*, 103–4.

CHAPTER 8

1 See, for example, the essays in Phillip McCann, *Popular Education and Socialization in the Nineteenth Century* (London 1977), and Carl F. Kaestle, *The Evolution of an Urban School System: New York City 1750–1850* (Cambridge, Mass. 1973).
2 The requirement that the governor license all teachers was contained in the

royal instructions of 1784; Katherine MacNaughton, *The Theory and Practice of Education in New Brunswick* (Fredericton 1947), 56–7. Even this small support exceeded that provided in Upper Canada, where grants were not made to common schools until 1816.

3 MacNaughton, *Theory and Practice*, 56, 63, 71

4 Ibid., 58, 70. The New Brunswick government's priorities paralleled those of the Upper Canadian government, which provvided grammar schools in each district in 1807. See J. Donald Wilson, Robert M. Stamp, and Louis-Philippe Audet, eds, *Canadian Education: A History* (Scarborough 1970), ch. 10.

5 See, for example, Robert Crookshank. R.W. Crookshank to R.J. Crookshank, 15 March 1838, Crookshank Papers, NBM; 1851 Saint John Census manuscript, PANB.

6 Young women's schools became quite common after 1815 but seem to have declined in popularity by 1830.

7 See the prospectus for Taylor's Mercantile Academy for youth, *The Courier*, 27 April 1816; Thomas Addison's Seminary on King's Square, *The Gazette*, 11 September 1818; and B.F. Foster's School, *The Courier*, 27 September 1823. Most were highly practical programs offering reading, writing, arithmetic, grammar, bookkeeping, globes, navigation, and surveying.

8 *The Courier*, 17 October 1819; 27 September 1823

9 The discussion over whether the English Sunday school was largely an instrument for the indoctrination of the working class into middle-class values is found in T.W. Laqueur, *Religion and Respectability, Sunday Schools and Working Class Culture 1780–1850* (London 1976); T.R. Tholfsen, *Working-Class Radicalism in Mid-Victorian England* (New York 1977). Phillip McCann and Simon Firth argue that the schools were set up by a middle-class bourgeoisie in an effort to ensure quietude among the working class but that many of the Methodist schools were often taught by artisans. See Phillip McCann, 'Popular Education, Secularization and Social Control: Spitalfield 1812–24,' in McCann, ed., *Popular Education and Socialization in the Nineteenth Century* (London 1977), 1–40; Simon Firth, 'Socialization and Rational Schooling: Elementary Education in Leeds before 1870,' in McCann, ed., Ibid., 67–92.

10 Most early Sunday schools were inter-denominational and viewed with antagonism by some New York churches until the 1830s when they tended to become extensions of individual congregations. See Kaestle, *The Evolution of an Urban School System*, 121–4.

11 J. Lawson and Harold Silver, *The Social History of Education in England* (London 1973), 240–87. H.C. Bernard, *A History of English Education from 1760* (London 1961), ch. 6

12 McNaughton, *Theory and Practice*, 65–7

13 *The Gazette*, 8 September 1819

14 Smythe to Bathurst, 5 August 1820, CO 188/26

15 RLE/823, rept 7, PANB. Report of Madras trustees to the lieutenant-governor, 8 January 1822, REX/PA, vol. 43, PANB

16 *The Gazette*, 15 July 1818

17 MacNaughton, *Theory and Practice*, 67

18 Common Council minutes, vol. VI, August 1827

19 RLE/830/4/ZZ/1/4, PANB

20 MacNaughton, *Theory and Practice*, 68
21 Royal charter of Madras School, REX/PA, vol. 43, 7/1, PANB
22 Anne Digby and Peter Searby make the same point in connection with the English Madras schools. They argue that the Church of England provoked the conflicts with all dissenters by insisting that they would educate all children. See *Children, School and Society in Nineteenth-Century England* (London 1981), 14–15. By contrast, the Newfoundland School Society permitted Methodists to participate in its administration until 1840. See Wilson, Stamp, Audet, *Canadian Education*, 132.
23 Report of trustees of Madras schools, 1 September 1822, REX/PA, vol. 43, 7/1, PANB
24 RLE/830/4/zz/1/4
25 RLE/830, pe. 37
26 RLE/836, pe. 26
27 *The Courier*, 9 July 1842
28 J.P. Partelow to Dollard, 25 March 1850, Dollard correspondence, no. 884, Chancery of the Diocese of Saint John
29 REX/PA, vol. 44, 7/29, 7/35; 412 of the 557 students were enrolled in the Saint John School.
30 The abilities of private masters were often publicly attested to by clergymen of particular denominations. See *The Gazette*, 11 September 1818; *The Courier*, 27 September 1823.
31 RLE/36, pe. 38, PANB. The infant schools were favoured philanthropies of English evangelicals. See McCann, 'Spitalfield 1812–24.'
32 As quoted by Lawson and Silver in *The Social History of Education in England*, 284–5
33 RLE/860, pe. 337; REX/PA, vol. 44, 7/34
34 RLE/824, pe. 25. The original funds had been provided by Lieutenant-Governor Stracey-Smythe who financed the school from his own pocket.
35 Common Council minutes, vol. x, 3 August 1832; *The Observer*, 6 January 1835. In Carleton this had been the case for years. Blacks on the west side had attended George Bond's Baptist Sunday School.
36 See the Common Council debate in *The Courier*, 31 October 1840.
37 Common Council minutes, vol. xiv, 21 September 1840
38 *The News*, 21 January 1841; RLE/841, pe. 53, PANB
39 RLE/844, pe. 125. There was apparently a break in the early 1850s followed by the creation of a new school. See *The Courier*, 13 March 1852; RLE/854, pe. 3, 71.
40 *Dictionary of Canadian Biography*, vol. ix (Toronto 1976), 277
41 RLE/839, pe. 136, PANB
42 Ibid., pe. 169
43 *The Courier*, 28 December 1839; *The News*, 23 October 1839
44 RLE/841, pe. 29. The building cost £1370, of which £875 was raised by subscription.
45 *The Courier*, 21 August 1841; *Dictionary of Canadian Biography*, vol. ix, 308–12. When Gesner fell into bankruptcy in 1843, his friends took over the Natural History Collection and donated it to the Mechanics Institute.
46 RLE/844, pe. 120
47 W.T. Wishart, *Extracts of Lectures on Political Economy* (Saint John 1845)
48 They argued that the Madras schools should be converted into a broadly

based non-sectarian system of subsidized public day schools. See RLE/
838, pe. 3, 67; *The Chronicle*, 7 October 1837; *The Courier*, 7 November 1837;
see also *The Courier*, 2 and 7 December 1850.
49 *The Courier*, 29 March 1845
50 Diane Ravisch, *The Great School Wars, New York City 1805–1973* (New York
1972), 22–40
51 *The News*, 18 April 1845
52 *The Courier*, 2 August 1845. A brief study of Duval's life and career by
Richard Rice is found in the *Dictionary of Canadian Biography*, vol. x, 268–9.
53 *The Courier*, 13 September 1845
54 RLE/846, pe. 248; RLE/848, pe. 336, PANB
55 See the letters to *The Courier*, 11 February 1845; MacNaughton, *Theory and
Practice*, 108
56 MacNaughton, *Theory and Practice*, 109–32. The act provided for three
classes of licences, each having its own salary scale and teaching requirements. Class III required only the ability to teach the three Rs. Class I in
addition had to be able to teach philosophy, algebra, geometry, trigonometry, mensuration, surveying, navigation, bookkeeping, geography,
and grammar.
57 RLE/849, pe. 258
58 MacNaughton, *Theory and Practice*, 139–40
59 See Michael Katz, *The Irony of Early School Reform: Educational Innovation in
Mid-Nineteenth Century Massachusetts* (Cambridge, Mass. 1968), esp. part II.
60 RLE/852, pe. 6; RLE/853, pe. 41; RLE/854, pe. 206; REX/PA, vol. 43, 7/25
61 Supporters of evangelical traditions composed a majority of the electorates
of nine counties returning 28 members of the Legislative Assembly in
1861.
62 Robert Cooney, *Autobiography of a Wesleyan Methodist Missionary* (Montreal
1856), 153–4; Common Council minutes, vol. XXI, 17 March 1853. REX/PA,
vol. 44, 7/36. The managers included Geo. and Ed. Lockhart, D.L. McLaughlin, E.T. Knowles, N.A. Robertson, Aaron Eaton.
63 T.W. Smith, *History of the Methodist church ...* (Halifax 1890), II, 390.
64 REX/PA, vol. 44, 7/31
65 RLE/849, pe. 205; Irvine to Mr Reed, 11 June 1849, Parks Papers, F no. 5, NBM
66 RLE/850, pe. 117
67 Free Christian Baptist Conference minutes book, 1858, report of the Committee on Education, UNBA
68 REX/PA, vol. 44, 7/31, Saint John High School 1861–1871
69 The 1858 provincial schools report, for example, reported that only 775 of
6717 school-age children were enrolled in the school system. Three years
later, the public schools reported 1716 enrolments, while the 1861 Census
reported 4384 children attending school. *Journals of the House of Assembly*
(1859), appendix p. DCXVI; (1862), Report of Public Schools, appendix p. xv;
Census of 1861, 96. The technique of employing statistical evidence to
imply a widespread ignorance was employed as well by Upper Canadian
promoters. See Allison Prentice, *The School Promoters: Education and Social
Class in Mid-Nineteenth Century Upper Canada* (Toronto 1977), 50.
70 About 55 per cent of the 101,000 children between five and fifteen years
living in New York City in 1850 were enrolled in some school. See
Kaestle, *The Evolution of an Urban School System*, 89.

71 Useful discussions of the views and activities of the Massachusetts and Upper Canadian educational reformers of the period are found in Katz, *The Irony of Early School Reform*, and Prentice, *The School Promoters*.
72 *The Courier*, 22 May 1851, 1 January 1853
73 *The Courier*, 7 November and 12 December 1857
74 *The Courier*, 16 January 1858. Issues of *The Freemen* for this period do not exist. *The Freemen* position has been reconstructed from quotations.
75 *The Courier*, 5 November 1857
76 Minutes of the General Conference of the Free Christian Baptist Church of New Brunswick (1856), report of the Education Committee, UNBA
77 RLE/858, pe. 212, 122
79 RLE/858, pe. 155, 156
80 W.S. MacNutt, *New Brunswick: A History: 1784–1867* (Toronto 1963) 365–6

CHAPTER 9

1 See Derek Fraser, ed., *Municipal Reform and the Industrial City* (Leicester 1982), 2–8, and Bryan Keith-Lucas, *The Unreformed Local Government System* (London 1980).
2 This fact made the Saint John experience unique in British North America. Efforts in other urban areas were usually directed at securing municipal institutions.
3 'One of the People,' in *The Courier*, 7 November 1835
4 Common Council minutes, vol. XII, 15 November 1836, 28 May 1839; vol. XIV, 24 October 1839, 18 April 1840; vol. XVII, 5 and 9 October 1844, SJCH
5 Ibid., vol. XI, 4 October 1835; vol. XV, 28 May 1841, vol. XXII, 16 April 1836, SJCH
6 Ibid., vol. XI, 1 and 3 April 1834
7 Ibid., vol. XI, 8 April 1834
8 RLE/835, pe. 7, PANB
9 Common Council minutes, vol. XI, 14 January 1835, SJCH
10 RLE/835, pe. 169, PANB
11 *The Chronicle*, 11 May 1838
12 *The New Brunswicker*, 14 April 1842
13 Common Council minutes, vol. XVII, 9 April 1845, SJCH
14 D.C.M. Platt, 'Financing the Expansion of Cities 1860–1914,' *Urban History Review/Revue d'histoire urbaine* XI (February 1983): 61
15 Details of the city accounts are generally found each year in the April minutes of Common Council. Rents and taxes surpassed £4000 for the first time in 1832. See Common Council minutes, vol. IX, 20 April 1831, SJCH.
16 Ibid., vol. V, 20 April and 8 July 1820; vol. VII, 9 May 1828; vol. IX, 26 November 1830; vol. XI, 10 June 1835
17 Ibid., vol. VII, 14 January 1828; vol. VIII, 20 April 1830
18 Ibid., vol. IX, 7 August 1830
19 Rising land values were the key to financing city modernization everywhere. Platt, 'Financing the Expansion of Cities,' 62
20 Common Council minutes, vol. XVI, 28 May 1842; vol. XIII, 14 March 1839; vol. XIV, 5 August 1839
21 Ibid., vol. XII, 12 October 1836; vol. VII, 15 April 1828; vol. XVI, 23 August 1842; vol. XVII, 24 January 1845; vol. XV, 23 and 30 August 1841
22 'Reporting on the Overseers Accounts,' *The Courier*, 19 February 1842

23 Common Council minutes, vol. xv, 4 and 24 November 1841, SJCH
24 Colebrook to Stanley, 27 September 1842, CO 188/79
25 Common Council minutes, vol. xv, 20 July 1841; vol. xvi, 22 August 1847; SJCH
26 Ibid., vol. xv, 23 August and 4 November 1841
27 *The New Brunswicker*, 10, 15 and 19 February 1842; *The News*, 21 February 1842
28 Common Council minutes, vol. xvi, 9 September 1842; Bondholders Committee report, Common Council supporting papers, vol. 4, 7/8–12/13 September 1842, PANB
29 Colebrook to Stanley, 27 September 1842, CO 188/79
30 Report of committee of Common Council preparatory to new trust deed, 3 October 1845, REX/PA, vol. 120, PANB. By 1845 the capital sum owed by the city to its bond holders had grown to £115,000.
31 At least part of this animosity toward Partelow was political. A long-time assemblyman for the city, he was a member of the executive council in 1842 and the financial adviser to the government.
32 Common Council minutes, vol. xviii, 22 July 1846, SJCH. As late as 1850, the council had revenues of £12,000 of which £6000 was paid to the trustees' accounts. Common Council minutes, vol. xx, 3 February 1851
33 Common Council supporting papers, vol. iv, 7/8–12/13 September 1842, PANB; Common Council minutes, vol. xvi, 7 September 1842, SJCH
34 Common Council minutes, vol. xiv, 18 July 1839; 19 November 1841, SJCH
35 *The News*, 23 November 1843
36 Common Council minutes, vol. xvi, 8 October 1842, SJCH
37 *The Courier*, 12 March 1842
38 *The New Brunswicker*, 30 December 1841
39 RLE/843, pe. 174, PANB
40 Petition of freemen and freeholders opposing any change in the elective franchise, Common Council supporting papers, vol. iv, 1 and 6 February 1843, PANB
41 RLE/843, pe. 173, PANB; Common Council minutes, vol. xvi, 15 February 1843, SJCH
42 *The Loyalist*, 2 February 1843
43 Common Council supporting papers, vol. 5, 21 February 1843, PANB. The act was 6 Victoria c. 35.
44 Ibid., vol. 6, 17 May 1843. These fees remained in effect until 1845 when they were reduced to £15 for alien merchants and £10 for alien artisans.
45 Common Council minutes, vol. xvii, 27 January 1844, SJCH
46 Ibid., vol. xvi, 13 December 1843; vol. xvii, 29 January 1845
47 *The News*, 5 April 1847
48 Common Council minutes, vol. xix, 15 July 1848, SJCH
49 Ibid., vol. xix, 3 August 1848
50 Ibid., vol. xix, 25 November and 23 December 1848
51 Ibid., vol. xix, 16 January 1849
52 Ibid., vol. xix, 9, 14, and 15 February 1849
53 *The Courier*, 24 February 1849; RLE/849, pe. 417, PANB
54 Common Council minutes, vol. xix, 3 July 1849, SJCH
55 Ibid., vol. xix, 7 August 1849

56 Ibid., vol. xix, 12 December 1849; vol. xx, 25 November 1849; 30 August, 28 September, and 21 October 1850
57 Ibid., vol. xx, 14 and 23 January and 17 December 1851; vol. xxi, 10 January 1853
58 Ibid., vol. xxi, 8 September and 17 November 1852. The final vote on the issue of the secret ballot was 7 to 4.
59 Petition of freemen living outside city, Common Council supporting papers, vol. 36, council concurrence 1/2 April 1856, PANB; RLE/856, pe. 403, PANB; Statutes of New Brunswick, 19 Victoria c. 53
60 By tradition, city freemen had been exempt from the provincial freehold requirement. Before 1855 they had only been required to show owner-ship of a personal estate of £25. The Elections Act of that year required that they be assessed for £25 or possess personal or personal and real pro-perty to a value of £100 or have an income of £100. See Statutes of New Brunswick, 18 Victoria c. 37.

CHAPTER 10

1 This point is made most strongly by D.C.M. Platt in 'Financing the Expan-sion of Cities 1860–1914,' *Urban History Review/Revue d'histoire urbaine* xi (February 1983): 61–6
2 See, for example, Elwood Jones and Douglas McCalla, 'Toronto Water-works, 1840–77: Continuity and Change in Nineteenth-Century Toronto Politics,' CHR lx (September 1979): 300–24; Francis Sheppard, *London 1808–70: The Infernal Wen* (London 1971), ch. 7; Derek Fraser, *Urban Politics in Victorian England* (Leicester 1976), ch. 7.
3 'Who Governed the Nation's Cities in the "Era of the Common Man"?' *Political Science Quarterly* lxxxvii (1972): 605
4 John Gerrard, *Leadership and Power in Victorian Industrial Towns* (Manchester 1983), ch. 3
5 This was not true in most major American cities. Philadelphia possessed a public water system from 1801, Boston from 1842, and New York from 1848. See S.B. Warner Jr, *The Private City: Philadelphia in Three Periods of Its Growth* (Philadelphia 1968), 102–11.
6 RLE/838, pe., PANB
7 Schedule of real estate belonging to Saint John, REX/PA, miscellaneous Saint John, PANB
8 Common Council minutes, vol. vi, 16 May 1827, SJCH
9 Of these 11 were in Kings Ward, 17 in Queens, and 5 in Dukes and Sydney. See Schedule of real estate belonging to Saint John, REX/PA, miscellaneous Saint John, PANB.
10 Common Council minutes, vol. v, 23 August 1819; 21 January 1820; vol. ix, 21 January 1832; vol. x, 5 September 1833. Rankine was required to pay an annual rental of £30, almost the amount paid by the other nine lessees combined.
11 Ibid., vol. vii, 14 May 1829; vol. xi, 13 August 1836
12 Ibid., vol. xii, 10 June 1837; vol. xxi, 4 and 17 January 1854
13 Ibid., vol. xix, 3 and 11 August, 11 October 1848; vol. xx, 19 September 1853
14 Statement of annual losses of north and south market wharves, Common Council supporting papers, vol. ii, 26/28 June 1842, PANB

15 There is little doubt that the councillors used the opportunity to settle a number of personal scores. Noah Disbrow had no difficulty obtaining his lease, while the Jarvis brothers were refused. Henry Gilbert and Nehemiah Merritt both applied at the same time; the former was refused and the latter granted. See Common Council minutes, vol. v, 21 January and 28 July 1823; 10 November and 27 December 1825, SJCH.

16 Common Council minutes, vol. VI, 23 September 1823; vol. VII, 9 and 31 May 1828; vol. IX, 7 and 25 August 1830

17 Ibid., vol. IX, 21 January 1832; vol. XIII, 14 February 1839; vol. XXI 9 March 1853

18 Ibid., 13 May 1839

19 RLE/835, pe. 54; RLE/835, pe. 185, PANB

20 Common Council minutes, vol. XIV, 30 January 1840; vol. XVII, 19 February and 8 April 1845, SJCH; RLE/845, pe. 326, PANB. Common Council supporting papers, vol. 10 and 19 February 1845, PANB. The promoters included I. Woodward, J. Kirk, J. Thurgar, J. Duncan, T. Millidge, F. Wiggins, W. Scovil, T. Walker, W. Perkins, D. McLaughlin.

21 RLE/845, pe. 323, PANB; Common Council minutes, vol. XVIII, 22 May 1846; 14 April 1847, SJCH; *The Courier*, 13 September 1845; 19 September 1846

22 *The Courier*, 2 February 1850; RLE/860, pe. 14, PANB

23 Common Council minutes, vol. IV, 11 September 1817; vol. VI, 12 June 1827; vol. VII, 18 July 1828; vol. XII, 28 April, 26 May, and June 1836, SJCH. Construction costs were at the rate of £1200 a mile in 1835.

24 Common Council minutes, vol. VII 15 June 1829, SJCH. This was the practice in London, where the sewerage systems were built only for surface water and street cleaning. See Sheppard, *London*, ch. 7.

25 Between 1850 and 1859 there were thirty-three applications, most of them in areas that had possessed common sewers for more than twenty years. For the most part they were from members of prominent families.

26 Common Council minutes, 24 January 1851, SJCH

27 *The Courier*, 6 June 1857

28 In this connection, note George Fenety's comment on the £7.10.0 that *The News* spent each year on water vendors; *The News*, 9 December 1839. Many vendors advertised that their water was procured from clear sparkling springs beyond the city, a claim that reflects the suspicion on the part of most knowledgeable townspeople that many city wells contained more than they should.

29 Common Council minutes, vol. X, 20 August 1832, SJCH

30 Ibid., vol. XI, 22 October 1835

31 RLE/837, pe. 96, PANB

32 *The Courier*, 3 July 1837. The development of the first Toronto water works in 1841–43 was undertaken by a Montreal proprietor who also held a franchise for gas distribution. Otherwise development problems and costs seem to have been comparable. See Jones and McCalla, 'Toronto Waterworks,' 302–5.

33 Common Council minutes, 10 June 1837; vol. XIII, 1 November 1837

34 Ibid., vol. XIII, 24 September 1838; vol. XIV, 15 January 1840; 29 May 1840

35 Ibid., 30 January, 13 February, 30 June, and 2 July 1840

36 Ibid., vol. XIV, 3 August 1840; vol. XV, 19 August 1841

37 Common Council minutes, vol. xiv, 5 and 10 August 1840, sjch; vol. xv, 8 April 1841
38 Ibid., vol. xv, 6 May 1841
39 Petition to legislature re Water Company, rle/842, pe. 79, Common Council supporting papers, vol. iv, 26/28 January 1842, panb. Common Council minutes, vol. xv, 22 January 1842, sjch. The company's 1841 balance sheet showed revenues of £530 and ordinary expenses of £500 on an investment exceeding £25,000.
40 Common Council minutes, vol. xvi, 28 May, 11 August, 31 October, and 17 November 1842; 27 September 1843; vol. xvii, 22 May, 5 June, and 18 September 1844
41 In 1846 it laid mains along Horsefield and along King from Germaine to Stone Church. In 1849 it was the turn of Brussels, Dock, Union, Mill, Germaine, St James, Carmarthen, and North St Andrew's streets; Common Council minutes, vol. xix, 13 June 1849, sjch.
42 rle/844, pe. 181, panb; Common Council minutes, vol. xvi, 28 May 1842, sjch. The £27,000 consisted of 2955 paid-up shares of £5 each, £5000 from forfeited shares, £5000 from the provincial loan. The remainder was owed to Barings and to provincial creditors.
43 Water Committee report, Common Council supporting papers, vol. iv, 23 December 1842, panb
44 Common Council minutes, vol. xvi, 1 and 8 February 1843, sjch
45 rle/844, pe. 86, 230, panb
46 New Brunswick, 7 Victoria c. 43
47 Common Council minutes, vol. xvii, 14 May 1844, sjch
48 *The News*, 6 August 1845
49 *The News*, 6 August 1845
50 New Brunswick, 8 Victoria c. 63
51 rle/846, pe. 152, panb; Common Council minutes, vol. xviii, 27 May 1846, panb
52 rle/850, pe. 297, panb
53 The resolution was carried on a 7 to 5 vote; Common Council minutes, vol. xx, 4 February, 29 April, and 30 August 1850, sjch. Needham, Nowlin, and Smith were among those offering to purchase the debentures.
54 *The Courier*, 18 December 1852
55 Common Council minutes, vol. xxi, 22 February 1853, sjch. Since par value of stock was £5, the company was asked to issue 1000 shares of which the city would take up 600.
56 Common Council minutes, vol. xxi, 17 March 1853, sjch
57 *The Courier*, 11 December 1853
58 Ibid., 17 March 1855
59 Ibid., 5 September 1854. The committee consisted of R. Jardine, F.A. Wiggins, Z. Wright, B. Robinson, Rev. W. Scovil, Wm Jack, R.F. Hazen, J.M. Robinson, John Owen, Robert Reed, H.G. Simonds, J.M. Walker, Dr Wm Bayard, Dr Botsford.
60 Ibid., 17 October 1854
61 Common Council minutes, vol. xxii, 17 October 1854, sjch
62 *The Courier*, 1 December 1854
63 Common Council minutes, vol. xxii, 9 February and 8 March 1855, sjch
64 Statutes of New Brunswick, 18 Victoria c. 38; 21 Victoria c. 7

65 Common Council minutes, vol. xxiii, 26 September 1857, sjch; *The Courier*, 28 November 1857
66 Statutes of New Brunswick, 18 Victoria c. 40
67 There were 5175 households in the city living in 2910 buildings in 1861. By contrast, the great majority of Toronto households were not connected to the waterworks system as late as 1874. See Jones and McCalla, 'Toronto Waterworks,' 320
68 Common Council minutes, vol. xxii, 17 October 1854, sjch; rle/858, pe. 4, 5; rle/860, pe. 2, 7, panb

CHAPTER 11

1 Eric H. Monkkonen, *Police in Urban America 1860–1920* (Cambridge 1981), 11
2 Francis Sheppard, *London 1808–70: The Infernal Wen* (London 1971), 30–40; Brian Barber, 'Municipal Government in Leeds 1835–1914,' *Municipal Reform and the Industrial City* (Leicester 1982), 65, 108
3 The first North American police force was created in Boston in 1838 following the Charlestown and Broad Street riots. See Roger Lane, *Policing the City: Boston, 1822–1885* (Cambridge, Mass. 1967), chs 1–3.
4 The system closely reflected its English roots. See John Field, 'Police, Power and Community in a Provincial English Town: Portsmouth, 1815–1875,' in Victor Bailey, ed., *Policing and Punishment in Nineteenth Century Britain* (New Brunswick, nj, 1981), 42–64.
5 The number of felons and miscreants delivered to prison increased from 49 in the last nine months of 1828, to 200 in 1833, and to 426 in 1836. In addition, there were 57 debtors committed to gaol in 1833 and 210 in 1836. See return of gaols for Saint John City and County 1828, 1833, 1834, 1836, 1839, rex/pa, statistics and returns 1, 2, panb. Creditors could maintain a debtor in prison by paying 4s. a week for the first six months and 5s. for the next six months.
6 Common Council minutes, vol. iv, 27 June 1812, 25 November 1814, sjch
7 *The Courier*, 17 October 1815, 9 February, and 12 January 1816
8 See discussions on the British watch in Sheppard, *London*, 30–4, and on the American in Monkkonen, *Police in Urban America*, 34–5, and Lane, *Policing the City*, 10–12. However, John Field found it quite effective in Portsmouth. See Field, 'Police, Power and Community.'
9 Common Council minutes, vol. iv, 29 April 1816
10 Ibid., 16 April 1836
11 In 1832, council sought approval for assessment of £500 for watch purposes, but no more than £5 could be assessed against any taxpayer.
12 The figures for 1816, 1835, 1842, and 1847 are found in the Common Council minutes; those for 1824 and 1839 are taken from the city accounts. See Common Council minutes, vol. xi, 9 June 1834; 2 and 10 July 1835; vol. xiv, 17 April 1841; 10 June 1842; vol. xviii, 11 October 1847, sjch
13 Common Council minutes, vol. xi, 16 April 1836, sjch
14 For example, James Small, an illiterate Irish immigrant, arrived in December 1842 with his wife and children. He was hired as a watchman on his arrival and had 50s. in freeman's fees deducted from his first month's wages; Common Council supporting papers, vol. vi, 12 July 1843, panb.

15 All constables petitioning for payment of fees in July 1843 were members of the watch; Common Council supporting papers, vol. VI, 26 July 1843, PANB.
16 RLE/839, pe. 55, PANB
17 Common Council minutes, vol. XIV, 15 August 1839, SJCH. Detailed watch records do not exist before 1841 but the record of expenditures would seem to indicate such an increase.
18 Notice of summons, 18 August 1839, Hazen Papers, mayor's correspondence 1830–1836, folder 2, NBM
19 *The News*, 25 September, 1839 and 7 February 1840
20 Common Council minutes, vol. XIV, 13 February, 12 march, and 8 June 1840, SJCH
21 The place of ritual violence in the Irish immigrant society of Upper Canada is discussed by Ruth Bleasdale in 'Class Conflict on the Canals of Upper Canada in the 1840's,' *Labour/La Travailleur* 7 (1981): 9–39.
22 *The Courier*, 5 December 1840
23 *The News*, 8 January 1841; *The Courier*, 9 January 1841
24 Presentment of grand jury, 28 January 1841, RJU (1841), 29, PANB
25 RLE/841, pe. 200, PANB
26 *The News*, 12 February 1841
27 *The Courier*, 12 June 1841; *The News*, 22 June 1841
28 Attempts were made to burn most of the city's Protestant churches. Mrs B. Gray died in the fire that destroyed Trinity Rectory.
29 *The News*, 1 and 3 December 1841
30 Ibid., 10 December 1841
31 *The Courier*, 6 February 1841
32 Common Council minutes, vol. XV, 5 February and 17 September 1841
33 Ibid., 12 November and 10 December 1841. Its members were Peters, Salter, Sandall, McLaughlin, Ray, and Greenwood. The committee proposed to pay each man £4.
34 RLE/842, pe. 110, PANB
35 Common Council minutes, vol. XV, 26 January 1842
36 *New Brunswicker*, 19 March 1842. Report of Legislative Committee Studying Police Bill for Saint John and Portland. Common Council supporting papers, 2, 26/28 January 1842, PANB; RJU S842 Z (9), PANB
37 *The News*, 19 January and 11 February 1842; Common Council supporting papers, 3 and 7 January 1842, PANB
38 Common Council minutes, vol. XVI, 10 June 1842, SJCH
39 See petition of the watch, Common Council supporting papers, 4, 28 September 1842, PANB; Common Council minutes, vol. XVI, 9 January 1843 (when the October and November wages were paid), 29 April 1843 (when £2 was given to each watchman on account), SJCH
40 By the third quarter of 1842 more than two-thirds of the 205 prisoners in the gaol were debtors. Over the course of the year, the prison population reached 540. See statistics and returns, 4 (1842), REX/PA, PANB.
41 G.W. Matthews to W.F. Odell, 25 June 1842, REX/PA emigration, PANB
42 Trial for riots of 12 July 1842, RJU S43Z(5), PANB. See Chapter 6 for a description of this riot.
43 *The News*, 22 January 1844
44 Donaldson to A. Reade, 8 March 1844, REX/PAC, MG9, vol. 10, PANB; *The*

Courier, 9 March 1844. Donaldson identified the combatants as Orange-men and ribbonmen. *The Courier* described them as 'evil disposed persons' whom S. Marks tried to disperse.

45 *The News*, 3 January 1845; *The Courier*, 4 January 1845; report of the Watch Committee, Common Council supporting papers, vol. 10, 10 January 1845, PANB

46 *The News*, 5 January 1845; *The Courier*, 4 January 1845

47 *The Courier*, 4 and 18 January 1845

48 Common Council supporting papers, vol. 10, 10 January 1845, PANB

49 *The News*, 3 February 1845

50 Common Council minutes, vol. XVII, 17 and 24 January 1845, SJCH. The vote on these proposals was 5 to 3 with the populist conservatives clearly in control.

51 Donaldson to Reade, 17, 22, and 29 March 1845, REX/PAC, MG9, vol. 122, PANB

52 *The Courier*, 17 May 1845; Whingates to Officer Commanding 33rd Regiment in New Brunswick, 20 March 1845, REX/PAC, MG9, vol. 122, PANB

53 'Legislative Review,' *The News*, 26 and 30 January 1846

54 See, for example, Common Council minutes, vol. XVIII, 9 December 1846, SJCH; Watch Committee, Common Council supporting papers, vol. 14, 25 January 1847, PANB

55 *The Courier*, 31 July, 11 and 25 September 1847; *The Loyalist*, 23 July 1847

56 Allan to Reade, 12 october 1847; Partelow to Saunders, 9 October 1847, REX/PAC, MG9, vol. 120, PANB

57 Ibid., Allan to Saunders, 11 November 1847

58 RLE/848, pe. 266, 426, PANB

59 The acrimonious debate among the four magistrates is detailed in the corre-spondence with the lieutenant-governor. See Colebrook to Simonds, 14 December 1847; J.S. Saunders to J. Allan, 21 December 1847; Allan to Saun-ders, 24 December 1847; Simonds to Colebrook, 25 December 1847, REX/PAC, MG9, vol. 120, PANB

60 Peace was not as easily accomplished as the correspondence might suggest. In early December, one policeman had a prisoner taken from him by a mob, which stabbed and nearly disembowelled him; RLE/848, pe. 80, PANB

61 *The Courier*, 5 August 1848

62 Common Council minutes, vol. XVIII, 11 October 1847, SJCH

63 Partelow to provincial secretary, 29 December 1847, REX/PAC, MG9, vol. 120, PANB. Monkkonen emphasizes the symbolic significance of uniforms. In American cities the uniform often produced protest against what was per-ceived as the imposition of a military system. See Monkkonen, *Police in Urban America*, ch. 1.

64 Common Council minutes, vol. XIX, 3 July 1849, SJCH

65 Report on police, J.R. Partelow to the mayor, 28 September and 1 October 1849; Common Council supporting papers, vol. 20, 10 October 1849

66 Ibid., Peters to J.R. Partelow, 25 September 1849

67 Common Council minutes, vol. XX, 25 February and 20 May 1850, SJCH

68 Peters to Partelow, 30 June 1851, REX/PAC, MG9, vol. 120, PANB

69 Common Council minutes, vol. XXI, 8 September 1852; vol. XX, 21 August 1851

70 Ibid., vol. XXI, 2 March and 27 April 1853

71 RLE/853, pe. 271; RLE/854, pe. 10, PANB
72 As a Church of Scotland Presbyterian, Johnston was prepared to imprison sabbath violators but not those who broke liquor laws.
73 Statutes of New Brunswick, 19 Victoria c. 52

CHAPTER 12

1 The occupational and ethnic composition of the population of the two west-side wards probably contained a higher proportion of native born and artisans than did that of the east side, but the small population of the west side could not significantly alter the social characteristics revealed in the east side.
2 A sample of this size should yield a 95 per cent certainty that the sample lies within a confidence of ±3.4 per cent. The standard error is 1.8 per cent.
3 The standard American work on this subject is Michael Katz, *The People of Hamilton, Canada West* (Cambridge, Mass. 1975); see also his 'Occupational Classification in History,' *Journal of Interdisciplinary History* III (Summer 1972): 63–88. A useful British discussion is W.A. Armstrong, 'The Use of Information about Occupation,' in E.A. Wrigley, ed., *Nineteenth-Century Society* (Cambridge 1972), 191–310.
4 A conclusion about the Irish that Katz reached in the Hamilton study, and one disputed by Darroch and Ornstein and by Burley. My contention here is not that there were no high-status Irish in the city – indeed, there were several great merchants among the Irish Protestants – but that they were few compared with the natives and that 93 per cent of all the labourers in the city were Irish, the great majority probably Irish Catholics. It should be noted that Darroch and Ornstein and Burley are dealing with origins, rather than birthplace. See Katz, *The People of Hamilton*, 67; A. Gordon Darroch and Michael D. Ornstein, 'Ethnicity and Occupational Structure in Canada in 1871: The Vertical Mosaic in Historical Perspective,' CHR LXI (September 1980): 305–33; Kevin Burley, 'Occupational Structure and Ethnicity in London, Ontario, 1971,' *Histoire Sociale/Social History* XI (November 1978): 390 410.
5 See Donald Akenson, 'Ontario: Whatever Happened to the Irish?' in Akenson, ed., *Canadian Papers in Rural History* III (Gananoque 1982): 402–56.
6 Katz came to similar conclusions in Hamilton using the results of municipal assessment (*The People of Hamilton*, 76).
7 Although Katz feels that servanthood was not degrading but an ordinary process through which young women from all ethnic and most social groups passed. See Katz, ibid., 289.
8 Donald Cole's study reveals that between 1855 and 1913 Irish-born men married Irish women in Lawrence in preference to native women in a ratio of 8:1 (682:86). As in Saint John, intermarriage between native men and Irish women rarely occurred (fewer than 9 cases out of 1300); *Immigrant City: Lawrence, Massachusetts 1845–1921* (Chapel Hill 1963), 103–6.
9 This argument accepts Akenson's proposition that the famine migrants arrived after 1844.
10 The Hamilton and Saint John process was similar, but Hamilton women generally began each about two years earlier than did their Saint John counterparts. Half had left home in Hamilton at 17, in Saint John at 19; 30

per cent were servants at 13 in Hamilton, in Saint John by 17; 60 per cent were married in Hamilton by 25, in Saint John by 26. See Katz, *The People of Hamilton*, 270.

11 This native-Irish dichotomy paralleled the one in Buffalo, where fewer than one native-born woman in five became a servant, while up to two-thirds of Irish-born women worked as live-in servants. The striking difference in the experience of Saint John women in comparison with those of Buffalo was the age of marriage. Half Buffalo's Irish-born and native-born women were married by 21, a figure that was not reached among Saint John women of any origin before 25. See Laurence A. Glasco, 'The Life Cycles and Household Structure of American Ethnic Groups: Irish, Germans and Native-born Whites in Buffalo, New York, 1955,' in Tamara K. Hareven, ed., *Family and Kin in Urban Communities 1700–1930* (New York 1977), 133, 135–6.

12 The marriage patterns of males in Buffalo, Hamilton, and Saint John were similar. Few married before 25 and most were married by 27. Boarding was a much more common experience in Hamilton, involving 45 per cent of all eighteen-year-old males. The Buffalo boarding experience more closely resembled that of Saint John than of Hamilton. Saint John males remained at home much longer than did those of Hamilton: most of the latter left before 18, the former by 24. See Katz, *The People of Hamilton*, 260; Glasco '... Buffalo, New York, 1855,' 123, 126.

13 The proportion of native boarders in Saint John corresponded closely to that found in Moncton in the same census. See Sheva Medjuck, 'The Importance of Boarding for the Structure of the Household in the Nineteenth Century: Moncton, New Brunswick and Hamilton, Canada West,' *Histoire Sociale/Social History* XIII (May 1980): 210.

14 Katz, *The People of Hamilton*, 316–81

Index